Praise for
GUIDE TO EASTERN CANADA

"An indispensable reference. . . . Canada-bound vacationers will quickly consider this handy compilation of facts and figures to be an important part of a trip to eastern Canada."
—**The Midwest Book Review**

"Will help you travel, eat, and enjoy your way through eastern Canada."
—**Philadelphia Daily News**

"An in-depth description of the part of Canada nearest us. . . . Extremely practical."
—**Erie (PA) Times**

"In *Guide to Eastern Canada* the Maritimes get some loving treatment."
—**Halifax Herald, Halifax, Nova Scotia**

"If you haven't already completed your plans for a group tour of Canada, hurry and pick up a copy. . . . For one who has seen Eastern Canada, I recommend it very highly. Aside from the fact it's a year-round, practical guide . . . it features up-to-date information on everything . . . information you can use no matter where you travel."
—**Northeast Detroiter, Harper Woods Herald, St. Clair Shores Herald**

Guide to
Eastern Canada
Third Edition

The comprehensive guide to year-round travel in:
Ontario • Quebec • New Brunswick • Nova Scotia
Newfoundland-Labrador • Prince Edward Island

by
Frederick Pratson

A Voyager Book

CHESTER, CONNECTICUT

About the Author

Frederick Pratson is author of several books, among them *Guide to the Great Attractions of Orlando and Beyond, Guide to Washington, D.C., and Beyond, Guide to Cape Cod, Guide to Western Canada,* and *Consumer's Guide to Package Travel around the World.* He has also published articles in many major magazines and newspapers including *The Boston Globe, Christian Science Monitor, Smithsonian,* and *Yankee.* Mr. Pratson is a member of the Society of American Travel Writers.

Cover photograph of Peggy's Cove, Nova Scotia, by Bill Brooks/Masterfile.
Text photos courtesy of the Canadian national and provincial tourism offices.

Manufactured in the United States of America
Third Edition/Second Printing

Library of Congress Cataloging-in-Publication Data

Pratson, Frederick John.
     Guide to eastern Canada : the comprehensive guide to year-round travel in Ontario, Quebec, New Brunswick, Nova Scotia, Newfoundland-Labrador, Prince Edward Island / by Frederick Pratson. — 3rd ed.
       p.   cm.
     "A Voyager book."
     Includes index.
     ISBN 0-87106-613-0
       1. Canada — Description and travel — 1981 — Guide-books.
2. Canada, Eastern — Description and travel — Guide-books.   I. Title.
F1009.P7 1989
917.13'04647 — dc19   89-30589
CIP

Contents

Part One—General Information

Part Two—Ontario and Québec

Part Three—Atlantic Canada

◄ Tranquil, beautiful land and seascapes offer bountiful inspirations to photographers and artists visiting Eastern Canada.

Maps in This Book

*I would like
to dedicate this book
to my good friends,*

Janet Aiton
Helen Jean Newman
Ralph Johansen
&
Linda Smidtke

Part One

General Information

Contents

◀ **Peggy's Cove, Halifax County, Nova Scotia.**

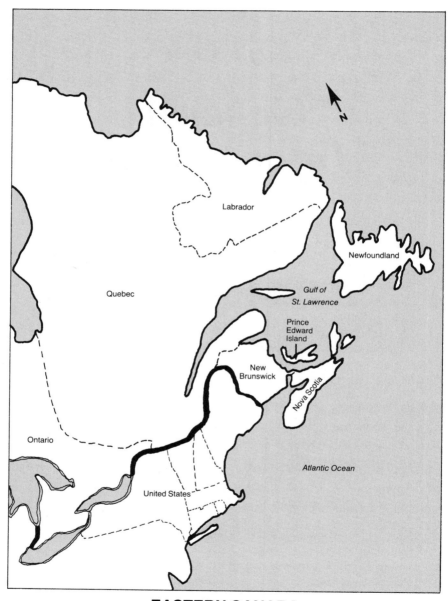

EASTERN CANADA

CHAPTER 1

Travel Sense

Introduction

Eastern Canada has everything you want for a splendid holiday: lively world-class cities, magnificent scenery, inspiring history, rich cultures, exciting sports, diverse recreational options, elegant accommodations, and the finest gourmet dining. Canada also offers greater travel value for your money than most other countries in the world. While the American dollar has decreased in value against many other major currencies, making international travel outside of North America considerably more expensive than it used to be, the dollar continues to hold its value in Canada (check with your bank for current rate of exchange). If you are using British pounds, French francs, Japanese yen, or West German deutsche marks, Canadian vacations and Canadian goods are among the world's best bargains.

The one Canadian quality I appreciate more than many others is the *civility* of most of the people. By civility I mean the extending of basic and traditional courtesies between friends and strangers, which makes for pleasant encounters for those of us who come for awhile into their midst. By civility I don't mean dullness. Canadians are as fascinating and colorful a people as any inhabiting this planet of ours. I have been traveling in Canada for more than twenty years and have seen a great deal of the country, from the Atlantic to the Pacific. During this time, I have seldom been bored and have always discovered many delightful surprises, even in places I've visited a number of times before.

I extend my best wishes to you as you travel through Canada. May every day be a pleasure and every experience rewarding. I also welcome your suggestions on improving this guide and your opinions about the quality of travel services (accommodations, restaurants, attractions, attitudes, and so on) in places you visit.

How to Use This Guide

Eastern Canada, as described herein, is a vast area, making it impractical for most people to visit its major points of interest during a single visit. Canada is, after all, the second largest country in the world. Only the Soviet Union is larger. With regard to this book, however, the term *Eastern Canada* is a misnomer, used more for the sake of brevity and convenience than absolute geographical accuracy.

This guide is not meant to be an encyclopedia on every area in Eastern Canada. It does, however, provide useful information about those places of keen interest to visitors that provide services, such as food, lodging, transportation, attractions, entertainment, and so on. This guide will also tell you where to find specialized information. All information has been checked for accuracy and updated as of this writing. When I wrote the first edition, my audience was primarily in the United States. Now, however, this guide is available throughout Canada and several other countries and has been rewritten to reflect the interests and needs of a growing international audience.

Guide to Eastern Canada can be used for the following:

1. As a year-round guide for people on holiday or business to major cities, such as Toronto, Montréal, Ottawa, Québec City, and Halifax.

2. As a guide for attractions and touring in areas adjacent to or not far from these large cities.

3. As a summer-season auto/camper/recreational touring guide through the various provinces.

4. As a sporting and adventure guide.

5. As a guide to top resorts and unique festivals.

When planning your visit to Canada, use this guide with detailed maps which you can obtain free of charge from the tourism organizations listed in this chapter.

This book is divided into three parts:
- Part 1 provides general information for travel to and in Eastern Canada.
- Part 2 focuses on Canada's two largest provinces—Ontario and Québec—and features the cities of Toronto, Ottawa, Montréal, and Québec City. Because these cities attract visitors throughout the year, Part 2 is essentially a "four seasons" guide. The Laurentian region and the Niagara Falls area are also "four seasons" recreational and sight-seeing places. In addition, Part 2 has summer

tours of the eastern townships, the Gaspé region, the Thousand Islands, and many other interesting areas of Ontario and Québec.

- Part 3 describes the provinces of Atlantic Canada: Nova Scotia, New Brunswick, Prince Edward Island, and Newfoundland-Labrador. Except for the "four seasons" city of Halifax, the appeal of Atlantic Canada for travelers is mainly during the warm weather months, from late May to the middle of October. Part 3 is, therefore, a summer touring guide.

Information on each vacation region is organized basically in the same manner: general comments, history and culture, transportation, special features (camping, hunting and fishing, skiing, festivals, and so forth), accommodations and dining, and tours of the province via major centers of attraction. All the sections on major cities are similarly organized: description, history, transportation, general information, attractions, accommodations, dining, and entertainment. Large cities, such as Montréal, Toronto, Ottawa, Québec, and Halifax, are described in greater detail. While absolute consistency has been the goal, relative consistency has been the reality. I have attempted to make this an easy-to-use, unconfusing guide, a tool for getting more value and pleasure out of your travels to Eastern Canada.

Your Travel Agent

Travel anywhere these days has become so complicated and costly that even the sophisticated traveler needs help to get through the maze of details and figures. You need go no farther than your local travel agent for help. A good travel agent can book your accommodations, meal plans, transportation, tours, rental cars, and many other aspects of your trip. And everything will be arranged to fit into the budget you specify. In addition, a good travel agent will give advice based on his or her own familiarity with a place. A good agent delivers a tremendous amount of service at *no* extra cost, though you may be charged for special services. Travel agents receive a commission from the hotels and transportation companies, but *you* pay the same rates as when you book yourself. Some of the best travel agents belong to the American Society of Travel Agents (ASTA); look for the ASTA symbol when you select your agent. Not all travel agents are as we would like them to be—top-notch professionals who place the well-being and satisfaction of their clients first. Ask your friends and business associates for recommendations.

Don't be afraid to shop around until you get the best. After all, it's your hard-earned money and your well-deserved vacation.

Package Tours

There are many different types of package tours available for Eastern Canada, originating in many major United States' and Canadian cities: bus tours of every kind, fly-and-drive packages, foliage tours, ski and resort packages, winter carnival and festival packages, big-city tour packages, romantic weekend getaways, big-game hunting and fishing packages, railroad tour packages, and cruise packages. Maupintour and Tauck Tours are two of the best in the business. Your local travel agent is your best source of information about tour operators who provide high-quality vacation packages to eastern Canada. In addition, most packages are usually booked through travel agents.

Free Information for U.S. Visitors

Provincial tourism organizations are your best resources for free information and advice on almost every aspect of travel to their communities and countryside. They will provide you with free brochures and maps and will answer your questions. The best way to reach these tourism organizations is by making a telephone call, in most cases toll-free, from your home.

The following provincial tourism organizations await your call:

TRAVEL INFORMATION ONTARIO
Queen's Park
Toronto, Ontario M7A 2E5
(800) ONT–ARIO (except
 Yukon, NWT, and Alaska)
From Toronto calling area and
 Alaska:
English (416) 965–4008
French (416) 965–3448
Telecommunication Device for
 the Deaf (416) 965–6027
Summer Campground
 Vacancies and Winter Skiing
 (416) 963–2992

TOURISME QUEBEC
C.P. 20 000
Québec City, Québec G1K
 7X2
(800) 443–7000 from eastern
 United States
(514) 873–2015 from rest of the
 United States; reverse the
 charges
(800) 361–6490 from Ontario
 and Atlantic Canada
(514) 873–2015 from rest of
 Canada; reverse the charges

DEPARTMENT OF TOURISM, RECREATION, AND HERITAGE NEW BRUNSWICK
P.O. Box 12345
Fredericton, New Brunswick E3B 5C3
(800) 561–0123 from United States and Canada
(800) 442–4442 from within New Brunswick

NOVA SCOTIA TOURISM
P.O. Box 456
Halifax, Nova Scotia B3J 2R5
(800) 341–6096 from continental United States, except Maine
(800) 492–0643 from Maine
(800) 565–7166 from Western Canada
(800) 565–7140 from central and southern Ontario
(800) 565–7180 from Québec and Newfoundland
(800) 565–7105 from Nova Scotia, New Brunswick, and Prince Edward Island
(902) 424–5000 in Halifax

PRINCE EDWARD ISLAND VISITOR SERVICES DIVISION
P.O. Box 940
Charlottetown, Prince Edward Island C1A 7M5
(800) 565–7421 (March 16 to October 31) from New Brunswick and Nova Scotia
(800) 565–0243 from eastern Canada
(800) 565–9060 from eastern United States
(902) 368–4444 in Charlottetown

NEWFOUNDLAND DEPARTMENT OF DEVELOPMENT AND TOURISM
Tourism Branch
P.O. Box 2016
St. John's, Newfoundland A1C 5R8
(800) 563–6353 from United States and Canada
(709) 576–2830 in St. John's

Travel information is also provided through Canadian Government consulates in the United States:

400 South Tower
One CNN Center
ATLANTA, Georgia 30303
(404) 577–6810

Suite 400, Three Copley Place
BOSTON, Massachusetts 02116
(617) 536–1731

Suite 3550
One Marine Midland Centre
BUFFALO, New York 14203
(716) 852–1345

310 South Michigan Avenue
CHICAGO, Illinois 60604
(312) 427–1031

55 Public Square
CLEVELAND, Ohio 44113
(216) 771–0150

715 North St. Paul
DALLAS, Texas 75201
(214) 922–9814

600 Renaissance Center, Suite 1100
DETROIT, Michigan 48243
(313) 567–2085

7

300 South Grand Avenue
Los Angeles, California 90071
(213) 687–7432

701 Fourth Avenue South,
Suite 900
Minneapolis, Minnesota 55415
(612) 332–4314

EXXON Building
1251 Avenue of the Americas
New York, New York 10020
(212) 586–2400

50 Fremont Street, Suite 2100
San Francisco, California
94105
(415) 543–2309

412 Plaza 600, 6th and Steward
Avenue
Seattle, Washington 98101
(206) 443–0476

1211 Connecticut Avenue,
N.W., Suite 300
Washington, D.C. 20036
(202) 223–9710

Tourist Information Outside North America

European and Japanese travelers can obtain free travel information, literature, and maps from these Canadian Government tourism offices:

Canadian High Commission–
Tourism Program
Canada House
Trafalgar Square
London SWIY 5BJ England
Tel. (011–44–1) 6299492

Canadian Embassy–Tourism
Program
37, Avenue Montaigne
75008 Paris, France
Tel. (011–33–1) 47230101

Canadian Tourism Office
D-6000 Frankfurt
Biebergasse 6-10
Frankfurt, Federal Republic of
Germany
Tel. (49–611) 280157

This office also provides service
to the German-speaking
regions of Switzerland.

Canadian Embassy–Tourism
Program
Sophialaan 7
2514 JP The Hague
P.O. Box 30820
The Hague, Netherlands
Tel. (011–31–70) 614111

Canadian Embassy–Annex
Yamakatsu Building 5F
8-5-32 Akasaka, Minato-ku
Tokyo 107, Japan
Tel. (011–81–3) 479–5851

Chapter 2

Visiting Canada

The Canadian Nation

Canadians are exceptionally well governed by a parliamentary form of democracy. Elizabeth II, queen of the United Kingdom, is also queen of Canada, a fact that comes as a surprise to many travelers, especially some Americans who perceive Canada as being similar in all respects to their country. The governor-general is the queen's representative and the symbolic chief of state, while the prime minister, who is also a member of Parliament and leader of his political party, is the chief executive officer of Canada. On the provincial level, lieutenant-governors, representatives of the queen under the governor-general, are also symbolic and ceremonial leaders. Political power on the local level resides with the provincial legislative assemblies and with the premiers, the chief executive officers who, like the prime minister, are members of the legislatures and leaders of the majority parties.

Canada is a member of the United Nations, NATO, and the Commonwealth of Nations. The two leading political parties in Canada are the Progressive Conservatives and the Liberals. There are several other parties, such as the New Democratic party, which has a national constituency, and the Parti Québecois, which once was the ruling party in the province of Québec. The federal capital is Ottawa, Ontario, although it is in a federal district that extends into Québec at the city of Hull. The provincial capitals of Eastern Canada are as follows: Toronto (Ontario); Québec City (Québec); Fredericton (New Brunswick); Halifax (Nova Scotia); Charlottetown (Prince Edward Island); and St. John's (Newfoundland-Labrador).

Canada has a population of more than twenty-five million, rapidly growing primarily through immigration. Close to two-thirds of this total reside in Ontario and Québec, and about 75 percent of all

Canadians live within a hundred miles of the U.S. border (most of the important urban centers of Canada are near the border). About 30 percent of all Canadians are French; more than 40 percent are of British stock; and the remainder are of various ethnic groups, such as Ukrainians, Poles, Italians, blacks, Asians, Greeks, and others. Unlike the United States, which thinks of itself as a "melting pot," where all groups tend to be assimilated into the dominant Anglo-Saxon culture, Canada considers itself a "cultural mosaic," where its citizens can be equally proud of their ethnic heritage and of being Canadians. (This concept has worked best in Ontario and the western provinces, where the opportunities for upward mobility have been greatest for immigrants, and less so in Québec where the French culture has been made legally preeminent by provincial government decree.)

In religion the vast majority of Canadians are Christian: Anglican, Roman Catholic, Presbyterian, United Church. There are, however, large concentrations of Jews in both Montréal and Toronto. The Anglican Church is the "established" church in many English-speaking communities, while the Roman Catholic Church is dominant with the French-speaking population and with various other ethnic groups from the European continent. Unlike the United States, where church and state are separate, church affiliation plays an important role in the life of the provinces. In Newfoundland, for example, the public education system is divided between Protestant and Roman Catholic schools, and a number of provincial holidays are established along religious lines (Saint Patrick's Day and Orangeman's Day). In recent years, Québec has become more secularized, now forming its socio-cultural divisions more according to language than to religion.

In April 1982, Canadians witnessed a historic event when Elizabeth II, queen of Canada, before a crowded assembly of the House of Commons and Senate of the Parliament of Canada in Ottawa, presided over the proclamation of the Constitution Act of 1982. This new act made important changes in Canada's constitution and is a milestone in the nation's political history. With the proclamation of the Constitution Act, Canada patriated its constitution and shed the last antiquated vestige of its colonial past. Patriation means the end of the role of the United Kingdom Parliament in the amendment process of the Canadian constitution. Canada is finally fully independent in the legal sense.

Canada is still very much a country in political transition. The encouraging note in this great national debate is that Canadians are among the most reasonable people on earth, and their political destiny will not be forged in violence, as in so many nations, but will evolve out of the innate good sense of the Canadian people themselves.

Entry into Canada

Important

Citizens or permanent residents of the United States do not require passports or visas and can usually cross the United States–Canada border without difficulty or delay. It is strongly recommended, however, that you carry some sort of valid personal identification, such as proof of residence and citizenship (birth certificate or similar documents). Naturalized U.S. citizens should carry a naturalization certificate or other evidence of citizenship. Permanent residents who are not citizens should carry their alien registration receipt card. Persons under eighteen years old who travel to Canada without an adult must have a letter of permission from a parent or guardian. U.S. citizens can also enter Canada from any other country without a passport or visa.

All other persons, except U.S. citizens or legal residents, citizens of France residing in Saint Pierre and Miquelon, and residents of Greenland, require a valid passport, visa, or other acceptable travel document to gain entry into Canada. If you are entering Canada from the United States, make sure that your travel documents are acceptable to the U.S. Immigration Service before you leave, so that you won't have trouble getting back into the country.

Employment or Study

If you want to work or study in Canada, you must obtain a student or employment authorization before coming to Canada. Employment authorizations are not issued if there are qualified Canadians or permanent residents available for the kind of work you are seeking. Persons wishing to work or study in Canada should contact the nearest Canadian Consulate for further information.

Clearing Canada Customs

By Car

The entry of vehicles and trailers into Canada for touring purposes, for periods of up to twelve months, is generally a quick, routine matter that does not require the payment of duty. Motor vehicle registration forms should be carried, as well as a copy of the contract if you are driving a rented vehicle. If you are driving a vehicle registered to someone else, you must carry that person's authorization to use the vehicle.

All national driver's licenses are valid in Canada, including the International Driver's Permit.

Important

All provinces in Canada require visiting motorists to produce evidence of financial responsibility in case of an accident. U.S. motorists are advised to obtain from their insurance agents a Canadian nonresident interprovincial motor vehicle liability insurance card, which is issued free of charge. If you have an accident in Canada and don't have this card, your vehicle can be impounded and other serious legal action can be taken against you. (Don't leave home without it!)

You are in violation of the law if you don't use seat belts throughout Canada. You can be subject to fines and other penalties if you violate Canada's seat belt laws.

The Canadian Automobile Association provides full member services to members of the American Automobile Association. Similar reciprocal services are provided by other auto clubs. Check with yours before traveling in Canada.

Gas and oil are sold in Canada by the liter: 1 U.S. gallon equals 3.78 liters; 1 Canadian imperial gallon, however, equals 4.5 liters. Canadian petroleum products tend to be costlier than in the United States but cheaper than in most other countries.

By Private Aircraft

Visiting pilots should plan to land at an airport that can provide customs clearance. You must report to Canada Customs immediately and complete all documentation. In emergencies, you can land at other fields, but then you must immediately report your arrival to the nearest regional customs office or the Royal Canadian Mounted Police. For more details on flying your own plane to Canada, contact your nearest Canadian consulate general.

By Private Boat

If you're planning to come to Canada on your own boat, contact your nearest Canadian customs office for a list of ports-of-entry that provide customs facilities and their hours of operation. When you arrive, you should immediately report to customs and complete all documentation. If you have an emergency and have to pull into a nonofficial port, immediately report your arrival to the nearest regional customs office or the Royal Canadian Mounted Police.

Personal Exemptions

Everything you bring into Canada must be declared and inspected by customs on your arrival in the country.

Tobacco. Persons sixteen years of age and older can bring in duty-free 50 cigars, 200 cigarettes, and 2 pounds of manufactured tobacco.

Alcoholic beverages. You can bring into Canada duty-free 40 ounces of liquor or wine or 288 fluid ounces of beer or ale.

Gifts. You can bring in duty-free bona fide gifts for friends and relatives provided that the value of each gift does not exceed $40 (Canadian funds) and that the item is not tobacco, liquor, or advertising material.

Regular duty fees and taxes must be paid on tobacco, alcoholic beverages, and gifts that exceed the above limitations.

Business equipment and materials. Printed materials, commercial samples, blueprints, charts, audiovisual materials, convention and exhibit displays, and the like brought into Canada may be subject to the full rate of duty and tax or a portion thereof or may be duty- and tax-free. Canada wants to make your business dealings in the country as easy and convenient as possible.

Pets. You can bring your dogs and cats into Canada provided each animal has a certificate from a licensed veterinarian that confirms vaccination against rabies within the preceding thirty-six months. Puppies and kittens under three months and seeing-eye dogs accompanied by their owners can enter Canada without certification or restriction.

Pet birds, songbirds, and birds of the parrot family, up to two per family, can be brought into Canada provided that the owner accompanies the birds and declares on arrival that the birds have been in his or her possession during the preceding ninety days and have not been in contact with other birds during that period.

Pet monkeys, other small pet mammals, fish, and most reptiles can come into Canada without restriction. Pet foxes, skunks, raccoons, and ferrets, however, can come into Canada without health certification or a Canadian import permit only when they are accompanied by the owner. Turtles and tortoises require an import permit before admission.

Livestock, horses, wild or domestic fowl, and commercial shipments of animals, including all species of birds, are subject to veterinary health inspection on arrival in Canada. Contact the Chief of Imports, Animal Health Division, Food Production and Inspection Branch, Agriculture Canada, Ottawa, Ontario K1A OY9, (613) 995-5433.

Plants, fruits, and vegetables. House plants can be brought into Canada without phytosanitary (plant health) certification when carried as a personal item. All other plants require phytosanitary certification, which is issued by the offices of the U.S. Department of Agriculture.

You can bring most fruits and vegetables into Canada; however, on certain types there are restrictions that change from time to time, and you should check with your nearest U.S. Department of Agriculture office for details.

Food. Food for two days' personal use can be brought into Canada from the United States duty-free.

Boats and recreational vehicles. Visitors to Canada can bring their boats, motors, trailers, snowmobiles, and so forth duty- and tax-free under a temporary entry permit, which is issued by Canada Customs on condition that such vehicles are for personal use only and are to be brought out of the country at the end of your visit.

Recreational equipment. You can bring in the following items duty- and tax-free in reasonable quantities provided they are only for your personal use: fishing tackle; camping, golf, tennis, scuba, and skiing equipment; radios, television sets, typewriters; camera equipment with a reasonable amount of film; and other hobby or recreational items.

Radio communication equipment. Radio equipment that has a power output of 100 milliwatts or less, operating in the 26.97/27.7 MH. band, may be operated in Canada without formal licensing.

Visitors to Canada are permitted to operate aircraft, ship, amateur, and citizens' band radio stations provided that such stations are properly licensed by the government of the United States. The following stations, which must have a U.S. license, require a Canadian permit for operation in Canada: citizens' band (CB) radiotelephone stations and radio-telephone stations in certain vehicles that move back and forth across the border or that are operated through a common carrier to connect with the telephone system. Permits may be obtained by writing the Director of Operations, Department of Communications, Ottawa, Ontario K1A 0C8. Visitors should carry their Canadian permit and U.S. license at all times.

Seasonal residents' household goods. A nonresident of Canada who purchases, constructs, owns, or leases for at least three years a seasonal residence (not a mobile home or other movable residence) may qualify for the duty- and tax-free entry of furniture and household goods.

Firearms. Firearms having no legitimate sporting or recreational use (e.g., handguns) are not permitted entry into Canada. Canada has extremely strong handgun laws, and they are strictly enforced. If you are traveling through Canada to get to Alaska, you must ship your prohibited or restricted weapons by commercial carrier and not bring them with you. Failure to report your weapons at customs can result in their seizure and forfeiture. If you are bringing in a handgun for competition shooting, you must obtain a permit in advance from a Canadian local registrar of firearms.

Long guns, those used for hunting and competition shooting, can be brought into Canada and used without a permit by visitors sixteen years or over. Nonresident hunters may bring in 200 rounds of ammunition per person duty-free. Nonresident marksmen competing in a meet recognized by the Amateur Trap Shooting Association, the Shooting Federation of Canada, the Dominion of Canada Rifle Association, or the National Skeet Shooting Association may bring in 1000 rounds of ammunition per person as personal baggage. Further details are available from your nearest Canadian Consulate General.

Explosives, ammunition, fireworks, and pyrotechnics. Blasting explosives and detonators, propellant explosives and ammunition, and all types of fireworks and pyrotechnic devices may not be brought into Canada without a special permit. For more information, contact the Chief Inspector of Explosives, Explosives Branch, Energy, Mines and Resources Canada, Sir William Logan Building, 580 Booth Street, Ottawa, Ontario K1A 0E4.

Sporting Regulations

Hunting

Hunting is governed by provincial laws. Nonresidents are required to obtain a hunting license from each province in which they plan to hunt. Weapons are forbidden in many of Canada's provincial parks, reserves, and adjacent areas.

Fishing

Fishing, like hunting, is governed by provincial laws. For freshwater fishing you must have a nonresident license for the province in which you wish to fish. No license is required for saltwater fishing. No permit is required to bring in your own gear.

A special fishing permit is required to fish in all national parks. These permits can be obtained at any national park site for a nominal fee and are valid in all the national parks across Canada.

National Parks

Any person entering a national park must seal firearms or any devices for capturing or killing game with seals that are provided at the entrance of the park. An exception is made in the case of persons traveling by motor vehicle through Fundy, Prince Edward Island, Cape Breton Island, or Terra Nova national parks during the hunting season of the province in which the park is located. In these cases, all firearms and devices are to be dismantled and kept within the vehicle.

Reentry into the United States

Important

To reenter the United States you have to satisfy U.S. Immigration authorities of your right to do so, which is usually accomplished by some form of identification and/or proof of citizenship (passport, birth certificate, or other document). You would do well to list all the purchases you are taking home before you confront the U.S. officials. Keep sales receipts and invoices handy and pack purchases separately for an easier inspection.

You can take out and bring into the United States up to $5,000 (U.S. funds). Any amount over this limit requires reporting with U.S. Customs.

Items of cultural, historical, or scientific value to the heritage of Canada that are more than fifty years old (for example, certain antiques) cannot be taken out of the country without special permission. For more information, contact the Secretary, Canadian Cultural Property Export Review Board, Secretary of State Department, Ottawa, Ontario K1A 0C8.

You can take into the United States plants of Canadian origin provided that you have a phytosanitary certificate for them. This can be obtained from any Plant Products and Quarantine Division office of Agriculture Canada, located in major centers across Canada.

Exemptions

If you have stayed in Canada for at least forty-eight hours, you can bring home up to $400 (U.S. dollars) of personal purchases duty-free. Members of the same family can combine their exemptions into a larger duty-free total. For example, if five of you are traveling together and Mother finds a terrific mink stole for $2,000 in Montréal, she can bring it back into the States duty-free (five family members times a $400 exemption per member equals $2,000). Duty-free purchases must accompany you back across the border.

Included in the duty-free exemptions are up to 100 cigars, so long as they are not Cuban, which are absolutely prohibited. You can also return with 200 duty-free cigarettes and 1 liter of liquor (minimum age is twenty-one).

Gifts can be sent to friends and relatives in the United States duty-free if the value of each gift does not exceed $50. The package should be marked "Unsolicited Gift."

Emergencies

In an emergency, simply dial 911 or 0 and ask the telephone operator for the police, who have been specially trained to handle and coordinate all types of emergencies. The larger towns and cities and the provinces of Ontario and Québec have their own separate police forces. The Royal Canadian Mounted Police (RCMP) provides security and traffic services in the other provinces, particularly on main roads, in small towns, and in rural areas. The famous Mounties are one of the best police forces in the world, even giving you a traffic ticket with a smile and courtesy.

If someone has an urgent need to get in touch with you but does not know where or how, this person should contact the RCMP in the area where you are traveling (leave your itinerary with a friend or relative back home). Several times each day many of the Canadian Broadcasting Corporation (CBC) radio outlets broadcast the names of individuals traveling throughout Canada, asking them to contact the nearest RCMP office for emergency messages.

You Need Health Insurance

No one wants to land in the hospital while on a trip, but the unexpected does happen.

Important

Make sure that your health insurance plan covers you and your family members while traveling in Canada and that you have adequate coverage to pay all or most costs for treatment. Although Canadians enjoy the benefits of an excellent, low-cost health care system, travelers from the United States must pay the going rate, which is as high as back home. Consult your insurance company or agent, your travel agent, or your nearest Canadian Consulate General on how best to handle your particular situation.

Important Numbers and Dates

Time Zones

All of Atlantic Canada, except for the island of Newfoundland, is on Atlantic Standard Time. Newfoundland is on Newfoundland Standard Time (6:00 A.M. Atlantic Time is 6:30 A.M. Newfoundland Time). Labrador, however, is on Atlantic Time. The easternmost portion of the Northwest Territories, east of Frobisher Bay, is also on Atlantic Standard Time.

Most of Québec and Ontario are on Eastern Standard Time (6:00 A.M. Atlantic Time is 5:00 A.M. Eastern Time), but easternmost Québec along the north coast of the Gulf of Saint Lawrence is on Atlantic Time. The westernmost portion of Ontario, west of Thunder Bay, is on Central Time. Most of the eastern portion of the Northwest Territories, between Frobisher Bay and Repulse Bay, is on Eastern Time.

Telephone Area Codes

Laurentians and most eastern townships:	819
London and west to Windsor area:	519
Montréal (metropolitan area and south):	514
New Brunswick:	506
Newfoundland:	709
Nova Scotia and Prince Edward Island:	902
Ottawa to the Saint Lawrence River region:	613
Québec City and eastern Québec:	418
Toronto (metropolitan area and west to Niagara):	416

National Holidays

New Year's Day (January 1)
Good Friday
Easter Monday
Victoria Day (mid to late May)
Dominion Day (July 1)
Labour Day
Thanksgiving Day (mid October)
Remembrance Day (November 11)
Christmas (December 25)
Boxing Day (December 26)

All these holidays mean that banks, government offices, factories, commercial offices, and many stores are closed for the day. Most hotels and motels and many restaurants are open for business.

The Metric System

All measurements in Canada now follow the metric system. Temperature is given in degrees Celsius; gas is sold by the liter, groceries by grams and kilograms; clothing comes in centimeter sizes; and road speeds are posted in kilometers per hour.

The Canadian government has prepared the following helpful conversion table:

Speed
15 miles per hour = approximately 25 kilometers (km.) per hour
30 miles per hour = approximately 50 kilometers (km.) per hour
50 miles per hour = approximately 80 kilometers (km.) per hour
60 miles per hour = approximately 100 kilometers (km.) per hour

Length
1 inch = 2.54 centimeters (cm.)
1 foot = 0.3 meters (m.) or 30 centimeters
1 yard = 0.9 meters or 90 centimeters
1 mile = 1.6 kilometers or 1600 meters

Mass
1 ounce = 28 grams (g.)
1 pound = 0.45 kilograms (kg.) or 450 grams

Volume
1 fluid ounce = 28 milliliters (ml.)
1 imperial pint* = 0.57 liters (l.) or 570 milliliters

1 imperial quart* = 1.14 liters or 1140 milliliters
1 imperial gallon* = 4.5 liters or 4500 milliliters
1 U.S. gallon = 3.78 liters or 3780 milliliters

Temperature
86°F = approximately 30°C (hot summer day)
68°F = 20°C (room temperature)
32°F = 0°C (water freezes)
−6°F = approximately −20°C (very cold winter day)

*Imperial size is larger than American measurement.

CHAPTER 3

Money Matters

Canadian Money

The monetary system of Canada, like that of the United States, is based on dollars and cents. There is, however, a difference in value between the two currencies, which works out to the benefit of U.S. residents and for travelers from other countries.

The value of the Canadian dollar has fluctuated in recent years from $.35 to $.20 *below* the U.S. dollar, depending on the current market rate. This means that Americans and others traveling in Canada have been getting more in Canadian money for each U.S. dollar.

This advantageous difference between Canadian and U.S. money is a strong incentive to travel in Canada and splurge a bit more than you would in other parts of the world.

Money Transactions and Banking

U.S. money is widely accepted throughout Canada for the purchase of goods and services, though hotels, restaurants, and stores usually offer a less favorable rate of exchange than banks. Most of the time you will receive your change in Canadian dollars and cents—make sure you receive the current market value for your American dollars in Canadian money. This conversion of money is done mainly as a convenience to you. Try to do most of your money transactions in Canadian currency. Most major banks in the United States carry some Canadian currency and Canadian traveler's checks. Take a small amount of Canadian money with you ($25 to $100 for minor expenses) when you leave home. When you come into Canada, convert what you'll need into Canadian dollars at a local bank, where you will receive the *best* rate of exchange. Hotels, for example, will give you several cents less per $1 than at a bank. On the other hand, hotel cashiers keep longer hours than banks and are more convenient. Most major traveler's checks are accepted throughout Canada.

Normal banking hours in Canada are 10:00 A.M. to 3:00 P.M. Monday through Friday. Many banks have extended hours of operation during the week, including Saturday. Automatic Teller Machines (ATMs) are located in urban areas throughout Canada.

Provincial Sales Taxes

All the Canadian provinces, except Alberta, the Northwest Territories, and the Yukon, have a sales tax, ranging from 4 to 12 percent, on most goods purchased in stores, on food in dining places, and in some cases on hotel and motel rooms. You can get a sales tax refund in Ontario when the goods you buy are taken out of Canada with you. Ask your salesperson or store manager about such refunds.

Special Fares in Canada

If you are over sixty-five, you may be eligible to receive reductions on air, rail, and bus fares within Canada, provided proof of age is supplied when you purchase your tickets. Young people between the ages of thirteen and twenty-one may also travel in Canada at reduced rates; other rate reductions may be available for children twelve and under. Proof of age (birth certificate or the like) is necessary when you purchase your tickets. Ask your travel agent for details.

Credit Cards

Most major credit cards are widely accepted throughout Canada, with Visa, MasterCard (and their international variations), and American Express being the most popular. You should ask your hotel, restaurant, or store before purchasing goods or services whether they accept yours. Most places display signs and decals, at or near entrances, cash registers, and so on, showing the cards they accept.

Major credit cards are necessary for renting automobiles. They are also a necessary form of identification at most places of accommodation.

Calculating Costs

Because of fluctuating prices, this guide uses a scale of relative prices—*expensive, moderate,* and *inexpensive*—to indicate costs for accommodations and restaurants. Here is how it works (all figures here represent Canadian dollars):

Accommodations

An *expensive* double room at a top hotel in Toronto, Ottawa, Québec City, and Montréal costs more than $100 a night. A *moderate* double would be more than $55, a decent *inexpensive* double $30 and up. There are variations in each of these categories, depending on the quality of the accommodations and when you want them. Toronto, Ottawa, Québec City, and Montréal are among the most expensive places to stay in Eastern Canada. Prices in other cities and towns of Eastern Canada are somwhat lower, depending on the location, season, quality of accommodation, and consumer demand. To cut some of the cost, ask about weekend or seasonal packages and special policies concerning children, senior citizens, groups, and commercial travelers.

Within each of the above cost categories, hotels and motels have a range of rates for doubles and singles. If you can make your booking well in advance, you should be able to get a more favorable rate. Also, if it's a slow week or season, you might be able to get some terrific bargains. The converse is also true: If you book at the last minute and if the city is filled with convention delegates and package tours, you may have to be content with whatever you can get at the price they want you to pay. It cannot be stressed enough that your travel agent can relieve you of much of the burden of booking accommodations when and where you want them and at the price you can afford to pay.

Dining

Again we use the relative categories of expensive, moderate, and inexpensive to indicate the price of dining in restaurants listed in this guide. The cost of meals throughout Eastern Canada is fairly consistent. The cost of meals in the countryside should be somewhat less, except at fine resorts and inns. While touring in rural areas and smaller cities and towns, you will often find the best dining in motels, inns, and hotels.

An expensive evening meal is one where the main course is

priced at $15 and up. The total cost of an expensive meal for two could go well over $100, when you figure in drinks and tips.

A moderately priced meal for two averages at about $60, while an inexpensive meal would cost below $25.

Fast-food places are everywhere in Eastern Canada.

Gasoline

Gasoline is plentiful throughout Eastern Canada. Gasoline is sold by the liter, and the Canadian imperial gallon is about one liter more than the American gallon.

Attractions

Many of the attractions mentioned in this guide are *free*. Others are marked *admission charge*. The amount charged can range from a voluntary donation to several dollars. Major attractions usually have several prices—for adults, children, senior citizens, groups, and tours. During the peak summer vacation season, from the end of June to Canada's Labour Day, most attractions are open every day from 10:00 A.M. to 5:30 P.M. Some major attractions (amusement parks, historical villages, and so on) offer evening hours during the peak season. Each attraction has its own method of operation: Sometimes when a historic home or local museum, for example, is closed on a Sunday or Monday, the curator just might open it for you. Don't be too shy to inquire if your interest is great.

Communications

Toll-free Calls

Most major transportation companies, hotel and motel chains, and rental car companies have toll-free reservation and information telephone numbers. Air Canada, Amtrak, VIA Rail, Eastern, Delta, and American Airlines, Canadian Pacific and Canadian National Hotels, Westin Hotels, Hilton Hotels, Sheraton Hotels, Holiday Inns, and others offer this service. In fact, most accommodations and many services listed in this guide have toll-free numbers. Before making a toll call, dial toll-free information—(800) 555–1212 in both the United States and Canada—to find out if the place you want to contact has a toll-free number that can be accessed from your location.

Postal Service

If you are mailing anything in or from Canada, you must use Canadian postage stamps. For mail from the United States to Canada, U.S. stamps are accepted.

Canada also offers an express mail service for more rapid delivery anywhere in Canada or in the United States.

Airport Services

International airports in Eastern Canada are located in Gander, Halifax, Montréal, Ottawa, and Toronto. American travelers returning to the United States from Toronto and Montréal clear U.S. Customs in the airports of these cities.

Special services offered at the international airports include foreign exchange, lockers, telephones, duty-free shops, bars, restaurants, newsstands, book and gift shops, drugstores, and so on. Most of these terminals have accommodations nearby.

All major airports have bus, taxi, and limousine services to and from the city centers. Rates for ground transportation are clearly posted in the terminals. Most of the major rental car companies also have desks at these terminals.

Most terminals have special facilities for persons with handicaps, such as ramps, washrooms, automatic doors, and other conveniences.

Free Culture

A treat while touring in Eastern Canada by auto is tuning into a Canadian Broadcasting Corporation (CBC) radio station. A government-operated network, CBC provides some of the finest news, discussion, cultural, and entertainment programming in North America. Its broadcasting of classical music is outstanding in variety and amount.

Part Two

Ontario and Québec

Contents

◀ **Eastern Canada's lighthouses are beacons of welcome for travelers to this diverse and fascinating region.**

◀ **Some 200 varieties of tulips bloom annually along scenic driveways in Canada's national capital region (Ottawa-Hull).**

CHAPTER 4

Toronto

Toronto Today

Toronto, one of Canada's most important cities, is a financial, commercial, and manufacturing center. Many of Canada's largest corporations have their home bases here, and many large foreign corporations have their Canadian headquarters in Toronto. Thousands of factories operate in and near the city. Toronto is also English-speaking Canada's center for broadcast communications, filmmaking, and publishing. Toronto has some of the best institutions for higher learning, research, and medicine in Canada. It is also the capital of Ontario, Canada's most populous and wealthiest province. Many of the economic decisions made in Toronto affect the entire country. And for this and other reasons, Toronto is frequently envied by the other provinces.

Toronto has always been economically strong. Its material success has been joined with a belief in predestination, a feeling that such success is a sign of being among the favorably chosen. With an increasing annual growth rate, based on a pragmatic attitude favoring the private sector, Toronto is one of the most dynamic cities in North America.

With a population of more than three million and rapidly growing, Toronto is Canada's largest urban center. Until the end of the Second World War, most Torontonians were of British stock (English, United Empire Loyalist, Welsh, Scottish, Ulster Irish), belonging to various Protestant denominations, with the Anglican Church being dominant.

There were also significant communities of Jews and Roman Catholic Irish. Although the Toronto area experienced several waves of immigration from Europe in the nineteenth and early twentieth centuries, most of the newcomers moved on to cheap land in West-

31

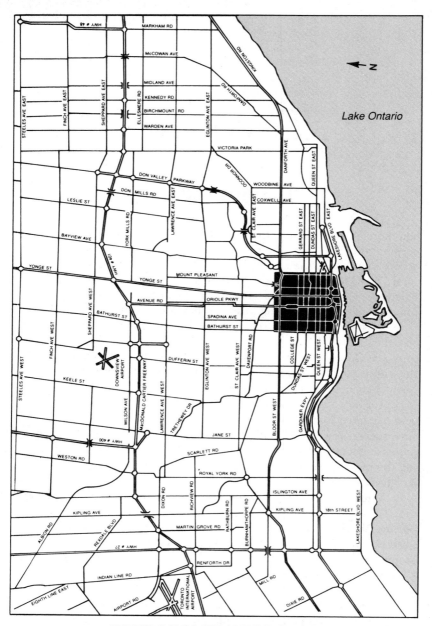

METROPOLITAN TORONTO

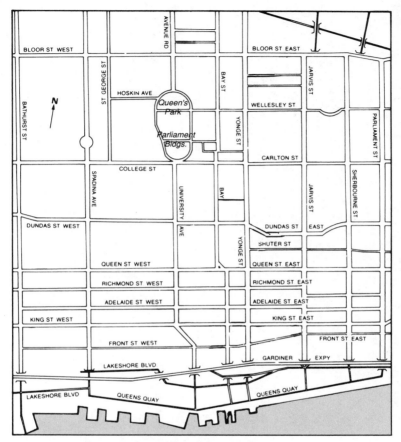

CENTER OF TORONTO

ern Canada. It was not until after 1945 that the ethnic character of Toronto changed dramatically. Immigrants from many different countries have settled in Toronto, worked hard, and shared in the economic prosperity of the city.

During the decades following World War II, Toronto went through a metamorphosis. Beautiful new buildings and complexes were added, including many fine hotels and excellent restaurants. Toronto's lively theater scene became second only to New York's in the quality, variety, and number of stage offerings. Its opera and ballet companies and its symphony orchestra were given new direction and energy, receiving international acclaim. Its public transportation system, metropolitan form of government, and urban renewal policies became models for growing cities throughout the world. Stunning new museums (for art, science and technology, and zoology) and libraries were opened to a delighted public. Run-down sections were refurbished into homey enclaves and fashionable areas lined with attractive boutiques and exotic places in which to eat, drink, and be entertained.

Toronto is not only one of the most modern cities in North America, it is also a highly disciplined place. Both work and law-and-order ethics are very much alive here. Visitors are surprised at how safe and clean Toronto is, considering that so many cities in North America are quite the opposite.

Toronto has so much to offer the vacationing traveler, the weekend tourist, the businessperson, or the convention delegate that one trip will just whet the appetite for more.

A Brief History

Until 1793 Toronto was a sparsely populated area on the north shore of Lake Ontario. It was visited in 1615 by the French explorer Etienne Brûlé, and by 1720 a trading post was established here, called Fort Rouille—later Fort Toronto (meaning "meeting place" in Algonquian). After the defeat of the French forces on the Plains of Abraham in 1759, the fort was destroyed so that the victorious English could not use it.

◀ **Toronto's modern and historic buildings give substantial evidence of the ongoing vitality of the city. To the left is the CN Tower, the world's tallest free-standing structure. There is excellent dining and viewing from the top of the tower.**

The American Revolution divided the continent into the United States and British North America. In 1793 Lieutenant-Governor John Graves Simcoe, a British army officer, selected the former site of Fort Toronto for the new settlement of York, which was to provide a defensive position for the British against their main enemy, the Americans. York became the capital of Upper Canada (Ontario) and a refuge for loyalists from the United States who wanted to continue to live under the British monarchy rather than in the new republic. British military families and loyalists formed the first permanent population of York and became the social, political, and economic elite of the community. Their position was strengthened through "family compacts" both in Toronto and in Great Britain and was maintained until well into the twentieth century.

During the War of 1812, York was captured, looted, and burned by American troops. In retaliation, the British burned Washington, D.C., in 1814.

York was incorporated as a city in 1834, at which time it also took on the name of Toronto. In 1837 Toronto's first mayor, William Lyon Mackenzie, a passionate nationalist who favored a republican system of government for the country, attempted a coup by armed force. Mackenzie's short-lived rebellion failed to rouse many citizens to his cause.

In 1841 Toronto ceased to be the capital of Upper Canada when that province was united with Lower Canada (Québec) into the Province of Canada. In 1849 the city became the capital of Canada, which did not then include the Maritime Provinces. With Canada's confederation in 1867, Toronto became the capital of Ontario.

Between the confederation and the end of the Second World War, Toronto occupied itself primarily with economic growth, as a burgeoning center for finance, manufacturing, and transportation. With continual expansion of population and economic activity, in 1954 the thirteen independent municipalities of the Toronto area, including the city itself, formed themselves into a federated metropolitan government to consolidate many of their public services and to plan more effectively for future growth. Metropolitan government has worked exceedingly well in Toronto, where it has earned the reputation of being uncommonly well managed and honest as well.

With the influx of immigrants after World War II, the population of the city ballooned and diversified. Magnificent new buildings changed Toronto's skyline from dowdy to splendid. And with these cultural and physical changes, Toronto entered a new period in its history in considerably better shape than most other big cities on the continent, and the transformation continues.

How to Get to Toronto

Toronto is located on the northwest shore of Lake Ontario, 98 miles/157 km. from Buffalo and 323 miles/517 km. from Montréal.

By Car

From New England, New York State, and Ohio, take Interstate 90 to Buffalo, then take the Queen Elizabeth Way (Q.E.W.) to Toronto. From the Detroit area, cross the bridge to Windsor, Ontario, and then take Highway 401 to Toronto.

From Western Canada, travel the Trans-Canada Highway to Orillia, Ontario, then take Highway 11, which becomes Highway 400 and goes into Toronto.

From Eastern Canada, travel the Trans-Canada Highway to Montréal, where you pick up Highway 20, which becomes Highway 401 at the Ontario border and goes into Toronto.

Driving distances to Toronto from:

Boston	545 miles/872 km.
Chicago	498 miles/797 km.
Detroit	221 miles/354 km.
Halifax	1073 miles/1717 km.
Montréal	323 miles/517 km.
New York City	531 miles/850 km.
Ottawa	239 miles/382 km.
Philadelphia	528 miles/845 km.
Rochester	160 miles/256 km.
Washington, D.C.	540 miles/864 km.

By Air

Many domestic and international airlines serve Metro Toronto from other areas of Canada, from the United States, and from other countries. Lester B. Pearson International Airport is located at Highway 427 and 401, 19 miles/30 km. northwest of the city center. Air Canada and Canadian Airlines International provide frequent, daily service from numerous domestic and international cities. The airport's general information number is (416) 676–3506. Contact your local travel agent for information on airlines flying to Toronto from your area.

Lester B. Pearson International Airport has both Canadian and U.S. Customs clearances, a duty-free shop, restaurants, lounges, book and magazine shops, and many other conveniences. There is frequent (every twenty minutes), low-cost express bus service to and from several leading downtown Toronto hotels, such as the Sheraton Centre, and to and from York Mills, Yorkdale, and Islington subway stations. Call (416) 979–3511 for bus schedules. In addition, there are taxi and limousine services to and from the airport. Near the airport are motels, restaurants, and shopping centers.

By Rail

VIA Rail provides passenger rail service to Toronto from major cities in Canada. Union Station, an architectural masterpiece from the peak days of railroading, is the main terminal for all passenger services. Located at Front and Bay streets and across from the Royal York Hotel, the station is also on the subway line and has its own stop. For more information on VIA Rail service, call (416) 366–8411.

Amtrak provides service from New York City to Toronto, through Niagara Falls (one train a day). Amtrak also has frequent service to Buffalo, where you can make easy bus connections to Toronto. Call Amtrak at (800) 872–7245 for details.

By Bus

Greyhound provides bus service to Toronto from throughout Canada and the United States. Travelways and Voyageur Colonial provide service to many Ontario and other Canada destinations. All out-of-town buses arrive and depart from the Bus Terminal, 610 Bay Street, at Dundas West (downtown). Call (416) 979–3511 for information.

Rental Cars, Limousine Services, and Taxis

Rental cars—Avis, Hertz, Tilden, Thrifty, and so on—are available at Toronto International Airport and at other city locations. You are advised to reserve a car ahead through your local travel agent or by calling the company toll-free number. Some companies, such as Thrifty, will deliver a car to your hotel and complete the paperwork there.

Limousines and taxis are available at the airport. While staying in Toronto, make limo and taxi arrangements through your hotel concierge.

General Information

Time zone: Eastern

Telephone area code: 416

Police: dial 911

Medical emergencies: dial 911 or call Community Information Centre of Metro Toronto for information on health and social services available in the city—(416) 863–0505 (access available twenty-four hours a day).

Weather information: dial (416) 676–3066; (416) 676–4567 for more detail

Tourist Information

The province of Ontario has a visitor information office, dispensing free information, literature, and maps, in the Eaton Centre Galleria on Level One, 220 Yonge Street. Open weekdays from 10:00 A.M. to 9:00 P.M., Saturdays from 9:30 A.M. to 6:00 P.M. There's another Ontario visitor office at Ontario Place, located at Lake Shore Boulevard, West.

Also contact the Metropolitan Toronto Convention and Visitors Association office located at Queen's Quay Terminal at Harbourfront, 207 Queen's Quay West, Suite 509, (416) 368–9821.

Accommodations in Metro Toronto can be booked ahead by calling this central reservations number: (416) 596–7117. This is a free service.

Toll-free Travel Information

Call (800) ONT–ARIO for information on Toronto and all other areas of Ontario. Free literature can be ordered through this toll-free number.

Also call the Metropolitan Toronto Convention and Visitors Association at (416) 368–9821.

Climate and Clothing

Toronto has a more moderate climate than most Eastern Canada cities. It is comparable with that of southern New England. The average low temperature in February is 17°F/8°C, the average high 31°F/0°C. The average high temperature in August is 78°F/25°C, the average low 60°F/16°C. Rainfall is similar to that of New England (26 inches/66 cm. annually).

If you're visiting Toronto for pleasure, good, fashionable casual clothes for the season can be worn during the day and the evening. Ties and jackets are recommended for men and elegant garb for women for an evening on the town, where style, elegance, and a certain degree of formality are expected in the better restaurants, lounges, and places of entertainment. Toronto is very style conscious, and the men and women here spend a lot of money to be à la mode.

Sweaters, raincoats, walking or jogging shoes, and knock-around clothes should also be packed. Warm topcoats are essential in the winter.

Sales Tax Exemption

You can claim exemption from the provincial sales tax on accumulated purchases of $100 or more. No tax will be added if goods are sent directly to your home. Be sure to keep original receipts. Out-of-province visitors can also claim rebates on the accommodations tax. Inquire at hotel or store for details.

Convention/Business Meeting Information

The Metro Toronto Convention Centre, located downtown at 255 Front Street West, is a comprehensive, modern facility. It is situated at the foot of the CN Tower and adjacent to the Skydome Stadium. Its main exhibition hall has 200,000 square feet of space. There are a grand ballroom of 28,000 square feet; a multimedia furnished auditorium accommodating 1,350 people; and 40 meeting rooms. It is within walking distance of more than 10,000 hotel rooms. Airport bus service is available at the front door. The deluxe L'Hotel is part of this complex.

Other convention/meeting facilities are Exhibition Place, Harbourfront Showplace, Maple Leaf Gardens, St. Lawrence Hall, O'Keefe Centre, Ontario Place, Ontario Science Centre, Roy Thomson Hall, Toronto International Centre of Commerce, and the World Trade Centre.

Some of the best convention/executive hotels are: Four Seasons, Holiday Inn—Downtown, Hotel Plaza II, The King Edward, L'Hotel, the Westbury, Park Plaza, Royal York, the

Sheraton Centre, Sutton Place, Harbour Castle Westin, and the Inn on the Park.

How to Get Around Toronto

The Central Area

Metropolitan Toronto is a sprawling urban area. The terrain is essentially flat, though creased with ravines, rivers, and streams. Toronto lies on the north shore of Lake Ontario, which has several offshore islands that are popular recreational areas for the city's residents and visitors. While Toronto is Canada's largest city, most of its attractions are concentrated in a central area, which can be easily covered by foot, subway, or taxi.

Nathan Phillips Square, on Queen Street, West, marks the center of the city. Inside this square are the unusual modern buildings of City Hall, and across Queen Street stands the Sheraton Centre complex. Nearby is the Eaton Centre.

Running south from this center is Bay Street, the financial district of the city, as well as Union Station, Harbourfront, and the ferry to the harbor islands.

East of the center, running north and south, is Yonge Street, famous throughout Canada for its many stores, restaurants, and places of amusement. Yonge, Toronto's most lively street, serves as a paseo for the young, for drifters and unusual characters, and for visitors. Yonge is also the world's longest street, running from the waterfront to far beyond the metropolitan limits.

West of the city center, University Avenue leads north to the buildings of Parliament and Queen's Park. To the west of Queen's. Park are the University of Toronto and many government buildings. To the north of Queen's Park, running from east to west, is Bloor Street, which is Toronto's Fifth Avenue, graced· with many fine stores, hotels, and restaurants. In the Bloor Street area are also the Royal Ontario Museum, the Yorkville section, and the handsome new library building.

Most of Toronto's attractions, hotels, and restaurants are within or near this grid of streets. Remember to keep Nathan Phillips Square, with the new City Hall, as your central landmark. South is toward Lake Ontario, and north is toward Queen's Park and Bloor Street. The main east-west streets are Front, King, Queen, Dundas, College, and Bloor. The main north-south streets are Yonge, Bay, University, Queen's Park, and Spadina Avenue.

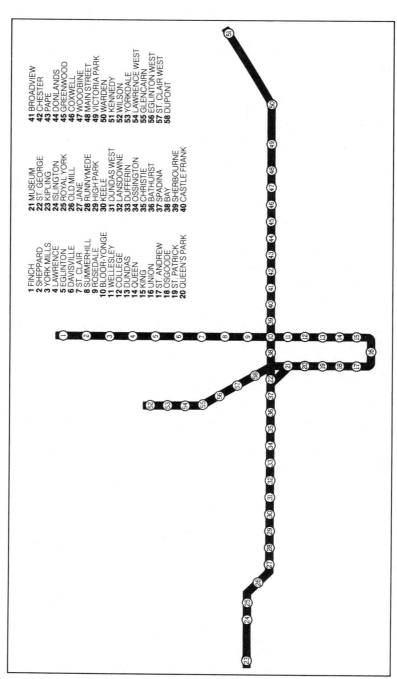

1 FINCH
2 SHEPPARD
3 YORK MILLS
4 LAWRENCE
5 EGLINTON
6 DAVISVILLE
7 ST. CLAIR
8 SUMMERHILL
9 ROSEDALE
10 BLOOR-YONGE
11 WELLESLEY
12 COLLEGE
13 DUNDAS
14 QUEEN
15 KING
16 UNION
17 ST. ANDREW
18 OSGOODE
19 ST. PATRICK
20 QUEEN'S PARK

21 MUSEUM
22 ST. GEORGE
23 KIPLING
24 ISLINGTON
25 ROYAL YORK
26 OLD MILL
27 JANE
28 RUNNYMEDE
29 HIGH PARK
30 KEELE
31 DUNDAS WEST
32 LANSDOWNE
33 DUFFERIN
34 OSSINGTON
35 CHRISTIE
36 BATHURST
37 SPADINA
38 BAY
39 SHERBOURNE
40 CASTLE FRANK

41 BROADVIEW
42 CHESTER
43 PAPE
44 DONLANDS
45 GREENWOOD
46 COXWELL
47 WOODBINE
48 MAIN STREET
49 VICTORIA PARK
50 WARDEN
51 KENNEDY
52 WILSON
53 YORKDALE
54 LAWRENCE WEST
55 GLENCAIRN
56 EGLINTON WEST
57 ST. CLAIR WEST
58 DUPONT

TORONTO SUBWAY SYSTEM

The Subway System

Toronto's metropolitan subway system (operated by the Toronto Transit Commission) is fast, frequent, safe, clean, and convenient. A single fare will take you anywhere in the system by rail, bus, or streetcar. The subway runs north and south under Yonge Street, makes a loop at Union Station, and runs north and south under University Avenue. It also runs east and west under Bloor Street, north and south under Spadina Avenue. A Light Rail Transit line will provide rapid public transportation between downtown and Harbourfront. For information about Toronto's subway system and fares, call (416) 393–INFO.

Subway stations provide access to many of Toronto's important sites:

Stations	Destinations
Bay	Bloor Street
Bloor-Yonge and St. George	Library, Bloor Street shopping area, connections on the Bloor-Danforth line to the Metropolitan Toronto Zoo and Lester B. Pearson International Airport
College	University of Toronto, Parliament buildings, provincial government offices, Kensington Market
King	Financial district
Museum	Royal Ontario Museum, Bloor Street, Yorkville shopping area
Osgoode	Nathan Phillips Square, City Hall, Chinatown, Sheraton Centre, Eaton Centre
Queen	Nathan Phillips Square, City Hall, Chinatown, Sheraton Centre, Eaton Centre
Queen's Park	University of Toronto, Parliament buildings, provincial government offices, Kensington Market

Saint Andrew   Financial district

Union   VIA Rail terminal, Royal York Hotel, and Harbourfront

The Toronto subway system operates from 6:00 A.M. to 1:30 A.M. Monday through Saturday, and from 9:00 A.M. to 1:30 A.M. Sunday.

Guided Tours and Cruises

Guided tours of Toronto are available through Gray Line, (416) 979–3511, which picks up passengers at major hotels and also has tours to Niagara Falls and other major attractions outside the city. Toronto by Trolley, (416) 869–1372, shows you the city from inside a charming 1920s Peter Witt trolley.

Central Airways provides aerial tours of Toronto and Niagara Falls (416) 363–2424. Toronto Downtown Heliport offers helicopter rides over the metro area and Niagara Falls, (416) 461–4633.

See Toronto by bike: City Cycle, (416) 466–6395, an organized tour, supplies bikes and helmets.

The following companies provide boat tours on Toronto Harbour and its islands: Toronto Harbour Tours, (416) 869–1372; PMCL Toronto Boat Cruises, (416) 283–3797; The Oriole, a Victorian-style riverboat, (416) 867–1051. All sailings depart from Harbourfront.

Niagara Falls tours are provided by Gray Line, (416) 979–3511, and Niagara Tours, (416) 868–0400.

Major Events

For more information on these major events, call the Metropolitan Toronto Convention and Visitors Association at (416) 368–9821.

International Caravan Festival, the best multicultural party anywhere, involves the entire metropolitan area for nine days in late June, when each ethnic group shows the best of its culture through art, music, dance, drama, food, and costumes. Pavilions to house the events are set up in the various neighborhoods, and visitors purchase passports admitting them to the different worlds of Caravan. One can sample the best of several foreign countries without leaving the city. Caravan has become one of Toronto's most popular annual events. If you're lucky enough to be in town when Caravan is taking place, buy a passport and just plunge in.

Caribana (Caribbean Festival), held in late June, celebrates the presence of Toronto's black population, who came from the islands of the British West Indies. Caribana features steel bands, calypso music, fruit and straw markets, a nightclub, parades, limbo dancing, art exhibitions, fashion shows, and the marvelous cuisine of the islands. The festival lasts about a week and is held on the Toronto Islands Park.

Canadian National Exhibition, which runs from mid August to early September, is the oldest and largest annual country fair in the world. It features many displays of agricultural, industrial, and cultural products, Canada's largest midway, an international air show, an aquatics show of swimmers and water skiers, and top star entertainment. Located at Lakeshore Boulevard, it offers great fun for the entire family. Admission is charged.

Festival of Festivals, ten days and nights in September, is one of the largest film festivals in North America. It's an international extravaganza of film showings, parties, and appearances by film and television stars.

The Queen's Plate, the oldest continuously run horse race in North America, is held in June at Woodbine Race Track.

The Royal Agricultural Winter Fair, held for ten days in November at Maple Leaf Gardens, features the Royal Horse Show, with international teams competing in various jumping and dressage events.

Attractions

Toronto's Parks

Toronto's lovely parks and recreational lands are open to the public for year-round enjoyment. These parks are generally clean and safe.

Marie Curtis Park, located at Forty-second Street off Lakeshore Road, west of Brown's Lane, offers swimming for adults, a wading pool for children, changing rooms, boat moorings, and launching facilities.

High Park, off the Queensway, Bloor Street, West, is available for hiking, touring, cross-country skiing, jogging, boat launching.

James Gardens, accessible via Edenbridge Drive, East, and Royal York Road, contains twenty-seven acres of lawns, flower gardens, pools, and streams. It is especially noted for its wildflowers and tulip garden.

Downsview Dells, via Sheppard Avenue, West, in beautiful Black Creek Valley, is a good place for hiking, picnics, jogging, cross-country skiing.

Toronto Islands Park is accessible by a ferry that leaves from the foot of Bay Street every twenty minutes. The park has areas for picnics, swimming, fishing, boating, jogging, and bicycling; for children, a farm with barnyard animals, swings, pony rides, and an amusement area; hiking walks, trails, and gardens; restaurants; and a magnificent view of the Toronto skyline. This splendid, low-cost recreational area should not be missed.

Taylor Creek Park, Dawes Road, south of Victoria Park Avenue, is a good area for hiking and nature study, especially birding.

Central Don Park, via Eglinton Avenue, East, offers hiking, nature study, horseback riding, picnic spots, and playing fields.

Edwards Gardens, via Lawrence Avenue, East, and Leslie Street, is a beautiful area of rolling lawns, stately trees, rock gardens, floral displays, and streams, with a rustic bridge—an exquisite park for walking and relaxing.

Morningside Park, via Morningside Avenue south of Ellesmere Road, is fine for hiking, picnics, jogging, cross-country skiing, and nature walks.

Historic and Cultural Attractions

Art Gallery of Ontario, 317 Dundas Street, West, has a permanent collection of more than seven thousand works of art. About half of these works are by Canadian artists, from both modern and early periods. The gallery has the world's largest public collection of works by the English sculptor Henry Moore, housed in a stunning wing of the museum, as well as the Klamer family collection of Inuit art, one of the most extensive in the world. The Art Gallery of Ontario is one of Canada's finest museums for painting and sculpture. Open throughout the year. Admission charge.

The Grange, built in 1817, is the oldest brick house in the city. Reached through the Art Gallery of Ontario, the Grange is an elegant Georgian-style mansion of beautiful rooms filled with antiques. Matthew Arnold was most pleased with his stay here.

CN Tower, 301 Front Street, West, at 1,815 feet high, is the world's tallest free-standing structure. The CN (Canadian National)

Tower has become Toronto's most familiar landmark and symbol. It's the best place in town, day and night, for breathtaking views of the metropolitan area, Lake Ontario, and the surrounding country- side. On especially clear days, you can see as far as Niagara Falls and the New York State shore of the lake. In the evening the lights of the city far below create an enchanting panorama. For a dramatic ex- perience, ride up the glass-enclosed outside elevators. You'll feel like Superman zooming up into the heavens. There is an observation deck on the 1,100-foot level, another one at 1,500 feet. On top of the tower is a revolving gourmet restaurant, lounge, and discotheque. Open throughout the year. Admission charge.

Tour of the Universe is at the base of the CN Tower, 301 Front Street. Within this new multimillion-dollar attraction, you enter the technological marvels of the future through a fully functioning space- port and become a passenger on a shuttle that tours the vast universe. Everything you experience—in sight, sound, sensations—simulates what space travel might be like in the twenty-first century. Tour of the Universe is an extraordinary experience for all ages. Open throughout the year. Admission charge.

Ontario Place is a cultural and entertainment complex built on three man-made islands on Lake Ontario, at 955 Lakeshore Boule- vard. A kind of mini-Expo, it supplies enough attractions to keep you and your family busy and interested throughout the day. It features the giant-screen Cinesphere, big star entertainment at the Forum, a children's village, three pavilion theaters, a northern On- tario theme pavilion, a super waterslide, picnic areas and parklands, pedal boats, a roller-skating rink, restaurants and pubs, miniature golf, and a variety of boutiques. Open from mid May to mid Sep- tember. Admission charge.

Casa Loma, 1 Austin Terrace, is Toronto's famous medieval- style castle, built in 1914 for $3 million. With its ninety-eight rooms, crenelated towers and turrets, secret passages, elaborate halls, and sumptuous bedrooms, Casa Loma is a freak on the North American landscape but immensely fun to visit. Open throughout the year. Admission charge.

Fort York, Garrison Road (entrance off Fleet Street), is a com- plex of blockhouses and ramparts dating from the War of 1812. The refurnished officers' quarters contain bedrooms, game rooms, and a sitting room. The Centre Blockhouse features an audiovisual pre- sentation on the history of Fort York and battles in the area. During the summer months, the Eighth King's Regiment, dressed in nineteenth-century uniforms, performs infantry drills and artillery salutes. Open throughout the year. Admission charge.

Black Creek Pioneer Village, on Murray Ross Parkway in the Downsview area of Metro Toronto, thirty minutes north of downtown, is the re-creation of a nineteenth-century, rural Ontario settlement. You can visit authentically restored and furnished buildings: log farm buildings; a church, firehouse, and schoolhouse; a museum housing the largest collection of nineteenth-century toys in Canada; and shops demonstrating such crafts as broom making, flour milling, weaving, gunsmithing, and blacksmithing. The staff, dressed in period costumes, perform household tasks and village trades. There are all kinds of barnyard animals, including oxen, geese, and chickens. An 1850s inn and stagecoach stop offers delicious full-course meals and afternoon tea. The 78th Fraser Highlanders show aspects of nineteenth-century military life. Open mid March to the end of the year. Admission charge. Call (416) 736–1733.

Riverdale Farm, River and Gerrard streets, is an old-fashioned working farm above the meandering Don River. Here you can see a wide variety of animals, watch people perform traditional farm chores and make handcrafts, and, in the fall, attend a typical country harvest celebration. Free.

George Scott Railton Heritage Centre, 2130 Bayview Avenue, is a fine museum devoted to the history and work of the Salvation Army in Canada and Bermuda. Free.

Todmorden Mills Museum, 67 Pottery Road, was the site of a nineteenth-century mill and has two restored pre-1867 houses, an old-time brewery, and the Old Don Train Station. Admission charge.

Colborne Lodge, at the south end of High Park, a fine nineteenth-century residence in a beautiful setting, was the home of John C. Howard, architect and city surveyor. Its picture gallery has more than a hundred of Howard's original drawings and paintings. Demonstrations of nineteenth-century crafts are also held at Colborne Lodge. Open throughout the year. Admission charge.

Museum of Ceramic Art, 111 Queen's Park, created by George and Helen Gardiner, features an excellent collection of porcelain and pottery: pre-Columbian pottery (2000 B.C. to fifteenth century), Italian Majolica (fifteenth and sixteenth centuries), seventeenth-century English Delftware, and Continental and English porcelain of the eighteenth century. Admission charge.

New City Hall is a complex of two curved office towers of different heights surrounding the saucer-shaped Council Chamber building. Until the opening of the CN Tower, New City Hall, designed by the Finnish architect Viljo Revell, was the main symbol for contemporary Toronto. While New City Hall is striking, it seems somehow incomplete, as the towers lack windows on the far side and thus appear to be turning their backs against parts of the city. New City Hall is located on Nathan Phillips Square, which has a fine Henry Moore sculpture and a reflecting pool that becomes a public ice-skating rink in the winter. Guided tours of New City Hall are provided every half hour daily. Free.

St. Lawrence Hall, located on the southwest corner of King and Jarvis streets, was established in 1850 as a hall for public gatherings. Jenny Lind, the "Swedish Nightingale," sang here in 1851. It is one of the more attractive historical buildings in Toronto and can be hired for meetings.

Royal Ontario Museum (ROM), Avenue Road at Bloor Street, is Canada's foremost public museum. The ROM's wide-ranging collection includes some of the finest pieces of ancient Chinese art in the world, as well as ancient Egyptian, medieval, Renaissance, and American Indian art. The museum also offers extensive displays of minerals, fossils, mammals, birds, fish, and other natural history areas. Special exhibitions—such as "Treasures of the Holyland"—are held all year. Open throughout the year. Admission charge.

McLaughlin Planetarium, part of the ROM, seats visitors in contoured armchairs and takes them on fantastic voyages through the heavens. This is one of the best planetarium shows in North America. Open throughout the year. Admission charge. Call (416) 586–5736.

Canadian Decorative Arts Museum, Sigmund Samuel Building, 14 Queen's Park Crescent, has a marvelous collection of antiques, artifacts, and historical documents from Ontario, Québec, and other parts of Canada. This interesting museum, across the street from the Parliament buildings, often overlooked by visitors, is well worth the visit. Open throughout the year. Free.

Parliament Buildings, located on Queen's Park, form the seat of government for the Province of Ontario. The huge Romanesque, sandstone buildings, designed by Boston architect H. H. Richardson, look down University Avenue and are a focus for many parades and ceremonies, such as a "royal progress," when the queen or members of the royal family visit. A fine statue of Queen Victoria graces the front of the buildings. The historic Legislative Chamber and precious mineral displays in the corridors are of interest, as are the interior decorations and portraits. Open throughout the year. Free guided tours are provided. Call (416) 965–4028.

Canada Sports Hall of Fame, Exhibition Place, off Lakeshore Boulevard, depicts the history of sports in Canada and features exhibitions about the nation's great athletes. Open throughout the year. Free.

Mackenzie House, 82 Bond Street, was home for William Lyon Mackenzie, Toronto's first mayor and leader of the rebellion of 1837. This restored home is furnished with mid-nineteenth-century antiques. Open throughout the year. Admission charge.

Marine Museum of Upper Canada, Exhibition Place, housed in the officers' quarters of an 1841 Stanley army barracks, shows Toronto's maritime history: ship models, relics of sunken ships, and Saint Lawrence Seaway lore. An old steam tug rests outside. Open throughout the year. Admission charge.

Metropolitan Toronto Library, 789 Yonge Street, designed by Raymond Moriyama, is one of the most unusual and appealing public reference libraries on the continent. Around a large atrium hung with plants are the floors for books and magazines. A stream flows through the main floor, and there are splashes of bright color everywhere. You may not have come to Toronto to visit a library, but this one is a must. Open throughout the year. Free. Call (416) 393–7196.

University of Toronto, across from Queen's Park, is where scientists discovered insulin and developed the first heart pacemaker and Pabulum. The University of Toronto is composed of several colleges, among them King's (the oldest) and Trinity (the most prestigious). The campus has a diverse collection of architectural styles: For example, Hart House is neo-Gothic, and University College is Romanesque. Feel free to stroll the campus. Many concerts, exhibitions, and special events are open to the public. Free guided walking tours of the historic midtown campus are available during the summer. Call (416) 978–2021.

Allan Gardens, at Sherbourne and Jarvis streets, is an extensive downtown greenhouse complex displaying tropical and semitropical trees, flowering creepers, and plants. This is a wonderful place in the winter. Open throughout the year. Free.

A visit to the stunning Metropolitan Toronto Library, designed by Canadian architect Raymond Moriyama, is a must. ▶

Montgomery's Inn, 4709 Dundas Street, West, built in 1832 and a fine example of loyalist or late Georgian architecture, has been restored and furnished in its period. A costumed staff works at the crafts of the mid-nineteenth century. Open throughout the year. Admission charge.

Osgoode Hall, Queen Street, West, next to the New City Hall, is a large neoclassical mansion, built in the early nineteenth century. The Law Society of Upper Canada has been housed here since 1830. Osgoode Hall is the finest example of historical architecture in Toronto. It is enclosed by a wrought-iron fence with special gates designed to keep cows from entering the grounds. There are no official visiting hours, but you may be permitted to see some of the interior. The Great Library on the second floor is the prize jewel of the building.

Campbell House, 160 Queen Street, West, a fine brick mansion, was the home of William Campbell, chief justice of Upper Canada from 1825 to 1829. It has period furnishings and features a model of the town of York as it was in 1825. Open throughout the year. Admission charge.

The SkyDome, located adjacent to the CN Tower, is Toronto's spectacular new venue for sports and entertainment. The SkyDome is the new home for the Toronto Bluejays baseball team (American League), the Argonauts football team (Canadian Football League), and a variety of other sporting and entertainment events. The Sky-Dome features a retractable roof that can open or close in just twenty minutes, providing ideal climate conditions for players and spectators. It also has a gourmet restaurant, the "world's longest cocktail bar," and many other amenities.

Harbourfront, a unique indoor-outdoor recreational and entertainment complex, is located on the shore of Lake Ontario. It includes Queen's Quay Terminal (an extensive shopping complex), antique market, a railway museum, Sunday flea market, art galleries, craft shops, hotels, restaurants, playgrounds for children, cinema, and plenty of beautiful space for walking, enjoying the waterfront, dancing, and listening to concerts—all in downtown Toronto. Ferries for the Toronto Islands leave from here.

Toronto Stock Exchange, 2 First Canadian Place, is the largest stock exchange in Canada. The TSE offers free tours and an audio-visual presentation of how it operates. Free.

Spadina, 285 Spadina Road, is the fine estate of James Austin, a leading Toronto "money man." Tours through this impressive mansion and its beautiful grounds are available. Admission charge.

Museum of the History of Medicine, 277 Bloor Street, has exhibits describing centuries of medical research and health care. Free.

Redpath Sugar Museum, 95 Queen's Quay, shows how sugar is refined and tells about the industry in Canada. Redpath family history is also shown. Free.

The Towers of Mammon

The Royal Bank Plaza, corner of Front and Bay streets, is probably one of the most beautiful and extravagant modern buildings in North America. Its serrated glass walls are imbedded with hundreds of thousands of dollars worth of gold dust, and its atrium contains a waterfall, trees, plants, flowers, and an unusual hanging sculpture consisting of nearly nine thousand aluminum tubes.

The Toronto Dominion Centre, with handsome black shafts designed by Mies van der Rohe, is nearby. The Toronto Dominion Bank Tower features art exhibitions and a gourmet restaurant on the fifty-fourth floor.

First Canadian Place, also nearby, has seventy-two stories and is the tallest office structure in the city.

All these complexes are part of the underground city of enclosed walkways replete with shops and restaurants.

Just Outside Toronto

Metro Toronto Zoo, 25 miles/40 km. northeast of downtown, via Highway 401 (and accessible by subway and bus), is an exceptional zoo and ranks with the best in the world. It is unique in that it re-creates in six zoogeographic regions the natural environment, including plants, soil, and climate, of the animals on display. Here you can see Siberian tigers, orangutans, gorillas, polar bears, and more. The Metro Zoo occupies a 710-acre site, displaying some 5,000 mammals, birds, reptiles, amphibians, and fish. The attractive pavilions that house the various zoogeographic regions are also equipped with audiovisual aids to enhance your visit. An elevated monorail train takes you through natural areas where magnificent wolves and other large North American animals make their homes. During the winter, visitors are encouraged to tour the zoo on cross-country skis (rentals are available). Open throughout the year. Admission charge. Call (416) 392–5900.

Ontario Science Centre, Don Mills Road at Eglinton Avenue, East (accessible by subway and bus), is considered one of the foremost museums of science and technology in the world. Designed by Raymond Moriyama, the facility is built on the top, side, and bottom of a steep ravine, and you take special escalators up and down the different levels. This unique museum features nearly 600 exhibits, many of which can be operated by visitors (touch 500,000 volts of electricity and have your hair stand on end). Museum displays explore space, earth, biology, communications, transportation, industry, and chemistry. Everyone in the family will enjoy the Ontario Science Centre and will learn a great deal as well. There is also a restaurant and gift shop. Open throughout the year. Admission charge. Call (416) 429–4100.

McMichael Collection of Canadian Art, located in Kleinburg (25 miles/40 km. north of downtown Toronto), is a beautiful museum, built from hand-hewn timbers and native stone, set in a 600-acre park overlooking a lovely river valley. Some of the gallery rooms focus on the works of Canada's immortal "Group of Seven" painters: Tom Thomson (the founder of the group and its most famous member), A. Y. Jackson, J. E. H. MacDonald, Lawren Harris, Arthur Lismer, Frederick Varley, Franklin Carmichael, A. J. Casson, Frank H. Johnston, Edwin Holgate, and Lionel Lemoine Fitzgerald. The museum also has Clarence Gagnon's paintings for the famous book *Maria Chapdelaine*, depicting early Québec rural life, and a large collection of original Inuit prints and carvings and Canadian Indian paintings. Tom Thomson's painting shack and the graves of several Group of Seven painters are on the premises. Special exhibitions are held throughout the year. This museum has a restaurant and a shop offering works of Canadian artisans for sale. Open throughout the year. Admission charge. (416) 893–ARTS.

Canada's Wonderland, located between Rutherford Road and Major MacKenzie Drive on Highway 400 (20 miles/32 km. north of downtown), is a 320-acre theme park featuring the Hanna-Barbera cartoon characters (Yogi Bear and his pals), a storybook mountain whose cascading waterfall is the central point in the park, the Crystal Palace, a medieval fair, an international street of shops and bazaars, and many exciting rides, including four rollercoasters. There are all

◀ Canada's Wonderland is the largest theme park in the country. It's fun for the entire family. Yogi Bear and the other Hanna-Barbera cartoon characters help to make it one of the most popular fantasy lands in Canada.

kinds of restaurants, including several selling ethnic foods, and much, much more. Canada's Wonderland is similar in quality to the large and very popular theme parks (such as Disneyland) in the United States. Open late May to early September. Admission charge. Call (416) 832–2205.

Parkwood, 270 Simcoe Street in Oshawa, is the fifty-five-room grand mansion of the late Colonel R. S. McLaughlin, founder of General Motors of Canada. This beautiful estate has an art gallery, teahouse, gardens, and a main house filled with many beautiful antiques. Admission charge. Call (416) 579–1311.

Hamilton

When you are traveling between Niagara Falls and Toronto via the Queen Elizabeth Way, consider stopping midway in the large industrial city of Hamilton to visit these major attractions:

African Lion Safari and Game Farm, Highways 8 and 52, 11 miles/18 km. northwest of Hamilton, allows you to drive your car through the domains of lions, cheetah, and other African and North American animals that roam free. A monkey jungle is home to a hundred African baboons. Open throughout the year. Admission charge.

Canadian Football Hall of Fame, City Hall Plaza, depicts the history of Canadian professional football over the past century. Open throughout the year. Admission charge.

Dundurn Castle, Dundurn Park, York Boulevard, is a splendid nineteenth-century mansion built by Sir Allan Napier MacNab, prime minister of the Province of Canada (1854–56). This thirty-six-room mansion, one of the finest in all of Canada, is furnished with period antiques, and the gardens and grounds are especially lovely. Open throughout the year. Admission charge.

Royal Botanical Gardens, via Highways 2 and 6, located at the westernmost tip of Lake Ontario, consists of some two thousand acres of gardens and nature walks and a four-hundred-acre arboretum. Visitors are encouraged to relax at the Tea House, overlooking beautiful scenery, and to hike the shoreline of Coote's Paradise Marsh and the trails along the wooded ravine lands. Open throughout the year. Free.

Recreational Sports

The metropolitan area has a number of public and private golf courses, tennis courts, swimming pools, and fitness facilities. There are also jogging routes and water sport areas. Your hotel concierge will be happy to make suggestions and reservations. Most major places of accommodation also have swimming pools and various recreational and exercise facilities.

Professional Sports

The Toronto Blue Jays, of the American League, play baseball at the SkyDome, adjacent to CN Tower in downtown. The sensational Blue Jays offer baseball fans the chance to see them as well as the Yankees, the Red Sox, and other American League teams play in Toronto. Call (416) 595–0077 for ticket and schedule information.

The Argonauts are fierce competitors in the Canadian Football League. They also play their home games at the SkyDome. Call (416) 595–1131 for ticket information.

The Toronto Maple Leafs, of the National Hockey League, have won the coveted Stanley Cup eleven times, which makes them one of the best teams in professional hockey history, though their record in recent years has not been up to their previous excellence. At any rate, tickets for home games sell out fast. The Maple Leafs play at Maple Leaf Gardens, 60 Carlton Street. Call (416) 977–1641 for information.

Horse races take place at the Woodbine Race Track, Rexdale Boulevard, at Highway 427. The Queen's Plate, Canada's most prestigious thoroughbred race, is held here in June. Call (416) 675–6110 for the schedule. There is also thoroughbred racing at Greenwood Race Track, 1669 Queen Street, East. Call (416) 698–3131 for details.

Accommodations

Toronto has a wide assortment of hotels and motels, both in the central city and in outlying areas. The Royal York has been a top Toronto hotel for decades, and sumptuous, full-service new hotels, such as the Sheraton Centre, Four Seasons Toronto, Harbour Castle Westin, L'Hotel, King Edward, and Inn on the Park, offer the sophisticated traveler deluxe comfort and first-rate conveniences. There are also plenty of moderately priced accommodations for those with more limited budgets. And U.S. and other foreign visitors can get good value because of the favorable exchange rate. In addition, many of the better hotels offer special weekend packages that give you splendid accommodations at about half the cost of the weekday rate, city tours, and other goodies. If you're traveling with children, ask whether they can stay in your room for free. Commercial travelers and senior citizens should also inquire about special rates. Most major credit cards are accepted in metropolitan hotels and motels, but inquire about yours ahead of time. And save yourself a lot of time and trouble by having your travel agent do the bookings for you. Because Toronto is busy throughout the year, advance reservations are highly recommended.

Accommodation Toronto will help you make the kind of reservations you want and at prices you can afford to pay. This is a free service. Call (416) 596–7117.

The following is a listing of recommended places to stay in Toronto:

The Very Best

Four Seasons Toronto, 21 Avenue Road, (416) 964–0411, offers excellent accommodations and services. The Four Seasons is Toronto's best hotel and has been consistently so through the years. Located in the chic Bloor-Yorkville area, with its vast array of smart shops and restaurants, and within walking distance of the Royal Ontario Museum and the stunning Metropolitan Toronto Library, the hotel features a swimming pool, health facilities, restaurants, and lounges. Truffles is its elegant, gourmet dining room, and La Serre is a relaxing place for cocktails and entertainment. Expensive.

The Sheraton Centre, 123 Queen Street, West, (416) 361–1000, has one of the best downtown locations: It's across the street from New City Hall, on top of the extensive underground city of shops and restaurants, and within a few steps of the fabulous Eaton Centre. It features its own inner park with a waterfall that flows into the lobby, a swimming pool with a South Seas motif, a health club, and several restaurants, such as the elegant Winter Palace, overlooking the city, and an authentic English pub that was shipped over, lock, stock, and Watney's, from the mother country. The Sheraton Centre, a favorite hotel for conventions, has adequate space for even the largest meetings. Expensive.

Inn on the Park, 1100 Eglinton Avenue, East, (416) 444–2561, is near the Ontario Science Centre and a fifteen-minute drive from downtown. Inn on the Park is the perfect place for those who want superb accommodations combined with many resort amenities. The Inn on the Park is set on beautifully landscaped acres. It offers swimming, skating, cross-country skiing, tennis, jogging, and raquetball, also five restaurants and lounges and shopping in fourteen boutiques. Seasons is its top restaurant. Expensive.

King Edward Hotel, 37 King Street, East, (416) 863–9700, fully restored to its former glittering magnificence, specializes in European-style service, the finest cuisine, and opulent decor. Among its features are twenty-four-hour room service, secretarial services, a whirlpool, and a sauna. Expensive.

The Windsor Arms, 22 Saint Thomas Street, (416) 979–2341, a small hotel that has been serving discriminating guests since 1928, is preferred by the rich and famous because of its high level of personal service. Every room is different and furnished with Canadian antiques. Its restaurants—the Courtyard Café and the Three Small Rooms—are regarded as among the very best in Toronto. Expensive.

Harbour Castle Westin, 1 Harbour Square, (416) 869–1600, set right on the edge of the waterfront and overlooking Lake Ontario and the harbor islands, offers first-class accommodations and service for the sophisticated traveler. It also is a favorite with businesspeople and conventions. An elegant restaurant sits atop the building, slowly revolving and providing magnificent vistas of the city skyline and of the lake; the restaurant's Sunday brunch offers a wide assortment of foods at a reasonable price. The hotel also features a swimming pool, health club, boutiques, and many other conveniences. Expensive.

The Royal York, 100 Front Street, West, (416) 368–2511, Toronto's largest hotel, has been an integral part of the city for many years. Across the street from Union Station and in the heart of the financial district, the excellent Royal York is popular with travelers and businesspeople. Among its outstanding restaurants is the Imperial Room, which features fine cuisine and a live floor show with top talent. The Royal York is connected to the shops and attractions of the underground city. Expensive.

Hotel Plaza II, 90 Bloor Street, East, (416) 961–8000, is built around a courtyard planted with trees, grass, and flowers, a delightful place, especially in the winter. A swimming pool, health club, and sauna are available to guests at the Bloor Park Club, which is in the building. Expensive.

Sutton Place, 955 Bay Street, (416) 924–9221, offers large rooms and outstanding personal service. Fine restaurants, swimming pool, health club, and sauna are some of its conveniences. Expensive.

Park Plaza, 4 Avenue Road, (416) 924–5471, is a favorite hotel with top entertainers and executives, stressing personal service and high quality. The Prince Arthur Dining Room is elegant and offers fine haute cuisine. Expensive.

Bradgate Arms, 54 Foxbar Road, in the St. Clair area, (416) 968–1331, is a small, elegant hotel. It's favored by those who want a pleasant urban refuge that's a bit removed from the frenetic pace of the city center. The hotel's restaurant is superior for its continental cuisine and fine service. The Bradgate has a lovely atrium, a library with comfortable leather chairs, and a lounge offering entertainment. There's a nice little park in front. Expensive.

L'Hotel, Front Street (next to the new Convention Centre), (416) 597–1400, is a new deluxe hotel,offering all the amenities, plus a convenient downtown location to all attractions and shops. Expensive.

Other Fine Accommodations

Delta Chelsea Inn, 33 Gerrard Street, West, (416) 595–1975, located in downtown Toronto, offers good value for your money in accommodations and conveniences, such as a swimming pool, restaurants, lounges, a health club, game rooms. Some rooms have balconies. Ideal for families. Moderate.

Holiday Inn Downtown, 89 Chestnut Street, (416) 977–0707, provides several restaurants and lounges, as well as swimming pools, sauna, game rooms, sun terrace. Moderate to expensive.

Ramada Inn Downtown, 111 Carlton Street, (416) 977–8000, located near Maple Leaf Gardens, features a rooftop restaurant, swimming pool, and saunas. Moderate to expensive.

Venture Inn/Toronto Yorkville, 89 Avenue Road, (416) 964–1220, a new hotel from an up-and-coming Canadian chain, located in the middle of chic Toronto. Moderate.

Westbury, 475 Yonge Street, (416) 924–0611, provides good accommodations in a centrally located hotel. Its restaurant offers fine French cuisine. Expensive.

The Brownstone, 15 Charles Street, East, (416) 924–7381. This European-style hotel in a strategic downtown location near Eaton Centre and Bloor Street provides many guest amenities, including free shoeshine service and morning paper. It has a good restaurant and cocktail lounge. Expensive.

Carlton Inn, 30 Carlton Street, (416) 977–6655, has comfortable rooms with small refrigerators, a swimming pool, and a sauna. Moderate.

Essex Park Hotel, 300 Jarvis Street, (416) 977–4823, offers nicely refurbished rooms in an older hotel, near downtown attractions and shopping. It has a restaurant and lounge. Moderate.

Airport Area Accommodations

Bristol Place, 950 Dixon Road, (416) 675–9444, is a super luxurious hotel, well regarded for its high level of personal service. It features gourmet restaurants and lounges, swimming pools, a health club, and saunas. Expensive.

Constellation Hotel, 900 Dixon Road, (416) 675–1500, features comfortable accommodations and fine dining, with a swimming pool, indoor tennis, health club, and game room. Moderate to expensive.

Cara Inn, 6257 Airport Road, (416) 678–1400, has comfortable rooms and a good restaurant, with a swimming pool in the garden area. Moderate to expensive.

Skyline Hotel, 655 Dixon Road, (416) 244–1711, offers modern accommodations and full hotel services at reasonable prices. Moderate.

Dining

In the not-too-distant past, Torontonians with a craving for truly fine haute cuisine would have to travel all the way to Montréal. Though Montréal still cannot be topped for French-inspired haute cuisine, its reputation for gastronomic superiority is being challenged by Toronto. And for variety of restaurants, no city in Canada can top Toronto, not even Montréal.

Toronto offers you elegant and expensive restaurants, ethnic restaurants representing the national cuisines of almost every country on earth, novelty restaurants, and every kind of low-cost, fast-food place ever invented. Toronto, a voracious consumer of all kinds of goods and services, attracts the best products from all of Canada's regions. Canadian western beef, for example, is considered by connoisseurs to be the finest in North America.

Dining habits in Toronto are similar to those in major cities throughout the continent. There is no essential difference between the business luncheon in Toronto and the one in New York City. The evening meal at a restaurant usually begins any time after 7:00 P.M., and while leisurely, it is not necessarily the lengthy ritual it can become in Montréal (Torontonians usually want to get on with other activities). Both men and women should dress well for dining in the better restaurants. Toronto is a highly fashion-conscious city. On the other hand, there are many excellent eateries that welcome you as you are—sometimes the more outrageous and eclectic, the better.

Toronto is a very active restaurant town throughout the year. Advance reservations are recommended for the better and more popular spots. Most restaurants accept major credit cards.

Liquor is served in lounges and most restaurants from noon to 1:00 A.M. The legal drinking age in Ontario is nineteen years old.

The following is a listing of recommended restaurants in Toronto:

Barberian's, 7 Elm Street, near Eaton Centre, (416) 597–0335, is the author's choice as the best steakhouse in Toronto. The meat—prime roast beef and steak—is so tender that it just about melts in your mouth, and all the fixings are delicious and generous. First-time visitors are made to feel like regulars, and the service is great. Expensive.

Sir Nicholas, 91 Roncesvalles Avenue, (416) 535–4540, is the best restaurant in Toronto for Polish cuisine and ambience with entertainment and dancing as well. Moderate.

Barmalay, 645 Bay Street, (416) 597–0923, specializes in Russian food, songs, and hospitality. Tea is served from a samovar, in a restaurant that looks like an old Russian country inn. Moderate.

Scaramouche, 1 Benenuto Place, at Avenue and St. Clair, (416) 961–8011, is a popular gourmet restaurant hidden away in the basement of an apartment building. Amusing eclectic decor and a menu of unusual dishes, the creations of chefs who combine flair with taste. Expensive.

Lobster Trap, 1962 Avenue Road, (416) 787–3211. Here you pick the live lobster you want, and the chef will cook it the way you want. Considering the price of lobster, the tab for what you get is fair and a better buy than at most top restaurants. Celebrities frequent the Lobster Trap, and you may get to snap open lobster claws near one. Moderate to expensive.

Fenton's, 2 Gloucester Street, (416) 961–8485. This is a restaurant of three rooms, of which the Garden is most favored by Torontonians. Lots of live flowers add beauty, color, and aroma to this charming dining place. Imaginative continental cuisine is practiced and well received at Fenton's. Expensive.

Auberge Gavroche, 90 Avenue Road, (416) 920–0956. Gavroche is a deluxe French restaurant, perhaps one of the finest of its genre in Toronto. It is located in a townhouse, and the decor, ambience, and service provide an ideal setting for the *haute cuisine* experience. Expensive.

Mövenpick, 165 York Street, (416) 366–5234, is a copy of a Zurich restaurant and offers great value for all kinds of Swiss specialties. Inexpensive to moderate.

Le Trou Normand, 90 Yorkville Avenue, (416) 967–5956. The fashionable Yorkville section of Toronto is where you can dine on Normandy-style cooking, such as *lapin* (rabbit). It's a nice change from the usual *cuisine de Française.* Expensive.

Hazelton Café, Hazelton Lanes in Yorkville, (416) 923–6944. This enticing restaurant is part of a chic shopping mall in smartypants Yorkville. It is famous for its brunches, a sumptuous array of foods, and bouquets of freshly cut flowers. Hazelton brings out the epicurean in all of us. Moderate to expensive.

Winston's, 104 Adelaide Street, West, (416) 363–1627, with an art nouveau decor and superb haute cuisine, attracts an affluent clientele. Expensive.

Top of Toronto, CN Tower, 301 Front Street, West, (416) 362–5411, is the world's highest revolving restaurant, offering Continental fare, steaks, and such. Sunday brunch is special. Expensive.

Ginsberg and Wong, 71 McCaul Street, is within the Village by the Grange, (416) 979–3458. Here you can order a pastrami on rye with an egg roll on the side; or matzoh balls with lobster sauce. Ginsberg and Wong serve up the best of two worlds exceedingly well for not much money. Inexpensive.

The Mermaid, 330 Dundas Street, West, (416) 597–0077, is an old favorite with Torontonians. Lobster bouillabaisse is a specialty. Moderate.

Underground Railroad Tavern, 225 King Street, East, (416) 869–1400, serves Old South-style soul food. Inexpensive to moderate.

Pink Pearl, 207 Queen's Quay, (416) 366–9162, is a cut above the usual Chinese restaurant; the word *elegant* is not inappropriate here. There is a much more interesting (exotic) selection of culinary concoctions. An ideal choice if you want an "upscale" Oriental dining treat. Moderate to expensive.

Masa, 195 Richmond Street, (416) 977–9519. Considered by many to be Toronto's "number one" Japanese restaurant, Masa has a bar for sushi mavens and a beautiful dining room where you can sit North American or *tatami* style and sup wonderfully on *yakiniku* and *mitsu mame.* Expensive.

Florentine Court, 97 Church Street, (416) 364–3687. When the folks at Florentine Court say, *"Mangia!"* (Eat!), they mean dig into a magnificent seven-course Italian feast—everything from salami to sweets. If you leave hungry, it's your fault. Moderate.

Bombay Palace, 71 Jarvis, (416) 368–8048. Tandoori, curry, and kabab are specialties of this attractive Indian restaurant. Bombay is thought to be the best of its kind in the city. Moderate.

Kiku, 214 King Street, (416) 598–5458, is the best place in town for Japanese and Korean cuisines. Moderate to expensive.

Le Canard, 12 Amelia Street (fashionable Cabbagetown section, east of city center), (416) 924–9901, quite naturally has duck (boned, served rare and with crisp skin) as its speciality—with orange sauce, cognac, and green peppercorns, sautéed with Armagnac and prunes, grilled with white turnips and small onions or with lime and dill. Chef/owner Benchitrit, from Paris, also offers bouillabaisse, boned pheasant, marinated salmon, chicken steak with herbs, and roasted quail. Fine cuisine in a room with many strange oil paintings—some quite erotic. Expensive.

Telfer's, 212 King Street, West, (416) 977–4447, has a varied menu of French, Italian, and North American dishes. This restaurant attempts to create an authentic Toronto cuisine for sophisticated palates by drawing on foods and concoctions from the city's many international flavors. Telfer's is highly regarded for its culinary efforts. It is located in a refurbished older building, right across the street from Roy Thomson Hall, which conveniently allows you to dine well before or after the symphony. Moderate to expensive.

Crispins, 64 Gerrard Street, East, (416) 977–1919, offers excellent Continental cuisine with a seasonal menu. The restaurant is located in the basement of a historic nineteenth-century building. Moderate.

Jacques' Omelettes, 126A Cumberland Street, (416) 961–1893. Jacques', a pretty place in colorful Yorkville, can give you a choice from close to twenty different omelets, and there are also quiches, sandwiches, salads, and many other good things to eat. Inexpensive to moderate.

Lichee Garden, 595 Bay Street, (416) 977–3481, is Toronto's oldest and one of its best Chinese restaurants, offering an extensive menu with many unusual as well as familiar dishes. Inexpensive to moderate.

Noodles, 1221 Bay Street, (416) 921–3171. There's far more to Noodles than pasta; try the osso buco, fried ice cream, snails, and goat cheese. Here is one of Toronto's more creative Italian restaurants—fun and delicious. Moderate to expensive.

The Keg at the Mansion, 515 Jarvis Street (at Wellesley Street), (416) 964–6609, offers good roast beef, steak, and seafood and a salad bar. The restaurant is in the former home of Vincent and Raymond Massey (King George V and Queen Mary stayed here). Inexpensive to moderate.

Maison Basque, 15 Temperance Street, (416) 368–6146, serves Basque cuisine. Inexpensive to moderate.

The Sultan's Tent, 1280 Bay Street, (416) 961–0601, offers Moroccan cuisine and ambience. Inexpensive to moderate.

Entertainment

Toronto has evolved into the entertainment capital of Canada. Today Toronto is second only to New York City in the performing arts: live theater, ballet, symphony, and opera. Toronto was the home of such great stars as Mary Pickford, Raymond Massey, and Lorne Greene. Many of today's top entertainers with Canadian roots, such as Donald Sutherland and Christopher Plummer, began their careers in Toronto.

There is some live theatrical or musical event being performed in Toronto almost every night of the week throughout the year; most often there are several excellent choices for an evening's entertainment. The larger hotels have services that provide information on current entertainment and assist you in getting tickets.

The following is a listing of performing arts centers, theaters, dinner theaters, cabarets, and discotheques in downtown Toronto:

O'Keefe Center, Front Street, East, at Yonge Street, (416) 872–2262, is home for the outstanding National Ballet of Canada and the Canadian Opera Company. It also presents a wide variety of popular dramatic and musical performances. Concerts by the National Ballet are especially recommended, as this troupe ranks among the top ballet companies in the world.

Royal Alexandra Theatre, 260 King Street, West, (416) 593–

4211, is the grande dame of live theater houses in Canada. Here you can see the most popular Broadway and London dramas and musicals with the world's leading entertainers.

St. Lawrence Centre, 27 Front Street, East, (416) 366–7723, presents performances by a resident repertory company and by visiting theater, opera, and dance companies.

The Roy Thomson Hall, 60 Simcoe Street, (416) 593–4822, is home for the Toronto Symphony Orchestra and the Mendelssohn Choir, also a venue for concerts by other groups and individuals. The magnificent 100,000-square-foot hall, designed by Arthur Erickson, features a sunken courtyard and an auditorium seating 2,800 people. Its unusual curvilinear shape is covered with reflective glass, which shimmers in daylight and becomes transparent in the evening as the interior lights shine through. The Roy Thomson Hall gives Toronto one of the foremost concert facilities in the world.

Leah Posluns Theatre, 4588 Bathurst Street, (416) 630–6752, shows innovative, avant-garde works in a modern facility.

Toronto Free Theatre, 26 Berkeley Street, (416) 368–7601, has two stages in its facility and presents new Canadian drama and revivals of past favorites.

Factory Theatre, 125 Bathurst Street, (416) 864–9971, stages contemorary Canadian plays.

Centrestage, St. Lawrence Centre, (416) 366–7723, presents contemporary and classical dramas.

Toronto Truck Theatre, 94 Belmont Street, (416) 922–0084, puts on Agatha Christie's *The Mousetrap.*

Ukrainian Caravan Restaurant Cabaret, 5245 Dundas Street, West, (416) 231–7447, features cossack dances, songs, and comedy, and cossack food.

Second City Comedy Theatre, 110 Lombard Street, (416) 863–1111, is highly recommended for zany humor. Dan Aykroyd and John Candy got started here.

Limelight Dinner Theatre, 2026 Yonge Street, (416) 482–5200, presents food and Broadway musicals.

Yuk Yuk's, 1280 Bay Street, (416) 967–6425, features stand-up comics. See new talent before they become hot.

Bamboo, 312 Queen Street West, (416) 593–5771, is the place for Latin and Reggae.

El Mocambo, 464 Spadina Avenue, (416) 961–2558, is one of Canada's top spots for rock music.

Shopping

Toronto is a shopper's mecca. There are enough attractive stores here to loosen your grip on your purse or wallet. The best way to deal with the temptations of Toronto's stores is to bring a few extra dollars and splurge on something unusual and extravagant. It's better to do this than to fill your bags with a lot of souvenir junk.

One of the best treats of being in Toronto, however, is vicarious shopping, poking in and out of the splendid stores and retailing areas. Here are some of the best:

Eaton Centre, 220 Yonge Street, has to be one of the most spectacular enclosed central city shopping complexes in North America. The million-square-foot Eaton store forms the northern end of the complex, which features a multilevel glass-ceiling Galleria, containing fountains, trees, gardens, benches, and even live birds. There are also many stores and restaurants. The Galleria's southern end connects with Simpson's, another large department store. The Eaton Centre is another way in which Toronto shows us how uplifting a modern city can be.

Kensington Market, Dundas Street, West, to College Street, Spadina Avenue to Augusta Street, is a fascinating area of stores selling every imaginable ethnic food. Here Poles, Greeks, Italians, Jews, Portuguese, Jamaicans, Germans, and others come to purchase those essential ingredients to make their national foods. Kensington Market is colorful, fragrant, and raucous; it's the crossroads of the world in Toronto. The best time to visit Kensington Market is Friday afternoon and evening and Saturday morning. There are several good restaurants and delicatessens in the area.

Village of Yorkville, between Yonge Street and Avenue Road, north of Bloor Street, West, was a run-down though architecturally interesting section of private residences. During the 1960s it became Canada's version of Greenwich Village for the young. Architects, designers, and builders who saw the potential in Yorkville restored the beauty of the buildings and gave them new life as fine boutiques, art and craft galleries, and restaurants.

Also in the Yorkville area is Hazelton Lanes, 55 Avenue Road, a large and attractive shopping complex of fifty-five stores and restaurants. At 2 Bloor Street is the Hudson Bay Centre, another huge complex consisting of the Hudson Bay Company, sixty shops, ten restaurants, and the Hotel Plaza II.

Chinatown, on Dundas Street, West, at Elizabeth Street, behind City Hall, and Spadina Avenue, is packed with Chinese restaurants, grocery stores, and curio shops. It's right in the center of the city and an exotic place in which to stroll anytime. Chinatown continues to grow and now extends west beyond Spadina.

Toronto Underground is a system of walkways and shopping complexes in the heart of Toronto. This underground system, attractive and safe, interconnects the Sheraton Centre, Eaton Centre, Richmond Adelaide Centre, First Canadian Place, Toronto Dominion Centre, Commerce Court, Royal Bank Plaza, Royal York Hotel, and Union Station. Within these walkways are countless shops, restaurants, and other conveniences. The subway system, with stations at Queen Street, King Street, Union, Saint Andrew's, and Osgoode, provides access to the shopping complexes in the Bloor Street area, Parliament buildings, the University of Toronto, and the Royal Ontario Museum. The beauty of this underground network is that it separates people from traffic and weather and gives them easy access to important places in the city in the most pleasant possible environment.

Mirvish Village, Markham Street, is lined with fine Victorian residences that have been converted into boutiques, antique stores, art galleries, bookstores, and restaurants. This charming section of the city was developed by Ed Mirvish, who made his fortune from Toronto's craziest store, Honest Ed's Discount Store, on the corner of Markham and Bloor streets.

Village by the Grange, McCaul Street at Dundas, West, is an Old World–style shopping and dining complex. Some one hundred stores and restaurants line cobblestone streets, and the atmosphere is human-scale and very comfortable.

Saint Lawrence Market, 95 Front Street, East, established in 1844, has many food stalls selling meat, fish, cheese, fruits, vegetables, and many other goodies in a noisy atmosphere where loud yelling and hard bargaining go together. Open Tuesday to Saturday. On Saturday, farmers sell their goods at the Farmers' Market across the street.

CHAPTER 5

Ottawa

Ottawa Today

Ottawa, Canada's national capital, spreads out along the west bank of the historic Ottawa River. The majestic neo-Gothic buildings of Parliament seem more European than North American. Their towers and spires dominate the city and give it a romantic feel.

Ottawa offers many outstanding attractions, such as its excellent national museums. If your touring itinerary includes Montréal or Toronto, Ottawa is close enough for a convenient two- or three-day visit.

The city is part of a federal district that also includes the city of Hull, Québec, across the Ottawa River, and a number of surrounding towns in both Ontario and Québec. Hull is an integral part of the federal district, having a number of major federal government offices, the extraordinary Canadian Museum of Civilization, and nearby Gatineau Park. When you take into account all the towns and cities in this quasi-independent area, the population reaches 800,000.

The main business of Ottawa is government; tourism ranks second. The offices of most federal agencies and departments are here. The embassies of most foreign countries and their resident nationals help to make Ottawa a cosmopolitan city. In addition, Ottawa has become one of Canada's centers for high-technology research and development, a fast growing one at that. Many high-tech laboratories and companies are situated within the metropolitan area, with new enterprises sprouting up like tulips in spring.

A Brief History

Samuel de Champlain sailed by the bluffs of Ottawa in 1613, and his log described Chaudière Falls and the surrounding coun-

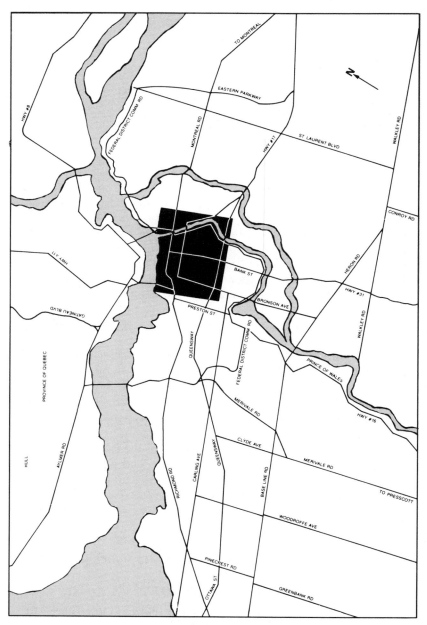

OTTAWA

tryside for future explorers. During the old French regime, the Ottawa River was part of the main fur-trading route that extended beyond the Great Lakes and across Canada. However, not until after the American War of Independence was any permanent settlement attempted here by whites. Philemon Wright, a Loyalist from Massachusetts, established a lumber mill on the Hull side of the river in 1800, and not much later Nicholas Sparks settled himself on the Ottawa side in lieu of pay from Wright.

From Wright's settlement to 1826, Ottawa was primarily a backwoods lumbering operation, populated by rugged woodchoppers who relaxed with hard liquor and loose women. In 1826, fearing American attack from the New York side of the Saint Lawrence River and needing a safe alternative water route between Montréal and Toronto, the British began construction of the Rideau Canal system, 124 miles/198 km. from Kingston to Ottawa. Colonel By, of the Royal Engineers, completed the project on schedule but the system was never used in time of war with the Americans. Instead, it became a major transportation route for lumber, agricultural products, and other supplies. Today it is a popular recreational boating area and, in winter, the "World's longest skating rink."

Ottawa was plucked from obscurity by Queen Victoria in 1857, when she selected it as the permanent capital of the United Provinces of Upper and Lower Canada. Earlier, the capital had shifted between Kingston, Toronto, Montréal, and Québec City, and there was constant bickering over just where the capital should be set. Queen Victoria's choice was a most astute one. Ottawa was an entirely new site—that is, nonpolitical in contrast to the others—and it was located on the knife's edge between Upper Canada (Ontario) and Lower Canada (Québec).

In 1860 the Prince of Wales (later Edward VII) laid the cornerstone of the Parliament buildings. They housed the first meeting of Parliament in 1865. In 1867 Ottawa became the capital of the new Dominion of Canada, with the confederation of the provinces, a role that it has admirably played since that time of new beginnings.

How to Get to Ottawa

By Car

The fast track from Montréal to Ottawa is the Trans-Canada Highway, Highway 40 to Highway 417, a distance of 127 miles/203 km. If you're traveling in the Laurentians, you can dip down to

Ottawa via Highway 105, off Highway 117. From Toronto, take Highway 401 to Highway 115 to the Trans-Canada east (Highway 7), a distance of 249 miles/399 km. You can also go along Lake Ontario and the Saint Lawrence River via Highway 401 to Highway 16 or 31.

By Air

Air Canada and Canadian Airlines International have frequent flights to and from Ottawa. First Air provides daily service from Boston. Contact your local travel agent for air service from your city to Ottawa.

There are taxis, limousines, and bus service from the airport to downtown locations. The terminal, expanded and modernized, is located about a fifteen-minute drive from city center.

Rental cars are available from Tilden, Avis, and Hertz.

By Rail

VIA Rail provides frequent daily service from Montréal and Toronto. The trains stop at a modern station at the southeastern end of Ottawa, at 2000 Tremblay Road. Call (613) 238–8289 for rail travel information. Taxis are available for the trip downtown.

By Bus

Bus service, provided by Voyageur Lines, (613) 238–5900, offers hourly Montréal service and frequent service to Toronto, including express.

General Information

Time zone: Eastern

Telephone area codes: 613 in Ontario; 819 in Québec

Police and medical emergencies: dial 911

Weather: (613) 998–3440

How to Get Around Ottawa

A shuttle bus service, making stops at attractions, takes visitors around Ottawa's core area on Confederation Boulevard and around Sussex Drive to the National Aviation Museum. Shuttle buses have information officers on board to assist visitors and sell tickets to main attractions. There is a small charge for this bus service. It operates from mid June to Labour Day.

The Central Area

Downtown Ottawa, containing most of the major attractions, is a relatively small area and compact enough so you can see almost everything on foot.

The buildings of Parliament are your central landmark. The tall Peace Tower can be seen easily from most parts of the city. Behind Parliament are the Ottawa River, Hull, Québec, and the Gatineau Hills. Wellington Street runs in front of the Parliament. The Rideau Canal bisects the city between the Parliament area and the Château Laurier. Elgin Street runs nearly parallel with the Rideau Canal and is perpendicular to Wellington Street. These streets converge at the National War Memorial. Sparks Street is parallel with Wellington and joins Elgin in the vicinity of the National War Memorial and the National Arts Centre.

To the northeast is Sussex Drive, which leads to Hull via the Alexandria and Macdonald bridges. Sussex also takes you to the Canadian War Museum, Royal Canadian Mint, Ottawa City Hall, Rideau Hall, Rideau Falls, and the exclusive Rockcliffe area.

Guided Tours and Cruises

Guided tours of attractions in the city and outlying areas are provided by Gray Line, (613) 748–4426, which picks up passengers at major hotels, and by Piccadilly Bus Tours, (613) 235–7674, which uses London-style double-deckers. Paul's Boats Lines, (613) 733–5186, offers sight-seeing cruises along both the Ottawa River and the Rideau Canal, as do Ottawa Riverboat, (613) 232–4888, and Capital Helicopter, (613) 822–2475. Tickets are available at the National Museum of Aviation. There are also many taxis and limousines in the city that can be hired for touring.

Tourist Information

Brochures and maps are available free in the National Arts Centre, at Elgin Street—open all year—and at other city locations, (613) 239–5000. You can also call toll-free (800) 267–0450 (accessible throughout Canada and continental United States). For convention and travel trade information, contact Ottawa-Canada's Capital Visitors and Convention Bureau, 222 Queen Street, Ottawa, Ontario K1P 5V9, (613) 237–5188.

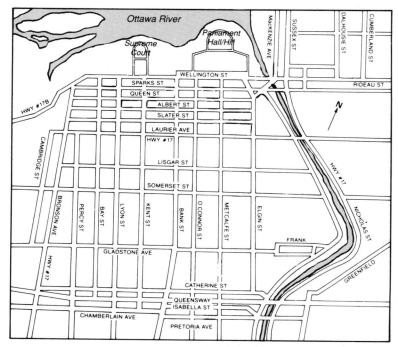

CENTER OF OTTAWA

For information on Hull, Québec, call the Association tour-
istque l'Outaouais at (819) 778–2222.

Major Events

For detailed information on the following events, call toll-free
(800) 267–0450 or (613) 239–5000. Also contact Ottawa-Canada's
Capital Visitors and Convention Bureau at the address and telephone number listed under "Tourist Information."

Festival of Spring, mid May, takes place when millions of
tulips and other floral displays burst into color throughout the city
and provide the occasion for several days of celebration. The original
tulip bulbs were given by the Netherlands government to the people
of Canada in gratitude for the refuge granted the Dutch royal family
during World War II. In addition to the magnificent flowering displays, the Festival of Spring includes parades, exhibitions, song-
fests, craft markets, and many other activities.

Canada Day Celebrations, July 1–3, celebrates Canadian
Confederation, featuring patriotic, cultural, sporting, and entertainment events.

Ottawa Winter Fair, in mid October, features many agricultural displays, a grandstand show with top entertainers, and a horse
show.

Festival of Lights runs from November 30 through January 1.
Decorative lights illuminate Parliament Hill and many other sites
throughout the city for the holiday season. There are special musical
concerts on Parliament Hill throughout December.

Winterlude, held in early to mid February, is ten days of fun
to break the back of winter. This outstanding festival features harness races on ice, an ice sculpture competition, parades, skating
races, dancing, singing, fireworks, hot air ballooning, canoe races,
great food and cheer, and all sorts of other activities to warm the
spirit.

Attractions

Confederation Boulevard—the Mile of History is a new ceremonial route that extends from Parliament Hill along Wellington
Street and Sussex Drive and goes as far as Rideau Hall, the
governor-general's residence. Attractions along this route include

renovated nineteenth-century homes, shops, galleries, and restaurants.

Parliament Buildings, off Wellington Street, are the seat of the Canadian government. The complex consists of three neo-Gothic buildings set on Parliament Hill. The Centre Block, holding the House of Commons, the Senate, and the Parliamentary Library, is graced by the 291-foot Peace Tower, with its carillon of fifty-three bells. The tower, which commemorates Canadians who gave their lives in the world wars, houses the Memorial Chamber with the Book of Remembrance. The Parliamentary Library is one of the most exquisite pieces of architecture in the city. It is all that remains of the original buildings, which were largely destroyed in a fire. The interior of the Centre Block is richly ornamented, and the House of Commons and the Senate chamber are especially worth seeing. (You can attend a session of Commons through advance arrangement with a member of the House.) The Centennial Flame in front of the buildings burns perpetually as a symbol of Canada's nationhood. The buildings on either side of the Centre Block are used as offices for the legislators, the prime minister, and members of his cabinet. Free tours of the buildings of Parliament are conducted throughout the year. During June, July, and August, you can make same-day reservations for a tour at the Infotent, located east of the Centre Block.

There are guided walking tours of Parliament Hill, from late June to early September. Call Parliamentary Guide Service at (613) 992–5042 for more information. Also attend the spectacle of the Sound and Light Show on Parliament Hill. This unusual show tells the dramatic story of Canada's past and hopes for her future through the voices of its great leaders. It runs from May to September; free. Concerts of the 53 bell Peace Tower Carillon are given on weekdays at 12:30 P.M., also on Sundays during June, July, and August.

Changing of the Guard, on the broad, lovely grounds in front of the Parliament Buildings, is one of the most splendid free shows in Canada. Patterned after the changing of the guard ceremonies in Great Britain, the Ottawa version features the spiffy Governor-General's Foot Guards and the Canadian Grenadier Guards. They perform a ceremony of precise maneuvers to stirring martial music.

Here are the houses of Canada's Parliament, majestically high over the ▶ Ottawa River. In the spring of 1982, Canada repatriated its constitution from Great Britain and became fully sovereign over its affairs.

This ceremony takes place daily, weather permitting, at 10:00 A.M., from the end of June to the end of August. Don't miss it!

Supreme Court of Canada, Wellington Street at Kent, allows visitors to see the building's beautiful lobby and court chambers, one for the Supreme Court and two for the Federal Court of Canada. You can attend proceedings. Free.

National Arts Centre, Elgin Street near Confederation Square, is a contemporary complex consisting of a 2,300-seat main auditorium, an 850-seat theater, a 350-seat studio, a 150-seat salon, and a gourmet café. The paintings, sculpture, and other artworks decorating the interior are interesting. Here is Ottawa's main venue for symphony concerts, opera, classical and experimental theater, and popular entertainment by top performers. The grounds around the arts center are graced with sculptures and flower gardens. This complex overlooks the Rideau Canal, where there are boat tours in summer and ice-skating in winter. Free tours of the National Arts Centre are offered.

National Gallery of Canada stands on Nepean Point overlooking the Ottawa River, Sussex Drive and St. Patrick Street, (613) 990–1985. The National Gallery of Canada has a new home in one of the most beautiful buildings in North America, designed by Moshe Safdie. This modern "crystal palace" houses the largest collection of Canadian art in the country, including works by the famous Group of Seven painters. It has a significant collection of art from the Middle Ages to the present, including works of Rembrandt, Van Gogh, and Picasso. Guest amenities include underground parking, a gallery shop, café and restaurant, guided tours, and wheelchair access. Open all year. Admission charge.

National Archives, 395 Wellington Street, has an extensive collection of original documents relating to Canada's history. Open throughout the year. Free. The National Library, a repository for Canadian publications, is also at this location. Open throughout the year. Free.

Canadian Museum of Civilization is located on Laurier Street in Hull, Québec, overlooking the Ottawa River, across from Parliament Buildings. The museum, reached from Ottawa via the Alexandra Bridge, is near the new home of the National Gallery of Art. This spectacular new museum, designed by Douglas Cardinal, perhaps the finest of its genre in the world, tells epic stories of the Canadians—where they came from, how they survived in a hostile wilderness, how they lived and worked, and how they created their various cultures, and how their nation progresses into the future. Visitors come into the Grand Hall, which houses a dramatic reconstruction of a Pacific Coast Indian village as it might have looked a hundred years ago. Other guest services include a children's museum, festivals and performances, an IMAX/OMNIMAX theater showing exciting films, educational programs, a resource center, a museum shop, two restaurants, and access for those with handicaps. Open throughout the year. Admission charge.

National Museum of Science and Technology, 1867 Saint Laurent Boulevard, has a large number of participatory exhibits where you can test your skills and learn more about various aspects of science. This complex also has excellent displays of locomotives, vintage cars, aircraft, and unique products of technology. A new astronomical observatory is open to the public by appointment. Open throughout the year. Admission charge.

National Aviation Museum, Rockcliffe Airport, housed in a new delta-shaped building, displays nearly a hundred historic aircraft, from the *Silver Dart*, one of the first Canadian-developed airplanes, to modern planes. Its exhibits include the history of the Royal Canadian Air Force, the heritage of wilderness bush flying, the age of transport, Canada's tradition of innovation in flight, and the opening of the nation's frontiers. Open throughout the year. Admission charge.

National Postal Museum, 365 Laurier Avenue, features an excellent collection of Canadian and British North American stamps. Stamps are sold to collectors here. Open throughout the year, Tuesday through Saturday. Free.

Canadian War Museum, 330 Sussex Drive, has many dramatic and interesting displays of weapons, uniforms, and medals relating to Canada's military heritage, from wars during colonial periods to its United Nations peacekeeping efforts. Open throughout the year. Free.

Royal Canadian Mint, 320 Sussex Drive, allows visitors to see the making of Canadian money. There is also a good collection of coins and medals from around the world. Open throughout the year. Free. Tours by appointment only, (613) 996–5393.

National War Memorial, at Elgin and Wellington, is Canada's official memorial, a heroic sculpture of twenty-two bronze figures, commemorating the nation's sacrifice and contribution to victory in World War I. King George VI unveiled this impressive monument in 1939, the year when World War II began. For a memorable

account of Canada's effort in World War I, read Pierre Berton's *Vimy*, an absorbing account of one of the world's greatest land battles.

Government House (Rideau Hall), on Sussex Drive, is the official residence of the governor-general of Canada, the head of state and the queen's representative. Built in 1838, by Thomas MacKay, a stonemason from Perth, Scotland, Government House is the ceremonial heart of Canada. Here the Order of Canada is awarded, and here visiting royalty and heads of state are received. Free tours of its grounds are offered to visitors throughout the year. Be sure to see the Changing of the Guard ceremony, which takes place on the hour from the end of June to the end of August, in front of this splendid building.

Laurier House, 335 Laurier Avenue East, was the home of Sir Wilfred Laurier and William Lyon Mackenzie King, both prime ministers of Canada. This Victorian mansion houses many personal items belonging to Laurier and King, as well as the contents of the study belonging to Lester B. Pearson, a more recent and much beloved prime minister who also won the Nobel Peace Prize. Open throughout the year. Free.

Nepean Point, Mackenzie Avenue, overlooking the Ottawa River, is site of the Astrolabe Theatre and a statue of Samuel de Champlain, who explored the river in 1613.

Nicholas Gaol, 75 Nicholas Street, was a grim prison in the 1800s. In 1869 the last public hanging in Canada took place here, when Patrick Whelan was executed for the assassination of Thomas D'Arcy McGee, a Father of Confederation. The Gaol now serves as an international youth hostel. Tours are offered on Sundays by appointment, (613) 235–2595.

Surveys and Mapping Branch, 615 Booth Street, produces topographic, geographic, and aeronautical maps and charts of Canada. It also houses more than four million aerial photos of Canada. Call (613) 995–4321. Open throughout the year. Free.

Museum of Canadian Scouting, 1345 Baseline Road, has a fine collection of the history of scouting in Canada and of Lord Baden-Powell, its founder. Open throughout the year. Free.

Major's Hill and the Noonday Gun can be found on Mackenzie Avenue. Major's Hill is a small park offering views of Rideau

◀ **Pomp and circumstance in Ottawa. The Changing of the Guard ceremony is performed during the summer on the grounds in front of the Parliament buildings. It is one of the best free shows in town.**

Canal locks. It is located between the Château Laurier hotel and the new National Gallery of Art. Colonel By's home was in the area; its foundations still exist. The Noonday Gun, a nine-pound ship's cannon from the Crimean War, is fired daily precisely at noon and at 10:00 A.M. on Sundays and holidays. Also in this area is the National Artillery Memorial.

Bytown Museum, on the west side of Rideau Canal, was the commissariat store, office, and treasury of Colonel By, the builder of the Rideau Canal. It contains more than 3,500 items relating to the history of the city. Open early May to mid October. Admission charge. The quay for Ottawa River cruises is at the far end of this park, just below Parliament Hill.

Bank of Canada Currency Museum, 245 Sparks Street, presents exhibits on the history and development of money, from prehistoric currency to the present. Open throughout the year, Tuesday through Saturday. Free.

Canadian Ski Museum, 457A Sussex Drive, has many interesting exhibits on the history of skiing in this country. Open throughout the year. Free.

St. Andrew's Kirk, 82 Kent Street, is the oldest church in Ottawa. The present building dates back to 1873, although a kirk was on this site from 1828.

Christ Church Cathedral, 439 Queen Street, is Ottawa's center for Anglican worship. This building also dates back to 1873.

St. Bartholomew's Church, 125 MacKay Street, the parish church for twenty governor-generals of Canada. It is also the chapel for the Governor-General's Foot Guards and is Queen Elizabeth's place of worship when she visits Ottawa.

Cathedral-Basilica of Notre Dame, Sussex Drive, was consecrated around 1840. In 1932 Colonel By gave the land on which it stands to Catholics so that they could have their place of worship. An Ottawa landmark, the Notre Dame's interior is lavishly decorated.

Ottawa City Hall, 111 Sussex Drive, overlooking the Ottawa River, invites visitors to tour the building and view its exhibits. Call (613) 564–1400. City Hall is built on an island above Rideau Falls, a double cataract at the confluence of the Rideau and Ottawa rivers. During the summer, royal swans, a gift from Queen Elizabeth, can be seen on the Rideau River. Not far from City Hall, at 174 Stanley Street, is the Ottawa Municipal Archives, which is open to the public for historical and genealogical research.

Rideau Canal and Locks, built under orders from the Duke of Wellington of Waterloo fame, were completed in 1832. Pleasure craft can cruise the Rideau Canal system from Kingston to Ottawa. The locks in Ottawa will bring boaters to the Ottawa River for a pleasant downstream sail to Montréal. Along the banks of the canal, in central Ottawa, you can stroll or jog. In the winter the canal becomes one of the world's longest skating rinks, particularly charming with the spires of Parliament and the Château Laurier as background.

Central Experimental Farm, on the Driveway, is a twelve-hundred-acre farm not far from downtown. Here you can see a blue-ribbon herd of dairy and beef cattle, take a horse-drawn wagon ride, and visit greenhouses, an arboretum, and a botanical garden. Open throughout the year. Free. Canada's National Agricultural Museum is also located here. Open all year. Admission charge.

The Log Farm, Cedarview Road, Western Greenbelt, is the re-creation of an early-nineteenth-century Canadian farm, where costumed guides tell you the story of rural life years ago. The special feature of this farm is that you and your children are invited to share in the chores—sheep shearing, gardening, maple sap collecting, haying, putting up preserves, helping at the forge, cooking, churning butter, and harvesting the crop. This is a wonderful vacation experience for all ages. Admission charge.

Gatineau Park, access through Hull, Québec, is a magnificent seventy-five-thousand-acre wilderness area with a system of touring roads, picnic sites, hiking trails, and many other recreational features. There are some excellent views of Ottawa's skyline from here. Be sure to watch your speed as you drive through the park, as the police are very strict. Open throughout the year.

"Moorside," located in Gatineau Park, was the summer home of the late William Lyon Mackenzie King, prime minister of Canada during the Second World War. There are a museum here containing his memorabilia, a nice public tea room, and lovely gardens. There are also stone relics on the grounds from the first Parliament buildings, which were destroyed by fire. King, an outstanding politician and national leader, had many strange aspects to his personal life, such as conversing with the spirit of his dead mother. Moorside and Gatineau Park are nice respites from urban Ottawa. Open afternoons from late May to mid October.

Rockcliffe Park Village, via Sussex Drive, is Ottawa's elite residential area. Here are the homes of the governor-general, prime minister, and leader of the opposition, and those of many foreign ambassadors and leading business executives. Also within Rockcliffe are the home barracks and stables of "N" Company of the Royal Canadian Mounted Police, who are famous for their exciting "Musical Ride."

Sports

Football and Harness Racing

The Rough Riders, of the Canadian Football League, play their home games at Lansdowne Park. Call (613) 563–1212 for schedule and ticket information.

Harness races are held at the Rideau-Carlton Raceway in South Gloucester, Ontario, (613) 822–2211, and at Connaught Park in Aylmer, Québec, (819) 771–6111.

Biking and Hiking

There are many kilometers of special biking trails in the Ottawa area maintained by the National Capital Commission. In the summer both the Colonel By and the Ottawa River parkways are closed to auto traffic on Sundays for the enjoyment of bike riders. Rent-a-Bike is located on Mackenzie Avenue, behind the Château Laurier, (613) 233–0268.

There are a number of hiking and nature trails in the Ottawa area, with the best ones in Gatineau Park. Ottawa has many active joggers, and the various trails are also widely used by runners. There is also excellent running in Gatineau Park and along the Rideau Canal.

Swimming and Boating

Most of the hotels and motels have heated outdoor swimming pools and/or indoor pools. There are public beaches at Moonie's Bay, on the Rideau River near Hog's Back, off Riverside Drive, and at lakes in Gatineau Park. Canoes can be rented at the Dows Lake Pavilion, on the Rideau Canal, 1001 Queen Elizabeth Drive, and in Gatineau Park.

Windsurfing

Windsurfing is permitted at all local beaches. Equipment can be rented at Britannia Beach in Ottawa, (613) 733–5100, and Lac La Pêche in Gatineau Park, (819) 684–1212.

White-water Rafting

Several companies offer white-water rafting expeditions down the thrilling Rocher Fendu Rapids. Wilderness Tours, (613) 646–2291, and Ottawa Whitewater Rafting, (613) 646–2501, are two of them.

Tennis and Golf

There are forty public tennis courts throughout the city. Call (613) 239–5000 for more information. The National Capital Commission operates the Canadian Golf and Country Club in Ashton, Ontario, (613) 836–6160, and the Capital Golf Course in Alymer, Québec, (819) 521–2621.

Horseback Riding

Horseback riding is available at the National Capital Equestrian Park, 401 Corkstown Road, in the Greenbelt, (613) 829–6925.

Skiing

The best skiing in the area is found in Québec at these Gatineau Park area locations: Mont-Cascades in Cantley, (819) 827–0301; Edelweiss Valley, in Wakefield, (819) 459–2328; Vorlage, in Wakefield, (819) 459–2301; Camp Fortune, in Old Chelsea, (819) 827–1717.

Accommodations

Ottawa has a number of good hotels and motels. As the national capital, Ottawa now attracts a great many conventions, and there are conferences on every conceivable topic almost every week of the year. In addition, salespeople continually stream in and out of town in quest of orders from federal agencies. All this means that advance reservations are absolutely necessary. A smart time to visit the city is on weekends, when there is a decreased demand for hotel space and a greater chance to take advantage of lower-cost packages. Many tour operators offer complete packages that include Ottawa. Check with your travel agent for details.

The following is a listing of recommended places to stay in Ottawa:

Four Seasons, 150 Albert Street, (613) 238–1500, is one of Ottawa's better hotels, located near government offices and a short walk from Parliament Hill. It features gourmet dining in the Carleton Restaurant, a wine bar and informal dining at the Sidewalk Café, and dancing at Sasha's. The hotel has a swimming pool and exercise facilities. Expensive.

Radisson Hotel Ottawa Centre, 100 Kent Street, (613) 238–1122, offers high-quality rooms, a central location, many facilities, and a high level of personal service. The hotel is connected to an underground shopping area of boutiques and restaurants. *La Ronde* is Ottawa's revolving rooftop restaurant. The food is excellent here, and so are the views of the city and surrounding landscape. Expensive.

Château Laurier, Confederation Square, (613) 232–6411, an impressive structure—with the look of a Loire Valley château—is Ottawa's most famous hotel, a bastion for politicians and wheeler-dealers. It has a gourmet restaurant and an indoor swimming pool. The Château Laurier is in a perfect location, across the street from Parliament Hill, the Rideau Canal, and the National Arts Centre. Expensive.

Skyline Hotel, 101 Lyon Street, (613) 237–3600, is a downtown hotel with fine accommodations, services, and restaurants, one of which is located on the top of this high rise and offers marvelous views of the city. The hotel is connected to the underground system of shops and restaurants and has an indoor pool. Expensive.

Holiday Inn Market Square, 350 Dalhousie Street, (613) 236–0201, provides basic Holiday Inn comfort, with a swimming pool and restaurant. Moderate.

Minto Place Ottawa Centre, 187 Lyon Street, (613) 232–2200, has four hundred deluxe suites with kitchens, also exercise facilities, swimming pool, and restaurant. Expensive.

Lord Elgin, 100 Elgin Street, (613) 235–3333, is a fine, newly renovated hotel that has a great location, comfortable rooms, and a stuffy lounge resembling an exclusive London gentlemen's club. Moderate.

Westin Hotel, 11 Colonel By Drive, (613) 560–7000, is the top accommodation in the city. It's close to everything and is connected to the convention and shopping center. The Westin offers all deluxe hotel amenities and many elegant touches. Expensive.

Venture Inn, 480 Metcalfe Street, (613) 237–5500, is comfortable and reasonable in price, but several blocks away from the center of the city. A good choice when the best are all booked. Moderate.

Delta Ottawa, 361 Queen Street, (613) 238–6000, is an excellent choice in a central location. Delta is one of Canada's better hotel chains, providing good value for a fair price. Expensive.

Hotel Roxborough, 123 Metcalfe Street, (613) 237–5171, offers good value and many nice guest amenities, with overnight shoe shines, the morning paper, and continental breakfast included in the price of the room. Centrally located, it has a restaurant and lounge. Moderate to expensive.

Howard Johnson Ottawa, 140 Slater, (613) 238–2888, has a convenient downtown location, restaurant, and lounge. Moderate to expensive.

Chimo Inn, 1199 Joseph Cyr Street, (613) 744–1060, though away from the center of town, is comfortable and offers many guest amenities. Moderate.

Aristocrat Hotel, 131-141 Cooper Street, (613) 232–9471, is an all suite hotel. Each suite has a separate bedroom, living room, kitchen, and baths. This hotel also offers a restaurant, lounge, and exercise facilities. A good choice for families. Moderate to expensive.

University of Ottawa, 648 King Edward Avenue, (613) 564–3902, May to late August, provides adequate accommodations in dormitories and is in a central location. Inexpensive.

Carleton University, 1233 Colonel By Drive, (613) 564–5510, May to late August, offers good accommodations in student residences. It also has a cafeteria, swimming pool, squash and tennis courts, jogging track, and sauna. The location is several blocks from the center of town. Inexpensive.

Nicholas Gaol International Hostel, 75 Nicholas Street, (613) 235–2595, is a former jail—gray and forbidding—and you sleep on cots in what were cells. The experience is unique and also about as cheap as you'll find in Ottawa. Inexpensive.

Ottawa Area Bed and Breakfast Association, 44 Hampton Avenue, Ottawa, Ontario K1Y 0N2, (613) 563–0161, inexpensive-to moderate-priced accommodations in Ottawa area private homes.

Hull, Québec Area Accommodations

Hotel Plaza de la Chaudière, 2, rue Montcalm in Hull, (819) 778–3880, is one of the best places to stay in the Ottawa-Hull area. It provides a shuttle service taking guests to and from downtown

Ottawa. The hotel offers high-quality personal service, a glass-enclosed pool, and many fine amenities. *Le Châteauneuf* is the hotel's outstanding restaurant, offering *French cuisine* at its best; excellent wine list, ambience, and service. Expensive.

Le Château Montebello is at 392, rue Notre Dame, in Montebello, Québec, (819) 423–6341. Le Montebello is one of Canada's premier resorts, once the exclusive bastion of the rich and powerful, offering superb accommodations and dining. Amenities include eighteen-hole golf course, swimming, tennis, marina, acres of woodland, frontage on the Ottawa River, cross-country skiing, and many other recreations. Highly recommended. Expensive.

Auberge des Gouverneurs is at 111, rue Bellehumeur in Gatineau, (819) 568–5252. Moderate to expensive.

Hotel Ramada is located at 35, rue Laurier in Hull, (819) 778–6111. Moderate to expensive.

Mont Sainte-Marie is at Lac Sainte-Marie, (819) 467–5200. Moderate to expensive.

Dining

Ottawa offers a diverse selection of restaurants, representing the traditional cuisines of many countries. There is something to satisfy almost every taste, from basic North American fare to exotic dishes.

The following is a listing of recommended restaurants in the Ottawa area:

The Restaurants at Dow's Lake Pavilion, 1001 Queen Elizabeth Drive, are Anchors for German and French specialties, moderate to expensive, (613) 236–5576; Rose's Cantina for Mexican food, moderate, (613) 232–1001. This contemporary dining and recreational facility has a terrace that overlooks the lake; a gift shop, and other amenities.

Little Hungarian Village, 164 Laurier Avenue West, (613) 238–2827, is the place if you crave good goulash and gypsy music. Moderate.

Mamma Teresa's, 300 Somerset Street, (613) 236–3023, fills you with great veal, homemade pasta, and antipasto. A lot of good soul food for a reasonable price. Moderate.

Japanese Village, 170 Laurier Avenue West, (613) 236–9519, serves tempting tempura, sushi, teriyaki, and other exotic Japanese dishes. Moderate to expensive.

Nate's, 361 Rideau Street, (613) 236–9696, has by now become a venerable Ottawa institution for its incomparable smoked meat sandwiches, latkes, blintzes, pierogies, kishke, and kreplach. You don't even have to be Jewish to adore Nate's offerings. Inexpensive.

Friday's Roast Beef House, 150 Elgin Street, (613) 237–5353, is a nicely appointed restaurant in a Victorian-era house. The prime roast beef here is excellent. Moderate to expensive.

Courtyard Restaurant, 21 George Street, (613) 238–4623, is located in an ancient stone building within the marvelous Byward Market district. Rack of lamb and beef Wellington are specialties. Expensive.

The Old Fish Market, 54 York Street, (613) 563–4954, offers fresh fish cooked without gimmicks. It's a good place for seafood purists. Moderate.

Le Soupçon, 408 Rideau Street, (613) 594–8808, serves excellent five-course *table d'hôte* dinners. Creative dishes use freshest ingredients. Expensive.

Bay Street, 160 Bay Street, (613) 234–1111, features California Italian cuisine—unique pasta, seafood, meat dishes, and "designer" pizzas. Moderate.

Le Brittany, 180 Cooper Street, (613) 238–3636, offers such gourmet specialties as skate fish with black butter and capers, flamed sweetbreads with calvados and artichokes, and lobster with Emmental cheese. Moderate to expensive.

Le Bistro, 1268 Wellington Street, (613) 728–3111, serves up eclectic gourmet fare; chefs use fresh ingredients and herbs they grow. Moderate to expensive.

The Mill, Ottawa River Parkway, (613) 237–1311, offers superb North American cooking in a historic mill overlooking Chaudière Falls and the Ottawa River. Roast beef with Yorkshire puffs is the specialty, and there are excellent homemade desserts. Moderate to expensive.

Guadala Harry's is at 19 York Street (in the Byward Market district), (613) 234–8229. Yes, there is a good Mexican restaurant north of San Antonio. Guadala Harry's may in fact be the one, at least in eastern Canada. Strolling mariachis liven up the atmosphere. Inexpensive to moderate.

Il Vagabondo, 186 Barrette Street, (613) 749–4877, is one of Ottawa's good restaurants, and serves superb Italian dishes in a modest setting. Moderate to expensive.

Hull, Québec Area Restaurants

Café Henry Burger, 69, rue Laurier in Hull, (819) 777–5646, offers fine French food and ambience. Moderate to expensive.

L'Orée du Bois, chemin Kingsmere in Old Chelsea, (819) 827–0332, has excellent French cuisine and the setting to go along with it. Moderate to expensive.

La Ferme Columbia, 376, boulevard Saint-Joseph in Hull, (819) 776–6484, has very fine French offerings and a nice dining room. Moderate to expensive.

Entertainment

Ottawa is a solid company town—and the company that dominates everything is the federal government. The major forms of entertainment in Ottawa are cocktail parties and receptions involving politicians, bureaucrats, business executives, and the diplomatic community.

Thanks to the National Arts Centre, cultural life is very much alive throughout the year and open to the general public. Here you can see the great ballet companies of Canada and other countries, grand opera performances, and both classical and experimental live theater. The National Symphony Orchestra plays at the Arts Centre, as do leading theatrical companies, musical groups, and entertainers from around the world.

Other theatrical venues in the Ottawa area are the Ottawa Little Theatre, 400 King Edward Avenue, (613) 233–8948; the Nepean Amateur Theatre, at the Centerpointe Theatre on Nepean Point, (613) 723–8715; Odyssey Theatre, Strathcona Park, (613) 232–8407; Théatre de l'Ile, 1 rue Wellington in Hull, (819) 771–6669; the Great Canadian Theatre Company, 910 Gladstone Avenue, (613) 236–5196; and the York Street Theatre, 12 York Street in Byward Market, (613) 236–5196.

There are also comedy, cabaret, and dinner theaters: Murder Mystery Evenings, at the Macdonald Club, 153 Gilmour Street, (613) 232–0507; Penguin Café, 292 Elgin Street, (613) 594–3201; and Skit Row, 601 Bank Street, (613) 233–9320.

Ottawa has a goodly share of bars and lounges featuring live entertainment, discos, and music places—rock and roll, new wave, country and western, blues. The bars and clubs in Hull, Québec, stay open until 3:00 A.M., hours longer than those in Ottawa. Ask the concierge at your hotel for recommendations on which places are currently hot. Also ask for copies of *What's on in Ottawa* and *Ottawa Magazine*, which provide listings of current entertainment offerings in the Ottawa area as well as more dining and shopping suggestions.

Shopping

Sparks Street Mall, off Confederation Square, is a car-free shopping street lined with boutiques, bookshops, and cafés. The mall also features open-air art exhibitions, fountains, and floral displays. Here's a Hyde Park–style "Speaker's Corner," where you are invited to get on a platform and expound on whatever subject you choose before an audience, which is amused most of the time, captivated occasionally.

Ottawa Congress Centre and Rideau Centre is a convention and shopping complex, conveniently located along the bank of the Rideau Canal, across from the National Arts Centre and facing Rideau Street. The Congress Centre provides facilities for conventions and association meetings of all kinds. The Westin Hotel is connected by passageways to this modern complex. Rideau Centre is Ottawa's top downtown, enclosed shopping mall. It has more than 200 shops, a cinema, and several restaurants.

Byward Market, one block north of Rideau Street, is where area farmers have been selling their fresh fruits, vegetables, meat, cheese, honey, jams, breads, and other products since the mid-nineteenth century. Byward Market is one of the most human and entertaining places in the city. There are many fine restaurants and interesting shops here. It is a great place for people-watching and carefree strolling.

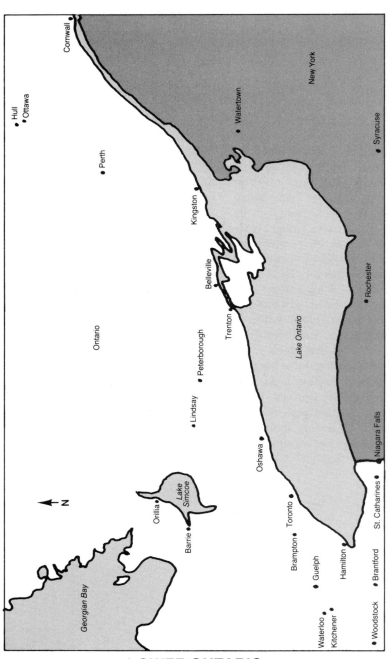

LOWER ONTARIO

CHAPTER 6

Vacation Regions Near Toronto and Ottawa

There is lots more to see in Ontario beyond the cities of Toronto and Ottawa. This chapter gives you some interesting and enjoyable options.

Ontario has some of Canada's best resorts, where you can enjoy all sorts of recreation and be pampered with fine accommodations and services. These resorts are located within magnificent scenery of lakes, hills, and forests. Many are open all four seasons of the year. Anytime is perfect for an Ontario resort vacation.

Niagara Falls is one of the natural wonders of the world. You can not only see the falls but also ride a boat that takes you right to where the waters explode at the bottom of the gorge. There is so much more to do and see in the Niagara area—family attractions and entertainments of all kinds, the Shaw Festival Theatre in historic Niagara-on-the-Lake, fortifications from the War of 1812, and charming inns reflecting the grace and traditions of a bygone time.

To the west of Toronto are Stratford, with its famous theater festival featuring the plays of Shakespeare and others, and the interesting cities of Guelph, Kitchener-Waterloo, and Brantford. In Kitchener-Waterloo, for example, you can attend one of the best German Oktoberfest celebrations on the North American continent and purchase fresh fruits and vegetables grown by Mennonite and Amish farmers.

About midway from Toronto and Ottawa is the old city of Kingston, once the capital of Canada, with its many historic attractions, such as Canada's military academy and hockey hall of fame. From Kingston you can cruise the beginning of the St. Lawrence

River and see the famous Thousand Islands with their castles. Not far to the east is Upper Canada Village, a working community caught in a time warp of the nineteenth century. Here you literally step back in time and experience how early Canadian pioneers lived.

For more information on the following vacation areas and other regions of Ontario, call toll-free (800) ONT–ARIO.

The Great Resorts of Ontario

Ontario has the largest collection of fine resorts in Canada, with most located an easy drive from Toronto, Niagara Falls, Windsor, Kingston, and Ottawa. All of these are lakeside resorts or are situated near recreational water areas. They offer swimming (in lake and heated pool), boating, canoeing, windsurfing, and fishing. Many have their own golf courses, tennis courts, and exercise facilities. There are special recreation programs for adults and for children. Some offer sports programs: fly-in fishing expeditions to remote lakes, rivers, and streams; equestrian sports; winter ice fishing, alpine skiing, cross-country skiing, horse-drawn sleigh rides, snow-shoeing treks, snowmobile touring, ice skating. Ontario's resorts are highly regarded for the quality and comfort of their accommodations, the excellence of their dining—North American home style cooking and international cuisines, the entertainment provided by singers, dancers, musicians, and comedians, and their many other guest amenities. For more information, contact your local travel agent, or Resorts Ontario, 10 Peter Street North, Orillia, Ontario, (705) 325–9115, toll-free from Ontario, New York State, Michigan, Ohio, and Pennsylvania.

This following is a listing of some of "the great resorts of Ontario," those providing deluxe accommodations and superior facilities, amenities, and services (all are moderate to expensive).

Georgian Lakelands Region

The Georgian Lakelands is one of Ontario's premier vacation areas, located directly north and northeast of Metro Toronto. The area is reached via Highways 400 and 11 from Toronto, about a four- to six-hour drive.

Blue Mountain Resort, in Collingwood, (705) 445–0231. Blue Mountain Resort, Ontario's largest Alpine skiing complex, also offering cross-country skiing. It has a giant summer waterslide, indoor pool, sandy beach, squash, racquetball, tennis, exercise facilities, and other recreations. The accommodations are excellent, as are the food and entertainment.

Cedar Rail Resort, in Port Carling, (705) 765–5789.

Clevelands House, in Minett, (705) 765–3171.

Deerhurst Inn and Country Club, on Peninsula Lake in Huntsville, (705) 789–5543.

Delwana Inn, in Honey Harbour, (705) 756–2424.

Fern Resort, in Orillia, (705) 325–2256.

Pinelands Resort, on Lake Muskoka in Port Carling, (705) 645–2191.

Rocky Crest Resort, on Lake Joseph in MacTier, (705) 375–2240.

Severn Lodge, on the Trent-Severn Waterway in Port Severn, (705) 756–2722.

Windermere House, on Lake Rousseau in Windermere, (705) 769–3611.

Central Ontario

The vacation region of Central Ontario is between Toronto and Ottawa, and is easily accessible to travelers touring this attraction- and recreation-rich area.

The Briars, on Lake Simcoe in Jackson's Point, (416) 722–3271.

Domain of Killien Resort, in Haliburton, (705) 457–1556.

Elmhirst's Resort, in Keene, (705) 295–4591.

PineStone Inn and Country Club, in Haliburton, (705) 457–1800.

Ontario Northeast

Ontario Northeast is that vacation area to the northwest of Ottawa, and to the northeast of Metro Toronto. Algonquin Provincial Park, located here, is the closest preserved wilderness area to the major population centers of eastern Ontario.

Arowhon Pines, at Algonquin Provincial Park in Huntsville, (705) 633–5661.

Rainbow Country

Rainbow Country faces Georgian Bay, which is part of giant Lake Huron. It is the place of "Manitou," the Indian name for God.

The Inn and Tennis Club at Manitou, on Lake Manitou-wabing in McKellar, (705) 389–2171.

Sunset Country

Sunset Country is located at the western end of Ontario, on the Manitoba border. Lake of the Woods is the favorite vacation and recreation area in this region.

Minaki Lodge, a Four Seasons Hotel, at Lake of the Woods in Minaki, (807) 224–4000.

Niagara Falls

No doubt Niagara Falls, reached via Queen Elizabeth Way (about a ninety-minute drive from Toronto), became a prime tourist attraction as soon as the first humans set eyes on them. They are still one of North America's most famous landmarks. And there is only one word necessary to describe them—awesome!

Niagara Falls form part of the border between Canada and the United States. The crescent-shaped Horseshoe Falls, 176 feet/54 m. high and 2,100 feet/641 m. wide, are in Ontario, while the American Falls, 182 feet/56 m. high and 1,076 feet/328 m. wide, are in New York State. The waters of nearby Lake Erie and the other upper Great Lakes flow through the Niagara River (of which the falls are a part) down into Lake Ontario, then through the Saint Lawrence River, which empties into the Gulf of Saint Lawrence and ultimately into the Atlantic Ocean. To the east of the Niagara River is the Welland Canal, part of the Saint Lawrence Seaway, which allows passage of ocean-going ships between Lakes Erie and Ontario.

The roar from Niagara Falls is so thunderous that it can be heard day and night for many miles into Ontario and New York State. On occasion, the waters freeze to a trickle during a particularly cold winter, the roar seems to stop, and local residents get an eerie feeling that nature has gone askew. The cascading waters create a perpetual boil at the bottom and send up thick mists, which catch sunlight and produce beautiful rainbows.

Niagara Falls has been a favorite attraction for honeymooners ever since Napoleon III's newlywed brother and his wife came up from New Orleans by stagecoach for a visit. It is unclear why a huge, noisy cataract enhances marital ardor, but somehow it seems to work.

Niagara Falls have also attracted an unusually large number of daredevils, who have gone over them in barrels or walked across on tightrope-wires. But most tourists come to Niagara Falls to be impressed by the power of nature; they leave astounded.

Niagara Falls can be visited throughout the year. In the evening they are illuminated with colored lights, making quite a beautiful sight, especially in winter, when the falls become sculpted in ice. A 25-mile/40-km. park system stretches from the falls down to the town of Niagara-on-the-Lake. This park offers many fine views of the falls.

The Niagara Parks People Movers is a bus system that will transport you to the main attractions all day for one low price, allowing you to get on and off as many times as you want. This shuttle operates from mid May to mid October.

For more information, contact the Niagara Falls, Canada, Visitor & Convention Bureau, 4610 Ontario Avenue, Niagara Falls, Ontario L2E 3P9, (416) 356–6061.

The following are ways in which you can experience the grandeur of Niagara Falls and its adjacent attractions:

Maid of the Mist, located at 5920 River Road, is a tough boat that pushes upriver against the strong current and takes you right into the Horseshoe and main falls. The noise is deafening, and the spray comes down on you like a rain storm (you are supplied with hooded raincoats to protect your clothing). The experience is a lifetime memory. The *Maid of the Mist* operates daily from mid May to mid October. Admission charge.

Table Rock Scenic Tunnels, Niagara Parkway, takes you into the falls through a system of tunnels so that you view the downpour of water from the inside looking out. You are issued raincoats to protect your clothing, as some of the viewing areas are splashed with spray. Open throughout the year. Admission charge.

Great Gorge Trip and Niagara Daredevil Gallery, 4330 River Road, has an elevator that takes you down into the Niagara River gorge below the falls. From here you go on a walkway to the famous Whirlpool Rapids. The gallery exhibits barrels and other daredevil methods of going over the falls. Open May to October. Admission charge.

Minolta Centre and National Marine Aquarium, 6732 Oakes Drive, features a 665-foot/203-m. observation tower above Niagara gorge, in which there are restaurants and lounges. It also has the National Marine Aquarium, the Bruning Springs Wax Museum, and a "waltzing waters" show. Open throughout the year. Admission charge.

Skylon Tower, 5200 Robinson Street, takes you up 520 feet/ 159 m. to an observation area above the falls. There is a revolving restaurant at the top, and there are shops, restaurants, and amusement stands at the bottom. Open throughout the year. Admission charge.

Niagara Falls IMAX Theatre, adjacent to the Skylon Tower, shows the majesty, thrills, and history of the falls on a movie screen six stories high, with a six-track sound system. Admission charge. Call (416) 374–IMAX.

Niagara Helicopters, 3731 Victoria Avenue, provide flights over the falls and surrounding area, throughout the year, weather permitting. Admission charge. Call (416) 357–5672.

Rainbow Tower Carillon, Rainbow Bridge, has fifty-five bells and gives concerts during the summer. Free.

Parks Commission Conservatory, Niagara Parkway, has year-round floral displays with special seasonal exhibitions. Open throughout the year. Free.

Maple Leaf Village, Rainbow Bridge, is a new shopping and amusement complex featuring a giant Ferris wheel from which you get great views of the falls. Open throughout the year. Free admission into the village; admission charge for amusements.

Marineland and Game Farm, 7657 Portage Road, South, features many different kinds of wildlife, an aquarium, and dolphin shows. Open throughout the year. Admission charge.

W. Kurelek Art Collection, Queen Elizabeth Way, is housed in a museum that also features the works of other Canadian, American, and European artists. The late William Kurelek was a world-famous Ukrainian-Canadian artist who painted on religious and allegorical themes. His *Passion of Christ,* consisting of 160 panels, is the highlight of this museum. Open throughout the year. Admission charge.

Niagara Falls Museum, 5651 River Road, is said to be one of North America's oldest museums. It contains an Egyptian collection, Oriental displays, and the Daredevil Hall of Fame. Open throughout the year. Admission charge.

The following places to stay in Niagara Falls are recommended:

Best Western Cairn Croft Hotel, 6400 Lundy's Lane, (416) 356–1161, has a dining room and swimming pool. Moderate.

Fiddler's Green Motel, 7720 Lundy's Lane, (416) 358–9833, features a swimming pool. Inexpensive.

Holiday Inn by the Falls, Murray and Buchanan Street, (416) 356–1333, offers fine accommodations and dining and has heart-shaped tubs and waterbeds for honeymooners. Moderate to expensive.

Ramada Inn Fallsview, 6455 Buchanan Avenue, (416) 357–5200, features excellent accommodations, dining, and recreational facilities. Moderate to expensive.

The Old Stone Inn, 5425 Robinson Street, (416) 357–1234, has a warm, charming ambience and gracious hospitality in what was a rustic flour mill at the turn of the century. Beautifully restored into an unique place of accommodation, it has a restaurant, lounge, swimming pool, health club, and many guest amenities. Moderate to expensive.

The Niagara Region Bed and Breakfast Service, 2631 Dorchester Road in Niagara Falls, (416) 358–8988.

Niagara-on-the-Lake

Niagara-on-the-Lake is one of the loveliest small towns in Canada. Just 8 miles/13 km. north of Niagara Falls, via the Niagara Parkway, Niagara-on-the-Lake is a favorite place for artists and writers. Niagara-on-the-Lake offers many attractions:

The Shaw Festival Theatre houses an outstanding professional acting company that presents the plays of George Bernard Shaw and others. The internationally famous Shaw Festival runs from early May to late September. Call (416) 468–2172 for ticket information.

Fort George defended British Canada from the Americans during the War of 1812. Its interesting Navy Hall Museum is housed in a structure built during the American Revolution. Open mid May to the end of October. Admission charge.

Laura Secord Homestead, off River Road, in Queenston Heights, was the home of a brave woman who warned the British of a forthcoming American attack in 1813. Laura Secord's heroism helped to win a victory in the Battle of Beaver Dam. Her home has been restored and furnished with priceless Upper Canada antiques. Open mid May to mid October. Admission charge.

McFarland House, Niagara Parkway, is a fine early-nineteenth-century Georgian-style brick house. During the War of 1812, it was used by both the Americans and the British as a hospital. Open mid May to mid September. Admission charge.

Niagara Apothecary, 5 Queen Street, is an authentic restoration of a late-nineteenth-century drugstore, complete with walnut

and butternut fixtures, crystal gasoliers, and a rare collection of apothecary glassware. Open mid May to Labour Day. Free.

Niagara Historical Society Museum, 43 Castlereagh Street, features items belonging to John Graves Simcoe, founder of Toronto; uniforms and weapons of the War of 1812; and personal possessions of Laura Secord. Open throughout the year. Admission charge.

Recommended accommodations in Niagara-on-the-Lake include the Oban Inn, 160 Front Street, (416) 468–2165, moderate, and the Prince of Wales Motel, 9 Picton Street, (416) 468–3246, expensive. Bed and Breakfast accommodations are also available in town.

Stratford

As in Shakespeare's England, the Avon River flows through Stratford, Ontario, site of the internationally acclaimed Stratford Festival. The repertory ranges from the great dramas of the Bard of Avon to contemporary works; there are also musical performances, including opera. The Stratford Festival, considered one of the outstanding cultural assets of Canada, attracts leading actors from America, Canada, and Great Britain. If you love the very best in live theater, don't miss *Richard III, My Fair Lady, Murder in the Cathedral, King Lear,* and many others. The Stratford Festival season runs from June to the end of October. For more information, contact the festival office in Toronto, (416) 363–4471.

In addition to the festival, Stratford offers other fairs and festivals, antique and crafts shops, a farmers' market, fine restaurants, bookshops, fashion boutiques, art galleries, and lots more.

Recommended accommodations in Stratford include Festival Motor Inn, 1144 Ontario Street, (519) 273–1150, moderate to expensive; Queen's Inn at Stratford, 161 Ontario Street, (519) 271–1400, moderate to expensive; Victorian Inn, 10 Romeo Street, (519) 271–4650, moderate to expensive; and the Jester's Arms Inn, 107 Ontario Street, (519) 271–1121, moderate to expensive.

Stratford also has many other motels, inns, and Bed and Breakfast places. For more information, call the Stratford Festival Accommodations Bureau at (519) 273–1600.

◀ **If you love live theater, a visit to Ontario would not be complete without taking in a performance at Stratford. Here the works of Shakespeare and other great dramatists come to life in one of the most renowned theaters in North America.**

Guelph, Kitchener, and Brantford

Guelph is the home of the University of Guelph (formerly the Ontario Agricultural College), largest agricultural school in the British Commonwealth, with the oldest veterinary college in North America. John Kenneth Galbraith graduated from here. Tours of the campus are available throughout the year. The Colonel John McCrae Home, 102 Water Street, is the birthplace of the author of the poem "In Flanders Fields," written during the Battle of Ypres in 1915. Open mid May to mid October. Admission charge. Guelph Civic Museum, 6 Dublin Street, houses collections relating to the history of the city. Open throughout the year. Free. The Church of Our Lady is modeled on the great cathedral of Cologne, Germany, and dominates the city from its site on the highest hill.

Kitchener-Waterloo are twin cities that have a common heritage. Many of the early settlers were German farmers and Amish and Mennonite people who came from the United States. Oktoberfest in this area is famous throughout Canada—nine days of beer drinking, sausage and kraut eating, oompah music, parades, amusements, and sporting events. Oktoberfest, one of the biggest festivals in North America, is held in mid October. Doon Pioneer Village, off Homer Watson Boulevard, has sixteen restored historic buildings depicting early rural life in this area of Ontario. It has a Conestoga wagon, an 1823 Eby Bible, and the first mass-produced car built in Canada. Open May to late October. Admission charge. The area's farmer's market is one of the best in Canada. Mennonite and Amish farmers sell homemade bread, preserves, cheese, sausage, and a vast array of fresh vegetables. Open Saturday throughout the year, early morning to early afternoon.

Brantford is named for the famous Mohawk Chief Joseph Brant, an important ally of the British in the early development of Canada.

Brant County Museum, 57 Charlotte Street, has a fine collection of items related to the Six (Iroquois) Nations and important figures in Brantford's history, such as Joseph Brant, Alexander Graham Bell, and E. Pauline Johnson, one of Canada's best-loved poets. Open throughout the year. Admission charge.

Chiefswood, via Highway 54, was built in 1853 by Chief Johnson, leader of the Six Nations, for his English bride, E. Pauline Johnson, to whose memory it is now dedicated. Open mid May to Labour Day. Admission charge.

Her Majesty's Chapel of the Mohawks, Mohawk Street, was built in 1785. It is the world's only royal Indian chapel and the oldest Protestant church in Ontario. Open April to November.

Woodland Indian Cultural Educational Centre, 184 Mohawk Street, has some excellent displays of Indian artifacts telling the story of the culture and history of native people in North America. Open throughout the year. Admission charge.

Bell Homestead, 94 Tutela Heights Road, is where Alexander Graham Bell lived as a young man and where he worked on his most famous invention—the telephone. Open throughout the year. Admission charge.

Glenhyrst Gardens, 20 Ava Road, is a sixteen-acre estate overlooking the Grand River. Here is a fine old house with gallery shows of paintings, prints, sculpture, and photography, set on beautiful grounds with a nature trail. Open throughout the year. Admission charge.

Kingston

Located on Lake Ontario and at the beginning of the Saint Lawrence River, Kingston can be reached via Highway 15 from Ottawa, via Highway 401 from Toronto and Montréal, and via Interstate 81 through upstate New York over the International Bridge.

Settlement of the Kingston area dates back to the seventeenth century. Kingston was once the site of Fort Frontenac, a major French fur-trading post. Because of its strategic location, Kingston was a key military stronghold in protecting British North America from the enemy to the south. It also served as the capital of Upper Canada and of the United Provinces of Canada. Kingston offers a number of attractions:

Bellevue House National Historic Park, 35 Centre Street, an 1840 Tuscan-style villa, was the home of Sir John A. Macdonald, the first prime minister of Canada. This fine mansion contains furnishings and personal possessions belonging to one of Canada's most illustrious political leaders. Open daily except holidays October to April. Free.

Old Fort Henry, a massive fortification, was once the principal stronghold of Upper Canada, as it guarded the entrance to both Lake Ontario and the Saint Lawrence River. Its museum houses an extensive collection of military uniforms, weapons, and equipment. The highlight of a visit is to watch the Fort Henry Guard, dressed in nineteenth-century uniforms, performing intricate drills, with fifes and drums, and artillery salutes. Highly recommended. Open mid May to mid October. At 7:30 P.M. on Wednesday and Saturday, weather permitting, a special "Sunset Ceremonial" is performed. Admission charge.

Canadian Forces Communications and Electronics Museum, Vimy Barracks, 1 mile/2 km. east on Highway 2, has displays relating to the history of the Royal Canadian Corps of Signals. Open daily, except Saturday, throughout the year, afternoons only. Admission charge.

Kingston City Hall, Ontario Street, built in the mid-nineteenth century, was once the capital building of the United Provinces of Canada. A domed structure built from limestone, it is considered one of the finest historical buildings in Canada. Open throughout the year, with daily tours mid June to Labour Day. Free.

Fort Frederick Museum (Royal Military College Museum), at La Salle Causeway, east of the city off Highway 2, has a fine collection of historic items relating to Fort Frederick and the Royal Military College (Canada's West Point) housed in a large Martello tower. It also contains the small arms collection of Porfirio Diaz, president of Mexico at the turn of the century. Open mid June to Labour Day. Admission charge.

Brock Street, in the center of Kingston, features nineteenth-century-style shops; a great place to stroll, sample the goodies, and buy souvenirs.

Pump House Steam Museum, 23 Ontario Street, is a restored 1849 steam-driven pumping station with a unique steam engine collection. Open mid June to Labour Day. Admission charge.

International Hockey Hall of Fame, York and Alfred streets, memorializes the top players of the National Hockey League and other professional and amateur leagues in Canada and the United States. Open daily mid June to mid September (on weekends the rest of the year). Admission charge.

Murney Tower Museum, McDonald Park, corner of Barrie and King streets built in 1846, is a Martello tower that was once part of the harbor defenses and the entrance to the Rideau Canal system. The museum houses a collection of early military and pioneer artifacts. Open late May to Labour Day. Admission charge.

Marine Museum, Ontario and Union streets, has a collection depicting the history of Great Lakes shipping from the seventeenth century to the present, including artifacts from old vessels sunk in the lakes. Open mid May to mid October. Admission charge.

Rideau Canal system goes for 124 miles/198 km. from Kingston to Ottawa and includes forty-nine locks. If you're traveling by or hauling a pleasure boat, a trip through the lakes, locks, and channels of the Rideau system is one of the great experiences of this area. The Duke of Wellington ordered Colonel By to construct the Rideau system, which he completed in 1832. It passes through the beautiful interior of Ontario, and there are many historic and cultural features along the way. For more information on taking your boat through the Rideau Canal from Kingston to Ottawa, call (613) 283–5170.

Cruise the beautiful Rideau Canal system on the 108-foot diesel-powered *Canadian Empress*. This vintage vessel offers five different cruises lasting three, six, or nine days. The *Canadian Empress* features first-class accommodations, good food, and a wide variety of on-board activities. For more information, call (613) 549–8091.

Agnes Etherington Art Centre, University and Queen's Crescent, on the campus of Queen's University, is an art gallery with a collection of more than 3,000 works. It has exhibitions of local, national, and international art. Open throughout the year. Free.

Tour Train, 209 Ontario Street, takes visitors on a one-hour, 10-mile sight-seeing tour of Kingston, including the Royal Military College, Fort Frontenac, Queen's University, Saint George's Cathedral, and the Kingston Penitentiary. Operates from the end of June to Labour Day. Admission charge.

Recommended accommodations in Kingston include the following:

Ambassador Hotel, 1550 Princess Street, (613) 548–3605. Moderate.

Best Western Fireside Inn, 1217 Princess Street, (613) 549–2211. Moderate.

Glen Manor, 1155 Princess Street, (613) 546–4285. Moderate.

Holiday Inn, 1 Princess Street, (613) 549–8400. Moderate to expensive.

Howard Johnson's Confederation Place Hotel, 237 Ontario Street, (613) 549–6300. Moderate to expensive.

Prince George Hotel, 200 Ontario Street, (613) 549–5440. Moderate.

Seven Oaks Motor Inn, 2331 Princess Street, (613) 546–3655. Moderate to expensive.

Walnut Grove Motel, 2327 Princess Street, (613) 546–2691. Moderate.

Thousand Islands Cruises

The best way to see the Thousand Islands is to take a boat cruise. Several operators offer cruises through these beautiful islands with their magnificent baronial mansions. Kingston and the Islands Boat Line, Brock Street Dock, Kingston, (613) 549–5544, has cruises of Kingston Harbour and the Thousand Islands on board the paddle-wheeler *Island Princess.* Operates mid May to mid October. Gananoque Boat Lines, Customs Dock, Gananoque, Ontario, (613) 382–2144, offers a three-hour tour on a double-deck vessel, covering the Thousand Islands area. Operates mid May to mid September.

Upper Canada Village

About 92 miles/147 km. east of Kingston, in Morrisburg, is Upper Canada Village, the re-creation of an early-nineteenth-century Ontario settlement. Upper Canada Village, which can be reached from Ottawa via Highway 31 (a distance of about 50 miles/80 km.), features an inn, a lovely Anglican church, a woolen mill, pioneer homes, a blacksmith shop, and a sawmill. There are forty buildings, corduroy roads, canals, a fort—all of which can be seen on foot. Or you can ride through the village on an ox-cart and sail through the canals on a bateau. In this working historic community the staff dress in pioneer costumes and perform the various household and community tasks typical of bygone days. Upper Canada Village is one of the outstanding living museums of Canada, and a visit here is highly recommended. Open mid May to mid October. Admission charge.

Other Morrisburg attractions include Crysler Farm Battlefield Park, right next to Upper Canada Village, which commemorates a British and Canadian victory during the War of 1812, and the Upper Canada Migratory Bird Sanctuary, both open throughout the year.

CHAPTER 7

The Province of Québec

Québec Today

The goals of contemporary Québec might be summarized as the preservation of its language, religion, laws, and traditions, with a passion for progress.

Today Québec's population exceeds six million, of whom more than 80 percent are French-speaking (mostly native-born Québecois). The remaining population is Anglophone, with 7 percent of this minority speaking other languages as well (mostly immigrants from Italy, Greece, and elsewhere).

Québec is a rich province with a diversified economy. The traditional industries (agriculture, forest products, fisheries, mining, and shoe and textile manufacturing) are still important factors in the economy. Québec is also a leading producer of automobiles, aircraft, and machinery. It is realizing wealth from its various hydroelectric projects, such as the one in James Bay, which are supplying power to New York State and New England.

Québec, with 963,000 square miles/2,504,000 sq. km., is the largest of Canada's ten provinces. If it were an independent country, it would rank 16th in size among the 150 nations of the world. As it is, several of the larger European countries could be placed inside Québec, and there would still be room to spare. From north to south, Québec extends from the Arctic Circle to the borders of New Brunswick, Maine, New Hampshire, Vermont, and New York State. Much of its western edge is on Hudson Bay and James Bay, while the southern section borders Ontario. To the east, Québec extends over the north coast of the Gulf of Saint Lawrence to the Labrador

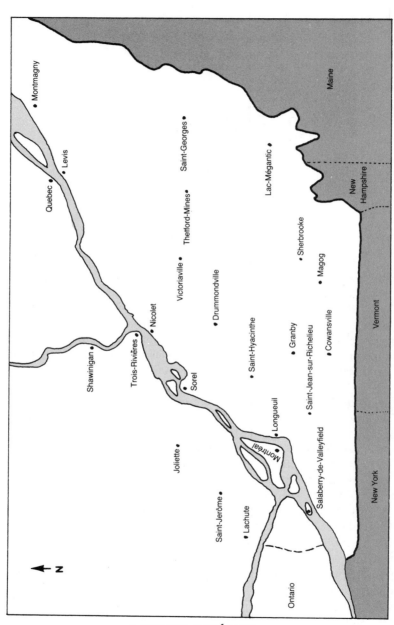

LOWER QUÉBEC

border. The Saint Lawrence, Ottawa, Saguenay, Saint Maurice, and Richelieu rivers are its major water routes. The Saint Lawrence, the most important, serves the ports of Montréal and Québec City and gives access to the Canadian and American hinterlands through the Saint Lawrence Seaway.

Most Québecois live in cities and towns in the southern portion of the province. Much of northern Québec is wilderness, with scattered small communities. This vast wilderness is a rich storehouse of minerals, forests, and hydroelectric energy, but the rugged terrain of the Canadian Shield and the bitter winter weather have inhibited settlement and extensive development. The land immediately to the south and east of Montréal is Québec's most fertile agricultural area, producing dairy products, fruits, vegetables, and grains. The Gulf of Saint Lawrence is a rich fishing area, and most of the people who live on the Gaspé, the Iles-de-la-Madeleine (Magdalen Islands), and the north shore of the gulf make their living from these waters.

Québec's inhabitants have achieved an exceptionally high standard of living. Publicly funded social services include all levels of education—even universities—most aspects of medicine and health care, special assistance to the poor, comprehensive programs for the elderly, and support for the advance of the culture.

The Province of Québec has contributed much to the quality of life in Canada: history, culture, imagination, style, economic and political progress. It would be difficult to imagine Canada without Québec.

History and Culture

The history of Québec is essentially a tale of two cities: Montréal and Québec City.

In 1534, during his second voyage to the New World, the French explorer Jacques Cartier landed on the tip of the Gaspé peninsula, planted the royal standard and a cross on the ground, and claimed all the territory before him for the king of France. In 1535 he wintered at what is now Québec City's Lower Town, which was then occupied by the Indian village of Stadacona. Cartier named the imposing headland above him *Cap Diamant* (Cape Diamond); on it the Citadelle and the rest of the city's Upper Town would eventually be built. In that same year he visited Hochelaga, an Indian village with about a thousand inhabitants. Cartier climbed to the top of a nearby mountain and again planted the cross of Christ. Hochelaga was where Montréal would begin, and a reminder of Cartier's cross stands today on the summit of Mont-Royal. When Samuel de Champlain, the greatest of the North American explorers, made his first visit, in 1603, to the spot that is now Montréal, the once-thriving Indian village of Hochelaga had disappeared.

In 1608, Champlain established Place Royale (Québec City), one of the earliest permanent settlements of Europeans in North America. This new settlement, founded twelve years before the Pilgrims landed at Plymouth, Massachusetts, consisted of a fortified area in Lower Town containing several dwellings and a trading post. In 1611 he attempted a settlement on the site of Hochelaga, an outpost that was later abandoned.

Champlain concentrated his efforts on Place Royale, which was flourishing below the cliffs of Cap Diamant. The King appointed him lieutenant general of New France, and in 1620 he began building the Château Saint-Louis, which became the palace for royal governors administering a territory extending from Hudson Bay to the mouth of the Mississippi River and from the Atlantic Ocean to the Great Lakes.

In 1629 English forces under Sir David Kirke attacked Québec and forced Champlain to surrender. The treaty of Saint Germain-en-Laye of 1632 returned Québec to the French, and Champlain returned as governor.

It was not until 1642 that a permanent settlement was established on the site of Hochelaga. Unlike Place Royale, which served primarily as a base for the Indian fur trade and for further commercial exploitation of the continent, Montréal was founded as a religious utopia. Paul de Chomedey de Maisonneuve, a military officer, and fifty others, including several Sulpician missionaries, built their community within a stockade and named it Ville-Marie. A flood almost destroyed the fledgling Ville-Marie during its first winter, and the settlement was subjected to repeated Indian attacks that did not cease until the Iroquois and the French made a treaty of peace in 1701. At this time Ville-Marie became known as Montréal. Although its early purpose as a religious utopia was altered by a more pragmatic one as a commercial and military stronghold, Montréal not only survived but grew increasingly important. By the end of the seventeenth century Montréal had a population of more than three thousand and was expanding far beyond its original stockade of Ville-Marie.

Two women stand out in this early history of Montréal. Jeanne Mance founded a hospital in 1645 and was a source of courage to the early settlers. Marguerite Bourgeoys founded the Congregation de Notre-Dame, established education for girls and young women, and helped to advance civilization in a frontier community.

In 1690 Québec City was again under attack, this time by Sir William Phips of Massachusetts. Phips wanted the city to surrender, but the governor, Comte de Palluau et de Frontenac, replied that the only prize Phips would receive would be out of the mouths of French cannons. Phips fired a few harmless shots in anger and then sailed back to New England.

In 1697 the Treaty of Ryswick gave most of the explored land north of Mexico to France. And in 1713 the Treaty of Utrecht transferred Newfoundland, Acadia (Nova Scotia), and Hudson Bay to the British. The British had a far stronger claim to Newfoundland than the French, and the treaty only formalized what had long been fact.

The Roman Catholic Church played a pivotal role in the development of New France. Bishop François de Montmorency Laval established higher education, cultural institutions, health care, and better treatment of the Indians. He brought in members of the Society of Jesus to spread the gospel among the Indians and to help explore the unknown reaches of New France. These black-robes, as the Indians called the Jesuits, became immortals in Québec and Canadian history. Inspired by the potential of an "uncorrupted" land, many outstanding men and women, among them Father Brébeuf and Marie de l'Incarnation, dedicated their lives to New France.

The British tried another time, in 1711, to capture Québec. But the fleet under the command of Admiral Hovedon Walker was almost completely destroyed by a storm in the Gulf of Saint Lawrence. It was not until 1759 that the conflict between the French and the English over possession of North America reached its climax. Defending Québec City (and the destiny of New France) was General Marquis Louis-Joseph de Montcalm with his force of 2,900 soldiers and 13,000 armed civilians and Indians. Opposing Montcalm was Major General James Wolfe with a British force of 27,000.

The British siege of Québec City began in June, but Montcalm's positions held against repeated assaults and artillery attacks into mid September. The approach of winter meant that the British fleet would have to sail for open water or be frozen into the Saint Lawrence River. A winter siege also meant being cut off from reli-

able lines of resupply. The victory that in June seemed so close was now beginning to slip from Wolfe's grasp. But young General Wolfe was a man of daring and imagination. During the night of September 12, Wolfe and his troops landed several kilometers west of Lower Town and climbed up the steep cliffs of Cap Diamant. There were French listening posts in this area, and historians still are not sure why an alarm was not sounded. The speculation is that the French were betrayed. At any rate, Wolfe assembled his forces on the Plains of Abraham. Québec City finally awoke to the emergency, and Montcalm marched forward to confront Wolfe. This battle lasted only a few minutes, but many men on both sides were killed and wounded, including Wolfe and Montcalm. On September 18, 1759, Québec City officially capitulated to the British. Although in April of the following year, Duc François Gaston de Lévis and remnants of the French and Indian forces attempted to retake Québec City, British reinforcements forced the French to retreat to Montréal. In 1763, by the Treaty of Paris, New France ceased to exist and the immense territory it once occupied became part of British North America.

The elite of New France sailed back to their homeland, leaving about 65,000 people, mostly farmers, trappers, priests, and nuns, to face British rule. The British were kinder to the Québecois than they had been to the Highland Scots and the Irish. The Québec Act of 1774, negating an earlier royal proclamation, reinstated the Roman Catholic religion and the French legal system. This infuriated the Protestant American colonies, which resisted paying their share of the high cost of the North American war against France because they felt betrayed by King George III and Parliament. The Québec Act was one of the main causes of the American War of Independence.

When that war did begin, one of the earliest American campaigns against the British took place in Québec. In 1775 American forces under General Richard Montgomery took control of Montréal and then moved northeast to conquer Québec City. At the same time General Benedict Arnold and his army came up through the wilderness of Maine to join Montgomery in setting a pincer on the city. Meanwhile, a delegation of Americans, led by Benjamin Franklin, took up residence in Montréal in an attempt to convince the Québecois to join their cause against the British. Although the Québecois had deep bitter feelings about being a conquered people,

◀ **The Gaspé Peninsula is a dramatic maritime environment. A tour of this region is considered a must by sophisticated travelers to Eastern Canada.**

they by and large resisted the entreaties of the Americans. The leading bishops and priests were confronted with what they considered two great evils: their new masters, the British, who allowed them their religion and way of life, and the Americans, who spoke of liberty but who also despised their religion and way of life. The British offered a certainty, the Americans an enticing promise but also the possibility of cultural disaster. The Québecois placed their destiny on the side of the British and joined in battle against the Americans. Arnold's and Montgomery's repeated attacks on Québec City failed. Montgomery was killed, and Arnold and his Americans retreated first to Montréal and then to Saratoga, where they were successful against the British.

During the early nineteenth century, the fortifications in and around Québec City were modernized and strengthened in anticipation of an American invasion, especially during the War of 1812. But after the American War of Independence, Québec City's history was relatively peaceful; the only real battles have been those of political ideas and between politicians. In 1791 Québec City became the capital of Lower Canada (today's Province of Québec). It was incorporated as a city in 1832. After the union of Upper and Lower Canada in 1841, the city became the capital of the United Provinces of Canada. In 1864 delegates from the British colonies in North America met in Québec City, and their deliberations led to the establishment of Canadian confederation in 1867.

Although Québec City continued as the center of political power during the nineteenth century, economic power shifted to Montréal. Montréal prospered because it attracted people and investments, becoming the transportation, commercial, and manufacturing hub of Canada, a position it maintained until the late 1960s.

In addition to the British and the Loyalists who fled north after the American Revolution, the population of Montréal expanded with large numbers of Scots, Irish, Germans, and Jews. Many came to Montréal, fleeing political oppression in other parts of the world or seeking a better life. Ironically, while economic opportunities were increasing for most of the new arrivals, the native Québecois were having very hard times. In the mid 1800s thousands of Québecois left the province for the New England states, where plenty of jobs existed in the textile mills. The majority of the people in Québec and Montréal were English speaking. During this period the Québecois were viewed mainly as manual laborers by the elite Protes-

114

tant families. The Québecois traditions of conservative, rural living in tight-knit communities, along with discrimination by the English-speaking oligarchies, made economic advancement difficult.

In the nineteenth century Montréal became a hotbed for radical political ideas. Louis-Joseph Papineau's Parti Canadien, which sought to create an American-style republic in Québec, was the first but hardly last attempt at separating the province from the rest of Canada. Papineau's party (usually called the Patriotes party) proposed reforms to the British, who rejected them. In 1837 he assembled an army and declared war against the British, but the rebellion was crushed, and Papineau fled to Vermont. The attempt failed in part because the clergy viewed Papineau as a radical liberal, a danger to the traditional religion and culture.

After the Papineau rebellion, Montréal and the rest of Québec settled into pursuing their economic goals, though the frictions and hatreds remained. In 1885 the transcontinental railroad was completed, linking Montréal to Vancouver on the Pacific coast, as well as to Toronto and New York City.

With the outbreak of World War I, Canada joined Great Britain against the kaiser. When the federal government instituted conscription, many Québecois resisted, stating that they would not fight in England's war. Others did serve, and of Canada's tremendous casualties on the battlefields of France, many were French-speaking Canadians. There was also resistance to conscription during World War II. Among the Québecois resisters was Québec's former premier René Lévesque, who refused to fight in a Canadian uniform, but joined the U.S. Army and served with distinction in Europe. And most Québecois did serve as Canadian soldiers or workers in the war effort.

Québec's most dynamic period began in the 1950s and continues to this day. Premier Jean Lesage launched what has been called the "Quiet Revolution," an effort to transform the old order. This revolution has meant the secularization of education, with an increased emphasis on training in economics, management, and the applied sciences; the assertion of government control over the electric companies and other key industries; the improvement and expansion of social services; and the transfer of powers from the federal to the provincial government. While the Quiet Revolution was accomplishing a great deal, radical Québecois were frustrated because progress was too slow, and violence erupted.

In 1968 Pierre Elliott Trudeau was elected prime minister of

Canada on the pledge that he would increase the rights of the Québecois and keep Québec within the Canadian confederation. Trudeau instituted a program of bilingualism in all federal government operations throughout the country and encouraged other levels of Canadian society to do the same. So far, only New Brunswick is officially bilingual on the provincial level. And in 1968 René Lévesque and others formed the Parti Québecois, pledging themselves to separation from Canada and a single official language for Québec—French.

In 1976 the Parti Québecois, under the leadership of René Lévesque, came to power in Québec. Premier Lévesque made French the official language of the province and put the issue of separation before the public as a referendum; in 1980 the voters rejected his proposal for "sovereignty-association," though they re-elected Lévesque and his party overwhelmingly the following spring.

During the summer of 1985, Premier Lévesque resigned from office. A turbulent era ended, and a new one, more dynamic, began in Québec's rich history.

Speak the Language

While you can get by in Québec without speaking a word of French, it is good manners and a source of pleasure to your hosts to acknowledge graciously, so far as you are able, their native tongue. Below are some basic words and phrases to help get you started speaking one of the world's most beautiful languages.

General Expressions

Bonjour.	Good morning or good day.
Bonsoir.	Good evening.
Bonne nuit.	Good night.
Bienvenue.	Welcome.
Merci (beaucoup).	Thank you (very much)
S'il vous plaît.	Please.
De rien.	You're welcome.
Pardonnez-moi.	Pardon me.
Comment allez-vous?	How are you?
Très bien.	Very well.
Je vais mal.	I am not well.

J'ai faim.	I am hungry.
J'ai soif.	I am thirsty.
J'ai froid.	I am cold.
J'ai sommeil.	I am sleepy.
J'ai mal à la tête.	I have a headache.
J'ai mal aux pieds.	I have sore feet.
Ici, nous parlons anglais.	English is spoken here.
Combien est-ce?	How much is it?
A quel prix?	What is the price?
La voiture est en panne.	The car broke down.
Bonne chance.	Good luck.

People

Monsieur	Mister
Madame	Mrs. (married or older woman)
Mademoiselle	Miss (young unmarried woman or girl)
Le garçon	The waiter or boy
La serveuse	The waitress
La dame	The woman
L'homme	The man
La jeune fille	The girl
Les enfants	The children
Le fonctionnaire	The civil servant
L'ouvrier	The workman
Le fermier	The farmer
L'homme d'affaires	The businessman

Places

La chambre d'hôtel	The hotel room
La salle de bain	The bathroom (for bathing)
La toilette	The bathroom (toilet)
La gare	The railroad station
La boîte de nuit	The night club
La centre ville	The city or town center
Le magasin	The store
La maison	The house
L'école	The school
L'église	The church
L'ascenseur	The elevator
Ouvert	Open

117

Fermé	Closed
Entrée libre	Free entrance
Sortie	Exit
Poussez	Push
Tirez	Pull

Food

Je voudrais un menu	I would like a menu
Le petit déjeuner	Breakfast
Le déjeuner	Lunch
Le dîner	Dinner
L'addition	The check
Le potage	The soup
Le fromage	The cheese
Le poulet	The chicken
Le poisson	The fish
Le bifteck	The beefsteak
Le porc	The pork
L'agneau	The lamb
Le veau	The veal
Le pain	The bread
Le beurre	The butter
Le vin	The wine
Le café	The coffee
Le lait	The milk
L'eau	The water
Le sucre	The sugar
La crème	The cream
La glace	The ice or ice cream
Le gâteau	The cake
Une fourchette	A fork
Un couteau	A knife
Une cuiller	A spoon
Une serviette	A napkin
Un pourboire	A tip

Days of the Week

Dimanche	Sunday
Lundi	Monday
Mardi	Tuesday

Mercredi	Wednesday
Jeudi	Thursday
Vendredi	Friday
Samedi	Saturday

Numbers

Un	One
Deux	Two
Trois	Three
Quatre	Four
Cinq	Five
Six	Six
Sept	Seven
Huit	Eight
Neuf	Nine
Dix	Ten

Weather

Le soleil	The sun
Le vent	The wind
La neige	The snow
La pluie	The rain

Traffic signs

Arrêt	Stop
Gauche	Left
Droite	Right
Tout droit	Straight ahead
Nord	North
Sud	South
Est	East
Ouest	West
Autoroute	Expressway
Défense d'entrer	No entry
Défense de passer	No passing
Défense de stationner	No parking
Stationnement	Parking
Zone de remorquage	Tow-away zone

General Information

Time zone: Eastern (most of Québec) and Atlantic (easternmost Québec)

Telephone area codes: Metropolitan Montréal and south to Granby and the New York State and Vermont borders: 514

The Laurentians, the Hull area, and most of Estrie (the Eastern Townships), including Sherbrooke: 819

Québec City and all the rest of the province north, south, and east of the metropolitan area: 418

Climate and Clothing

Southern Québec summers are warm and pleasant. Generally, there is very little humidity in Montréal and Québec City. They are refreshing refuges for people coming up from sweltering Boston, New York, Washington, D.C., or Philadelphia. The average high temperature in August is 77°F/25°C in Montréal, 74°F/23°C in Québec City. The evenings are mostly cool.

You get a taste of autumn around the end of August. The Laurentians and Estrie come ablaze with color in September.

The first snows come in November and can last into late April. Québec winters are long, cold, and snowy. In February, Montréal averages 18 inches/58 cm. of snow and a high of 26°F/−3°C, while Québec expects 23 inches/46 cm. and 24°F/−5°C. Montréal's underground city and Québec City's Winter Carnival take some of the bite out of the cold season. The province is well known as a center for winter sports.

A very lovely but all-too-brief spring comes in mid May.

Casual clothing is appropriate for vacationers in the cities, at resorts, and while touring; however, both men and women should be careful about what they wear into churches, shrines, and cultural institutions. Most Québecois dress up for evenings in fine restaurants and at cultural events. Keep in mind that Montréal is one of the most fashionable cities in North America and bring clothing that shows respect for your hosts and that will gain you respect in return. Top-coats, sweaters, and light windbreakers are necessary for all seasons in Québec.

The Québecois have learned to make winter a joyous time. Every kind of ▶ winter sport is played throughout the province. Just bring a good spirit, and you won't be disappointed.

The best recommendation for business travelers is to dress as you would at your office or while visiting New York, London, Paris, or Tokyo on business. The Québecois businessperson is very aware of fashion and the status it conveys, perhaps more so than people in other parts of Canada. Women on business trips would do well to bring some chic cocktail dresses. Flair and good taste are much appreciated in Montréal, and women visitors can have a good time looking their best.

Tourist Information

For brochures and maps on the eighteen tourist regions of Québec, contact Tourisme Québec, C.P. 20 000, Québec City, Québec G1K 7X2.

Call toll-free (800) 443–7000 from eastern United States; toll-free (800) 361–6490 from Ontario and Atlantic Provinces; (514) 873–2015 from Montréal; and (800) 361–5405 from elsewhere in Québec.

For special-interest sports vacations in the province of Québec, ask for these brochures:

Québec Snowmobiling Guide
Québec Boating Guide
Québec Camping Guide
Québec Skiing Guide
Québec Golf Guide
Québec Provincial Parks Guide
Québec Hunting and Fishing Packages

The government of Québec recommends that hunters and anglers use the services and facilities of licensed outfitters who control some of the better territories under lease arrangements with the province. In addition to guiding you to some of the best hunting and fishing, many outfitters also provide food, transportation, accommodations, and equipment. Many of the guides also draw on their own experiences, sharing tall tales of adventure in the wilds and of legendary characters.

The north coast of the Gulf of Saint Lawrence offers the big-game hunter and especially the Atlantic salmon fisher some superb opportunities. In many instances you will need the assistance of bush pilots to get you into remote areas, a service that outfitters can provide.

Nonresidents of Québec are required to obtain permits for all freshwater fishing and special permits for salmon. You can obtain permits from game wardens, fish and game outfitters, and most sports shops. Certain parks and reserves require their own special permits.

Game in Québec includes deer, black bear, moose, caribou, hare, duck, goose, partridge, fox, and wolf. Fish species include bass, pike, walleye, trout, landlocked salmon, Atlantic salmon, and Arctic char.

Accommodations

Québec has everything you want in accommodations. The major hotels and motels in Montréal and Québec City compare with the best anywhere. The resorts of the Laurentians are among the finest in North America. While many of the better hotels and motels are of recent vintage, many older places, such as the Château Frontenac and the Ritz-Carlton, are highly regarded for their elegance and sophistication. Québec accommodations come in all price ranges and are considerably cheaper than in other international cities. You will also find a high standard of service. The Québécois take special pride in being excellent hosts, and the visitors greatly benefit from this traditional hospitality.

The Québec government enforces strict standards for accommodations throughout the province. Every hotel, motel, and resort serving the public is subject to frequent inspection by the government, and each accommodation is rated on the standard of quality, service, and value it offers. Their dining rooms or restaurants are also rated by the government on the basis of the food, service, ambience, and value. All places of accommodation are required by law to post the price of each room on the back of the main door. Discrimination based on religion, race, or ethnic background is prohibited under provincial law.

Dining

Eating in Québec is fabulous! Montréal, for example, is a gastronomic capital. In Québec fine dining has four aspects: art, pride, pleasure, entertainment. Well-prepared food is savored over a long sitting, its finer points discussed seriously. Although the hours for meals are the same in Québec as elsewhere in North America, the approach to food is similar to continental Europe's. The exceptional restaurants of Montréal would be exceptional in

Paris, Rome, and London. Fine wines and spirits, mostly from France, accompany most luncheons and dinners; the wine selection at the better restaurants is extensive. A meal for two with wine at a top-notch restaurant will be expensive, but it will also be memorable. Outside Montréal and Québec City, many of the best restaurants are connected with hotels and motels. Check the dining facilities where you are staying.

Traditional Québec cuisine, which emphasizes pork and seafood, thick pea soup, and desserts made with dense maple syrup and fresh cream, enabled the people to survive hard work and cold weather. Of the native foods, try Matane shrimps, cod from the Gulf of Saint Lawrence, Québec cider, anything made from maple syrup, cheeses from the monasteries at Oka and Saint-Benoît du Lac, landlocked salmon, and venison. When you are touring the countryside (the Laurentians, Estrie, the Gaspé), be sure to ask for the specialty of the area (for example, the bouillabaisse is far more splendid on the Gaspé than in the big cities).

French cuisine, both Continental and Québecois style, is to be expected throughout a predominantly French-speaking province. There are, however, especially in Montréal, many different kinds of ethnic restaurants and just about every brand of fast-food spot you love at home.

CHAPTER 8

Montréal

Montréal Today

There is a tendency to describe Montréal (*Mo-ray-el*) as the Paris of North America, but except for its French heritage, Montréal is no more like Paris than Boston is like London. Montréal is a distinctly North American city, an important point to remember because so many visitors compare the city with Paris, in its language, cultural traditions, and ambience. For travelers who know Paris, Montréal will become a welcome surprise: The people here are very friendly to visitors and pride themselves on their warm hospitality. This is quite a contrast to Paris!

Montréal is the financial, manufacturing, and transportation capital of Québec and is second only to Toronto as a Canadian economic center. The current population of greater Montréal is about three million, nearly half the population of the entire province.

Most Montréalers are French-speaking Québecois, and most are fluently bilingual. An Anglophone population lives in the western section of the city (Westmount) and in the western suburbs. Montréal has always had one of the largest concentrations of Jews in Canada. In addition, there are large communities of other ethnic groups, including blacks and Asians.

The history of Montréal would not be complete without mentioning the contributions of a former mayor, the late Jean Drapeau. In the 1950s Drapeau was an energetic public prosecutor who cleaned up much of the corruption in places of power. He was elected mayor in 1954, a position he held until the 1980s. No big city mayor in North America ever had such a long tenure in office. He was responsible for making Montréal the site of the highly successful 1967 World's Fair (Expo), the 1976 Summer Olympic

METROPOLITAN MONTRÉAL

Games, the 1980 International Floral Exposition, and other major events. It can be said that Jean Drapeau was largely responsible for creating contemporary Montréal. Montréal is a well-run city of stunning high-rise buildings, featuring one of the best public transportation systems on the continent and a dynamic urban environment.

Montréal's impressive skyline of high rises is set against beautiful Mont-Royal and along the the Saint Lawrence River, Canada's lifeline. Although a thousand miles from the Atlantic Ocean, Montréal has always been one of Canada's major ports. Its harbor can accommodate scores of ocean-going vessels, including the largest luxury liners. It has two international airports; the one in the suburb of Mirabel is the largest in Canada. The city is served by VIA Rail, Canada's passenger rail system, and AMTRAK from the United States. Excellent highways and roads give easy access to the city.

Montréal has some of the finest hotels and restaurants in Canada. Its French cuisine, in particular, is considered exceptional by leading gourmets from around the world. The city is also the French-Canadian center of fashion, movie production, book publishing, and architectural and interior design. The second largest French-speaking city in the world, Montréal is the capital of French (distinctly Québecois) culture in the western hemisphere.

So much happens in the city that Montréal never seems to sleep. Montréal accepts a wide range of lifestyles, from the most conservative to radical chic. Yet religion, particularly the Roman Catholic faith, is evident everywhere—in an abundance of churches and shrines.

Montréal is a four-seasons city. In the winter, you can enjoy the weather-protected and attractive "underground city," and the excellent skiing and plush resorts of the Laurentians are only a short drive away. Spring, though brief, is a time of sultry breezes and colorful flowers—most pleasant days for a visit. Summer offers fun at La Ronde, one of the largest amusement parks in Canada. You can enjoy a special treat in the autumn through foliage tours of Estrie and the Laurentians.

Most visitors come away raving about their stay in Montréal, and you surely will too.

Tourist Information

For additional information write or call the Greater Montréal Convention and Tourism Bureau, 1010, rue Sainte-Catherine, ouest, Suite 410, Montréal, Québec H3B 1G2, (514) 871–1595. The Bureau invites you to visit their Information Centre, located in Old Montréal, Place Jacques Cartier, 174, rue Notre-Dame, est. There are information booths at the airports and at Dorchester Square (June to September). The Province of Québec has a visitor center, Maison du Tourisme, at 2 Place Ville-Marie, Suite 70, at the corner of University and Cathcart, (514) 873–2015.

How to Get to Montréal

By Car

From New York City take Interstate 87 to Autoroute 15. From western New York State, take Interstate 90 to Interstate 81 as far as Highway 401 in Ontario, which goes east to Montréal. Visitors from central and western New England can go from Interstate 91 to Interstate 89 and then to Autoroute 10, or from Vermont they can take Interstate 91 directly to Autoroute 10 (Sherbrooke, Québec). Eastern New Englanders (from eastern Massachusetts, Rhode Island, and New Hampshire) can take Interstate 93 to Interstate 89, then pick up Autoroute 10.

From Western and Eastern Canada, travel the Trans-Canada Highway, or from Toronto, Highway 401. An alternative for travelers from the Maritimes is to cut across Maine, New Hampshire, and Vermont using Interstate 95, 89, or 91.

For current road condition information, call (514) 873–4121.

Driving distances to Montréal from major cities

Boston	307 miles/512 km.
Chicago	850 miles/1,417 km.
Detroit	585 miles/975 km.
New York City	365 miles/608 km.
Philadelphia	458 miles/763 km.
Québec City	162 miles/270 km.
Toronto	324 miles/539 km.
Vancouver	2,881 miles/4,801 km.

◀ An overview of Montréal, looking south. Montréal is a business and tourist city with a great deal of flair.

Ottawa	114 miles/190 km.
Winnipeg	1,445 miles/2,408 km.
Calgary	2,246 miles/3,743 km.
Halifax	750 miles/1,249 km.
Washington, D.C.	586 miles/977 km.
Seattle	2,848 miles/4,747 km.
Los Angeles	3,015 miles/5,025 km.

Driving in Montréal

Drivers should have no problem driving in and around Montréal. The highways are well marked, maintained, and illuminated, as are the city streets. Obey all signs and speed limits. The Montréal police are not tolerant of traffic violations.

By Air

Many domestic and international airlines, including Air Canada and Canadian Airlines International, provide daily service to Montréal. Contact your local travel agent for information on airlines providing direct or connecting service from your area.

Montréal International Airport at Dorval, in a suburb west of Montréal, is 14 miles/22 km. from downtown. Dorval airport is used for domestic flights and flights to the United States. The terminal has a gourmet restaurant, cafés, gift and duty-free shops, book and magazine stores. Returning American travelers clear U.S. Customs at Dorval rather than back in the United States. Taxis and limousines are plentiful. Frequent service is available to and from the city (the Queen Elizabeth Hotel is a major pick-up point). There are several excellent motels nearby.

Montréal International Airport at Mirabel, located 34 miles/55 km. to the north of downtown, is one of the world's largest airports. This airport is primarily used for flights by domestic and other country carriers to and from the European continent and other international destinations. Mirabel has a number of conveniences for the traveler, including places of accommodation, restaurants, lounges, and boutiques. Frequent bus service operates between downtown Montréal and Mirabel. Taxis and limousines are also available.

Rental Cars

Rental cars are available at Dorval and Mirabel airports and at other city locations from Avis, Hertz, Tilden. Because of the demand for rental cars during busy tourist and convention periods, you

131

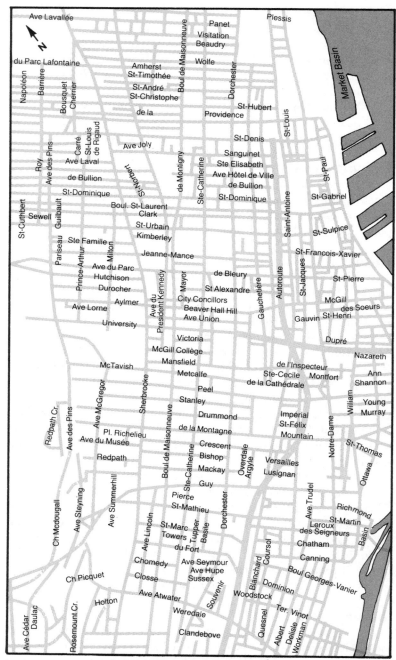

CENTER OF MONTRÉAL

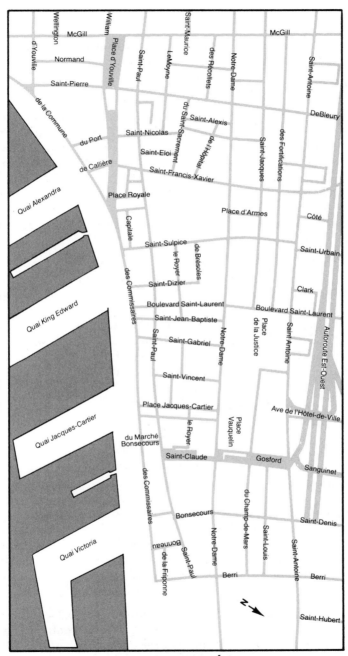

OLD MONTRÉAL

are advised to make reservations before you leave home, a service that your local travel agent will provide.

By Rail

VIA Rail, the Canadian passenger rail system, provides service to Montréal from points west in Canada and from the Maritimes, with frequent daily service from Québec City, Ottawa, and Toronto. VIA Rail trains arrive and depart Gare Centrale (Central Station), located next to the Queen Elizabeth Hotel and across the street from Place Bonaventure. From Montréal call (514) 871–1331 for VIA Rail information and reservations; from the United States call toll-free (800) 361–3663 or –3667.

The Bonaventure métro station, located in Place Bonaventure, is a short walk from Central Station.

By Bus

Greyhound provides frequent daily service to Montréal from the United States and from other cities in Canada. Check with your local Greyhound agent for details.

Terminus Voyageur, (514) 842–2281, the city's main bus terminal, is located next to the Berri-Uqam métro station, where subway trains radiate to almost every section of the city. Bus service is available from here to many destinations in Canada.

General Information

Time zone: Eastern

Telephone area code: 514

Fire, Police, and medical emergencies: dial 911

Weather information: (514) 636–3302

English-language Newspapers and Television

Most major English newspapers and magazines published elsewhere are available throughout the city. In addition to French-language stations, Montréal receives a large number of English-language American and Canadian stations.

Sales Tax and Tips

There is no tax on hotel rooms or on clothing, textiles, and furniture with a value under $500. There is a 9 percent sales tax on most other goods and a 10 percent sales tax on meals over $3.25. The customary tip is 15 to 20 percent of the food and drink bill.

Convention Centre

Montréal's impressive new Montréal Convention Centre is located at 201, avenue Viger, between avenue Viger and rue Saint-Antoine, just below the Vieux (Old) Montréal section. It is one of the largest convention facilities in North America. Its main exhibition hall has 100,000 square feet of space; there are an additional 50,000 square feet on the Convention Level, a large number of meeting rooms, a cafeteria, and a first-class restaurant. The Convention Centre is situated in the heart of Chinatown with its many fine restaurants and colorful shops. This section is becoming one of the more appealing areas of the city and a wonderful place in which to roam about after the hoopla of a convention or association meeting.

Other convention and business meeting facilities in Montréal include Place Bonaventure, Queen Elizabeth Hotel, Château Champlain, Hôtel Meridien, Montréal Airport Hilton, Olympic Stadium, Montréal Forum, Place des Arts, McGill University, Concordia University, and the University of Montréal.

Montréal's top downtown hotels for convention goers are the Queen Elizabeth, L'Hôtel de la Montagne, Le Centre Sheraton, Bonaventure Hilton, Château Champlain, Holiday Inn Downtown, Le Quatre Saisons, the Ritz Carlton, Hôtel Meridien, and Le Grand Hôtel.

How to Get Around Montréal

The Central Area

Although Montréal is a large metropolis, the visitor will find it easy to get around. Much of what you'll want to do and see is in a rather compact area, which can be covered on foot and via the métro subway system.

From a visitor's point of view, the center of the city is Place Ville-Marie, a complex of high-rise buildings on boulevard Rene-Levesque. Other landmarks in this area are the Queen Elizabeth Hotel, Cathedral Marie-Reine-du-Monde, Gare Centrale, Place du Canada-Château Champlain Hotel, Place Bonaventure, and Dorchester square. To the north is Mont-Royal, to the south the Saint Lawrence River.

The street just north of Rene Levesque and running parallel to it is rue Sainte-Catherine, which is lined with big department stores: Eaton's, the Bay, Simpson's. There are also many small shops and inexpensive places to eat, including familiar fast-food places.

Two or three streets north of Sainte-Catherine is rue Sherbrooke. Sherbrooke has high-fashion shops, art galleries, the McCord Museum, business offices, the campus of McGill University, the Museum of Fine Arts, and the venerable Ritz Carlton Hotel.

North of Sherbrooke is Avenue du Mont-Royal and beautiful Parc Mont-Royal. On the other side of Mont-Royal is the campus of the Université de Montréal and Saint Joseph's Oratory, one of Québec's important religious shrines.

To the south of Place Ville-Marie flows the Saint Lawrence River. The lovely Ile Sainte-Hélène, site of La Ronde amusement park, the Montréal Aquarium, and the David M. Stewart Museum at the Old Fort, can be reached by the métro.

To the east of Place Ville-Marie is Old "Vieux" Montréal, the city's preserved historic section, also Place des Arts (the performing arts center), the Convention Centre, Complexes Desjardins and Guy Favreau, Maison de Radio-Canada (CBC production and broadcasting facility), and Chinatown. Further east are Olympic Park and the Botanical Gardens, both easily reached by métro.

To the west of Place Ville-Marie are rue Crescent, rue Mackay, and rue Bishop, with their trendy restaurants, boutiques, lounges, and discos. Westmount is a cozy area of mansions, residences of Montréal's "power elite."

Montréal's Subway System

Montréal's métro can take you to most downtown attractions, fast, inexpensively, and efficiently. Each station is a work of art, beautifully decorated, clean, and safe. Easy-to-read maps of the system are posted on the station walls and inside the trains. You'll see that the métro interconnects everything in the "underground city."

Although the métro serves a large metropolitan area, most visitors mainly use the following stops:

Stations	Destinations
Atwater Le Forum	Westmount Square shopping area
Berri-Uqam (central station, where all lines converge, and the bus terminal)	Latin Quarter/rue Saint-Denis area, train to Ile Sainte-Hélène

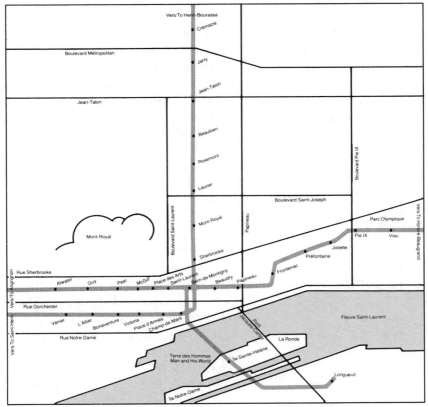

MONTRÉAL SUBWAY SYSTEM

Stations	Destinations
Bonaventure	Downtown Montréal, Place Ville-Marie, Place du Canada, Place Bonaventure, Central Station (rail)
Champs de Mars	Old Montréal (Place Jacques Cartier), City Hall, Longueil train to Ile Sainte-Hélène and attractions
Guy Concordia	rue Sherbrooke, Ritz Carlton, Museum of Fine Arts, rue Crescent boutiques and restaurants
McGill	rue Sherbrooke, McGill University, rue Saint-Catherine department stores, central Montréal, Place Ville-Marie
Peel	rue Sherbrooke, Ritz Carlton, Museum of Fine Arts, rue Crescent boutiques and restaurants
Pie-IX	Olympic Park, Botanical Gardens
Place d'Armes	Convention Centre, Complexe Guy Favreau, Complexe Desjardins, Old Montréal, Chinatown, alais de Justice
Place des Arts	Place des Arts performing arts center, Place Desjardins, Square Victoria, Place Victoria, Montréal Stock Exchange, rue Saint-Jacques to Vieux (Old) Montréal

Guided Tours and Cruises

Guided tours of Montréal are available from Murray Hill (514) 937–5311 and Gray Line (514) 280–5327—both pick up guests at major hotels; Guidatour (514) 844–4021; Les Montréalistes (514) 744–3009; and Visites de Montréal (514) 737–3519.

Another way to see Montréal, perhaps the most romantic way of all, is to hire a calèche (a horse-drawn carriage and driver), which can be found around Dominion Square, Place Jacques Cartier, Parc Mont-Royal, and Place d'Armes.

Cruises on the Saint Lawrence River are offered by Montréal

Montréal's extensive subway is not only modern, clean, efficient, and safe; ▶ it is also beautiful, with works of art in the forms of murals and colored glass.

Harbor Cruises, (514) 842–3871. Lachine Rapid Tours (514) 284–9607, provides thrilling jet boat and rafting trips down through the churning, historic Lachine rapids. This is an excellent wilderness adventure right next to the city. The boarding area for Saint Lawrence River trips and cruises is at the Victoria Pier on the waterfront, near Place Jacques Cartier.

Major Events

Montréal thrives on shows, galas, spectacles, and grand events that capture the attention of the world. The following is a brief listing of significant annual events in Montréal (for more information on these and upcoming special events, contact the Greater Montréal Convention and Tourism Bureau at (514) 871–1595):

Montréal Canadiens hockey at the Forum, from autumn through spring

Montréal Symphony Orchestra, performances at various times throughout the year, at Place des Arts

Montréal Snow Festival, late January to beginning of February

Les Grands Ballets Canadiens, performances at various times of the year, at Place des Arts

Montréal Expos baseball at Olympic Stadium, from April to October

International Benson & Hedges Fireworks Competition at La Ronde, late May to June

Grand Prix Molson of Canada Formula 1 racing, in June, at Ile Notre-Dame

Tour de l'Ile Cycling Competition, in June (departure from Olympic Park)

The Du Maurier Classic Ladies Professional Golf Association, in late June to July at Golfe Club Beaconsfield

The Montréal World Film Festival, late August to September

The Player's International Canadian Open Tennis Championship (men's in odd years, women's in even years), in August, at Parc Jarry

Montréal International Marathon (42 km.), in September

Attractions

The Underground City

Montréal's biggest year-round attraction is its so-called underground city (Montréal souterrain), a vast complex, consisting of clusters of modern buildings, located in various parts of the city, and connected by the métro subway system, shopping promenades, and passageways. The "underground city" incorporates many conveniences: residences, offices, stores, restaurants, theaters, hotels, recreation, and public transportation. It is quite possible to live, work, and enjoy life here without ever setting foot outdoors, especially important during Montréal's long, cold winters. This concept has been copied in a number of other cities.

Montréal's "underground city" began in the 1960s with the opening of Place Ville-Marie, a complex of office high rises built over a labyrinth of boutiques, restaurants, and service establishments. Place Ville-Marie was connected by attractive, often glittering, passageways to the Queen Elizabeth Hotel, Central Station, the métro, and Place Bonaventure, another massive complex of offices, eateries, boutiques, hotel, and exhibition areas. As the city continued to modernize through the 1970s, more complexes were connected: Place des Arts, Westmount Square, Place Victoria, Complexe Desjardins, Complexe Guy Favreau, the Convention Centre, Place du Canada, and several others. The métro links all these complexes plus many other stores and office buildings together into an attractive, enclosed, climate-controlled, urban living network nearly 8 miles/13 km. long.

Touring the underground city is a pleasure. There seems to be an infinite number of shops and boutiques, selling everything from high fashion to the bizarre. The window displays and interiors of many of the shops are nearly works of art—most are at least entertaining. You can spend many delightful hours just window-shopping and poking in here and there. In the Place des Arts you can attend symphony, opera, ballet, and dramatic performances. And you can experience another unique pleasure—riding an attractive, clean, safe subway to almost anywhere in the underground city.

Old Montréal (Vieux Montréal)

Although Montréal is one of North America's most modern cities in appearance and spirit, it has not turned its back on a distinguished heritage. Much of Montréal's past has been lovingly preserved and restored in a section known as Old Montréal. The architecture in Old Montréal is predominantly eighteenth and nineteenth century, and the section is dotted with superb French restaurants, cafés, bistros, boutiques, and handicraft shops. Place Jacques Cartier, a sloping, cobblestone open area ringed by cafés, shops, and restaurants, is where young people and lovers of all ages come to sip wine and espresso and listen to songs, poetry, and political ideas. Many of the buildings around the Place have been recently renovated. However, Place Jacques Cartier, the most intimate public place in the city, has long been and continues to be a central meeting place for Québecois intellectuals, artists, and literati. At the top of Place Jacques Cartier, on rue Notre Dame, is the Nelson statue (1809) and across from it is the baroque edifice of Montréal's City Hall, which has frequent cultural exhibits for the public.

Château Ramezay, 280 rue Notre-Dame and built in 1705, is one of the city's oldest buildings. The Norman-style structure has housed French and English governors, offices of the West India Company, General Benedict Arnold during his retreat from Québec City, and Benjamin Franklin and his party during their mission to convert the Québecois to the American revolutionary cause. Today it houses one of Québec's best collections of historical artifacts and documents. Open throughout the year, closed Monday. Admission charge.

Basilique Notre-Dame, 116 Place d'Armes, was designed by New York architect James O'Donnell and features twin towers, a neo-Gothic style, and a lavish, ornate interior. The elaborate carvings, the paintings, and the dramatic lighting make for an impressive liturgical show. Opened in 1829, Notre-Dame has been the spiritual locus (Roman Catholic) for the city ever since, though it no longer serves as the ecclesiastical seat of the diocese. Notre-Dame is where the Luciano Pavarotti Christmas music special, broadcast annually on television, was filmed. There is an interesting little museum of local and church history here. Admission charge for the museum.

Place d'Armes itself is a square marked by a fine heroic statue of Paul de Chomeday de Maisonneuve, founder of Ville-Marie (as Montréal was first called). Next to the church is a 1658 stone wall protecting the Sulpician Seminary (the Sulpicians predate the Jesuits in Québec). And across Place d'Armes is the nineteenth-century edifice of the Bank of Montréal, which has a museum on early banking practices that is open to the public. (A substantial sum of money was deposited here by the Confederates during the American Civil War.) Free.

Marguerite d'Youville Museum, 1185, rue Saint-Mathieu, a Romanesque-style chapel, contains memorabilia of the Grey Nuns. Open throughout the year, Wednesday to Sunday. Free.

Marché Bonsecours, on rue Saint-Paul, whose handsome dome and colonnade are reminiscent of the Palladian style, is one of the most outstanding pieces of historic architecture in the city, but unfortunately it is not open to the general public.

Notre-Dame-de-Bonsecours, the sailor's church, is next to Marché Bonsecours on 400 rue Saint-Paul. Montréal's oldest church (circa 1657), it was founded by Sister Marguerite Bourgeoys, an immortal in Québec history. Visit the church museum honoring this great educator and religious leader and climb up into the spire to see the city and the harbor.

Parc Historique National Sir George-Etienne Cartier, 458, rue Notre Dame, is the home of one of the fathers of Canadian Confederation. The Cartier family lived here from 1848 to 1871. Open throughout the year. Free.

Montréal History Centre, 355, rue Saint-Pierre, at Place d'Youville, has exhibits on the development of the city from its early beginnings. Open throughout the year. Admission charge.

Old Montréal is a compact area, and everything is within walking distance. Automobiles here are a nuisance, and parking is difficult. Take a taxi from your hotel or the métro to either Champs de Mars or Place d'Armes station. Another nice and romantic way of experiencing Old Montréal is by calèche (horse-drawn carriage), which can be hired in Place Jacques Cartier.

Other Major Attractions

Parc Mont-Royal, on the top and slopes of Mont-Royal, is the city's favorite and most beautiful green space. Designed by Frederick Law Olmsted, the great American landscape architect, the park offers magnificent vistas of the city and the Saint Lawrence River. This is a perfect place to bring a picnic; to stroll along Beaver Lake; to ride in a calèche under majestic trees; to see an art exhibition or enjoy music from itinerant players. There is a nature center here. At the summit of Mont-Royal a huge cross, illuminated at night, marks the spot where in 1535 Jacques Cartier planted the cross in honor of his king. In the winter there is cross-country skiing, ice-skating on Beaver Lake (an old tradition in Montréal), and sledding and skiing on the slopes. Open throughout the year.

La Ronde, on Ile Saint-Hélène, is Montréal's spectacular amusement park. There are exciting rides of all kinds, games, entertainment, and restaurants. A visit to La Ronde is a must if you are bringing children. Open mid May to Labour Day. Admission charge.

David M. Stewart Museum, at the Old Fort on Ile Sainte-Hélène, is an old British arsenal, containing artifacts from the early seventeenth century to the mid 1800s. During the summer, the Compagnie Franche de la Marine and the 78th Fraser Highlanders, dressed in period costumes, perform eighteenth-century military drills. Open throughout the year, except on Mondays. Admission charged.

Montréal Aquarium, near La Ronde on Ile Sainte-Hélène, has an extensive collection of fish and other marine life. Open throughout the year. Admission charge.

Museum of Contemporary Art, in Cité du Havre, features recent works by Canadian and international artists. Open throughout the year, Tuesday to Sunday. Free.

Olympic Park, 4545, avenue Pierre de Coubertin, is the massive complex of sports facilities first used for the Summer Olympic Games of 1976. Tours are given of the main stadium, the swimming pavilion, and the Vélodrome (a cycling track). Today the main stadium is used for baseball home games of the Expos, and other entertainment events requiring seating for many thousands of people. Open throughout the year. Admission charge for tours. Tickets for sports events can be ordered through Ticketron, (514) 288–3651.

Place des Arts, 175, rue Sainte Catherine, ouest, is, like New York City's Lincoln Center, a complex of theaters and other facilities that accommodate performances by symphony orchestras, dance and opera companies, drama troupes, and individual entertainers. Tickets for symphony, ballet, and opera events can be ordered through Ticketron, (514) 288–3651.

Botanical Garden, 4101, rue Sherbrooke, est, near Olympic Park, is a beautifully landscaped, extensive open space, with thirty gardens containing some twenty-five thousand species of plants and flowers. Ten greenhouses display flowers and plants from all the world's climatic regions. Open throughout the year. Admission charge.

Canadian Historic Wax Museum, 3715, chemin Reine Marie,

has costumed wax figures of famous historical personages. Open throughout the year. Admission charge.

Canadian Guild of Crafts, 2025, rue Peel, is a main showplace for artisans. The gallery displays pottery, weaving, carving, furniture, jewelry, and the work of native Indian and Inuit artisans. All these wares are for sale at attractive prices. Open throughout the year, Tuesday to Saturday. Free.

Dow Planetarium, 1000, rue Saint-Jacques, ouest, presents the entire universe to the general public. This is a must place to visit if you are interested in science or if you have never seen a first-rate planetarium before. Open throughout the year. Admission charge. Call (514) 872–4530.

McCord Museum, 690, rue Sherbrooke, ouest, across the street from McGill University, is the best anthropological museum in the province, specializing in American Indian and Inuit cultures. Open throughout the year, Wednesday to Sunday. Admission charge.

Montréal Museum of Decorative Art, Château Dufresne, boulevard Pie-IX and rue Sherbrooke, est, is a turn-of-the-century hotel with a permanent collection of decorative arts of Québec. Open throughout the year, Wednesday to Sunday. Admission charge.

Montréal Museum of Fine Arts, 1370, rue Sherbrooke, ouest, is Québec's leading fine arts museum and one of Canada's finest. It has a superb permanent collection of Canadian and European paintings, sculpture, furnishings, and other rare and exotic objects. It is also the gallery for important traveling international exhibitions. One should not leave the city without spending some time in this outstanding museum. Open throughout the year, Tuesday to Sunday. Admission charge. Tickets for important international exhibitions can be ordered through Ticketron, (514) 288–3651.

Saidye Bronfman Centre, 335, boulevard de Maisonneuve, est, features exhibitions by Canadian and international artists. Open all year, closed Saturdays. Free.

Musée du Cinéma, 335, boulevard de Maisonneuve, est, houses a collection of film-making equipment from the late 1800s to the present. Films are shown daily. Closed Mondays. Free (admission charge for seeing films).

Ferme Saint-Gabriel, 2146, rue Favard, is a Montréal architectural jewel dating from the beginning of the eighteenth

145

century. Open mid February to mid December; closed Mondays. Donation.

McGill University, rue Sherbrooke, ouest, is a venerable institution of higher learning, with its campus right in the middle of the city, just below Mont-Royal. You are welcome to stroll the campus and to visit the Redpath Museum of Natural History.

Bibliothèque Nationale du Québec, 1700, rue Saint-Denis, has manuscripts from 1643 to the present, including notarial deeds, family papers, maps, original drawings, and photographs. If you are doing some genealogical research, it can be an important resource. Open throughout the year. Free.

Saint Joseph's Oratory, 3800, chemin Queen Mary, built through the inspiration of Brother André, is one of the world's largest basilicas and Montréal's most important religious shrine, drawing thousands of pilgrims annually. Religious services are held every day. Even if you are not a Roman Catholic, the oratory is worth seeing for its huge dome set on the northern slope of Mont-Royal. It is one of the great landmarks of Montréal.

Christ Church Cathedral (Anglican), on rue Sainte-Catherine in the heart of the downtown shopping district, is a fine neo-Gothic structure with a lovely interior. Open daily for worship to all.

Université de Montréal, chemin Queen Mary and avenue Marie Guyard, is near Saint Joseph's Oratory. It is the second-largest French-speaking university in the world.

Views from on High: The best views of the city and surrounding countryside are from the summit and slopes of Mont-Royal Park, from the restaurants and lounges high in the main tower building at Place Ville-Marie, and from the revolving restaurant on top of Le Grand Hotel.

Zoological Garden—Jardin des Merveilles, at Lafontaine Park, 4000, avenue Calixa-Lavallée, has live animals, rides, games, a dolphin show, and other entertainment for children and their parents. This is a delightful place for the kiddies. Open mid May to the end of September. Admission charge.

Cathedral of Marie-Reine-du-Monde (Mary Queen of the World), on boulevard René Lévesque, ouest, across from the Queen Elizabeth Hotel and in front of Place du Canada, is supposed to be a scaled-down replica of Saint Peter's in Rome. Built in 1870, this elegant house of worship has an interior less frenetic than Notre-Dame's in Old Montréal. Visitors of all faiths are welcome.

Saint-François Xavier Mission and Saint-Louis Museum and

Fort, at the Kahnawake (Caughnawaga) Mohawk Reserve in nearby Caughnawaga, via the Mercier Bridge, is famous with Roman Catholic pilgrims for its relics of Blessed Kateri Tekakwitha, a Mohawk maiden who converted to Christianity in the eighteenth century. The Mohawks here sing the Mass in their own language at 11:00 A.M. There are many items of historical interest at Kahnawake. The men from this reserve are world famous as steel workers on highrise buildings. Open throughout the year. Free.

Saint Lawrence Seaway, via the Victoria Bridge and Highway 15 to Saint Lambert Lock, gives visitors a close look at large ships making their way through the complicated but efficient locks that allow them to pass to and from the major ports on the Great Lakes. There is a splendid view of the Montréal skyline from here. Observation deck open from May to October.

Recreational Sports

The metropolitan area has a number of public and private golf courses, tennis courts, swimming pools, and fitness facilities. There are also jogging and biking routes, water sport areas, skating, and rafting. Your hotel concierge will be happy to make suggestions and reservations. Most major places of accommodation also have swimming pools and various recreational and exercise facilities.

Professional Sports

You can see the Montréal Expos play at Olympic Stadium. Call (514) 253–3434 for ticket information.

Harness races are run at Blue Bonnets Raceway, 7440, boulevard Décarie; throughout the year, except on Tuesdays. Call (514) 739–2741 for information.

Les Montréal Canadiens of the National Hockey League are a blue-chip team of professional hockey and one of the best sports teams of any kind in Canada. Les Canadiens are a sporting legend, and they play their home games at the Forum, a legendary place in itself. Tickets for home games go fast. Call (514) 932–6131 for information. The regular season runs from October through April.

Tickets for major sports events may be purchased at Ticketron, (514) 288–3651.

Accommodations

Montréal has accommodations for every budget, from deluxe hotels to intimate Bed and Breakfast places. Most major hotels offer less expensive weekend and holiday packages and lower rates to senior citizens and commercial travelers. Some allow children to stay in the same room with their parents free of charge. Do inquire about packages, special rates, and discounts when booking your rooms. Your travel agent can be very helpful in this regard.

Here is a listing of recommended hotels and motels in the Montréal area:

La crème de la crème

Le Quatre Saisons (The Four Seasons), 1050, rue Sherbrooke, ouest, (514) 284–1110, is Montreal's best hotel; expensive. It is the recipient of AAA's coveted "Five Diamond Award" and has a "Four Star" rating from the *Mobil Travel Guide*. This Four Seasons is a very elegant accommodation, located on Montréal's most fashionable street, right across from the campus of McGill University. The rooms are spacious and well appointed. There are many guest amenities, including fully stocked refrigerator bars and bathrobes. The service is first-rate and friendly. The hotel has a fitness facility, swimming pools, and massage and suntan rooms. Le Réstaurant is the hotel's top spot for gourmet dining, expensive. L'Apéo is its popular piano bar for after-hours relaxation and for grand buffets on weekends.

Hotel Le Reine Elizabeth (The Queen Elizabeth), 900, boulevard René Lévesque, ouest, (514) 861–3511, offers the best location in town. It is linked to Place Ville-Marie and the underground city and convenient to the Gare Centrale. The Queen Elizabeth, now a Canadian National Hotel, has a long-standing reputation for excellent service. Its Beaver Club dining room is considered one of the best places to eat in North America. Expensive.

Le Grand Hotel, 777, rue Université, (514) 879–1370, is a beautiful hotel with a revolving rooftop restaurant. This hotel features a gourmet restaurant, an indoor pool, and a health club. Expensive.

Le Centre Sheraton, 1201, boulevard René Lévesque, ouest, (514) 878–2000, offers luxury guest rooms and suites, including its exclusive "The Towers" section. Le Centre Sheraton is a fine business hotel. It features an indoor swimming pool that opens onto a broad outdoor terrace, a health club and sauna, a games room, meeting rooms, an exhibition hall, a concourse of boutiques, and several restaurants and bars. Le Point de Vue is their gourmet dining room, and L'Entretemps is an intimate place punctuated with glitzy entertainment. Expensive.

Le Château Champlain, 1, Place du Canada, (514) 878–9000, is a Canadian Pacific hotel, the most architecturally interesting hotel in Montréal: a slender high rise with half-circle windows, offering good views of the city and a central location, next to the Canadian Pacific rail station and the underground city complex. La Caf' Conc is a popular supper club, and Le Neufchatel serves French cuisine in an elegant environment. This is a favorite hotel with those who can afford the best. Expensive.

Méridien, 4, Complexe Desjardins, (514) 285–1450, is part of Place Desjardins, a massive but extremely attractive complex of boutiques, restaurants, and offices. Le Club is the hotel's excellent gourmet restaurant. The hotel is across the street from Place des Arts and linked to the rest of the underground city by the métro. The rooms here are spacious and attractive, and the service is good. Its Le Club President provides added services and amenities. There is an indoor pool in a greenhouse setting. Expensive.

Montréal Aeroport Hilton, Dorval Airport, (514) 631–2411, offers deluxe accommodations, a swimming pool, a private flower garden, excellent restaurants, a disco, and full facilities for business meetings. There is also a health club and free shuttle service to downtown Montréal. Expensive.

Ramada Renaissance du Parc, 3625 avenue du Parc, (514) 288–6666, next to Parc Mont-Royal, has swimming pools, squash and tennis courts, saunas, whirlpool baths, a gourmet restaurant, a disco, and complete facilities for conventions and business meetings. It is also connected to a shopping arcade that contains many boutiques, restaurants, and cinemas. Expensive.

Bonaventure Hilton International, 1 Place Bonaventure, (514) 878–2332, is one of Montréal's most unusual hotels. It is located on top of Place Bonaventure, a titanic building of stores and exhibition space. The rooms look out either on the city or on beautiful gardens. The heated outdoor pool can be used even on the coldest winter's day or during a snow storm. Le Castillon is the hotel's award-winning gourmet restaurant. Expensive.

Ritz Carlton, 1228, rue Sherbrooke, ouest, (514) 842–4212, is Montréal's most famous hotel. Here the rich, famous, and powerful have stayed. The hotel continues to have an "establishment" aura.

Le Café-de-Paris is famous for its gourmet cuisine, and the Maritime Bar is also well known to discriminating travelers. When the weather is good, Jardin-du-Ritz, an outdoor restaurant in a lovely garden, offers elegant alfresco dining. Expensive.

Hotel de la Montagne, 1430, rue de la Montagne, (514) 288–5656, is an elegant hotel emphasizing the continental approach to personal service. It has one of the most splendid lobbies in Montréal—opulent Art Deco—and a "four star" restaurant, Lutetia. Thursday's disco is very popular. Expensive.

Other Fine Accommodations

Holiday Inn Crowne Plaza, 420, rue Sherbrooke, ouest, (514) 842–6111, is the best Holiday Inn in the area, offering gourmet dining, an indoor pool, a sauna, and convention facilities. Moderate to expensive.

Château de l'Aéroport, Mirabel Airport, (514) 476–1611, is an excellent hotel with full facilities, gourmet dining, boutiques, and a disco; a convenient choice for international travelers. Expensive.

Le Pavillon Hotel Deluxe, 7700 Cote de Liesse, Dorval Airport area, (514) 731–7821, a nice hotel in the European manner, provides shuttle service to business meetings within an 8 km. radius. Expensive.

Hotel Place Dupuis, 1415, rue Saint-Hubert, (514) 842–4881, features an indoor swimming pool, saunas, and several restaurants. Moderate to expensive.

Holiday Inn Richelieu, 505, rue Sherbrooke, est, (514) 842–8581, provides a swimming pool and sauna, connections to the underground city, restaurants, and a bar. Expensive.

Delta Montréal, 450, rue Sherbrooke, ouest, (514) 286–1986, excellent downtown location; good accommodations, dining, and amenities. Expensive.

Ruby Foo's Hotel, 7655, boulevard Décarie, (514) 731–7701, features excellent accommodations and access to Ruby Foo's restaurant, which is famous in Canada for Chinese and French cuisine. Expensive.

Auberge Ramada Montréal Downtown, 1005, rue Guy, (514) 866–4611, has a central location, swimming pool, restaurant, and lounge. Expensive.

Hôtel Château Versailles, 1659, rue Sherbrooke, ouest, (514) 933–3611. This is an excellent value for your money; good location and nice amenities. Moderate.

La Tour Centre-Ville, 400 boulevard René Lévesque, ouest, (514) 866–8861. Luxury furnished apartments available by the week or the month are close to everything downtown. Apartments have kitchens and dining rooms. There is a swimming pool on premises. Moderate to expensive.

Montréal Bed & Breakfast, 4912, rue Victoria, (514) 738–9410, is a network of inexpensive to moderately priced B&Bs in central Montréal. It also provides discounts on sight-seeing tours and restaurants. You can also book apartment rentals and country B&Bs with them.

Montréalers at Home, 3458 avenue Laval, (514) 289–9749, helps place you in excellent, inexpensive B&Bs in Montréal.

Dining

Montréal has thousands of restaurants, many of them exceptional. This is only natural where dining is considered a high art—not just a means for bodily survival. For the most part, restaurants stress continental cuisine, though a few serve traditional Québecois dishes, which are mostly rich and heavy (pork, potatoes, maple syrup) because they were meant to sustain hard-working men and women through long winter months. Today's Montréaler eats far more lightly. Many of the chefs at the top restaurants learned their art in Europe, though increasing numbers of native-born and -trained Québécois chefs have been winning international culinary competitions. Montréal is such a great place to eat that gourmets travel to the city just for that purpose.

Montréal also has a wide range of ethnic restaurants. For those who crave the fare of delicatessens and fast-food places, the city offers everything you could want, from the best smoked-meat sandwiches in North America to southern fried chicken.

For those dining in style, a dinner with wine, tip, and tax can be as expensive as in New York City. Reservations are essential in the better places. Friday and Saturday evenings are especially busy as Montréalers and visitors compete for tables at the best restaurants. The evening dining period begins at 7:00 P.M. Since Montréal is one of Canada's most fashionable cities, men and women dress to the hilt. Obviously, there are many informal places where casual clothes are welcomed. Montréal's brasseries (pubs), for example, offer good food, beer, and wine at reasonable prices.

An evening on the town can consist of drinks at an attractive

lounge, dinner at a gourmet restaurant or supper club, entertainment at a show, sports event, or concert, dancing at a disco, an early morning snack at a bistro, and bed by 4:00 or 5:00 A.M. Unlike most Canadian cities, Montréal displays no Puritan or Presbyterian constraints about pleasure—it delights in being epicurean.

Liquor (including beer and wine) can be obtained in government stores from 9:00 A.M. to 5:00 P.M. Monday through Saturday. In addition, many grocery stores sell wine, beer, and alcoholic cider seven days a week. Many bars and restaurants serve until 3:00 A.M. seven days a week. The legal drinking age is eighteen.

It is impossible to name all the good restaurants in Montréal. But this listing will give you a start in dining well in Montréal, and you can discover other places on your own.

Old Montréal

Gibby's, 298, Place d'Youville, (514) 282–1837, is a popular steakhouse in historic Youville Stables (circa 1716). Expensive.

Auberge Le Vieux Saint Gabriel, 426, rue Saint-Gabriel, (514) 878–3561, is an excellent restaurant in Vieux Montréal, serving excellent haute cuisine in a seventeenth-century inn. Expensive.

A la Catalogne, 311, rue Saint Paul, (514) 866–9180, is one of Montréal's oldest and finest French restaurants. Expensive.

Stash Café Bazaar, 461, rue Saint-Sulpice, (514) 861–2915, is Montréal's popular Polish restaurant. Stash's provided "old country soul food" to Pope John Paul II when he visited the city in autumn of 1984. Pierogies, bigos, hunter's stew, and golabki are specialties. Inexpensive to moderate.

Le Saint Amable, 188, rue Saint-Amable, (514) 866–3471, is considered one of Montréal's (some say North America's) finest restaurants, offering lobster Victoria, sole soufflé, and tournedos opéra. Expensive.

La Marée, 404, Place Jacques Cartier, (514) 861–8126, serves fine cuisine in an elegant eighteenth-century house. Expensive.

Le Fadeau, 423, rue Saint-Claude, (514) 878–3959, offers French dishes, seafood, and fine wines in a beautiful seventeenth-century house. Expensive.

Les Filles du Roy, 415, rue Saint-Paul, est, (514) 849–3535, is Vieux Montréal's best-known restaurant for traditional Québecois

◀ Excellent restaurants and chic boutiques please Montréalers and visitors alike in the rue Crescent area.

food and ambience. You are served by costumed waitresses dressed as "les filles du Roy" (daughters of the King). This restaurant is a must for many first-time visitors to Montréal. Expensive.

Modern Montréal

Les Mignardises, 2037, rue Saint-Denis, (514) 842–1151, is one of Montréal's best French restaurants. It is owned and operated by Chef Jean-Pierre Monnet, who worked wonders at another superb city restaurant, Les Halles. Highly recommended. Expensive.

Les Halles, 1450, rue Crescent, (514) 844–2328, is a premier French restaurant, located near the Ritz Hotel, exclusive shops, and art galleries. Trout with sorrel in pastry, pike soufflé, Chateaubriand with Bearnaise, and veal Normande are specialties. Expensive.

Desjardins Seafoods, 1175, rue MacKay, (514) 866–9741, is a top seafood place in business since 1892. Lobster is a specialty. Expensive.

Katsura, 2170, rue de la Montagne, (514) 849–1172, offers fine Japanese food in a beautiful contemporary interior. Expensive.

La Medina, 3464, rue Saint-Denis, (514) 282–0359, specializes in the lamb-centered cuisine of Morocco. Moderate.

William Tell, 2055, rue Stanley, (514) 288–0139, offers Swiss and French dishes, such as Zurich-style scalloped veal. Moderate to expensive.

Le Pavillon de l'Atlantique, rue Alcan Building, 1188, Sherbrooke and Stanley Street, (514) 285–1636, has a seafaring decor and a wide selection of seafood. Moderate to expensive.

Le Caveau, 2063, rue Victoria, (514) 844–1624, is an intimate French restaurant with good food. Moderate to expensive.

Vieux Kitzbuhel, 505, boulevard Perrot, (514) 453–5521, is the place to go for wienerschnitzel, Tiroler rostbraten, dorschfilet mit mandeln, kalbsschnitzel cordon bleu, and other good things to eat à la Austria. Moderate.

Vespucci, 124, rue Prince Arthur, (514) 843–4784, features an extensive menu of enticing Italian dishes. Moderate to expensive.

Montréal Hebrew Delicatessen and Steak House (Schwartz's), 3895, boulevard Saint-Laurent, (514) 842–4813, is the best deli in French Canada. Schwartz's smoked-meat sandwiches, washed down with Dr. Brown's soda, bring tears of joy to the eyes of deli addicts. Inexpensive.

Ruby Foo's, 7815, boulevard Décarie, (514) 731–7701, is a culinary institution in Montréal and famous throughout Canada for mouth-watering Chinese and French specialties. Moderate to expensive.

Les Chenets, 2075, rue Bishop, (514) 844–1842, features a multi-course gastronomic dinner, a special dining experience, rare in North America. The restaurant is also famous for its extensive wine list, with some bottles priced in the high four figures. Expensive.

Restaurant Rancho Grande, 2074, rue Clark, (514) 842–6301, serves some of the best Mexican food in Montréal. Moderate.

Troika Restaurant, 2171, rue Crescent, (514) 849–9333, is Montréal's only Russian restaurant, in business since 1962. It features fresh Russian caviar, roast rack of lamb, beef stroganoff, and Russian vodkas and brandies. Strolling musicians play sentimental songs while you spoon your borscht. Expensive.

La Maison Kam Fung, 1008, rue Clark, (514) 866–4016, offers a score of delicious Chinese specialties from which to choose. Dim-sum served at lunch. Inexpensive to moderate.

Le Taj, 2077, rue Stanley, ouest, (514) 845–9015, offers North Indian cuisine—tandoori and curries. Moderate.

Restaurant Hélène de Champlain, on Sainte-Helen's Island, (515) 395–2424, is a top restaurant serving continental dishes in an elegant room of traditional Québec decor, located adjacent to the site of the 1967 World's Fair. Moderate to expensive.

Entertainment

Certainly fine dining serves as a major form of entertainment in Montréal, but there are other forms too. The discotheque was well established in Montréal long before it became the rage in the United States and elsewhere. Montréalers are avid patrons of the symphony, opera, ballet, and live theater. The city attracts star entertainers and touring groups from all over the world. The Canadiens and the Expos make Montréal a big league professional sports city. Glittering supper clubs, such as Caf' Conc, present Las Vegas–style productions. There are boites à chansons in Old Montréal, where folksingers serenade you with the ballads of Québec. Cinemas can be found in every section of the city, featuring the latest major productions from Hollywood and from, yes, Montréal. Montréal is one of the film-making centers of Canada, and its productions have won top awards at Cannes and other film festivals.

The only problem you'll have is to make a choice: The entertainment possibilities in Montréal, on any given day, are quite extensive.

Ask your concierge or the visitor services person at your hotel for suggestions and help in making reservations. You can purchase tickets to major cultural events—such as a performance of the marvelous Les Grands Ballets Canadiens or the Montréal Symphony Orchestra—and for sporting events over the phone by calling Ticketron at (514) 288–3651. Tickets for the dinner theaters can also be purchased over the phone by calling Les Enterprises Dupont et Dupond at (514) 843–3177. Various free brochures and magazines are available at your hotel. Most place them in your room. They contain up-to-date listings of special events and entertainment happenings throughout the city.

English-language theater is presented at the Centaur Theatre, 453, rue Saint-François Xavier, (514) 288–3161. Compagnie Jean Duceppe stages French-language productions at the Place des Arts, (514) 842–2112.

For an evening of free entertainment, go walking and people-watching along rue Saint-Catherine and in the rue Crescent area and rue Saint-Denis. These streets and those in Old Montréal never seem empty of people, even in the early morning hours.

Le Caf' Conc, Chateau Champlain, rue la Gauchetière, (514) 878–9000, is a French-style cabaret with cancan dancers and big-name entertainers. Expensive.

Thursday's, 1449, rue Crescent, (514) 288–5656, is Montréal's top bar for cruising—for both sexes. The well-heeled yuppie crowd considers Thursday's their chic watering hole, at least as of this writing. Expensive.

Winnie, 1455, rue Crescent, (514) 288–0623, has music and dining in an Olde English atmosphere. Moderate.

Biddle's, 2060, rue Aylmer, (514) 842–8656, is Montréal's place for jazz.

Vol de Nuit, 14, Prince Arthur, (514) 845–6243, is a dance club catering to professionals and artists.

Old Munich, 1170, rue Saint-Denis, (514) 288–8011, features thumping German music and singing. Moderate.

Le Festin du Gouverneur, at the Old Fort on Sainte-Helen's Island, (514) 879–1141, is an unusual dinner theater, where you are part of the cast. You take part in a seventeenth-century banquet in old Québec. It is a lot of fun.

L'Air du Temps, 191, rue Saint-Paul, (514) 842–2003, offers jazz in a quasi-Victorian setting. A popular, sophisticated night spot.

Shopping

There are thousands of stores in Montréal, one thousand shops just within the "underground city." You can find some good values in Canadian-made clothing and furs, as well as Canadian arts and crafts. If money is not a pressing concern, Montréal offers high-fashion clothing, jewelry, furs, and cosmetics from the world's leading designers and makers. Montréal is Canada's haute couture capital, not just because of its imports but also because of its many highly talented Québecois designers, not just French inspired but also Italian. The Québecois, regardless of their ethnicity, adore glamour and pay top dollar to look their best.

The huge, enclosed shopping complexes—Place Ville-Marie, Place Bonaventure, Complexe Desjardins, Place du Parc, Plaza Alexis Nihon, and Westmount Square—offer a tremendous variety of specialty shops and boutiques in glamorous environments. Rue Saint-Catherine features large department stores, such as Eaton's, Simpson's, the Bay, also the shops at Les Terrasses. Rue Sherbrooke has expensive Holt Renfrew, antique shops, and art galleries. The rue Crescent area sparkles with many boutiques offering dresses, shoes, jewelry, and other attractive, expensive goods.

Le Faubourg Sainte-Catherine is a colorful marketplace selling fresh and prepared gourmet foods. This is a wonderful area to stroll about and sample all the good things to eat. Prince Arthur Street is an enclave of ethnic restaurants and small shops, and on Laurier Street you'll find Greek goods and food. St.-Lawrence Boulevard, also called "The Main," is another area of ethnic shops and restaurants. It seems that almost every nationality has a bit of commercial turf here—Jewish, Polish, Hungarian, Spanish, Portuguese, and so on. Mont-Royal Avenue has seventeen blocks of shopping from Avenue du Parc to Papineau Street, offering just about every kind of merchandise, many at bargain prices. In addition, there are many interesting shops in Chinatown and in Old Montréal. Antique shops are found on Saint-Denis Street, north of Sherbrooke; Sherbrooke Street West, near the Museum of Fine Arts, and sides streets in this area; and Notre Dame Street West, from Guy Street to Atwater Market. There are about seventy-five art galleries in Montréal. Most of them are in the Sherbrooke Street West area, and in Old Montréal.

CHAPTER 9

Québec City

Québec City Today

One word best describes Québec City: romantic. Old Québec City looks as if it had been plucked from some charming area in France and gently reassembled on and around an imposing, high-cliffed headland jutting into the powerful Saint Lawrence River.

Québec City is an eminently human habitation of winding streets and ancient buildings that exude more than four centuries of history. Unlike flashy and frenetic Montréal, Québec City is sedate, elegantly establishmentarian, completely secure in its position as the spiritual and political capital of French Canada.

Some 95 percent of its half-million people are of French descent. Not many years ago, the city's elite were mostly of Anglo-Saxon stock, but their number has greatly diminished with the rise of the Québecois and the assertion of their right to be "masters of their own house." Luckily for the visitor, most of the people who work in the city will try to help you in your own language.

Winston Churchill, who visited Québec City in the early 1940s to plan the Allied invasion of France, called this ancient settlement the "Gibraltar of North America." Churchill was not just being kind to his hosts but was precisely describing the city's terrain and military history. Québec City is built on and around a steep palisade that juts into the Saint Lawrence River like a sharp spear, poised to thrust into any enemy daring to pass into the hinterland of Canada. In the seventeenth and eighteenth centuries Québec City was of such strategic importance that no invader could hope to win the northern half of the continent until it was taken. This is why Québec City was a prime target for Britain's General James Wolfe in 1759. Once his forces were victorious on the Plains of Abraham, New France became part of British North America.

As the capital of Québec, the city's main business is government: Several thousand civil employees work here. While most people think of Québec City only as a historic town, the modern community encompasses a metropolitan area with several suburbs. It is a major educational center, with the sprawling campus of the Université Laval and its thousands of students, an important seaport, and a manufacturing and tourism center. Sometimes its romantic image clouds the fact that Québec City is one of Canada's most dynamic generators of economic activity.

But for the visitor, the economic life of Québec City is far less important than the pleasure of being in a city that hides its mundane business so well. Québec City is one of those special places where you would like to stay a bit longer—to have a romantic affair, to paint lovely pictures, or to write a novel. In Québec City the air always seems clear and fresh. The slower pace of life can be savored like old brandy. Magnificent vistas of river, mountains, cliffs, and islands appear in every direction. In Québec City the illustrious ghosts of the past seem to whisper with every step you take: "Here I governed a people, here I fought my enemy, here I set out to explore a wilderness, here I prayed, and here I died." To fall in love with Québec City is not unusual—it is expected.

In 1985 UNESCO designated the historic district of Old Québec City as a World Heritage site. Québec City is the first North American city to be so honored. A monument commemorating this honor is located on the Dufferin Terrace.

How to Get to Québec City

By Car

Most traffic to Québec City originates in Montréal. The quickest route from Montréal, a distance of 240 miles/384 km., is to take the Louis-Hippolyte-Lafontaine Tunnel, east of Montréal's center, which crosses the Saint Lawrence River and immediately connects with Autoroute 20, the highway to Québec City. Near the city you cross back over the Saint Lawrence River, via the Québec or Laporte bridges, which bring you into Sainte-Foy, the western suburb of Québec City. Boulevard Laurier takes you right into the heart of the city.

A more scenic but slower route is to follow the north shore of the Saint Lawrence River, via Highway 138, which passes through pleasant farm country, lovely small villages and towns, and the historic city of Trois-Rivières. Some of the river views along this route are splendid. This trip can be shortened, without sacrificing scenery, by taking Autoroute 40 from Montréal to Trois-Rivières, then scenic Highway 138 to Donnacona, and from there Autoroute 40 again to Sainte-Foy and Québec City.

U.S. travelers coming directly to Québec City through Maine can take Interstate 95 to Route 201 (just north of Waterville), which goes north and merges with Highway 173 at the border, near Jackman, Maine. Highway 173 goes through the Beauce region of Québec and connects with Autoroute 73 north of the town of Sainte-Marie. Autoroute 73 leads directly to the Québec or Laporte bridges at Sainte-Foy.

Canadian and U.S. travelers coming from the Atlantic Canada provinces can follow the Trans-Canada Highway to Québec City.

By Air

Air Canada and other domestic airlines provide frequent daily service to Québec City. Québec Airport is located northwest of Québec City in Ancienne Lorette, 14 miles/23 km. Taxi and low-cost bus service is available to and from major hotels in the city.

Rental cars—Hertz, Tilden, Avis—are available at the airport and at other locations in Québec City.

By Rail

VIA Rail provides frequent daily service between Montréal and Québec City. The train makes a stop in the western suburb of Sainte-Foy, and at the Central Station in downtown. Call (418) 692–3940 for all train information in Québec City.

By Bus

Voyageur Lines provides hourly service between Montréal and Québec City. The bus terminal in Québec City is at 225 boulevard Charest, est; call (418) 524–4692 for information. Voyageur buses also make connections at the New Brunswick border with buses for those traveling into Atlantic Canada.

General Information

Time zone: Eastern

Telephone area code: 418

Police: (418) 691—6911

Medical emergencies: (418) 648–2626

Weather information: (418) 872–2859

Road Condition Information: (418) 643–6830

How to Get Around Québec City

The Central Area

Happily, you can see most of Québec City on foot. You can visualize the city as consisting of a level plain set high above the Saint Lawrence River (Upper Town), its steep cliffs skirted below by historic Lower Town. The massive Château Frontenac can be used as your central landmark. If you stand in front of the château on the Terrasse Dufferin (Dufferin Terrace), facing the Saint Lawrence River, Lower Town will be immediately below you. You can reach Lower Town by taking the elevator a few steps from where you are standing or by walking down steep Côte de la Montagne. There are many important old buildings in Lower Town's Place Royale, including the historic church of Notre-Dame-des-Victoires.

Back on the Terrasse Dufferin, looking toward the château, you will see the Promenade des Gouverneurs, the Parc des Gouverneurs, and the Citadelle on your left. To your right are the Place d'Armes, rue du Trésor, the Quartier Latin (Latin Quarter), and Québec Seminary.

Walking west on rue Saint-Louis, away from the château, you will notice on both sides streets with many historic buildings, such as the Kent House and the Ursuline Convent. Continuing on rue Saint-Louis, you will pass through the old stone wall that encircles the historic area. To your left is access to the Citadelle, with its Changing of the Guard ceremony, and Battlefields Park, where you can stroll the famous Plains of Abraham. To your right are the handsome buildings of the Québec National Assembly.

Public Transportation

Québec City's buses will take you throughout the city and into nearby suburban communities, such as Sainte-Foy, which has the campus of the Université Laval, massive shopping malls, and many motels. Taxis are available all over town, but they are rarely needed because of the close proximity of most attractions.

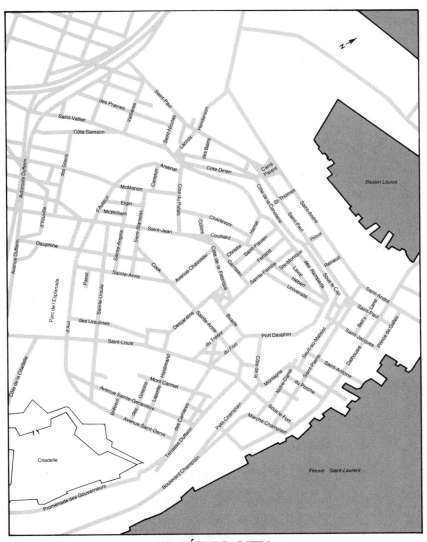

QUÉBEC CITY

Calèches, horse-drawn carriages, with bilingual drivers who are knowledgeable tourists guides, offer a slow-paced, comfortable, and romantic way to see North America's most romantic city. Whereas automobiles seem out of place in Old Québec City, the calèches are as much a part of the tapestry as the venerable Château Frontenac itself. Calèches can be hired at Place d'Armes at any time of the year.

The ferry to and from the city of Lévis is an inexpensive cruise on the Saint Lawrence. It sails every half hour and takes passengers and cars. The terminal is located near Place Royale in Lower Town.

Guided Tours and Cruises

Guided bus tours of Québec City are provided by Grayline-de-Québec, (418) 622–7420; Maple Leaf Tours, (418) 687–9226.

Sonore Tours sells self-guided tours using tape recorders they provide, (418) 627–2351. Les Visites Culturelles Baillargé provides guided tours through the city on foot; (418) 658–4799.

The M/V *Louis-Jolliet*, (418) 692–1159, offers cruises from May to October on the Saint Lawrence River to Ile d'Orléans, Montmorency Falls, and the Québec Bridge. It also offers night cruises with music and dancing. The boarding point is in front of Place Royale.

Cité Express, (418) 872–1931, provides flights over Québec City and the nearby countryside.

Tourist Information

Maps for walking tours, brochures on attractions, and other information can be obtained from the Québec City Region Tourism and Convention Bureau, 60, rue D'Auteuil, (418) 692–2471.

Major Events

For more information on the following events, contact the Québec City Region Tourism and Convention Bureau mentioned in the preceding section.

Carnaval de Québec (Winter Carnival) starts the first Thursday in February and lasts ten days. The only winter bash comparable to Québec's carnival is the Mardi Gras in New Orleans. Carnaval de Québec is a joyous celebration of the human spirit over the harshness of the winter season; it is also the last bacchanal before the somber season of Lent. Perhaps at no other time of the year do so many thousands of people pack into the city. The carnival attracts visitors from all over Canada and the United States. Even if the temperature plunges way below zero and Québec City is blanketed by a snowstorm, the carnival goes on, and whatever nature hands out only makes Québec City more lovely. As a matter of fact, Québec City is at its most beautiful in the snows of winter.

The carnival features glittering parades in both Upper and Lower Town, a snow sculpture competition, grand balls, the crowning of a queen, fireworks, canoe races across the frozen Saint Lawrence, and much more. The giant snowman figure, Le Bonhomme Carnaval, is the official host, delighting all ages. Chefs go out of their way to prepare great feasts. Streets, homes, and hotels are decorated with bright colors, and there is singing, dancing, hugging, and kissing in the streets. Wine and spirits never cease to flow—to keep out the cold and to enhance the joy of the moment. In short, there's nothing like Québec's carnival anywhere.

Plan ahead, if you would like to attend. Some of the best space (such as the Château Frontenac, which is at the center of many events) is reserved a year in advance. Call at least several months ahead of time for reservations, before accommodations become scarce.

Le Festival d'Eté de Québec (Summer Festival) takes place in early July and is the largest Francophone cultural event in North America. It features folk singing and dancing, art exhibitions, theater, sports events, and many other entertainments.

Expo Québec (Provincial Exhibition) is held from late August into early September at Exhibition Park. This is an agricultural and industrial fair with a midway, live entertainment, and contests. Québécois farmers display their prize animals and produce.

International Pee Wee Hockey Tournament, mid February to March.

Eastern Canada Ski Jumping Championships, in February.

Attractions

Québec City is the only walled city in North America. Walls have protected it from unwanted intruders ever since Samuel de Champlain's settlement. The walls you see today were built by the British in the early nineteenth century to protect Québec City from invading American armies. Though American forces, under Generals Benedict Arnold and Richard Montgomery, unsuccessfully as-

saulted the earlier log walls at the beginning of the American War of Independence, no defender has ever shot at an enemy from these present granite ramparts. To the contrary, through the historic Saint-Louis Gate, these old walls have welcomed millions of visitors into the most charming and romantic human habitation in all of North America.

Mont Sainte-Anne, one of Québec's best winter sports– summer recreational areas and important attractions, located a short drive from the city, northeast via Highway 138, is described in the next chapter. Also included are recommended accommodations for that area. These accommodations should also be considered when visiting the nearby Sainte-Anne-de-Beaupré shrine.

Lower Town

During the 1759 British siege of Québec City, most of its buildings were destroyed by artillery fire. Old engravings show Lower Town, in the area of Notre-Dame-des-Victoires, filled with ragged shells of buildings, rubble, and despondency everywhere. But a great human habitation, like the mythical phoenix, arises from its ashes and despair, rebuilds an even better place, and recreates the best of its former glory.

Place Royale, on the site of Champlain's 1608 settlement, is an outstanding example of modern archaeologists, architects, builders, historians, and artisans working together to bring back the seventeenth- and eighteenth-century beauty and ambience in what had become a run-down section. Open throughout the year. All the attractions on the following list are free. There are a number of good restaurants and gift shops in the Place Royale area. The car and passenger ferry for Lévis operates from its nearby terminal.

Notre-Dame-des-Victoires (Our Lady of Victory), named to honor the people's faith and ability to survive, is the gem of Place Royale. It is an exquisite little church, with an attractive facade and a bright interior decorated with gold and many religious statues and paintings. Be sure to see the Chapel of Sainte-Geneviève and the model of an eighteenth-century sailing vessel hanging from the ceiling of the nave. The oldest stone church in Québec (circa 1688), it

◀ Québec City is the only walled city in North America. The stone walls were constructed by the British as a defense against possible invasion of Canada from the United States. One of the best ways to see this historic city is to be driven in a calèche.

continues to be an active parish throughout the year. In the wide cobblestone square in front of the church, frequently used for folk singing and folk dancing, is a fine bust of King Louis XIV, one of the last remaining relics of the French monarchy.

Maison-des-Vins, across the square from the church, sells fine wines and lets you see its wine cellars, brick vaults illuminated with candles.

Maison Jolliet was the home of Louis Jolliet, who along with Father Jacques Marquette explored the Mississippi River in the late seventeenth century. In his house is the *ascenseur* or funicular (elevator) that, for a small price, will take you up to the Terrasse Dufferin at the Château Frontenac. I highly recommend that you use this elevator to get back to Upper Town, as the walk up the stairs and the Côte de la Montagne can be huff and puff for some.

Maison Fornel has foundations constructed in 1658 and vaulted cellars built in 1735. Exhibits show the mechanics of the Place Royale restoration project: the methods used and the findings revealed through the digs and examinations of the old buildings.

Maison Chevalier, a seventeenth- and eighteenth-century complex built for entrepreneur Jean Baptiste Chevalier, now serves as a very interesting and attractive museum of Québec historical artifacts, furniture, and works of art.

Quartier Petit-Champlain is considered one of the oldest residential and commercial districts in North America. In the early seventeenth century, it was a place of elegant homes and diverse shops. Over the years it became a rather squalid area until recent renovations turned it into a charming riverside village in the heart of the city, a special place of flowers, restored homes, street musicians, clowns, jugglers, fine restaurants, and handcraft shops. Open all the time; free access.

Musée de la Civilisation has exhibits on various aspects of culture and also features musical and theatrical performances. Open daily from 10:00 A.M. to 5:00 P.M. Admission charge.

Upper Town

Hotel Château Frontenac stands on the site where Governor Louis de Frontenac and subsequent governors lived in the Château

The famous "Breakheart Stairs," which lead into Lower Town, the most ▶ historic part of Québec City. Here, French culture in North America took root and spread beyond the Mississippi River and down to the Gulf of Mexico.

Saint-Louis. The Norman-style château, with its slanted green copper roofs, has dominated Québec City since the late 1800s, and it is one of Canada's most beloved landmarks. Almost every visitor to the city takes a stroll through its beautiful dark-paneled lobby.

Terrasse Dufferin, in front of the hotel, is an extensive boardwalk set on the edge of the high cliffs overlooking Lower Town. The terrace offers excellent views of the high cliffs of Lévis, the broadening Saint Lawrence River, the tip of Ile d'Orléans and the peaks of the Laurentians in the distance, and the quaint rooftops of Lower Town below. It displays a heroic statue of Samuel de Champlain. The elevator takes you down to Lower Town and a large congregation of calèche drivers hawking their tours of Vieux Québec City. The Terrasse Dufferin was designed so that people could enjoy strolling in an inspiring setting high above the river. Often, during the summer season and the winter carnival, singers and musicians provide free entertainment.

Parc des Gouverneurs, off the terrace and next to the château, was once a private garden and is now a public park. It contains a significant monument to Generals James Wolfe and Louis-Joseph de Montcalm, with a memorable inscription: "Their courage gave them the same lot;/history the same fame;/posterity the same monument."

Promenade des Gouverneurs merges with the Terrasse Dufferin beyond the Parc des Gouverneurs. The promenade is a protected walkway that skirts the cliffs of Cap Diamant and the walls of the formidable Citadelle, rising to the Plains of Abraham near the site of the fateful battle between Wolfe and Montcalm. It offers an exceptional view of the Saint Lawrence River and the steep cliffs of its southern shore. Climbing this path to the Plains of Abraham can be strenuous. If you have a health problem, start the walk atop the Plains and stroll down to the Terrasse Dufferin.

Place d'Armes, across rue Saint-Louis from the château, holds an impressive monument in honor of the Récollet missionaries who came to New France in 1615.

Holy Trinity Anglican Cathedral, 31, rue Desjardins, nearby across rue du Trésor, was built in 1804, the first Anglican cathedral to be built outside the British Isles. This structure has beautiful stained-glass windows and many historic memorials along its interior walls. A special pew is reserved for the British monarch. Though Québec City's Anglophone population has dwindled considerably, the cathedral continues to hold worship throughout the year, and all are welcome.

Rue du Trésor, the place of treasurers, is one of Québec City's more interesting streets. Located across from Anglican Cathedral, it is inhabited by a flock of artists who display their paintings and drawings on the walls of flanking buildings and create a festive atmosphere. There is something here for everyone and at quite inexpensive prices.

Musée du Fort, near the Champlain statue on the Terrasse Dufferin, features a light and sound show depicting the various sieges of Québec City and the battle on the Plains of Abraham. This is a good place to get a quick and interesting history of the city. Open throughout the year. Admission charge.

Basilica of Notre Dame, a gray baroque edifice in the so-called Quartier Latin (Latin Quarter), is the ecclesiastical seat of the archdiocese of Québec City. It was once responsible for the religious administration of all of New France, stretching to the Mississippi River. The interior of the basilica is lavishly decorated, albeit a bit gloomy for some tastes.

Québec Seminary, adjacent to the basilica, was founded by Québec's first bishop, François de Montmorency Laval, in 1663. Here was the original campus of the Université Laval, which now occupies its own contemporary academic city in Sainte-Foy. Within the seminary is an exquisite Jesuit chapel (Laval brought in the Jesuits in preference to the original Sulpician missionaries), a hidden treasure of which many visitors are unaware. The chapel contains the tomb of Bishop Laval, covered in a marble effigy. Pope John Paul II pronounced Laval "Blessed," a step toward sainthood in the Roman Catholic Church. The spires and buildings of the Québec Seminary have been distinctive features of the city's skyline since its early years. Of the old buildings, only the Château Frontenac and the Citadelle on Cap Diamant are more prominent. The seminary, built when most of North America was sparsely settled, imposed highly sophisticated European architecture on an entirely new landscape. The only counterpart at that time was hundreds of miles south in Spanish-controlled Mexico City. Within the seminary, the University Museum houses an eclectic collection of religious items, historical artifacts, old coins, and even an Egyptian mummy. Open throughout the year. Admission charge.

Rue des Ramparts, behind the seminary, has stone fortifications on the high ground overlooking the harbor. Ancient pieces of artillery, poking their muzzles out of the ramparts, are today nice decorative touches in a city that has known mostly peace since the late eighteenth century.

Parc Montmorency is also near the Québec Seminary and borders Côte de la Montagne. Artists and young people congregate in this small park, graced with statues (such as that of nineteenth-century politican Sir Georges Etienne Cartier), and more artillery. Across from Montmorency Park, on Côte de la Montagne, is a heroic statue of Bishop Laval.

Côte de la Montagne, a steep street, winds down to Lower Town, past some intimate French restaurants and shops selling the creative work of artists and artisans (much better, but also much more expensive, than those on rue du Trésor). Côte de la Montagne will bring you to the Breakneck Stairs, which lead to the special world of Place Royale Lower Town.

The Quartier Latin has many good restaurants, lounges, cafés, fashionable boutiques, department stores, and Libraire Garneau, an excellent French language bookshop. The area is compact, and every place is easy to reach on foot. If you must bring a car into this congested area, there is underground parking at the Hôtel de Ville (City Hall), and space is sometimes available at the Château Frontenac's garage.

The area west of the Château Frontenac and the Quartier Latin, toward the wall and its Saint-Louis and Saint-Jean Gates, is a mélange of narrow streets flanked by old buildings that exude the atmosphere of past centuries. It's fascinating to explore these streets to the accompaniment of the clopping, reverberating sounds of the hooves of calèche horses. Rue Saint-Louis, for example, has several good hotels and good restaurants.

The Ursuline Convent, 12, rue Donnacona, was founded in the seventeenth century by the immortal Blessed Marie de l'Incarnation. The convent is an important place of worship for pilgrims. The chapel, which is open to the public, is the most elegant house of prayer in the city. In an adjacent building the Ursuline nuns operate a historical museum that houses General Montcalm's skull. Montcalm's body is buried in the chapel, as is Marie de l'Incarnation. Open May through October, Tuesday to Saturday. Free.

Outside the Central Section

The Citadelle is on the tip of Cap Diamant. The present fortress, built by order of the Duke of Wellington, of Waterloo fame, superseded earlier French fortifications here. The Citadelle continues to be an active military installation, manned by members of the Canadian armed forces. Although built to repulse American invaders, its great moment in history came during the Second World War, when Winston Churchill and Franklin Roosevelt resided here for a time and planned the invasion of France. You may tour the inside of the Citadelle. Its military museum displays a good collection of uniforms, weapons, decorations, documents, and insignia. The highlight of a visit to the Citadelle takes place on the main parade, where the colorful and exciting Changing of the Guard ceremony is performed daily at 10:00 A.M. from mid June until Labour Day. The Beating the Retreat ceremony is held on Tuesday, Thursday, Saturday, and Sunday, during the summer. During early June, there are moonlight concerts by a regimental military band. A tour of the Citadelle is a must when in Québec City. Admission charge. Call (418) 648–3563.

Québec Fortifications National Historic Park has pedestrian paths so that visitors can walk along and inspect these walls and their decorative gates. There is nothing else like them in North America. The powder magazine is open to the public. The fortifications also make a dramatic background for photos of yourself and your companions.

Artillerie Park consists of barracks and other buildings used by the British and Canadian armies on a site formerly used by the French King's army. There are an interpretation center, an exhibition of early Québec fortifications. Open from April to October.

Plains of Abraham Battlefields Park (Parc-des-Champs-de-Bataille) is an extensive park running along the southern edge of the city, high above the Saint Lawrence River, beginning just west of the Citadelle. Here is where the fate of Canada was decided in 1759 and where both Wolfe and Montcalm received their mortal wounds. Signs throughout the battlefield indicate the positions of the military forces and where the important engagements took place. Other monuments here (for example, a beautiful rose garden and a magnificent equestrian statue of Jeanne d'Arc) honor famous moments and personages in French or Québec history. Passenger cars are permitted on park roadways. It is a romantic place for walking and lounging during the warm days and evenings of summer, for pushing a baby carriage, or for jogging. In the winter the Québecois use its rolling terrain for cross-country skiing and for sledding.

Musée du Québec, at the western end of the Plains of Abraham, has a large permanent collection of paintings, sculpture, prints, furnishings, and religious objects relating to the history of the province. In addition, galleries feature the works of contemporary Québec artists. The museum is a major showplace for new and established talent and plays an important role in the development of the people's culture. Open throughout the year. Free.

Cartier-Brébeuf Park, 175, rue de l'Espinay, is where Jacques Cartier had his winter encampment in 1535–36 and where the Jesuits established their first mission in 1626. You can visit a full-size replica of Cartier's ship *La Grande Hermine* and an interpretation center where you can learn more about Cartier and the early history of Québec. Open throughout the year. Free.

Hôtel du Parlement, Québec National Assembly, just west of the Saint-Louis Gate and near the Québec Hilton—huge, gray, and baroque—houses the provincial government. Bronze statues of famous persons in Québec history, such as Cartier and Champlain, decorate the facade. The richly decorated legislative chambers contain oil paintings of scenes from Québec's history and beautifully carved wood paneling and furnishings. You are invited to dine in the excellent Parliament Buildings Restaurant, where you can rub elbows with the politicians. Free guided tours are available. Open throughout the year. Call (418) 643–7239.

Complexe G, 1037, rue de la Chevrotière, is the tallest government building in the city. From an observatory on the thirty-first floor you can see the panorama of Québec City, the river, and mountains. Open throughout the year. Free.

Grand Théâtre de Québec, 269, boulevard Saint-Cyrille, est, a handsome contemporary building both inside and out, is noted for its Louis Frechette and Octave Cremazie Halls. You can see Jordi Bonet's stunning mural, which shocked some conservative citizens when it was first unveiled. Here you can enjoy the symphony, ballet, opera, live theater, and top entertainers from all over the world. Free tours are available from late June to mid September. Events are held throughout the year. Call (418) 643–8131 for a schedule of events and ticket information.

Université Laval is the first French language Catholic institution of higher learning in North America. Its new campus is actually a city in itself, located on a five-hundred-acre site in the suburb of Sainte-Foy. Though mainly a secular university today, it was founded by Bishop Laval in the seventeenth century and remained a stronghold of the Roman Catholic faith for many generations. The beautiful chapel in the center of the campus is a reminder of this heritage. The university has an enrollment of more than twenty-four thousand full-time students. Of particular interest on campus is the sports complex, whose Olympic-size pool is open to the public. Laval's buildings interconnect through underground tunnels, and students often roller-skate to cover long distances quickly. Laval offers an excellent intensive French language course in the summer for non-French-speaking students. Laval is close to Sainte-Foy's several huge and very attractive enclosed shopping malls, which you might want to visit after touring the campus.

Québec Aquarium, 1675, avenue du Parc, in Sainte-Foy, has a good collection of fish and other marine life. Open throughout the year. Admission charge.

Québec Hôtel Dieu Museum Les Augustines, 32, rue Charlevoix, in Québec City, has an important historical collection of art and objects relating to Québec and the first hospital in America north of Mexico City. Open throughout the year. Free.

Maison des Jesuites, 2320 chemin du Foulon, in the Sillery section, dates back to the beginning of the eighteenth century and is one of the oldest historic sites in North America. The first Jesuit mission was founded in 1637.

Chapelle des Jesuites, 14 rue Dauphine, is dedicated to the Roman Catholic religious martyrs of Canada. It contains relics of several saints. The chapel features beautiful sculptures and a high altar made from native pine. Open daily. Free.

Port of Québec National Historic Park, 100 rue Saint-Andre, has interesting exhibits that tell stories of early shipbuilding and timber trading in this important seaport.

Chalmers Wesley United Church, 78, rue Sainte-Ursule, is one of the most beautiful neo-Gothic structures in the city. It has superb stained-glass windows and handcrafted woodwork, as well as a century-old organ. Evening concerts are held during the summer months.

Outside Québec City

Québec Zoological Park, via Highway 15, has more than 564 birds, representing 165 species, and some 214 mammals of 57 different species. There are lions, tigers, bears, camels, owls, eagles, beavers, wolves—more than enough wildlife, exotic and domestic, to delight everyone. The grounds of the zoo are nicely landscaped. Open throughout the year. Admission charge.

Montmorency Falls, via Highway 138, is on your way to Ile d'Orléans and Sainte-Anne-de-Beaupré. You can't miss them because the falls are so near the highways and so awesome that the plunging water seems about to deluge the road. Montmorency Falls are almost as famous as those at Niagara. In the winter the surface freezes and forms a huge cone of ice. You can view the thundering water from the bottom or the top at a park. At the top is also the Duke of Kent's Lodge, a palatial retreat built for Queen Victoria's father, which has had a variety of uses ever since. It is now a hotel.

Ile d'Orléans, via Highway 138 through Beauport, (or Autoroute Dufferin-Montmorency), is a special place for Québecois. Its rural beauty and simplicity remind them of their past seen through romantic perspectives. The towns display some superb examples of old Québec architecture, and the little eighteenth-century churches, such as those in Sainte-Famille and in Saint-François, are gems. For the visitor, this is a great place to picnic in a meadow or on the bank of the Saint Lawrence, to read poetry and be in love. Saint-Pétronille offers the best view of Québec City across the water. There are several excellent and unusual restaurants on the island and many places where you can buy fresh vegetables and fruits (strawberries), delicious maple syrup, and long loaves of fresh, crusty bread.

Sainte-Anne-de-Beaupré, via Highway 138, is the most important Roman Catholic shrine in all of Canada. Through the decades, millions of pilgrims have come here from all over the world to pray and to seek relief from their suffering. A large number of miraculous cures have been attributed to Sainte Anne here. The massive and magnificent basilica has hundreds of crutches left behind as evidence of cures. Like Lourdes, Sainte-Anne-de-Beaupré holds candlelight processions during summer evenings. Masses are held every day at the basilica. On a nearby hillside are the Fountain of Sainte Anne; The Holy Stairs, where the pilgrims climb on their knees in prayer; beautiful little chapels (Scala Santa Chapel and the Old Chapel); and Stations of the Cross set in a grove of trees. The Cyclorama presents biblical Jerusalem in a 360-degree painting. Admission charge. There are accommodations and restaurants in the area, though most people stay in Québec City; and there are various facilities for persons with handicaps, such as ramps, special rest rooms, and medical assistance.

Recreational Sports

The metropolitan area has a number of public and private golf courses, tennis courts, swimming pools, and fitness facilities. There are also jogging routes and water sport areas. Your hotel concierge will be happy to make suggestions and reservations. Most major places of accommodation also have swimming pools and various recreational and exercise facilities.

Professional Sports

The Nordiques, of the National Hockey League, play home games at the Colisée. Call (418) 694–7110 for information. Harness races are held at the Québec Hippodrome on the Exposition grounds, 2205, avenue du Colisée, throughout the year. Call (418) 524–5283 for information.

Accommodations

Québec City offers accommodations for every taste and budget. Inquire about special rates for senior citizens, commercial travelers, and children with parents, and for off-season periods. Your travel agent is your best resource for information and making arrangements tailored to your needs. One period of the year when accommodations are almost impossible to book is during Carnaval, in February. The better places, such as the Château Frontenac, are booked a year in advance, though even this famed hotel might have some space for late reservations. If you want to attend the winter carnival, call your travel agent as soon as possible.

Here is a listing of recommended places of accommodation in the Québec City area:

Québec City

Hilton International Québec, 3, Place Québec, (418) 647–2411, is a large, modern, and complete hotel catering to conventions, touring groups, and individual travelers. Located next to key government offices and overlooking the old city, the hotel has many fine facilities, including a heated outdoor pool, sauna, health club, gourmet restaurants, and lounges. Le Croquembroche is this hotel's top restaurant, and l'Eden is its popular disco. It is connected to the Convention Centre via an arcade of expensive boutiques. Expensive.

Le Château Frontenac, 1, rue des Carrières, (418) 692–3861, is more than a great hotel—it is Québec City's most important landmark and symbol. Every visitor to Québec City stops here. Through its long history, the Château Frontenac has played host to royalty from many countries and the famous from all walks of life. During the Second World War, while Churchill and Roosevelt stayed in the nearby Citadelle, it accommodated the Allied officers who planned the invasion of France. Today, it offers fine accommodations, excellent service, and gourmet dining to the discriminating traveler. **Expensive.**

Loews Le Concorde, 1225, Place Montcalm, (418) 647–2222, is one of the best hotels in Québec City. It offers spacious rooms with highly contemporary furnishings. Most of the rooms have splendid views of the old city, the Plains of Abraham, or the Saint Lawrence River. This hotel is across the street from the Plains of Abraham, with its beautiful green areas, gardens, and vistas. Le Concorde features an outdoor heated pool, sauna, gym, a rooftop revolving restaurant, and lounges. Expensive.

Auberge des Gouverneurs Downtown, 690, Saint-Cyrille, est, (418) 647–1717, is next to the Parliament buildings and historic Vieux Québec City. This beautiful high-rise hotel offers excellent accommodations, services, gourmet dining, lounges, and a disco. It also has a heated outdoor pool and is connected to the Convention Centre. Expensive.

Holiday Inn Downtown, 395, rue de la Couronne, (418) 647–2611, offers a central location convenient to attractions, restaurants, and lounges. Expensive.

Hôtel Fleur de Lys, 115, rue Sainte-Anne, (418) 694–0106. Moderate.

Hôtel Clarendon, 57, rue Sainte-Anne, (418) 692–2480, features an excellent restaurant. Moderate.

Hôtel Château Laurier, 695, rue Grande Allée, est, (418) 522–8180. Moderate to expensive.

Sainte-Foy

Auberge Ramada Inn, 1200, rue Lavigerie, (418) 651–2440, offers a swimming pool and an excellent restaurant. Moderate to expensive.

◀ Canada's most famous landmark, the Château Frontenac on the heights of Québec City.

Château Bonne-Entente, 3400, chemin Sainte-Foy, (418) 653–5221, has a swimming pool, tennis courts, and a good restaurant. Moderate to expensive.

Auberge Universe Wandlyn, 2955, boulevard Laurier, (418) 653–8721. Moderate to expensive.

Hôtel-Motel Le Châteaubriand, 3225, rue Hochelaga, (418) 653–4901, near the Québec Bridge, features a heated outdoor pool, playground, gourmet restaurant, and lounge with entertainment. Expensive.

Auberge des Gouverneurs Sainte-Foy, 3030, boulevard Laurier, (418) 651–3030, offers a terraced garden, outdoor pool, gourmet restaurant, and disco. Expensive.

Auberge Quality Inn, 3115, boulevard Laurier, (418) 658–5120, has a heated outdoor pool, restaurant, and lounge. Moderate to expensive.

Beauport

(This eastern suburb is on the way to Sainte-Anne-de-Beaupré shrine.)

Hôtel-Motel Le Voyageur, 2250, boulevard Sainte-Anne, (418) 661–7701, is one of the best in this area. Moderate.

North of Québec City

Manoir du Lac Delage, 40, avenue du Lac, Lac-Delage, (418) 848–2551, is a complete resort about twenty minutes from Québec City via Highway 175. It features a heated pool, tennis courts, badminton, volleyball, a golf course, horseback riding, boats, skiing, skating, and sleigh riding, as well as a fine dining room and cocktail lounge. Expensive.

Manoir Saint-Castin, 99, chemin Tour du Lac, Lac-Beauport, (418) 849–4461, is a superb resort, about 12 miles/19 km. north of Québec City via Highway 175. It has a golf course, swimming pool, indoor and outdoor tennis courts, racquetball, canoeing and boating, Alpine and cross-country skiing. Its restaurant, Salle Saint-Castin, is considered one of Québec's finest for French haute cuisine. Expensive.

Dining

The emphasis in Québec's capital is on French, Québecois, and Canadian-American cuisine. The top restaurants here are a match for the best in Montréal, and in North America, for that matter. The people of Québec, like those in Montréal, consider fine dining an art and demand perfection from their chefs. The price for a fine meal, with wine, tips, and taxes, is similar to what you'd pay in Montréal. People dress for dinner in their best and latest fashions. Meals, which start at 7:00 P.M. or later, often last a good part of the evening. Most of the better restaurants accept credit cards.

Each year more and more fine restaurants open for business in Québec City, much to the delight of residents and visitors. The following is but a small sample:

Québec City

Le Champlain, Château Frontenac, 1, rue des Carrières, (418) 692–3861, offers elegant, gourmet dining (under crystal chandeliers and to live harp and violin music). One of the best places in the city. Expensive.

La Crémaillère, 21, rue, Saint-Stanislas, (418) 692–2216, prides itself on its European cuisine and fine service. Moderate to expensive.

Café de Paris, 66, rue Saint-Louis, (418) 694–9626, has a menu of French and Italian specialties, also Beef Wellington and rack of lamb. Moderate to expensive.

Aux Anciens Canadiens, 34, rue Saint-Louis, (418) 692—1627, serves Québec meat pie and hare stew in one of Québec's oldest houses. Moderate.

La Caravelle, 68 ½, rue Saint-Louis, (418) 694–9022, is a Spanish restaurant, unique in Québec City, specializing in seafood, paella, and gazpacho andalouse. Moderate to expensive.

Chez Guido, 73, rue Sainte-Anne, (418) 692–3856, is the best Italian restaurant in town, serving scampis, pears in Pernod. Moderate to expensive.

Le Croquembroche, Québec Hilton, 3, Place Québec, (418) 647–2411, offers superb dining with ambience of elegance. Expensive.

Le Bonaparte, 680, avenue Grande-Allée, est, (418) 647–4747, is an extra-special place for romantic dining. Expensive.

L'Astral, Hotel Loews Le Concorde, 1225, Place Montcalm, (418) 647–2222, is a revolving rooftop restaurant offering good food and the best views of the city and the surrounding countryside. Expensive.

Le Saint-Amour, 48, rue Sainte-Ursule, (418) 694–0667, is

181

considered by many Québecois to be one of the finest new restaurants in the city. Specialties include fillets of sole with salmon stuffing and shrimp sauce, grilled lamb cutlets cooked with split garlic buds and marinated in olive oil, a special chicken pâté, and fish soup with garlic toast. In good weather there is dining in an outdoor garden—well worth the visit. Moderate.

Serge Bruyère, 1200 rue Saint-Jean, (418) 694–0618, near the Latin Quarter, is noted for superb continental cuisine. Expensive.

These are a few recommended moderately priced restaurants:

Le Chalet Suisse, 26, rue Sainte-Anne, (418) 694–1320.

Le Marie Clarisse, 12, Petit-Champlain, (418) 692–0857.

Le Vendôme, 36, Côte de la Montagne, (418) 692—0557.

Café d'Europe, 27, rue Sainte-Angèle, (418) 692–3835.

Au Petit Coin Breton, 1029, rue Saint-Jean, (418) 694–0758.

Ile d'Orléans (Orleans Island)

L'Atre, 4403, Chemin Royal, Sainte-Famille, (418) 829–2474, prepares superb old-fashioned Québec dishes and serves them in traditional style in an ancient farmhouse (circa 1680) with an open hearth. You are brought to the door by a horse-drawn carriage. Expensive.

Auberge Chaumonot, 425, Chemin Royal, Saint-François, (418) 829–2735, offers fine dining in a beautiful setting on the banks of the Saint Lawrence. Moderate to expensive.

Le Moulin de Saint-Laurent, 754, Chemin Royal, Saint-Laurent, (418) 829–3888, serves central European dishes in this old mill (circa 1635), accompanied by gypsy music. Expensive.

Outside Québec City

Manoir Saint-Castin, 99, chemin du Tour du Lac, Lac-Beauport, (418) 849–4461, is reputed to serve outstanding haute cuisine, in elegant style, in its main dining room—well worth the short trip to scenic Lac Beauport to dine well here. Expensive.

Entertainment

Québec City's best entertainment in the evening is its own romantic ambience. Stroll through historic Upper and Lower Town, along the Terrasse Dufferin and onto the green fields of the Plains of Abraham, or dine elegantly in a fine gourmet restaurant and then linger over old brandy to savor the romantic essence of Québec City.

Most of the better hotels and motels feature live entertainment and dancing in their dining rooms and lounges.

Discos in Québec City include L'Eden at the Hilton, Le Cabaret at Le Concorde, also Brandy's at 690 Grand-Allée. Ask the concierge at your place of accommodation for suggestions for taking in the current hot spots in town.

Drama and music are vibrant in Québec City at the Grande Théâtre de Québec, 269, boulevard Saint Cyrille, est; call (418) 643–8111 for information. Musical and dramatic performances are also held at Palais Montcalm, 995, Place d'Youville; call (418) 670–9011.

Shopping

If you would like souvenirs, your best bet is to patronize the young artists who display their paintings and drawings in rue du Trésor. Their work is inexpensive, and you will go home with something original and the memory of the person who created it. Within the Quartier Latin are gift shops selling wood carvings from Saint-Jean-Port-Joli and soapstone carvings from the far north, bookshops, boutiques, and department stores. There is also a complex of very expensive boutiques in the small underground city at the Québec Hilton and Convention Centre. Sainte-Foy's boulevard Wilfrid Laurier has several enclosed shopping malls.

CHAPTER 10

Other Popular Vacation Regions in Québec

Québec is Canada's largest province in terms of territory. It is so huge, in fact, that several European countries can be placed within Québec and still have room left over for more. It would be impossible to visit most of Québec during one trip. This is good because you will want to return again and again to see what you have missed. Although many visitors to the province spend most of their time in Montréal and Québec City, there are other fascinating vacation regions that can be experienced within one visit. This chapter describes several of the most popular vacation regions of Québec.

Just a short drive to the north of Montréal is the Laurentian mountain resort region. This is a four-seasons area where you can hike, swim, horseback ride, and go canoeing during the summer, and ski at some of the finest downhill runs or go cross-country in winter. The resorts here are world famous for their accommodations, services, and food, especially their cuisine and après-ski fun.

To the south of Montréal is Estrie, also called the Eastern Townships, where there are picturesque towns, fine inns, an imposing monastery overlooking a majestic lake, and pleasant touring of the lovely countryside. Estrie is also a popular winter sports region.

Between Montréal and Québec City is a region called the "Heart of Québec." Here are the historic cities of Trois-Rivières and

◀ Ah, Québec, C'est magnifique!

Drummondville with their many attractions, parks, and religious shrines.

Along the north shore of the St. Lawrence River to the east of Québec are the regions of Charlevoix, Manicougan, and Duplessis. On this side of the river is Mont Sainte-Anne ski center, one of the finest winter sports facilities in North America. There are challenging downhill runs and extensive trails for cross-country ski touring. During the summer, there are hiking, swimming, and other recreation. The St. Lawrence River continues to widen as you travel farther east, and the slopes of the mountains plunge down into the water, making for dramatic vistas from every turn of the road. There are wonderful inns and famous resorts within Charlevoix, also quaint villages that have become favorite haunts of artists. In the regions of Manicougan and Duplessis, you enter a special world of small fishing settlements, traditional values, and a way of life reminiscent of earlier decades.

On the south side of the St. Lawrence is one of the most popular tours in all of Canada, that of the Gaspé peninsula. The scenery of mountains, broadening river, and sealike Gulf of St. Lawrence is to be remembered for years to come. Here are the traditional fishing villages of Québec, places of strong family and community ties and a history that begins with the earliest European exploration of this continent. There are national parks where you can experience the ecological wonders of this region, its wildlife, birds, and marine life. Gaspé is also a region that offers superb dining, excellent accommodations, and countless attractions made by both a generous nature and creative humans.

For more information on the Québec vacation regions described below, call Tourisme Québec: from eastern United States, (800) 443–7000; from Ontario and the Atlantic Provinces, (800) 361–6490; from all other areas in the United States and Canada, (515) 873–2015. Or write Tourisme Québec at C.P. 20 000, Québec City, Québec, Canada G1K 7X2.

Laurentides

What the Catskills are to New York City, the Laurentians are to Montréal. The Laurentians are a four-seasons recreational region

The splendid work of talented craftspeople can be found throughout the ▶ province of Québec. The question becomes not whether to buy but how to make the best selection from the vast array.

of steep mountains, beautiful lakes, deep forests, and cozy valleys. This terrain provides the best Alpine and cross-country skiing in Eastern Canada, plus every other winter sport you can name and lively Québecois après-ski fun. During the warmer months, you can enjoy all sorts of outdoor activities: camping, canoeing, sailing, hiking, rock climbing, auto touring, horseback riding, swimming, golf, and tennis. The Laurentians have fabulous resorts with luxurious accommodations, gourmet dining, and top star entertainment. The Laurentians are only an hour's drive from the central city. This means you can come up here just for the day or stay an entire season.

The Laurentians have been called the "Switzerland of Eastern Canada." They are part of the Canadian Shield, a vast, relatively uninhabited area north of the Saint Lawrence River Valley and the Great Lakes, composed of rugged mountains, thousands of waterways, and endless forests. Agriculture and forestry, once the backbone of the Laurentian economy, are still important, though leisure-time businesses now provide a substantial portion of the region's employment and income. The Laurentians serve as magnificent recreational areas for millions of people and as secure sanctuaries for many species of wildlife. They offer a splendid respite from touring the big cities. Here you can refresh yourself in an inspiring natural environment that also has a great many modern conveniences. In the Laurentians you can really rough it in the wilderness—or you can live it up in style.

The Laurentians were settled by French-speaking Roman Catholics, and the towns of this region continue to reflect this heritage. But because of their proximity to Montréal and major cities in the eastern United States, affluent English-speaking Canadians and Americans have also made this area into a popular vacation refuge. So, though French in flavor, the Laurentians are cosmopolitan enough for everyone.

For more information on this vacationland, contact the Association touristique des Laurentides, Saint-Jérôme, Québec J7Z 5T4, (514) 436–8532.

The fastest highway access to the Laurentians from Montréal is Autoroute-des-Laurentides 15, a toll road that ends in Sainte-Agathe-des-Monts. From Sainte-Agathe to Saint-Jovite and Mont-Tremblant, Highway 117 is the main access road. From the Ottawa-Hull area, take Highway 105 to 117 at Mont-Laurier.

Voyageur buses, operating from Terminus Voyageur in Montréal, service the Laurentians with several runs a day, (514) 842–2281.

Highway 15 passes through **Saint-Jérôme,** the "Gateway to the Laurentians." A bronze monument in town honors Father Labelle, an inspiring force in the economic development of this area in the nineteenth century. Also in Saint-Jérôme is the Vieux Palais Art Gallery, which features works by artists living in the region. Open throughout the year.

At the municipality of **Prévost,** secondary roads lead to Echo, Connelly, and de l'Achigan lakes.

Saint-Sauveur and **Mont-Gabriel** have several resorts, eight ski centers, seventy-two slopes—some with 213-meter vertical drops—and eighty chair lifts. Saint-Sauveur has live theater, craft shops, antique boutiques, and good restaurants. Accommodations and dining are available at the Auberge Saint-Denis, 61, rue Saint-Denis, (514) 227–4766, a top-rated place and moderate to expensive; Motel Le Nomade, on Highway 117, Piedmont, (514) 227–5181, with a swimming pool and skiing nearby, moderate; Motel Mont Habitant, 12, boulevard des Skieurs, Saint-Sauveur, (514) 227–2637, with a swimming pool, skiing on site, tennis, and access to a lake, expensive.

Sainte-Adèle is another popular vacation center, featuring four downhill ski centers and miles of cross-country trails. Visit Village-de-Séraphin, a re-creation of a nineteenth-century Laurentian community, consisting of twenty buildings, a costumed staff, and displays of crafts. Open mid May to mid October. Admission charge. There are also a number of studios in town where you can watch artisans make beautiful handicrafts, which you can buy. Accommodations and dining are available at the following:

Motel Altitude, Highway 117, (514) 229–6616, offers a swimming pool and sauna. Expensive.

Motel Champêtre, 1435, boulevard Sainte-Adèle, (514) 229–3533, has a swimming pool. Moderate.

Hôtel Le Chantecler, chemin du Chantecler, Lac Rond, (514) 229–3555, is a famous resort that offers great accommodations, excellent dining, golf, tennis, swimming pools, lake beaches, boats, skiing on site, and tennis. Expensive.

Highway 370 from Sainte-Adèle goes into the resort community of **Sainte-Marguerite Station.** The Hôtel Alpin Inn, chemin Sainte-Marguerite, (514) 229–3516, features good accommodations in a beautiful setting, plus gourmet dining, swimming pools, beaches, tennis, and skiing on site. Expensive.

Highway 370 continues to **Estérel**. L'Estérel, boulevard Simard Fridolin, (514) 228–2571, is one of the fine resorts in the Laurentians. At L'Estérel you can ski (both downhill and cross-country), sail and swim on a beautiful lake, play tennis and golf, sweat off in a health club the calories you consumed the night before, and enjoy the magnificent scenery around you; expensive (Modified American Plan).

Back via Highway 15, you come to the villages of **Val-Morin** and **Val-David,** noted for their artisans. Nearby Mont-Condor attracts expert rock climbers from throughout North America. At Val-David is Santa Claus Village, exit 76 on Highway 15, an entertaining theme park for young children. Open mid June to mid October. Admission charge. **Théâtre-de-Val-David**, 2554, rue Monte, (514) 322–2818, offers live drama. Accommodations and dining are available at Hôtel La Sapinière, Highway 117, Val-David, (819) 322–2020, a superb resort with outstanding cuisine (wine cellar has 25,000 bottles, featuring 200 different labels), a swimming pool, skiing on site, tennis, and other recreational facilities, expensive. In 1982 this resort was the site for NATO's first meeting in Canada. Also try Auberge du Vieux Foyer, 3167, chemin Donscater, Val-David, (819) 322–2686, with a good restaurant and accommodations, moderate; and Hotel Far Hills Inn, rue Far Hills, Val-Morin, (514) 866–2219, an excellent resort with cross-country skiing, swimming, sailing, tennis, and other recreational offerings, as well as an excellent dining room, expensive.

The largest community within the Laurentians is **Sainte-Agathe.** It is on Lac-des-Sables, which has beaches, swimming, and boats for rent. Théâtre Le Patriote, chemin Tour du Lac, presents live drama and exhibits handicrafts in a tourist pavilion. Visit the village of Mont Castor, which has many restored historic houses. Recommended accommodations include Motel Sainte-Agathe, 1000, rue Principale, (819) 326–2622, moderate; Motel Saint-Moritz, 1580, rue Principale, (819) 326–3444, moderate; Chalets Domaine Chanteclair, on Highway 117, (819) 326–5922, expensive. Fully furnished condominiums are available from Les Mansardes Condos De Luxe, 74, rue Desjardins, (819) 326–4850, expensive.

Highway 117 takes you to **Saint-Jovite,** and from here a secondary road, Highway 327, takes you to the best-known and most popular recreational area in the Laurentians, **Mont-Tremblant Provincial Park.** Here you can downhill ski on the highest mountain in the region, cross-country ski, ice-skate, snowshoe, camp, canoe, rock climb, swim, auto-tour, and hike. Fall foliage touring through the park is a favorite way to spend weekends for Montréalers and visitors.

The Mont-Tremblant area has the largest concentration of top-notch resorts and motels in the Laurentians. For additional information and reservations, call (800) 567–6760 (winter) and (800) 425–8681 (summer). The following is a listing of recommended accommodations and dining:

Auberge Gray Rocks Inn, located on the shore of Lac Ouimet, Highway 320, nord, Saint-Jovite, (819) 425–2771, is one of the best known of the great Laurentian resorts, particularly popular with U.S. visitors. It offers excellent accommodations and dining and a wide variety of recreational facilities: skiing on site, swimming in a pool and at the lake, tennis, golf, seaplane rides, and much more. It has a new indoor sports and fitness complex. Expensive.

Auberge Cuttle's Tremblant, on Lac Tremblant, (819) 425–2731, provides excellent accommodations and dining, cross-country skiing, golf, tennis, sailing, and swimming. Expensive.

Auberge Le Château (Gray Rocks), on Lac Ouimet, (819) 425–2771, is similar in quality and features to Gray Rocks Inn. Expensive.

Auberge Villa Bellevue, on Lac Ouimet, (819) 425–2734, offers good accommodations and dining, on-site skiing, and swimming in the lake. Moderate to expensive.

Le Pinoteau Village, on Lac Tremblant, (819) 425–2795, provides good accommodations and dining, easy access to great skiing, tennis, and swimming in a pool and the lake. Expensive.

Chalet-des-Chutes, on Lac Tremblant, (819) 425–2738, features good accommodations and dining and swimming in a pool and the lake. Moderate to expensive.

Station Mont Tremblant Lodge is the only resort complex located on Mont Tremblant, (819) 425–8711. There are fine accommodations in the main lodge, in chalets, and in efficiency apartments. This super resort offers gourmet restaurants, après-ski fun, a ski school, and immediate access to some of the best downhill skiing in North America. Expensive.

Auberge Château Beauvallon, Montée Ryan, (819) 425–7275, is a beautiful lodging offering seclusion but convenient access to all recreational features in the area. It has its own beach on a lake. Moderate.

From Saint-Jovite and the Mont-Tremblant area, Highway

117 continues on to the town of **Mont-Laurier,** where it meets Highway 105 from Ottawa-Hull. Highway 117 leads to *La Vérendrye Provincial Park,* an extensive wildlife refuge. **La Vérendrye Wildlife Reserve** offers camping, canoeing, fishing, moose hunting, cottages, and cross-country skiing.

Laurentian Area Alpine Ski Centers

With five months of ice and snow each year, winter sports and Québec go together. It's no exaggeration to say that Québec has the best skiing east of the Canadian Rockies and north of Stowe and Lake Placid. Excellent ski centers, with good facilities and well-tended slopes, are located close to Montréal—the famed resorts of the Laurentians, for example, are only a hour's drive away. What makes skiing in Québec different is the special liveliness of the Québecois themselves. Not only do they survive the long winter months, they make a joyful art out of living in a frigid zone. You'll feel their joie de vivre out on the slopes and especially at the many après-ski activities. Skiing in Québec also means having superb accommodations, gourmet dining, and easy access to Montréal. When you get tired of the downhill runs, you can ice-skate, cross-country ski, snowshoe, ice-fish, and snowmobile amid some of the most magnificent scenery in the world. You can come to Québec alone or book a package that includes almost everything.

The following lists the top alpine ski centers in the Laurentians:

Mont Avila, in Saint-Sauveur, (514) 227–4671.
Mont Olympia, Piedmont, (514) 227–3523
Mont Saint-Sauveur, Saint Sauveur, (514) 227–4671
Mont Habitant, Saint Sauveur, (514) 227–2637
Mont Christie, Saint Sauveur, (514) 226–2412
Ski Morin Heights, Morin Heights, (514) 226–1333
Mont Gabriel, Mont Rolland, (514) 229–3547
Le Chantecler, in Sainte-Adele, (514) 229-3555
Cotes 40/80, Sainte-Adele, (514) 229–2921
L'Avalanche, Saint-Adolphe-d'Howard, (819) 327–3232
Belle Neige, Val Morin, (819) 322–3311
Mont Sauvage, Val Morin, (819) 322–2337
Vallée Bleue, Val David, (819) 322–3427
Mont Alta, Val David, (819) 322–3206
Mont Blanc, Saint Faustin, (819) 688–2444
Gray Rocks, Saint-Jovite, (819) 425–2771

Mont Tremblant, Mont Tremblant, (819) 425–8711
Mont Daniel, Labelle, (819) 597–2388

Estrie (The Eastern Townships)

Estrie (the Eastern Townships) is an extensive rural area southeast of Montréal, near the Vermont border, with rolling farmland, charming small towns, sparkling lakes, and medium-size mountains. About an hour's drive from downtown Montréal, Estrie has long been a favorite vacation haunt. This is also equestrian country, and jumping and dressage are a way of life here. During the summer, Estrie becomes a tranquil haven for artists, writers, musicians, and actors, many of whom participate in the region's many cultural programs.

Much of the Estrie region was originally settled by Loyalists after the U.S. Revolution and by British soldiers who were given land grants by the crown. Because of this heritage, some of the communities resemble those in nearby New England. The fields are broad, in the English manner, while those of the Québecois are long and narrow strips, in the French tradition. In recent years, the Anglo-Saxon population has declined, and the Québecois have come to dominate the towns. They changed the region's name from the Eastern Townships to Estrie. A few farmers from Switzerland have moved into the region, bringing their agricultural expertise and their strong traditions of hard work and frugality.

Estrie nourishes the fattest and most fecund milk cows in the province. A congregation of monks living above Lac Memphremagog has become world famous for their cheeses. Some of the lushest apple orchards in Canada thrive here, their fruits making a delicious but potent cider. Ducks for gourmet dishes grow plump on local farms. Vast stands of sugar maples are tapped in the spring, and the resulting crystal liquid is rendered into some of the best maple syrup made in North America.

Estrie is very much a four-seasons vacation area. In winter it offers great downhill and cross-country skiing. In spring you can tour a countryside awakening from the deep sleep of winter and bursting with life and color. Summer is enlivened with swimming, golf, hiking, horseback riding, art, music, and theater. In autumn, try touring the magnificent landscape, which has become scarlet, gold, and tan, visit country harvest fairs and sample from their bountiful fruit and vegetable harvests.

Estrie is easily reached by taking Autoroute 10, east toward Sherbrooke, the largest city in the region. From Vermont, Interstate 91 and then Highway 55 take you right into the heart of Estrie, at Magog and Sherbrooke. If you are driving back into New England after visiting Montréal and Québec City, you can enjoy your trip more by traveling through this lovely region.

On the way to Estrie, Highway 10 crosses the Richelieu River just south of **Chambly.** In early colonial days, the Richelieu was an important waterway giving Montréal and Québec City easy access to Lake Champlain and the English settlements in New York State and New England. General Montcalm and his French forces made frequent use of this route for his attacks during the Seven Years (French and Indian) War. The Richelieu was also used by General Benedict Arnold and his American troops in their retreat from Québec. See old Fort Chambly, which played an important role in the early history of Canada and in Papineau's rebellion in the mid-nineteenth century. Open during the summer. Free.

The "gateway" city to Estrie is Granby, well known as the Townships' Gastronomique Capital. From late September to the end of October, the Festival Gastronomique takes place in Granby. Various restaurants participate in this event by preparing and serving to visitors their haute-cuisine specialties. Also in mid September is Festival de la Chanson, a national competition featuring performances by amateur singers and musicians. Visit the Granby Zoo, 347, rue Bourget, a ninety-five-acre park with animals from all continents and a farm where children can handle tame animals. Open May to mid October. Admission charge. The Hôtel Le Castel de l'Estrie, 901, rue Principale, (514) 378–9071, is highly recommended for accommodations and especially its superb cuisine, moderate. Motel Le Granbyen, 700, rue Principale, (514) 378–8406, also has fine dining, moderate. Hôtel Le Monde 400, rue Principale, (514) 372–1705, with another good dining room, offers inexpensive accommodations.

As a side trip, take Highway 139 and explore the countryside down to **Cowansville** and then take Highway 104 to Lac Brome, where they raise ducks for gourmet chefs. There is also an interesting museum of local history.

Bromont, near Granby, is horse country, with an equestrian festival in mid July, hunter trials and riding competitions in September. The Auberge Bromont, 95, rue Montmorency, (514) 534–2200, is recommended for fine dining and accommodations. Moderate to expensive.

Magog and **Mont-Orford** are the prime recreational areas in Estrie. Magog is on the northern tip of Lac Memphremagog, a large body of water that extends well into Vermont. There are public beaches on Lac Memphremagog and cruises. *Mont-Orford Provincial Park* offers all kinds of recreational activities—the best downhill skiing in the region, cross-country skiing, camping, hiking, and swimming. The Orford Art Centre, located off Highway 10, is well known for its summer educational program in music, art, and theater, especially in the training of young talent. Its season runs from May to September. During this period the faculty and students hold their Festival of Music. Concerts and recitals are held at the art center and at the Abbey of Saint-Benoît-du-Lac.

Near Magog is the unusual and beautiful Benedictine Abbey of Saint-Benoît-du-Lac, dramatically set out on a peninsula high over Lac Memphremagog. To reach Saint-Benoît from Magog, take the road to Austin and then follow the signs for the side road to the abbey. Its architecture is Renaissance in style, distinctly European on a distinctly North American site. Orchards, fields, and pastures surround the abbey. The entire scene is exceptionally lovely and, frankly, quite stunning when one first comes upon it. The monks make jams, honey, and cheeses for sale. Their gourmet L'Ermite blue cheese is well known in sophisticated cheese circles. The public is welcome to visit the abbey and to attend religious services, which feature Gregorian chants. Men are also welcome to make spiritual retreats at the abbey. There are also lodgings for women.

Recommended accommodations and dining in the Magog area include Auberge Cabana, 1460, rue Principale, (819) 843–3313, moderate; Auberge de l'Étoile, 1133, rue Principale, ouest, (819) 843–6521, with good food and accommodations, moderate to expensive.

At nearby Lake Massawippi are three of Estrie's finest inns: Hovey Manor, in North Hatley, (819) 842–2421; Ripplecove Inn, in Ayer's Cliff, (819) 838–4296; and the Hatley Inn, in North Hatley, (819) 842–2451. These inns offer superb accommodations, dining, recreation, and guest amenities. Hovey Manor, within a secluded lakefront area, has English gardens. Ripplecove Inn, also on the lake, has one of the best dining rooms in the entire region. Hatley Inn overlooks the lake and is decorated with antiques. Some rooms have a fireplace and Jacuzzi. All three are expensive.

Sherbrooke, the largest city in Estrie, is located on the Saint-François River. Sherbrooke's economy is based on forest products and other forms of manufacturing. The University of Sherbrooke's

Art Gallery, within its Cultural Centre, on boulevard Université, exhibits paintings, drawings, and sculpture. Open throughout the year. Free. The campus itself is quite attractive and worth a visit. Sherbrooke Seminary Museum, 195, rue Marquette, has an extensive natural history collection, antiques, paintings, coins, medals, and firearms. Open throughout the year. Admission charge. Also visit Saint-Michel Cathédrale, on rue de la Cathédrale, and the Beauvoir Shrine. In August Sherbrooke holds its Agricultural Exhibition, one of the largest in the province.

Accommodations and dining are available at the following:

Auberge des Gouverneurs, 3131, rue King, ouest, (819) 565–0464, is the best in town for accommodations and dining. Expensive.

Hotel Le President, 3535, rue King, ouest, (819) 563–2941, is a good place to stay. Moderate to expensive.

Motel Le Baron, 3200, rue King, ouest, (819) 567–3941, is also recommended. Moderate to expensive.

To the south of Sherbrooke is **Lennoxville,** via Highway 147, the site of Bishop's University, founded in 1843. You are welcome to stroll the lovely campus and to attend English-language dramas during the summer. Also visit the internationally known experimental farm. Open May through early September. Lennoxville is also known for its antique shops. Recommended accommodations and dining include the Motel La Paysanne, 42, rue Queen, (819) 569–5585, noted for its cuisine, moderate, and Motel La Marquise, 350, rue Queen, (819) 563–2411, moderate to expensive.

Estrie Area Alpine Ski Centers

Mont Orford, Magog, (819) 843–8882
Owl's Head, Mansonville, (514) 292–5592
Mont Sutton, Sutton, (514) 538–2345
Bromont Ski Centre, Bromont, (514) 534-2200

For more detailed information on accommodations, dining, and recreation in Estrie, contact Tourisme Québec (see beginning of chapter for telephone numbers and address).

Coeur-du-Québec
(The Heart of Québec)

In haste to travel between Montréal and Québec City, many visitors miss the attractions of Trois-Rivières and Drummondville. Trois-Rivières is midway between Montréal and Québec City on the northern route (via Highways 40 and 138). Drummondville is midway on the southern route (via Highway 20).

Trois-Rivières

This old city has many historical attractions. The Saint-Maurice Ironworks (Les-Forges-du-Saint-Maurice), 10150, boulevard des Forges, is where the Canadian iron industry began under the French. Open May to September. Free. The Pierre Boucher Museum, at the Séminaire Saint-Joseph, 853, rue Laviolette, features art exhibitions throughout the year. Free. The Museum of Archaeology of the Université-du-Québec, 3351, boulevard des Forges, has a collection of fossils and artifacts from Indian and European settlements in the region. Open throughout the year. Free.

Other walking tour attractions in the center of the city include the Museum of the Ursulines; St. James Anglican Church; the Roman Catholic cathedral, the only Westminster-style church in North America; statue of Maurice Duplessis, a legendary and controversial premier of Québec; the eighteenth century Manoir de Tonnancour; and Maison Hertel-de-la-Fresnière. There are also a number of art galleries and antique shops in the city.

The M/S *Jacques Cartier* offers cruises on the Saint Lawrence River during the summer.

Adjacent to Trois Rivières, at Cap-de-la-Madeleine, is the important religious shrine of Notre-Dame-du-Cap, which features a huge circular basilica decorated with beautiful stained-glass windows, an old historic chapel, and a large outdoor area for worship, including stations of the cross and a gigantic rosary carved out of granite. Call (819) 374–2441.

The following is a listing of recommended accommodations and dining:

Auberge des Gouverneurs, 975, rue Hart, (819) 379–4550, offers excellent accommodations and dining, and many conveniences. Expensive.

Motel Montclair, 7331, rue Notre-Dame, (819) 377–1252, is a good choice for accommodations and dining. Moderate.

Motel Castel de Prés, 5800, boulevard Royal, (819) 375–4921, is well known for its excellent cuisine. Inexpensive to moderate.

Hôtel-Motel Le Baron, 3600, boulevard Royal, (819) 379–3232, is a large modern facility with good dining room. Moderate to expensive.

Nearby Parks

Trois-Rivières is the gateway to the Mastigouche and Saint-Maurice Parks, north via Highway 55:

Mastigouche Wildlife Reserve offers camping, canoeing, fishing, touring, moose and small-game hunting, snowmobiling, cross-country skiing, and cottages.

Saint-Maurice Wildlife Reserve has camping, cottages, canoeing, fishing, touring, sailing, moose and small-game hunting, cross-country skiing, and snowshoeing.

Shawinigan Falls, between Shawinigan and Shawinigan South via Highway 138, welcomes hiking and cross-country skiing.

Drummondville

While in Drummondville visit Des Voltigeurs Park. Within this park is the Trent Manor House and Estate (circa 1836), which displays antiques and other historical artifacts in a lovely setting. Admission charge. The park also welcomes camping, swimming, touring, cross-country skiing, and snowshoeing. Another major attraction in Drummondville is Le Village Québécois d'Antan, on rue Mont Plaisir, Highway 3. Its buildings, costumed staff, and activities depict life in a nineteenth-century Québec community. Open June to Labour Day. Admission charge. The village is a major historical and cultural attraction in the province and should not be missed.

Recommended accommodations and dining include Motel Universel, 915, rue Hains (819) 478–4971, moderate to expensive; Hôtellerie Le Dauphin, 600, boulevard Saint-Joseph, (418) 478–4141, the best accommodation and restaurant in town, moderate.

Mont Sainte-Anne and the Charlevoix Coast

For the serious skier, Mont Sainte-Anne, located thirty minutes' drive from Québec City, via Highway 138 east, is the province's best downhill venue. This super facility has forty-three trails spread over three sides of the mountain; fourteen ski lifts that can serve more than seventeen thousand skiers per hour. Eighty-five percent of the total skiable surface on the mountain is backed by a snowmaking system, although this area is heavy snow country in the winter. There are seven night skiing trails, with the highest vertical drop for night skiing in Canada. Various skiing championships are held here each year, such as the Canada Cup in 1987. There are six chalet-type restaurants on the mountain itself. During the summer, Mont Sainte-Anne offers two 18-hole golf courses, a golf school, a gondola ride to the top of the mountain, hiking and mountain cycling trails, and many other recreations. This is an area of many fine accommodations, restaurants, and lounges. Accommodations range in price from moderate to expensive. Package plans are available. You can get more information on accommodations and make reservations throughout the year by calling toll-free (800) 463–1568 (accessible from the rest of Québec, Ontario, Atlantic Canada, and the United States), or call Tourisme Québec (see beginning of this chapter). For more information on the park, call (418) 827–4561. For the latest ski conditions at Mount-Sainte Anne, call (418) 827–4579.

The Charlevoix coast, via Highway 138, from Sainte-Anne-de-Beaupré to Saint-Siméon, offers one of the most scenic drives along the ever-widening Saint Lawrence River. Along this route the rugged Laurentians extend their fingers into the river. There are breathtaking vistas and many examples of traditional Québecois architecture (homes, barns, churches) along the way. This is a rich area for the photographer.

Cap Tourmente National Wildlife Reserve, with 5,000 acres of mudflats, tidal marsh, farm land, and mixed forest on the north shore of the Saint-Lawrence River, is habitat to 250 bird species, including the greater snow goose that can be seen by the thousands during spring and fall migration. The reserve includes a nature center and several miles of hiking trails. It is open to the public from mid April to early November. Admission charge.

Baie-Saint-Paul is a pretty town favored by artists. The Galerie d'Art Clarence Gagnon has works by this great Québecois artist. His paintings of rural life in Québec are highly prized and in major museums throughout Canada. The artist A. Y. Jackson also liked Baie-Saint-Paul and did many paintings here. At **Saint-Joseph-de-la-Rive** you can take the short ferry ride to **Ile aux Coudres,** which has charming inns for accommodations and dining, museums of local history, lovely churches, spots where you can see porpoises in the river, and friendly islanders who welcome visitors.

Back on the mainland at **Pointe-au-Pic** is one of Québec's most famous resorts, Manoir Richelieu, (418) 665–3703, which resembles a French château. The Manoir Richelieu offers golf, tennis, swimming, fishing, fine accommodations, gourmet dining, lounges, and entertainment. This was once a popular watering hole for wealthy Americans and English-speaking Canadians. Today it is more egalitarian, but the quality remains high. The views of the Saint Lawrence River and surrounding mountains from the front are magnificent, especially when shafts of sunlight plunge dramatically from the clouds and spread over the water. Expensive.

Highway 138 continues up the Charlevoix coast to the mouth of the Saguenay River, which is a favorite cavorting area for whales. You can go on whale-watching trips sailing the schooner *Marie-Clarisse*, which departs from the Hotel Tadoussac dock, (418) 235–4421. Here you can take a ferry to the historic town of **Tadoussac** and continue on the north shore into the regions of Manicouagan and Duplessis.

Most people touring the Charlevoix coast from Québec City try to make it a one- or two-day trip, turning back at Pointe-au-Pic or continuing from Saint-Siméon to the Gaspé via the ferry to Riviere-du-Loup on the south shore, (418) 862–5094.

The following inns are recommended in the Charlevoix region for the quality of their accommodations, dining, and guest amenities, and their romantic ambience:

Auberge les Sources, in Pointe-au-Pic, (418) 665–6952. Expensive.

Auberge des Peupliers, in Cap-a-l'Aigle, (418) 665–4423. Expensive.

Auberge La Pinsonniere, in Cap-a-l'Aigle, (418) 665–4431. Expensive.

Auberge La Maison Donohue, in Pointe-au-Pic, (418) 665–4377. Expensive.

Auberge des 3 Canards, in Pointe-au-Pic, (418) 665–3761. Expensive.

Hotel Cap-aux-Pierres, on the Isle-aux-Coudres, (418) 438–2711. Expensive.

The Manicouagan Region

The Manicouagan region goes along the Saint Lawrence River from Tadoussac on the east shore of the Saguenay River to Baie Trinité. Tadoussac, via Highway 138 from Québec City, is reached by ferry across the Saguenay. This portion of the north shore of the Saint Lawrence is connected to the shore by ferries between Les Escoumins to Trois Pistoles on the south shore, between Baie Comeau, the principal community in this region, and Matane, and between Godbout and Matane. These ferries allow you to tour the north shore as far as Godbout and still have access to the Gaspé and the Atlantic provinces. At Godbout, the Saint Lawrence River empties into the Gulf of Saint Lawrence. For students of natural history, north of Baie Comeau is the site where a gigantic meteor smashed into earth thousands of years ago. Some scientists believe that the impact of this meteor so changed the earth's environment that it was a cause for the disappearance of many species of animal life on our planet, including the dinosaurs. You can see the circular shape of this meteor by looking at a map or space satellite photo, and you can drive up to this area on Highway 389, which goes past the mammoth hydroelectric complex called Manic Five, with its Daniel Johnson dam. There's excellent fishing in the lake and rivers surrounding the meteor, which is now simply a mound topped with thick woods. There's also good hunting. The use of local outfitters and guides is required.

There are many good places of accommodation in the Manic-ouagan region, including the Hotel Tadoussac, (418) 235–4421 in Tadoussac, and the Hotel Le Manoir, (418) 296–3391, in Baie Comeau. Both offer excellent accommodations and dining, and both are expensive. Be sure you book a room ahead of arrival.

Duplessis Region

Highway 138 continues northeast along the north coast of the Gulf of Saint Lawrence, through the Duplessis region, all the way to Havre Saint-Pierre. The road stops at Havre Saint-Pierre. There is no connecting road from here to the Québec and Labrador border at Blanc Sablon. At Blanc Sablon, a paved road does go a few miles east to the village of Vieux Fort and west to Pinware, Labrador. A ferry, operating when the waters of the Strait of Belle Isle are free of ice, provides access between Blanc Sablon and St. Barbe on the northern tip of the huge island of Newfoundland. Commercial aviation companies provide regularly scheduled flights to many of the communities along the north coast of the Gulf of Saint Lawrence, with the city of Sept-Iles (Seven Islands) being their principal destination. Sept-Iles is a major port for the ocean shipment of iron ore and is the largest and most important of the communities on the coast. Ferries also provide service to the remote fishing communities along the coast. During the summer, travelers have enjoyed the leisurely cruises and the opportunity to visit the picturesque villages to meet the people and to purchase their local handicrafts. A number of these fishing villages, such as Harrington Harbour, are inhabited by English-speaking people. Ferries from Sept-Iles also provide service to Anticosti Island, an extensive wilderness preserve in the

Gulf of Saint Lawrence, and back west to the city of Rimouski on the south shore of the Saint Lawrence River and just a few hours' drive to Québec City. Duplessis is most famous for its salmon fishing rivers and for hunting. Anticosti Island, once a private domain of one man and off-limits to casual visitors and sportsmen, is now a prime place for salmon fishing and deer hunting. You can also hike and camp on Anticosti. The hiring of local outfitters and guides is required. There are good accommodations and restaurants in Sept-Iles, and Bed and Breakfast–style places in most of the smaller communities.

The Gaspé Peninsula Tour

On a map, the Gaspé looks like Québec's proud but remote lower lip jutting into the Gulf of Saint Lawrence. With Montréal and Québec City, the Gaspé is one of the "must see" areas in Canada.

The greatest delight of a Gaspésian trip is the feel of an ever-present sea; but the sea must contend with spectacular mountains, steep cliffs, the Saint Lawrence Gulf and River, the islands, snug valleys, picturesque villages, and a way of life that remains close to nature and to the traditions of an earlier time. The Gaspésian trip is a constantly changing panorama of the moods of nature and humanity.

Allow three to five days for your Gaspésian tour. You can do it in two days, but your trip will be all driving. There are public and private picnic and camping areas along the entire route. If you find yourself in an interesting village and your French is rusty or non-existent, don't worry—there's sure to be a bilingual person around to recommend points of interest, accommodations, and places to eat. The local shopkeeper and the parish priest should also be helpful.

The accommodations mentioned in the guide are in logical stopping points. By and large, the best dining on the Gaspé can also be found at these lodging places. It is recommended that you call ahead for reservations, especially in the popular tourist town of Percé.

Most people prefer to begin their Gaspésian tour from Québec City, traveling along the south shore of the Saint Lawrence River and around the peninsula in a clockwise direction, then entering the province of New Brunswick at Campbellton (the gateway to Atlantic

Canada) around the Baie des Chaleurs. The total distance is about 665 miles/1,064 km. Alternatively, you can follow the Charlevoix coast on the north shore from Québec City to Saint Siméon, where a ferry crosses to Rivière-du-Loup on the south shore. The Charlevoix coast route is far more scenic, but it also requires more time.

Experienced travelers have found that the best vistas of sea, mountains, fishing villages, and forests are seen by going around the Gaspé peninsula clockwise. Stretches of the road are set on narrow terraces with steep cliffs rising on one side and the pounding waves of the Saint Lawrence below on the other. The clockwise direction gives you a greater sense of security because you are driving on the inside of the road, hugging the sides of mountains. Sometimes, when the gulf waters are particularly rough, waves smash against the low sea walls and send spray high into the air, so keep your window washers full of cleaning solution.

Our Gaspésian tour follows the south shore of the Saint Lawrence River from Québec City. You can leave Québec City via the Québec or Pierre Laporte bridges at Sainte-Foy or cross over on the ferry to Lévis. Get on Highway 20, a superhighway, and continue until it merges with Highway 132, which goes around the peninsula.

Saint-Jean-Port-Joli, 64 miles/102 km. from Québec City, is a major handicrafts center of the province. Shops and studios managed by craftspeople working in wood sculpture, jewelry, textiles, graphic arts, and pottery abound. This little riverfront town was launched into the field of handicrafts by the famous Bourgault family, master woodcarvers and teachers. The Saint-Jean-Port-Joli artisans exhibit their work throughout town and offer it for sale at attractive prices. The Musée Les Retrouvailles houses a collection of weaving looms, spinning wheels, and other tools. Open end of June to mid September. Admission charge. Visit the richly decorated wood church built in 1776. Also visit the Musée des Anciens Canadiens with its exhibits of wood carvings. Open mid May through October. Admission charge.

Rivière-du-Loup is a large community, where the Trans-Canada Highway turns inland toward Edmundston, New Brunswick, another gateway to Atlantic Canada, with access to eastern Maine at Fort Kent and Madawaska. Points of interest include the Seigniorial Manor of the Frasers, on rue Fraser, the Park of the Luminous Cross, the lookout at the summit of Mont Citadelle, the beach at Côte-des-Bains, and the lighthouse on the Ile Blanche.

Also visit the Musée du Bas-Saint-Laurant, which has interesting art and ethnology exhibitions. Open end of June to early September at various times. Admission charge. Les Carillons touristiques is a private collection of bells of different sizes. Open from May to November. Admission charge. Recommended accommodations include Motel Universel, 311, boulevard Hôtel de Ville, (418) 862–9520, moderate; Motel Lévesque, 171, rue Fraser, (418) 862–6927, moderate; and Motel Auberge-de-la-Pointe, Highway 132, (418) 862–3514. Moderate. The Motel Lévesque and the Motel Auberge-de-la-Pointe have excellent dining rooms.

Trois-Pistoles is a popular resort town and port for fishing. Visit La Maison du Notaire, 168, rue Notre Dame, a century-old home that contains a handicafts boutique and art gallery. Open throughout the year. Free. Also visit the Musée Saint-Laurent for local history. Open June to mid September. Admission charge. You can take a ferry from Trois-Pistoles to the north shore of the river at Escoumins. At Ile Razades is a bird sanctuary, and Ile-aux-Basques is said to have been used by Basque fishermen even before the time of Cartier.

Rimouski, the largest city east of Québec City, is a center of religious, educational, and commercial activity for the Bas-Saint-Laurent and Gaspé regions. Its facility of the Québec National Archives houses a collection of family records, legal documents, maps, engravings, and photos. Open throughout the year. Free. Visit the Rimouski Regional Museum, 35, rue Saint-Germain, which features a permanent collection and itinerant exhibitions of contemporary and traditional art. Open throughout the year. Admission charge. Also visit the Rimouski Conservatory of Music, 22, rue Sainte-Marie, which features concerts by students and teachers throughout the year. The Museum of the Sea has exhibits of marine life typical of the Gaspé area. Open mid June to early Septmber. Admission charge. Nearby is Rimouski Park for camping and picnics. Recommended places for both accommodations and dining include Auberge des Gouverneurs, 155, boulevard René Lepage, est, (418) 723–4422, expensive; Motel Normandie, 556, boulevard Saint-Germain, (418) 723–1616, moderate to expensive; Auberge Universal, 130, rue Saint-Bernabé, (418) 724–6944, moderate. All offer fine dining.

Rimouski Wildlife Reserve, 30 miles/48 km. south of Rimouski

◀ Traditional domestic Québecois architecture, pleasing to the eye and perfect for the climate and terrain.

via Highway 232, provides camping, cottages, fishing, touring, deer and small-game hunting, (418) 722–3779.

Grand Métis is the site of the Métis Floral Garden at the Reford Estate, off Highway 132. This exceptional garden, a major attraction on the Gaspé tour, covers forty acres and has more than five hundred species of trees and shrubs and a large variety of flowers. Open June to mid September. Admission charge.

Matane, famous in big-city restaurants for its shrimp, is a major fishing port, and you can hire boats and equipment here for catching salmon and other species. There are nice views of the river, the lighthouse, and the islands. Ferry service operates between Matane and Baie Comeau and Godbout on the north shore.

Matane Wildlife Reserve, 25 miles/40 km. south of Matane via Highway 195, has camping, cottages, canoeing, fishing, nature interpretation, hiking, touring, moose and small-game hunting, and cross-country skiing. For information, call (418) 224–3345.

Sainte-Anne-des-Monts is the site of Château Lamontagne, off Highway 132, built in 1873 in the Anglo-Normand style. Here you can see how the elite once lived. There are dining and entertainment on Sunday. Open late June to September. Sainte-Anne-des-Monts also provides access to the rugged beauty of the provincial de la Gaspésie Park.

De la Gaspésie Park (now a national park) is a great favorite with the Québécois, 10 miles/16 km. south of Sainte-Anne-des-Monts via Highway 299, features camping, cottages, salmon and other fishing, nature interpretation, hiking, touring, cross-country skiing, and snowshoeing. There are accommodations and exceptional dining at l'Auberge le Gîte du Mont-Albert (advance reservations are absolutely essential). For information and reservations, call (418) 763–2288. Open early March to early November.

Between Sainte-Anne-des-Monts and Cap-aux-Os you drive along the base of steep mountain walls and next to the waters of the Gulf of Saint Lawrence, each turn of the road offering a breathtaking view of the meeting of land and sea. For a long stretch, the road twists and turns on its flat narrow bed, but at times it climbs inland into forests and past rushing streams. Small fishing villages along the way, such as Mont Sainte-Pierre, Grand-Vallée, and l'Anse-a-Valleau, are a photographer's delight. Split cod can be seen drying outdoors on flakes (wooden beds), and some of the villages sell fresh-baked bread from ancient outdoor ovens. Be sure to notice the canals that enable fishermen to dock their boats near their homes and stop at some of the lighthouses along the way to enjoy the vistas.

Take your time and stop also at de la Gaspésie Provincial Park and Forillon National Park. Many people speed by this region, but this section offers more of the true spirit of Gaspé than any other.

Parc National Forillon is land's end on the Gaspé peninsula, (418) 368–5505. The cliffs here rise more than 600 feet above the sea. The arctic Alpine flora of Cap-Bon-Ami and the pioneer plants at Penouille are unique to the region. At the top of the Forillon peninsula, whales can sometimes be seen cavorting and spouting in the gulf water; gray seals and common seals also can be seen. You can hike, swim, and picnic and arrange cruising and fishing expeditions and deep-water scuba-diving excursions. Camp sites are available at Cap-Bon-Ami and Petit Gaspé.

From the village of **Cap-aux-Os** to the city of Gaspé, the coastline (except for Forillon Park) is less dramatic, but nevertheless lovely. The area's culture changes here. Between Québec City and Cap-aux-Os, you have driven through quintessential French communities, but from here to Matapédia you will pass through many communities that, though predominantly French, have sizable English-speaking populations. Anglican and United Church spires stand alongside the towers of the Roman Catholic churches. Many of these English-speaking people are descendants of the U.S. Revolutionary War Loyalists and British troops who took part in Wolfe's campaign against the French.

Gaspé, a city of more than 20,000 inhabitants, is the administrative center for this end of the peninsula. A monument commemorates Cartier's landing and his claiming of all the land before him for his king. The Regional Museum, on Highway 132, features exhibits of local history, displays the work of area artists, and holds concerts of folk, popular, and classical music. Open all year at various hours. Admission charge. Also visit the contemporary Cathedral of Gaspé, in the center of town, and the fish hatchery, off Highway 132. Fishing trips and boat rides can be arranged in Gaspé. There is also direct air service to the Iles-de-la-Madeleine (Magdalen Islands). Recommended accommodations and dining include Auberge des Commandants, 178, rue de la Reine, (418) 368–3355, moderate; and Motel Adams, 2, rue Adams, (418) 368–2244, moderate.

Fort Prével is a provincial park offering accommodations (difficult to book because of the park's popularity), a superb dining room, where the meals are prepared by master and student chefs, and a fine golf course. Highly recommended. Call (418) 368–2281 for reservations.

Percé is the most popular resort community on the Gaspé. Besides a number of excellent vistas of Percé Rock, a famous Canadian landmark, and Ile-de-Bonaventure (both now a national park), daily cruises take passengers to and around Ile-de-Bonaventure, a well-known bird sanctuary, with a rookery for gannets, gulls, puffins, and other species, (418) 782—2240. In Percé itself there are live theater, folk song and dance festivals, concerts, and so on. You can take a mini-bus ride around Mont Sainte-Anne, go deep-sea fishing, visit the exhibits of artisans and painters, and enjoy excellent French cuisine. Recommended accommodations and dining include:

Hôtel-Motel Le Bonaventure, Highway 132, (418) 782–2166, has excellent dining. Moderate.

Hôtel-Motel La Normandie, Highway 132, (418) 782–2112. Moderate.

Hôtel Bleu Blanc Rouge, Highway 132, (418) 782–2142, has excellent dining. Moderate.

Motel Manoir Percé, Highway 132, (418) 782–2022, Moderate.

Auberge du Gargantua, Route des Failles, (418) 782–2852, is considered to have the best restaurant in Percé. Moderate accommodations, expensive dining.

Port Daniel Reserve, 50 miles/80 km. southwest of Percé via Highway 132, features camping, cottages, salmon and other fishing, and hiking. For information, call (418) 396–2789.

The coastline from Percé to Chandler begins to turn in a southwesterly direction and forms the north shore of the Baie des Chaleurs. You will pass through several interesting fishing villages such as l'Anse-à-Beaufils, Cap d'Espoir, and Grand Rivière, where more split cod can be seen drying on flakes. **Chandler** is a mostly English-speaking community, where the main industry is pulp and paper. It offers fishing, swimming, tennis, and golf.

Bonaventure's Gaspé Zoological Garden displays exotic animals from around the world. Open June to September. Admission charge. Also visit the Acadian Museum, off Highway 132, for local history. Open June to September. Admission charge.

Many of the towns along this part of the coast provide deep-sea fishing and boat cruises for tourists.

New Carlisle, the hometown of Québec's late Premier René

Lévesque, is the administrative center for the Baie des Chaleurs area. Its population has a substantial loyalist element. This section of the coast also has a large population of French-Acadians whose ancestors were expelled from Nova Scotia by the British and several communities of Micmac Indians. At **Maria,** for example, you can purchase Indian baskets, weavings, and snowshoes and see a church shaped like a tepee.

At **Saint-Siméon**, there is a panoramic view of the Baie des Chaleurs and the distant coast of New Brunswick.

When you reach **Carleton,** a pleasant resort town, you are near the end of your Gaspésian tour. The main attraction here is to drive to the top of 1,959-foot/555-m. high Mont Saint-Joseph for great views of the bay, the New Brunswick shore, and the surrounding countryside. On the summit is the Notre Dame Oratory, a religious shrine noted for its colorful mosaics and stained-glass windows. Carleton also offers saltwater swimming, horseback riding, golf, tennis, windsurfing, fishing excursions, and handicraft boutiques. Recommended accommodations and dining include Motel Baie Bleue, 482, boulevard Perron, (418) 364–3355, the best accommodations and dining in town, moderate to expensive. Also in Carleton is Aqua Mer, Canada's first Thalassotherapy center, offering various water therapies for tired bodies, also fine lodging and dining, (418) 364–7055.

At the village of **Miguasha** is **Parc National Miguasha,** a rich reserve containing prehistoric fossils. Guided tours are given from early June to Labour Day. Free. From Miguasha, you can take a ferry across the Baie des Chaleurs to **Dalhousie,** New Brunswick. If you prefer not to wait for the ferry, continue further to **Pointe-à-la-Croix,** where you can cross over on the bridge to **Campbellton.**

If you are going back to Québec City and points west, continue on to **Matapèdia,** where Highway 132 cuts through the Matapédia Valley and comes out on the south shore of the Saint Lawrence River at **Mont-Joli.** Rimouski is just a few miles south of Mont-Joli, and Québec City is west beyond Rimouski.

Iles-de-la-Madeleine (Magdalen Islands)

Souris, Prince Edward Island, is a terminus for the passenger and car ferry service, on the M/V *Lucy Maud Montgomery,* to the **Iles-de-la-Madeleine (Magdalen Islands),** which operates April 1 to the end of January, depending on weather and ice conditions. The crossing time is five hours. For more information, call (902) 687–

2181, or Tourisme Québec. There is daily air service to the islands from Charlottetown, P.E.I., and the town of Gaspé. Tilden has a car rental agency on the islands. Make reservations before you go.

The Iles-de-la-Madeleine are in the Gulf of Saint Lawrence (180 miles/288 km. from the Gaspé, 70 miles/112 km. from Prince Edward Island, 55 miles/88 km. from Cape Breton). The archipelago's twelve islands are part of the Province of Québec. The main islands are Hâvre-Aubert, Etang-du-Nord, Hâvre-aux-Maisons, Grande-Entrée, Grosse-Ile, Ile d'Entrée, Ile Brion, Ile-aux-Cochons, and Rocher-aux-Oiseaux. On the seven inhabited islands, most of the residents are of French-Acadian stock, though there are about a thousand of English and Scottish descent. The Madelinots are fishing people who make their living from lobster, herring, and cod. They have formed cooperatives and operate the canneries, smokehouses, and freezing plants as owners.

The main reason for going to the Iles-de-la-Madeleine is, quite frankly, to enjoy the pleasure of long sandy beaches, drawing closer to nature with its myriad seabirds, undulating dunes, and moody seas of the Gulf of Saint Lawrence. Bring a bike for transportation and a sleeping bag for accommodations. The islands also have organizations that provide diving expeditions, deep-sea fishing trips, land and air sight-seeing, windsurfing and boat rentals, bike rentals, horseback riding, golf and tennis, harness racing. There are history museums, nature preserves (seals, gannets, puffins), warm-water swimming areas, an aquarium, art galleries, and handicraft shops.

Almost all the restaurants here specialize in freshly caught seafoods—lobster, cod, mussels, haddock. There is even an Italian restaurant. Recommended accommodations include Auberge Chez Denis & François, in Hâvre-Aubert, (418) 937–2371, moderate; Hôtel Château Madelinot, in Cap-aux-Meules, (418) 986–3695, expensive; and Auberge La Jetée, in Cap-aux-Meules, (418) 986–4446, inexpensive to moderate. All offer fine dining. Tourisme Québec will provide you with information on Bed and Breakfast places and camping facilities, or call the tourism office on the islands direct at (418) 986–2245.

Part Three

Atlantic Canada

Contents

◀ The Cabot Trail on dramatic Cape Breton Island in Nova Scotia is one of the most popular tourist attractions in all of Atlantic Canada. Here high mountains rise from an uncompromising sea. If Cape Breton Island reminds you of the Highlands of Scotland, you are not alone: Thousands of Scots settled this area partly because of the similarity.

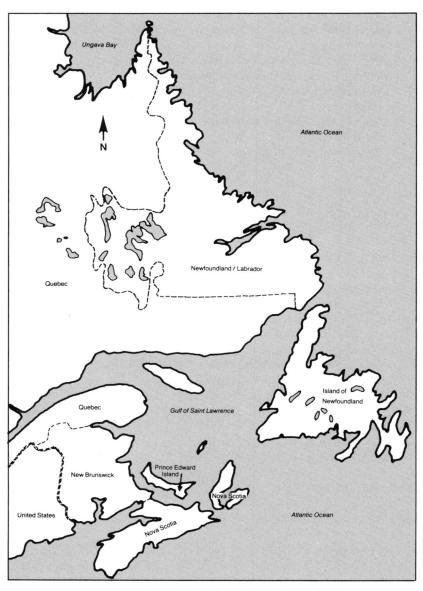

OVERVIEW OF ATLANTIC CANADA

CHAPTER 11

Introduction to Atlantic Canada

The Discovery of a New World

Centuries before Columbus planted the flag of Spain in the warm sands of a lush Caribbean isle, Viking explorers erected their longhouse overlooking the golden marsh of L'Anse-aux-Meadows, on the northern tip of Newfoundland. And thousands of years before then, aboriginal Eskimos and Indians had made this region their home.

Today's explorer of Atlantic Canada can see the communities of many of the early settlers of this region, such as the Maliseets of the Saint John River Valley of New Brunswick; the Micmacs of eastern New Brunswick, Prince Edward Island, and Nova Scotia; and the Naskaupi Indians and the Eskimos of Labrador. Add to these peoples the Acadians of Nova Scotia, New Brunswick, and Prince Edward Island, as well as the French, Scots, English, Irish, and Germans who are now deeply rooted throughout Atlantic Canada, and you have some idea of the rich ethnic and racial diversity of this large region.

Atlantic Canada's geographical, environmental, and cultural range is enormous: icebergs in the north and warm, Gulf Stream currents, ideal for swimming, in the southern areas; harness racing, and Scottish dancing; simple, isolated fishing outposts and sophisticated cities that offer almost every convenience and diversion. The landscape is a pleasing conglomerate of thick forests, empty beaches, steep cliffs, powerful seas and tides, peaceful lakes, salmon-filled rivers, and rushing trout streams. It is, too, a wilderness of moose, bear, fox, caribou, and deer. And its dark blue oceans boast spouting whales and innumerable lobster, mackerel, herring, sole, haddock, cod, and seal.

To explorers past and present, the dominant features of Atlantic Canada have been its 17,000 miles/27,200 km. of coastline and the sea. Cold Arctic waters flowing south from Labrador intermingle with the warm Gulf Stream and moderate the temperature of the water in the southern portion of the coasts, where craggy, granite-edged capes, inlets, and cliffs rise up to frame long stretches of fine sandy beach. Perhaps most important, the sea has shaped a way of life in many communities which has remained virtually unchanged for hundreds of years.

But the sea must also compete in significance with the terrain of Atlantic Canada. In some places the land rises to become mountains of awe-inspiring majesty and beauty, particularly on Cape Breton Island and in Newfoundland. There are dense forests, productive farmland, and ore-rich earth. Lakes, rivers, and streams abound for the pleasure of sportspeople, campers, and nature lovers.

Whether you prefer the slow, congenial pace of life offered by the small villages of Atlantic Canada or the lure of big cities such as Halifax and Saint John, whether you prefer the historic past or contemporary vitality, the peace and harmony of Atlantic Canada, its deep roots and powerful, natural rhythms will make your visit a memorable personal discovery.

The Geography of Atlantic Canada

Atlantic Canada extends from approximately parallel 43° north at Clark's Harbour, Nova Scotia, to above parallel 60° north at Port Burwell, Labrador. The Atlantic Canada covered in this guide consists of the provinces of Nova Scotia, New Brunswick, Prince Edward Island, Newfoundland, and Labrador.

Terrain

The terrain of Atlantic Canada is largely hilly, with the rugged mountains of the Canadian Shield running along the northern coast of the Gulf of Saint Lawrence and into Labrador. The Appalachian Range, which forms the Catskills, Adirondacks, and the Green and White mountains of the United States, also extends into Canada and shapes the land of the Gaspé, New Brunswick, Nova Scotia, Newfoundland, and the Iles-de-la-Madeleine (Magdalen Islands). The high hills of northern Nova Scotia are called the Cape Breton Highlands, to many the Highlands of Scotland. In Newfoundland, the Long Range Mountains form the strong backbone of that province.

The smallest of Canada's ten provinces, but one of the most beautiful, is Prince Edward Island, seemingly at first to be a flat plain, but actually rolling, fertile farmland. Other agricultural areas of scenic and historic interest lie in the orchard-dotted Annapolis Valley of Nova Scotia and the lush green Saint John River Valley of western New Brunswick.

Dense forests occupy much of the hinterland of Atlantic Canada, providing New Brunswick, Nova Scotia, and Newfoundland with considerable annual revenue from lumber and paper-pulp operations. The land of these provinces also contributes great riches in coal, iron ore, gold, salt, gypsum, copper, and zinc. Mines and mine-related operations, including smelting plants and steel works, are familiar though usually unobstrusive sights in the region.

Climate

Many travelers head to Atlantic Canada in the summer in order to get away from their steaming cities. Summer days are warm enough for all outdoor activities, including swimming, golf, tennis, and sightseeing. Usually there is very little humidity, except for some inland areas. The waters of the Gulf of Saint Lawrence, particularly on the eastern coast of New Brunswick, the Northumberland coast of Nova Scotia, and all around Prince Edward Island, are to be the warmest in this part of Canada.

Much of Atlantic Canada is a hay fever sufferer's paradise, with little pollen floating in the air. The Passamaquoddy Bay area of New Brunswick is one such place.

From early July to mid October is the best time to visit Atlantic Canada. The days are mostly bright and sunny, and the nights are pleasantly cool. You should, however, bring some warm sweaters and jackets to wear in evenings. One problem you may encounter is the dense fog that often covers the coast during the late spring (May and June). Your best bet then is to head inland, where the sun is usually shining.

While summer is Atlantic Canada's most popular vacation time, all the provinces are promoting the autumn months as the best season to visit them: The pace of life has slowed, and people have more time to spend with you. And the foliage is spectacular.

The winters throughout the region are cold and raw, although skiers and snowmobilers consider the state of things to be just right.

Waterways

The sea brought settlement to Atlantic Canada and for several centuries has contributed decisively to the development of its economy, culture, and political destiny.

The Atlantic Ocean, the most important and dominant force, directly and indirectly influences every island and province. While modern technology and the growth of inland urban centers have shifted a great deal of Canada's emphasis away from the Atlantic, the ocean will always influence the nation's future.

The coastlines of these provinces are granite and sandstone, with countless indentations that form safe harbors and sites for both small fishing villages and large modern cities, such as Halifax in Nova Scotia, Saint John in New Brunswick, and St. John's in Newfoundland. These three cities are year-round open-water ports, vital when the Saint Lawrence River and Seaway freeze above Québec City. While paved highways reach most places, there still remain long stretches of coastline, such as the coast of Labrador and parts of Newfoundland, where the traveler must journey via sea routes to visit the remote villages and outports.

The Gulf of Saint Lawrence is second only to the Atlantic Ocean in importance to the life of this region. Its waters touch all the land areas of Atlantic Canada. The province of Prince Edward Island is surrounded by the gulf, with the Northumberland Strait separating it from New Brunswick and Nova Scotia. Into the gulf flows the 900-mile/1,440-km. Saint Lawrence Seaway, a lifeline from Canada's heartland to the sea. The Saint Lawrence River has been the scene of much of Canada's exciting history, particularly during the struggle between France and England for control of this vast North American empire.

During the age of sail, European explorers, settlers, clerics, soldiers, and merchants traveled every water route leading to and from the settlements we now call Québec City, Montréal, Ottawa, and Toronto. In the iceberg-free months of summer, voyagers sailed through the hazardous Strait of Belle Isle, which separates Newfoundland from Labrador and which has claimed countless vessels and human lives over the centuries. More recently mariners have preferred the Cabot Strait, lying between Cape North, the northern tip of Cape Breton Island, and Cape Ray, Newfoundland, the southwestern tip of that island. The Cabot Strait has always offered a broader and safer passage for navigation. Today, one can sail this water route to Québec City, Montréal, Toronto, and the Great Lakes cities of the American Midwest.

The long, broad Bay of Fundy separates a large portion of Nova Scotia from New Brunswick. Its tides are the highest in the world. At Barncoat Head in the Minas Basin of Nova Scotia scientists have measured the tide difference at 55 feet/17 m. In a Bay of Fundy coastal village, for example, a large cargo ship may float normally in deep water during part of the day and sit high and dry on a mud flat a few hours later. The new high tide comes in the form of a tidal bore, a singular wave that moves unhesitatingly toward the shore at places such as Moncton, New Brunswick, and Truro, Nova Scotia. These tides are so powerful that Nova Scotia is harnessing them to produce hydroelectric energy for portions of Atlantic Canada.

A Capsule History

Thousands of years ago Indians and Eskimos from the Asian continent migrated to Atlantic Canada. Little is known of these very early aboriginal peoples, although archaeological digs in northern Newfoundland are beginning to put together some clues regarding their vanished cultures. Substantive evidence of a Viking settlement in northern Newfoundland establishes European habitation of North America at about A.D. 100

While the land must have looked forbidding to these people, the sea—particularly the Grand Banks off the eastern coast of Newfoundland—teemed with an apparently unlimited supply of fish. Fishermen from Portugal, Spain, the British Isles, and France labored anonymously in these waters long before other explorers, such as Champlain, arrived on the scene.

Of the many explorers and adventurers who came to northern North America, John Cabot and Jacques Cartier are the best known. Cabot is said to be the founding father of Nova Scotia and New-foundland, while Cartier has that honor in Québec. King Henry VII, the founder of the British navy, commissioned the Italian-born Cabot to seek new lands and riches for England in the New World. Cabot rewarded the king's faith by discovering New-Founde-Land (Newfoundland), with its tremendous wealth of fish, a prize Great Britain did not relinquish until recent times. In 1497, Cabot landed on Cape Breton Island and claimed all of Nova Scotia for the king, which later gave the British legal justification for reclaiming it from French occupation. Cartier, who came on the scene about forty years after Cabot, sailed through the Strait of Belle Isle and called the north coast of Québec the "land God gave to Cain" because it appeared inhospitable. Cartier went on to discover Prince Edward Island, which he called "Ile Saint Jean," and the Gaspé, where he planted the fleur de lis and claimed all the land to the west in the name of the king of France. He called this new land *Kannata*, an Indian word that means settlement.

In 1605 the French mariner, explorer, and writer Samuel de Champlain, who later founded the permanent colony of New France, joined with the Sieur-de-Monts to establish one of the first habitations on the Atlantic seaboard. At first they chose Saint Croix Island, in the river of the same name, at the southwest corner of New Brunswick at the eastern border of the state of Maine, for their winter camp. But the harsh weather killed many of their men, and those who survived moved on to the more congenial environment of Nova Scotia, where they founded Port Royal (now Annapolis Royal), the first permanent European settlement in this part of the New World. Here Champlain created the L'Order-de-Bon-Temps (The Order of the Good Time), the oldest social club in North America, to mellow the long winter nights of Nova Scotia.

These settlements in "Acadie," as Nova Scotia and New Brunswick were called by the French, were intended to serve primarily as bases for exploration of the fabled northwest passage to Cathay's riches and for trade in virgin timber and fur with the Indians. As the fur trade became more profitable, the British wanted a share. While the northwest passage seemed elusive, the fur trade brought the two great European powers into a bitter, bloody struggle that lasted decades.

As England and France fought to protect their interests in North America, the settlers cleared the trees, built their homes, and planted the fertile fields of the Annapolis Valley. These quiet farmers preferred to cherish their new land and their good life rather than participate in a struggle that seemed so remote. They were not left in peace. Instead, the French-Acadians were expelled from their homelands, a tragedy so poignantly portrayed in Henry Wadsworth Longfellow's epic poem *Evangeline*. After the Treaty of Paris, signed in February 1763, many Acadians returned to resume a way of life deeply rooted in the land and sea.

Today, Atlantic Canada is predominantly Anglo-Saxon in language, law, business, education, and culture. The English, assisted by immigrants from the American colonies, overcame the French following their victories at Fort Louisbourg and the Plains of Abraham. Not long after the musket smoke cleared, English colonization of Atlantic Canada increased, and to the numerous immigrants from the United Kingdom were added thousands of American colonials who remained loyal to the crown.

This significant migration of United Empire Loyalists included families of English, Irish, Dutch, and Scottish stock. Thousands settled in New Brunswick, Nova Scotia, and Ontario. They were enterprising people, many of them members of professions and of the commercial and social elite. Despite great hardships in wilderness conditions, they founded prosperous urban centers in Atlantic Canada, such as Saint John and Fredericton in New Brunswick. They also established themselves as leaders in business, education, medicine, religion, and in the arts. Descendants of the Loyalists, particularly in Nova Scotia and New Brunswick, continue to form a large segment of the elite and substantially influence the continuing life and progress of the region.

In addition to the English, French, and Loyalists, a sizable population of Irish, Welsh, Scots, and Germans migrated to Atlantic Canada. More than two thousand people from the Hanover region of Germany alone came to Nova Scotia in 1753 and helped to found the world-famous fishing and shipbuilding center of Lunenburg, where many French Protestants (Huguenots) also settled.

With the landing of the vessel *Hector* at Pictou, Nova Scotia, in the eighteenth century, the great migration of Scottish people into the region began. The Scots fled oppression at home, a fact their descendants recall passionately. These hardy people brought their customs and language, their enterprise, and their religion. Scottish festivals, during the summer, feature piercing bagpipe music, colorful tartans, and exciting Highland dances. Countless oatcakes are eaten, many glasses of Scot's whisky are drunk, and sweet Keltic voices sing the poetry of Robert Burns. The Scots are everywhere in Atlantic Canada, with most living in Nova Scotia and Prince Edward Island.

In Nova Scotia, Prince Edward Island, New Brunswick, and Newfoundland the Irish are also in strong force. St. John's, Newfoundland, speaks like the Emerald Isle because the brogue of the people is so thick.

The Irish and the Scottish peoples of Atlantic Canada display the religious paradoxes of their ancestral lands. While the Scots in Pictou County, Nova Scotia, are staunch Presbyterians, those a few

223

miles away in Antigonish County and on Cape Breton Island are strong Roman Catholics. The Catholic Highlanders are descendants of Bonnie Prince Charlie's supporters in the Jacobite rebellion. On Prince Edward Island you find Orange Ulster Irish and Catholic Irish.

In addition to these ethnic groups, today's Atlantic Canada includes citizens from Greece, Scandinavia, China, Italy, Poland, Russia, Africa, India, and the Middle East—a United Nations of people who are making a better life for themselves and their children. For many immigrants, entry into Atlantic Canada, especially through the port of Halifax, has been a doorway to the dream of a new and more promising future.

Making the Most of Your Time

If you are visiting the provinces of Atlantic Canada for the first time and have limited time, you will want to focus on places that are easily accessible. Plan one or two side trips to special points of interest, such as a festival or a cruise to one of the islands. A vacation passes all too quickly, and you do not want to spend the entire time driving. There are waits for ferries and slow-moving traffic on two-lane highways during peak summer months. Be sure to make reservations for all accommodations well in advance. The object of your trip is to savor what is best about Atlantic Canada.

CHAPTER 12

New Brunswick

New Brunswick Today

New Brunswick is the gateway to Atlantic Canada. The diversity of leisure and recreational options here will make you want to spend a few days in this beautiful maritime province.

New Brunswick (Nouveau-Brunswick), shaped like a huge heraldic shield, is a place of many contrasts. Here you will find an extensive interior of dense forests, abundant with game, and rich salmon rivers; the world's highest tides; broad salt-hay marshes; fertile agricultural river valleys and historic cities; diverse cultures; flourishing arts and humanities; and a wide variety of natural curiosities.

In the 1800s, the United States felt that a large portion of the province, then part of British North America, should belong to the state of Maine (New Brunswick had similar designs on Maine territory), and for a while there was talk of war to settle the issue. While no guns were fired, a paper war was fought, called the Aroostook War, and the boundaries that exist today were officially established by the Ashburton-Webster Treaty in 1842.

New Brunswick's borders join those of Maine on the west, Québec on the north, and Nova Scotia at the Isthmus of Chignecto. The province has more than 1,400 miles/2,240 km. of coastline. On the northeast, the border forms the southern shoreline of the Bay of Chaleur (Baie des Chaleurs—Bay of Warmth). The east coast, with its excellent beach areas, is on the Gulf of Saint Lawrence and the Northumberland Strait, which runs between the province and Prince Edward Island. The south coast faces the Bay of Fundy, opposite the north coast of Nova Scotia. The Saint John River, whose source is in Maine, is the province's most important waterway. Along the Saint John are located the cities of Edmundston,

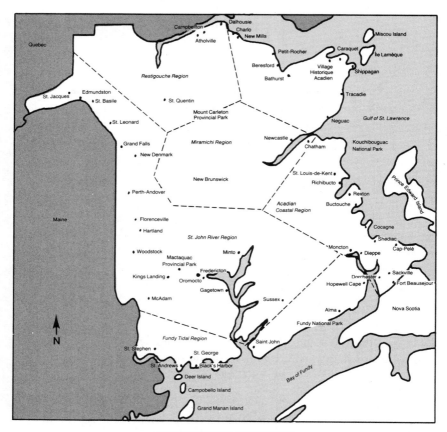

NEW BRUNSWICK

Fredericton, and Saint John. The Miramichi, long famous for its superior salmon fishing, is another important river.

New Brunswick consists of 28,354 square miles/73,437 sq. km., 85 percent of it timberland. Lumber and paper pulp are among its major industries. Extensive mining operations are also carried on in the interior. The highest mountain in the province is Mount Carleton at 2,693 feet/820 m.

The Saint John River Valley is a highly productive agricultural area, ideal for growing potatoes and other crops, also for dairy and beef cattle. The Saint John River Valley is a recreational and scenic asset, offering swimming, fishing, and boating. If you come into New Brunswick via the Trans-Canada Highway, which follows the Saint John River, take time to enjoy the beautiful surroundings and adjacent historic and recreational sites.

New Brunswick is famous with sportspeople around the world for its excellent fishing and hunting—trout, bass, Atlantic salmon, black bear, and deer. In the winter, there are several ski areas, and snowmobiling is a major sport. Swimming, sailing, tennis, golf, windsurfing, canoeing, and horseback riding are popular summer activities.

New Brunswick's Passamaquoddy Bay area, on the Bay of Fundy, contains the special islands of Deer, Grand Manan, and Campobello. You can see huge whirlpools spinning in the bay when you take the island ferries. The Bay of Fundy coast is serrated with many coves and inlets, and it is strung with some of the more picturesque fishing villages in the province, such as Maces Bay and Dipper Harbour. Be sure to see the fishing weirs, an ancient method of fishing. From Fundy National Park to near the city of Moncton the coast has several unusual topographical features, such as the Hopewell Rocks (giant natural flowerpots carved from the land by the sea), the coastal caves at St. Martins, and broad salt marshes near the city of Moncton. The Northumberland coast, or eastern shore, has the best beaches and warmest saltwater swimming.

History and Culture

Before European explorers and settlers came to New Brunswick, the Maliseet Indians of the Saint John River Valley and the Micmacs of the eastern shore lived here for thousands of years.

The first notable Europeans to spend time in New Brunswick were Samuel de Champlain and the Sieur-de-Monts, who in 1604

set up an ill-fated habitation on Dochet's Island in the St. Croix River. These intrepid explorers misjudged the severity of the winters in this part of the world, and about half their company perished by the following spring.

The French were too busy establishing trading posts, creating the settlement at Saint John (so named by Champlain), and keeping Québec out of the hands of the British to exploit the vast interior. When the Acadians were expelled from Nova Scotia, many escaped into the forests of New Brunswick (then a part of Nova Scotia) or moved to the northern Saint John River Valley and to the Caraquet area.

Once peace was established between the French and English, after Québec City fell to Wolfe, more Acadians moved back from the American and French colonies and settled along the Saint John River and along the eastern shore. Today, most of the people living from Moncton north to Campbellton, and west to Saint Léonard, are descendants of these early Acadians. The French language, religion, and customs of the Acadians continue to play essential parts in their lives. Some 35 percent of the province's population speak French. New Brunswick is Canada's only officially bilingual province.

Once Britain had firm control of Acadia, British settlers came into the province to create their own communities. However, it took the American War of Independence to give the province its greatest boost in population. In 1783, 3,000 United Empire Loyalists landed at Saint John. In the American colonies the Loyalists had been part of the elite, but their decision to support the king of England cost them almost everything, and they had to begin life anew.

The Loyalists applied their intelligence and enterprise to the difficult task of building a new society with such zeal that they not only survived but prospered. New Brunswick was separated from Nova Scotia and became a province in 1784. Saint John, Canada's first incorporated city, became an important shipbuilding, trading, and commercial center, and Fredericton became the cultural, intellectual, religious, and political capital of the province. Today the descendants of the Loyalists hold many positions of leadership. The

◀ **Nature's flowerpots, carved from the sea, are one of the many surprising oddities in beautiful New Brunswick. Be sure to have your picture taken against one of these wonders to show the folks back home.**

city of Saint John continues to be a bastion of support for the English crown. While some complain that the Loyalists have too much control over the destiny of New Brunswick, one can only admire their accomplishments.

The more than 714,800 inhabitants of New Brunswick are primarily concentrated in its six cities—Saint John, Moncton, Fredericton, Bathurst, Campbellton, and Edmundston—with the rural population scattered throughout the province. The labor force works in farming, lumbering, fishing, manufacturing, mining, shipbuilding and repair, commerce, finance, education, tourism, and government. New Brunswick has a very aggressive economic development program to attract new industries.

One of Canada's most important conglomerates of diverse industries was created by K. C. Irving, who is regarded by many as a modern Horatio Alger and whose name is connected with almost every industry in the province: petroleum products, newspapers, radio stations, pulp and paper, lumbering, and so on. William Maxwell Aitken, known to the world as Lord Beaverbrook, is another famous son of New Brunswick. He founded a great publishing empire and was a well-known member of Winston Churchill's wartime cabinet. The cultural life of the city of Fredericton owes much to Lord Beaverbrook. The Beaverbrook Art Gallery, the Playhouse, and many buildings of the University of New Brunswick were his gifts to the city. Funds from the estate of Sir James Dunn, also a native New Brunswicker, helped establish the Canada Council for the Encouragement of the Arts, Humanities and Social Sciences, one of the major stimulants to the cultural life of the nation.

New Brunswick maintains a sophisticated cultural life, stimulated by its several fine institutions of higher learning. The University of New Brunswick, established more than two hundred years ago, was the first provincial institution of higher learning in North America. Founded by Loyalists, it set its standards to match those of Harvard and Columbia universities. The university's Poet's Corner of Canada monument honors such well-known poets as Francis Joseph Sherman, Bliss Carmen, and Sir Charles Roberts, all natives of Fredericton. Mount Allison University, in Sackville, has one of the loveliest campuses in all of Atlantic Canada, and the University of Moncton is considered the intellectual center for Acadian life in Atlantic Canada.

Fredericton's Beaverbrook Art Gallery is the most important art museum in Atlantic Canada, exhibiting the works of Salvador Dali,

George Romney, Joseph Turner, Sir Joshua Reynolds, Thomas Gainsborough, and others. The city's Playhouse is an important arts venue in the province, producing a wide variety of musicals, dramas, and comedies. It is also the place for symphony and the ballet.

New Brunswick has an excellent reputation encouraging the creation of handicrafts—pewter, weaving, pottery, and glassware. The work of the artisans is distinquished by superb design, materials, and execution. Some of Canada's best workshops are located on remote New Brunswick rural roads. They are worth seeking out, and the experience of discovery is part of an excellent vacation.

New Brunswick's spirit combines the dynamism of economic progress with a Victorian-Acadian feel and a sophisticated ambience. Its people convey a sense of substance and permanence in today's world of shifting values.

How to Get to New Brunswick

By Car
From the state of Maine, the most widely used route takes Interstate 95 to Houlton and connects with the Trans-Canada Highway 2. For a more scenic but longer ride, take Route 9 from Bangor to St. Stephen or Route 1 along the coast of Maine to St. Stephen, with a side trip to Campobello Island.

From western Canada, take the Trans-Canada Highway 2, which brings you to Edmundston. From Québec's Gaspé region, cross into the province from Matapédia, and head toward Campbellton on Highway 11, which will take you south toward Moncton.

New Brunswick's roads and highways are well maintained and marked. Some secondary roads are unpaved, but they invite exploration, particularly along the coasts. Be careful on the unpaved roads in the interior, as many are used by heavy trucks in lumbering, farming, and mining operations.

Rental cars—Hertz and Tilden—are available at major airports and cities.

By Ship
From Digby, Nova Scotia, to Saint John, take the M/V *Princess of Acadia* (see page 287). From Borden, Prince Edward Island, a ferry goes to Cape Tormentine (see page 363). From Miguasha, in Québec's Gaspé region, a ferry to Dalhousie operates late June to early September, every hour until the last sailing at 8:30 P.M. It

takes autos, trailers, and buses. Call (506) 684-4280 for more information.

By Air

Air Canada and Canadian Airlines International serve New Brunswick. The major airports are located in Saint John, Fredericton, Charlo, and Moncton. Rental cars are available there.

By Bus

Increasingly people are visiting the province on tour buses. Check with your own travel agent for details on these comprehensive tours.

There is daily bus service to St. Stephen from the United States through Maine on Greyhound and from the Québec area on Voyageur buses. SMT buses, (506) 658-6501 in Saint John, will transport you within New Brunswick.

By Rail

VIA Rail service goes along the eastern coast of New Brunswick from Rivière-du-Loup to Matapédia to Moncton; also from Moncton to Saint John to Fredericton through the state of Maine, and then to Montréal.

General Information

Time zone: Atlantic

Telephone area code: 506

Police and medical emergencies: dial 911

Climate and Clothing

Summer weather in New Brunswick is pleasant and warm both in the interior and along the coasts—perfect for all summer activities. The Passamaquoddy Bay area is a haven for those who suffer from hay fever. The Fundy coast has dense fogs in the late spring and early summer. Autumn is an especially lovely time in New Brunswick, when the maples and other deciduous trees turn the landscape into tapestries of red, yellow, and orange. It is well worth a special trip into New Brunswick in autumn just to savor the colorful foliage and the bountiful harvests from the farms. The winters are cold, with lots of snow, but New Brunswickers live it up in great style through various cold weather sports and warming festivities.

Casual clothes of almost any kind are acceptable throughout the province. Some of the better eating places require men to wear jackets and ties and women to dress up. Tweeds and woolen sweaters are wise for cool, crisp nights and for foggy days along the Fundy coast.

Tourist Information

You can receive free travel literature before you leave home by contacting Department of Tourism, Recreation, and Heritage New Brunswick's toll-free at (800) 561–0123, or by writing them at P.O. Box 12345, Fredericton, New Brunswick E3B 5C3.

Major Events

Summer is festival time in New Brunswick, when residents pull out all stops to celebrate everything from their noble heritages to the princely lobster. Here are some interesting festivals:

June

New Brunswick Highland Games, Oromocto, mid June
Pioneer Days, Oromocto, late June to July
Railroad Days, Moncton, late June to first week in July
Salmon Festival, Campbellton, late June to first week in July

July

River Jubilee, Fredericton, early July
Hospitality Days, Bathurst, mid July
Lobster Festival, Shediac, early to mid July
Canada's Irish Festival, Chatham (the largest in the northeast), mid July
International Festival of Baroque Music, Lamèque, early to mid July
Fisheries Festival, Shippagan, mid July
Loyalist Days, Saint John, mid to late July
Old Home Week, St. Martins, mid to late July
Old Home Week, Woodstock, late July
Miramichi Folk Song Festival, Newcastle, late July to early August

August and September

Foire Brayonne, Edmundston, early August
International Festival, St. Stephen, early August
International Hydroplane Regatta, Cocagne, early August
Acadian Festival, Caraquet, early to mid August
Festival by the Sea, Saint John, early to mid August
Chocolate Festival, Saint Stephen, early to mid August
Sand Sculpture Contest, Parlee Beach, mid August
Atlantic National Exhibition, Saint John, late August
Mactaquac Craft Festival, Mactaquac, early September
Fredericton Exhibition and Provincial Livestock Show, Fredericton, early September

Accommodations are difficult to book in the host communities during popular festivals. Make reservations in advance.

Special-Interest Vacations

New Brunswick has been innovative in developing special-interest vacation packages. These packages include accommodations and activities. Some also include meals and entertainment. For more information, call the listed organization or Tourism New Brunswick. The following lists some unique holiday package offerings in the province:

A vacation on a Micmac Indian Reserve: Indian storyteller, Indian dancing, trips to historic sites, Indian crafts and food, warm water swimming, (506) 523–9676.

Canoeing on the Jemseg River, also Grand Lake, the lower Saint John River, (506) 488–3113.

Canoe tours on the St. Croix River, see eagles and moose; stay at Loon Bay Lodge, (506) 466–1240. Also white-water tubing trips on the St. Croix River.

Trail riding in Albert County timberland; trout fishing and swimming, (506) 882–2349.

Golfing by the sea in St. Andrews; eighteen-hole championship course in New Brunswick's prettiest town, and accommodations at the deluxe Algonquin Hotel, (506) 529–8823.

Norwood Farm holidays, lake swimming, canoeing, horseback riding, great scenery in Loyalist country, (506) 488–2681.

Houseboat vacations on the Saint John River, (506) 433–4801.

Treasure hunt adventure in St. Martins; fine accommodations and dining at charming country inn, (506) 833–4772.

Bird-watching expeditions on the Jemseg River, (506) 488–3113.

Rocklyn Inn and bicycle touring in Dorchester area, (506) 379–2205.

Photography workshops conducted by Freeman Patterson and Doris Mowry in Gagetown, (506) 763–2271.

Printmakers workshops on Grand Manan Island, (506) 662–3187.

Cruise and learn-to-sail program in Gagetown, (506) 488–2979.

Learn to windsurf on Lac Baker, (506) 992–2439.

Canoe and kayak clinics on the St. Croix River (Loon Bay Lodge), (506) 466–1240.

Tidal tours of Hopewell Cape, (506) 734–2975 or (506) 734–3121.

Relaxation by the sea and gourmet package at La Fine Grobe, (506) 783–3138.

Hunting and Fishing

New Brunswick has long been popular with hunters and anglers from around the world. The province is easily accessible and has many miles of wilderness and waterways for both game and fish. New Brunswick has good hunting for black bear, deer, grouse, woodcock, and many species of duck. All nonresident hunters are required by law to hire licensed guides. There is also excellent fishing, and the province is famous for its Atlantic salmon, which can be caught in its Miramichi and Restigouche rivers. Salmon fishing is restricted to fly fishing only, and you must hire a licensed guide. You can also fish for trout and bass in inland waters and hire boats and gear for exciting deep-sea fishing excursions. A list of outfitters and information on hunting and fishing is available from New Brunswick's Department of Tourism, Recreation, and Heritage.

Provincial Parks and Campgrounds

Parks and campgrounds (both government and private) are located throughout New Brunswick. All parks are open during the summer and a few (such as Mactaquac, Sugarloaf, and Mount Carleton) are open throughout the year. No reservations for camp sites at provincial parks are accepted: Spaces are allotted on a first-come/first-served basis. The maximum stay at a provincial camp site is fourteen days. There are also two national parks in New Brunswick—Fundy and Kouchibouguac—and the Roosevelt-Campobello International Park; camping is not permitted at the Roosevelt Park.

Most parks have lavatories and facilities for cooking, washing, and so on. Many have recreational activities, such as swimming, nature trails, festivals, and the like. For more information on provincial and private campgrounds, contact New Brunswick's Department of Tourism, Recreation, and Heritage.

Accommodations

New Brunswick offers a wide selection of accommodations for every budget—resorts, motels, elegant country inns, hotels, Bed and Breakfast places, and camp sites. Advance reservations are recommended during the peak season, from about the end of June through Labour Day.

Take advantage of the free Dial-a-Nite service, which connects you with hotels, motels, farm vacation hosts, and privately operated campgrounds throughout the province. You are encouraged to use this service at all government-operated Tourist Information Centres, which are strategically located at border crossings, such as St. Stephen and Woodstock. You can also make toll-free reservations in the province through the major chains, such as Wandlyn, Keddy's, Holiday Inn, and Howard Johnson.

If you have any complaints concerning accommodations, contact the Coordinator of Accommodations, New Brunswick's Department of Tourism, Recreation, and Heritage, (506) 453–2730, or write to P.O. Box 12345, Fredericton, New Brunswick E3B 5C3.

New Brunswick Farm Vacations

If you want to get to know real New Brunswickers, live with them on their farms. You will get a clean, cozy bedroom, wholesome meals, plenty of fresh air, and a chance to take part in the activities of the farm, the family, and the local community. Best of all, it's a high-value vacation at an outrageously inexpensive price. For full details on New Brunswick farm vacations, contact New Brunswick's Department of Tourism, Recreation, and Heritage.

Dining

The native foods of New Brunswick present the traveler with some delicious treats: potatoes from the Saint John River Valley, fiddleheads (the first buds of ferns, used as a vegetable), mushrooms from the Tantramar area, lobster from Shediac and the Northumberland shore, herring and sardines from Blacks Harbour, Miramichi salmon and trout, oysters and crabs from the Caraquet area, and lobster from coastal areas.

There is a good choice of restaurants in most areas: Some, such as York's in Perth-Andover, 88 Ferry in Fredericton, Cy's Seafood in Moncton, and La Fine Grobe in Nigadoo, have achieved an excellent reputation far beyond New Brunswick's borders.

Liquor by the bottle is sold only in government stores and by the glass only in licensed restaurants, dining rooms, and lounges. The legal drinking age is nineteen. Government liquor stores, located in major cities and towns, are open Monday through Saturday.

Touring New Brunswick

Though there is so much to see and do in New Brunswick by following the established tourist routes, be adventuresome and take the less traveled roads. You will be surprised at some of your discoveries: a hidden cove, perfect for a picnic; a majestic Victorian farmhouse gracing a gentle, sloping hill; a country store that carries about every knickknack you ever wanted plus plenty of good conversation; children drying dulse on the ground and offering you a bit of this sea tang to chew. The possibilities are endless because of New Brunswick's great variety. Don't be in a rush to pass through this beautiful province. Stay a while and allow its enchantments to work their magic on you.

For your convenience New Brunswick has organized itself into six tourist regions: the Saint John River Valley, from Edmundston to just above Saint John; the Restigouche Uplands, including the Campbelltown area; the Miramichi Basin, from Newcastle and Chatham, along the river and into the heartland of the province; Fundy Coast, from Saint Stephen to Fundy National Park; Acadian Coast, from Belledune to Bartibog Bridge; and Southeast Shores, from Kouchibouquac National Park to Fundy National Park.

The Saint John River Valley

The Saint John River begins its flow in the northern wilderness of Maine. It forms the upper western border between that state and New Brunswick (also the international border between the United

States and Canada). The river moves into the heartland of the province and past the provincial capital of Fredericton and rushes out to sea into the Bay of Fundy at New Brunswick's largest city, Saint John. Most of the land in the river valley is devoted to agriculture: potatoes, other vegetable crops, dairy and beef cattle. The scenery along the entire valley is exceptionally beautiful. It is often called the "Rhine area of Canada," albeit without castles and vineyards.

Most Canadians enter New Brunswick via the Trans-Canada Highway 2, a few miles north of **Edmundston.** There is a border crossing here for Americans from Madawaska, Maine. Edmundston is a large city and its principal economic activities are lumbering, paper, and pulp. The majority of residents speak French, as do most of the people in this region on both sides of the international border. In the nineteenth century, the residents here became fed up with the squabble between the United States and Great Britain over the location of the international border and decided to form their own République de Madawaska. This idea continues in the mythology of the region.

While in Edmundston, visit the Madawaska Museum, featuring the history and development of this part of the Saint John River Valley. Open all year. Admission charge. Near Edmundston (in Les-Jardins-de-la-République Provincial Park) is the Antique Automobile Museum, a collection of classic cars. Open mid June to Labour Day. Free. This park itself is a major recreational facility offering swimming, tennis, and other recreation.

The skyline of Edmundston is dominated by the Cathedral of the Immaculate Conception. Another point of interest is La Galerie Colline at Saint Louis Maillet College, which holds art exhibitions.

Accommodations and dining in Edmundston are available at the following places:

Wandlyn Inn, south of the city heading toward Fredericton, on the Trans-Canada Highway, (506) 735–5525, has an indoor pool, dining room, and lounge. Moderate to expensive.

Lynn Motel, 20 Church Street, (506) 735–8851, in the city center, is convenient to in-town attractions and has a coffee shop. Moderate.

◀ **New Brunswick has some of the richest farmland in all Eastern Canada. Consider a farm vacation in this province, where you can share in the everyday life of a farm family or relax as you see fit. Excellent meals and accommodations are offered at a price you can not afford to pass up.**

Praga Hotel, 127 Victoria Street, (506) 735–5567, comfortable, has a dining room and lounge. Inexpensive.

Howard Johnson Motor Lodge, 100 Rice Street, (506) 739–7321, in the city center, has an indoor pool, dining room, and lounge.

Le Baron Restaurant, 174 Victoria Street, (506) 739–7822, is one of the best in town, serving steaks and varied cuisine with a French flair.

At the town of **Saint Basile,** just south of Edmundston on the Trans-Canada, is the Saint Basile Chapel Museum, a replica of a chapel built in the early 1800s, and a nearby cemetery dating back to 1785. Open July and August. Free.

Saint Leonard, on the Trans-Canada, is the home of the internationally famous Madawaska weavers. You can visit their gift shop and select choice knitted woolen goods of exquisite patterns and colors. There is a border crossing here for Americans from Van Buren, Maine. You can also go up to Campbellton via Highway 17 from here. You can stay at Daigle's Motel, off the Trans-Canada on Highway 17, (506) 423–6351, with an outdoor pool, dining room, and lounge; moderate.

Grand Falls is where the Saint John River becomes a miniature Niagara Falls, plunging many feet. Scenic lookouts provide good views of the falls and the gorge. Grand Falls is in the center of the potato-producing belt. Visit the Grand Falls Historical Museum. Open July to September. For accommodations and dining, try the Motel Pres-du-lac, on the Trans-Canada, (506) 473–1300, with a heated pool, dining room, and lounge, moderate; or La Grange Rouge, on the Trans-Canada, (506) 473–3747, with a heated pool, moderate.

Take a side trip, via Highway 108, to **New Denmark,** founded by Danish settlers, and visit their museum of pioneering history. Open mid June to Labour Day. Free.

Perth-Andover, off the Trans-Canada, has one of the province's most popular restaurants, York's, in the center of town, (506) 273–2847, where everything is fresh, homemade, and ample. Americans can enter the province here from Fort Fairfield, Maine.

Hartland is the site of the world's longest covered bridge, 1,282 feet/391 m. long. It makes a great photo for your vacation scrapbook.

Woodstock is where most Americans enter the province, via Interstate 95 from Houlton, Maine. Here you can visit the Old

Carleton County Court House (circa 1833), on Highway 560, in Upper Woodstock, used as a seat of justice and a stagecoach stop. Open July to Labour Day. Donations. For accommodations and dining, try Stiles Motel, 827 Main Street, (506) 328–6671, which has a dining room, moderate; Wandlyn Inn, on the Trans-Canada and Interstate 95, (506) 328–8876, with many conveniences, a swimming pool, and dining room, moderate to expensive; or Panorama Motel, Trans-Canada and Interstate 95, (506) 328–3315, a good value, with an indoor pool, dining room, and lounge, moderate. There's a duty free shop in Woodstock, located at the Trans-Canada and Interstate 95.

Kings Landing Historical Settlement, at **Prince William,** via the Trans-Canada, is the major attraction in this part of the province and has something of interest for the entire family. Kings Landing depicts the life of a loyalist settlement in the river valley from the late eighteenth through the nineteenth century: how the people lived, worked, worshiped, and entertained themselves. This large site has sixty buildings (including homes, farmhouses, barns, workshops, and an Anglican chapel where service is still held) and more than a hundred people dressed in period costumes who do the chores of an earlier time, while answering visitors' questions. Kings Landing has a beautiful setting high above the Saint John River, and the only traffic in the settlement consists of visitors and horses. The Kings Head Inn offers visitors hearty traditional meals in a historic environment. There is live, professional entertainment at the King's Theatre. There are tours for children and special events for all ages throughout the summer. Open June to November. Admission charge. Special family rates. Call (506) 363–3081.

Also in this general area and convenient to the Trans-Canada are Woolastook Recreation Park, popular with children during its summer season, and *Mactaquac Provincial Park*, open throughout the year. Mactaquac has everything: swimming, boating, an eighteen-hole golf course, a dining facility in an elegant lodge, hiking, camping, nature trails, entertainment, and much more. If you intend to camp there, however, be warned that during the summer season this is one of the most popular provincial parks in all of Atlantic Canada, and on weekends it is best to arrive before noon to

◀ Hartland, New Brunswick, has the world's longest covered bridge. New Brunswick has a magnetic hill, sea-carved flowerpots, reversing falls, a tidal bore, and a giant frog stuffed and waiting to greet you in Fredericton.

avoid a long wait. But give it a try anyway, or use private camp-grounds and then the public facilities of the park. There is a dining room at Mactaquac Lodge.

Fredericton, the "city of stately elms," became the capital of New Brunswick in 1785. Lying along the west bank of the gently flowing Saint John, Fredericton may be the most beautiful city in Atlantic Canada, with its river, elms, and large Victorian mansions. Fredericton has generally escaped the ugly wounds of industrialization by remaining a place where the main activity is essentially that of the mind—scholarship and politics.

Here are the most important attractions in Fredericton.

Christ Church Cathedral, Brunswick and Church Streets, was built in the mid 1800s. The first cathedral foundation on British soil since the Norman Conquest, this is perhaps architecturally the finest Anglican cathedral in all of Canada. Its landscape is graced by tall elms, and the building resembles Salisbury Cathedral. Tours during the summer months. Free.

Legislative Assembly Building, on Queen Street, the province's seat of government, has a stunning, ornate interior and houses an excellent portrait of King George III, a collection of Audubon bird prints, Hogarth prints, and a copy of the original Domesday Book (1087) printed in 1783. Tours are available. Free.

Guard House, off Carleton Street, within a military compound, is a restored military post, with a costumed guard on duty. Open June to Labour Day. Free.

Soldiers Barracks, also within the military compound, is a three-story building that has been restored and furnished to show what barracks life was like in the mid 1800s. Open June to Labour Day. Free.

Pioneer Princess III, a replica paddle-wheeler, provides scenic and evening dinner cruises along the beautiful Saint John River. It sails from a quay located near the back of the Beaverbrook Hotel. Call (506) 357–5646.

National Exhibition Centre and New Brunswick Sports Hall of Fame, at Queen and Carleton streets, has exhibitions of provincial interest on the first floor and the New Brunswick sports memorabilia on the second floor. Open throughout the year. Free.

Officers' Square, in the center of the city, features the Old Officers' Quarters, which houses the York-Sunbury Historical Society Museum. This fine museum has many interesting displays from Fredericton's military and civilian past, including items from the

Boer War and World Wars I and II, colonial furniture, and Indian artifacts. Open all year. Admission charge. At 10:00 A.M. Monday through Friday from mid July to late August the colorful Changing of the Guard ceremony takes place in the square. The guards wear scarlet tunics, blue pants, and white pith helmets, and they are usually inspected by some distinguished citizen or guest. The square contains a statue to Lord Beaverbrook, the city's great benefactor, and a memorial to John F. Kennedy.

Saint Dunstan's Church, on Regent Street, between King and Brunswick, was the first Roman Catholic cathedral built in New Brunswick. The original cathedral was demolished and replaced by the current structure. The episcopal throne of the first bishop has been preserved and there is a beautiful painting entitled *The Crucifixion.* Though primarily an English-speaking parish, a mass is celebrated in French every Saturday at 5:00 P.M.

The Playhouse, on Queen Street, (506) 458–8344, directly opposite the Lord Beaverbrook Hotel, is the center of the performing arts in the Maritime Provinces. It is home for Theatre New Brunswick, a professional company that plays locally and tours the region. It also features symphony concerts, ballet, and special guest performers.

The Craft House, 610 Queen Street, sells New Brunswick pottery, wood crafts, pewter, jewelry, glassware, carved birds, and folk art. Open all year.

Beaverbrook Art Gallery, on Queen Street, is the finest facility of its kind in Atlantic Canada, featuring Salvador Dali's massive *Santiago el Grande* and works by Sir Joshua Reynolds, Thomas Gainsborough, John Constable, William Hogarth, Graham Sutherland, Walter Richard Sickert, Augustus John, and others. The gallery has the largest single collection of the nineteenth-century Canadian artist Cornelius Krieghoff. In addition to this permanent collection, the gallery has changing shows featuring the works of contemporary artists from New Brunswick and other parts of Canada. Open throughout the year. Admission charge.

The Green, next to the Beaverbrook Gallery, is a lovely grassy, tree-shaded area along the bank of the Saint John River. A statue of the poet Robert Burns, a fine marble fountain donated by Lord Beaverbrook, and a memorial to the Loyalists who settled Fredericton grace the green.

University of New Brunswick, on University Avenue, overlooks the city and the river. Its many historic buildings and their exhibitions are open to the public free. You can arrange a tour of the Brydone Jack Observatory, the first astronomical observatory in Canada. Visit the old Burden Academy on campus, a one-room schoolhouse of the mid 1800s. At Head Hall see an exhibit of early electrical implements. The Old Arts Building is the oldest university building (circa 1825) still in use on any campus in Canada. The Provincial Archives, of historical records, maps, photographs, plans, and drawings relating to the history and development of New Brunswick, are located in the Bonar Law–Bennett Building—open every weekday. Sports events, concerts, and conventions are held at the modern Aitken Centre. Saint Thomas University, which grants its own degrees, uses many of the University of New Brunswick's facilities.

Be in Fredericton on Saturday morning and visit the *Boyce Farmers' Market,* which operates from 7:00 A.M. to noon. Farmers, artisans, and others offer all kinds of good things for sale: fresh fruits and vegetables, homemade baked goods and relishes, maple syrup, unique pottery, flowers, and more: The browsing is free, and no doubt you'll find something to buy.

Other features include public tennis courts and swimming and wading pools. Call the Recreation Department, (506) 458–8530, for locations and hours of operation. If you're the betting type, there's harness racing on Mondays and Thursdays, from mid May to mid October, at the Fredericton Raceway. Band concerts are held most Tuesday evenings during the summer in Officers' Square at 7:30 P.M.

The city has a number of modern shopping centers: Fredericton Shopping Mall, Brookside Mall, Regent Mall, and Kings Place are enclosed and have all sorts of boutiques, gift shops, and clothing stores.

The following is a listing of accommodations in the Fredericton area:

Condor Motor Lodge, at the junction of Highways 2 and 102, (506) 455–5537, has a swimming pool and dining room. Moderate.

Diplomat Motor Hotel, 225 Woodstock Road, (506) 454–5584, popular with travelers, features a heated pool and a good Chinese restaurant. Moderate to expensive.

Carriage House B&B, 230 University Avenue, (506) 452–9924, an imposing Victorian home located near cathedral, art gallery, shops, and restaurants, serves home-style breakfast.

Lord Beaverbrook Hotel, 659 Queen Street in the center of the city, (506) 455–3371, is an "establishment" place, close to everything, with indoor swimming pool, good restaurants, and lounges. Moderate to expensive.

Fredericton Motor Inn, 1315 Regent Street, (506) 455–1430, has swimming pool, a restaurant, and a lounge. Moderate to expensive.

City Motel, 1216 Regent Street, (506) 455–9900, provides a swimming pool, restaurant, and lounge. Moderate to expensive.

Wandlyn Inn, 58 West Prospect Street, (506) 452–8937, features many conveniences, a swimming pool, restaurant, and lounge. Moderate to expensive.

University of New Brunswick, off Highway 2, (506) 453–4666, offers dormitory rooms during the summer—the best value in town. Inexpensive.

Keddy's Motor Inn, 368 Forest Hill Road, off the Trans-Canada, (506) 454–4461, features a swimming pool, dining room, and lounge. Moderate to expensive.

Howard Johnson's Motor Lodge, Lower Saint Mary's on the Trans-Canada south of the city, (506) 472–0480, has traditional Howard Johnson conveniences, including a restaurant and pool. Expensive.

Many of the hotels and motels listed above have good dining rooms, where you can relax and have a drink, dine on well-prepared foods, and enjoy live entertainment. The Lord Beaverbrook Hotel, for example, has the Terrace Dining Room, noted for its elegance, service, and menu. It overlooks the Saint John River. The hotel's Maverick Room serves steak and beef dishes, and its River Room is patterned after an English public house. All restaurant and lounge services at the Beaverbrook are moderate to expensive. The dining room at the Diplomat Motel, with an extensive menu of Chinese and Canadian dishes, is one of the city's better Chinese restaurants, and it's convenient for hotel guests to have a take-out service so close at hand. The Wandlyn Acadian dining room offers great buffets and sparkling dinner theater.

Also consider the following Fredericton restaurants:

Bannister's, 546 King Street, (506) 458—5819, popular with Frederictonians, has an elegant interior and serves a varied menu. Inexpensive to moderate.

88 Ferry, 88 Ferry Avenue, (506) 472–1988, is an excellent restaurant with a charming decor, where you go to spend an evening. Specialties of the house include salmon, beef, duck, and many unusual dishes, such as edible flowers. Moderate to expensive.

La Vie en Rose, 594 Queen Street, (506) 455–1319, specializes in light meals and desserts. Moderate.

Victoria and Albert, 642 Queen Street, (506) 458–8310, next to the Playhouse and across from the Lord Beaverbrook Hotel, features elegant decor, excellent seafood and beef dishes, and irresistible desserts. Moderate to expensive.

Goofy Roofy's Restaurant, located in Boyce Market, on George Street, (506) 455–9020, is probably the most unusual restaurant in Fredericton. Open on Saturday morning in conjunction with Boyce Farmers' Market, it offers delicious country food and is frequented by politicians, professors, artists, and just about everybody else. Inexpensive to moderate.

Excelsior, 1185 Smythe Street, (506) 452–1098, offers steaks and seafood. Moderate.

Martha's, 625 King Street, (506) 452–1533, serves good Hungarian goulash and cabbage rolls, also wienerschnitzel. Moderate.

Into the Miramichi Basin

From Fredericton, Highway 8 leads to the Miramichi Region. It follows the famed Miramichi River and passes through lovely farm country and small towns. This area is famous for tall legends of extraordinary lumberjacks. At **Boiestown** visit the Central New Brunswick Woodmen's Museum, which depicts the life of early woodchoppers, hunters, and trappers. Open mid May to end September. Admission charge. Highway 8 leads to Newcastle and Chatham and the warm-water beaches along New Brunswick's east coast.

Continuing down the Saint John River Valley

To see more of the Saint John River Valley, take Highway 102 south from Fredericton. This leisurely drive along the river to the city of Saint John offers the best scenery in this valley. Several river ferries cross the river along the way. At **Oromocto** you are welcome to come into the huge Canadian Forces Base and visit its Gagetown Military Museum. It has exhibits relating to the Royal Canadian Dragoons, the Black Watch, and the Eighth Canadian Hussars. Open throughout the year. Free. Also in Oromocto is the Fort Hughes Blockhouse, a historical reconstruction. Open end of June to Labour Day. Free. The place to stay is the Oromocto Hotel, 100 Hersey Street, (506) 357–8424, moderate to expensive.

The village of **Gagetown** is a charming, historic riverside community. The Queens County Museum, with many Loyalist furnishings, is housed in the birthplace of Sir Leonard Tilley, a father of Canadian confederation. Open July to mid September. Admission charge. Here also is the workshop of the Loomcrafters, well-known artisan weavers of fine woolen goods and tartans. Their studio is in the oldest building on the Saint John River, built in 1761 by the British for trade with the Indians. You can buy tartans, ties, linens, and suitings here or have something woven to order. Open mid May to the end of September. Free. There are also several other craftspersons in the area.

Steamers' Stop Inn, Front Street, (506) 488–2903, is a charming country inn, serving hearty home cooking at moderate prices. There is a sailing school at Colpitt's Marina. A free ferry at Gagetown takes you across the river to explore the lovely countryside around Grand Lake and the Kingston peninsula.

Highway 102 continues along the west bank of the river. At **Oak Point** the river broadens at Long Reach. Many of the houses along this route were built by Loyalists in the early 1800s. And at **Westfield** it begins to widen even more into Grand Bay. Highway 102 connects with Highway 7, which leads to the city of **Saint John,** at the southern end of Grand Bay. The Saint John River flows through the narrow Reversing Falls Rapids section at low tide into Saint John Harbour and ultimately into the Bay of Fundy.

The Fundy Coast

The Fundy Coast extends from Passamaquoddy Bay to beyond Fundy National Park. Here you have the islands of Grand Manan and Campobello, affluent resort towns, modern cities, and natural curiosities. Highway 1 begins at the U.S. border, connecting St. Stephen with Saint John. Highway 1 joins with the Trans-Canada Highway 2 at Sussex, providing a link between Saint John and Moncton.

This is the most dramatic coast in New Brunswick—high cliffs, intriguing coves, fascinating islands steeped in history, rookeries for puffins, the highest tides in the world, and picturesque fishing villages. You can hire boats and gear for fishing expeditions. Swimming is possible for the hardy.

Campobello Island, on Passamaquoddy Bay, is where President Franklin Delano Roosevelt had his summer home. His cottage and estate are part of the Roosevelt Campobello International Park, jointly administered by the federal governments of the United States and Canada. FDR's office contains many of his personal belongings. Open late May to mid October. Free. Also visit the Campobello Island Library and Museum, which contains Roosevelt memorabilia and artifacts of the Owen family, early settlers. Open all year. Free.

Take the time to explore the rest of the island. Herring Cove Provincial Park offers a nine-hole golf course and camping. Accommodations and dining are available at Friar's Bay Motor Lodge, in Welshpool, (506) 752–2056, moderate; and Owen House, in Welshpool, (506) 752–2977, once the home of some of the island's original settlers. Moderate. The Lodge at Herring Cove serves seafood, freshly caught from local waters. The only land access to Campobello Island is through Lubec, Maine, from U.S. Highway 1 to 189.

A ferry connects Campobello to Deer Island, and then a free ferry takes you to the New Brunswick mainland. This is a satisfying ride amongst the islands in the bay. Only a limited number of autos can be transported per sailing, and you should plan your itinerary accordingly.

St. Stephen is the principal entry point for travelers coming up the Maine coast via U.S. Highway 1 or from Bangor, Maine, via U.S. Highway 9. While in town, visit the Charlotte County Historical Society Museum. Open June to the end of August. Donations accepted. One of St. Stephen's main attractions is Ganong's Candy Factory and Shop. It was the first to make lollipops in Canada and the first to sell chocolates in Valentine heart packages. Watch chocolate dipping demonstrations and see the world's tallest jelly bean display. Ganongs chocolatier shop is located on Milltown Boulevard. St. Stephen's annual Chocolate Festival takes place in early August. In early August the International Festival is held to celebrate many generations of friendship between St. Stephen and Calais, Maine.

Accommodations and dining are available at Wandlyn Inn, on Highway 1, (506) 466–1814, comfortable, with a good restaurant, moderate; Fundy Line Motel, 198 King Street, on Highway 1, (506) 466–2130, comfortable, with a coffee shop, moderate; and Scoodic Motel, on Highway 1, (506) 466–1540, with a swimming pool, inexpensive to moderate.

Take Highway 127, off Highway 1, to reach the resort community of **St. Andrews,** overlooking Passamaquoddy Bay. St. Andrews, one of New Brunswick's most beautiful towns, was founded in 1784 by Loyalists who floated their homes here from Castine,

Maine. The town has an early nineteenth-century New England look. It has long been a popular summer vacation place and a refuge for hay fever sufferers. The Huntsman Marine Science Centre Aquarium/Museum has live marine specimens and displays and films on marine ecology. Open the end of May to October. Admission charge. The Henry Phipps Ross and Sarah Juliette Ross Memorial Museum, in an 1800s Georgian-style home, exhibits a collection of Chinese porcelains and other antiques. Open mid May to early October. Free. St. Andrews Blockhouse National Historic Site, a War of 1812 fortification, has displays and tours. Open June to mid September. Free. Also visit the Sunbury Shores Arts and Nature Centre, the Pansy Patch thatched-roof cottage, the 1822 Greencock Church (in each of the four corners of the ceiling is a large Scottish thistle), and the 1840 courthouse. The town invites strolling its tree-lined streets and browsing in its many gift and handicraft shops. St. Andrews has one of the best golf courses in the province, also tennis, beaches, boat tours, fishing, whale watching cruises, and many other recreational opportunities.

Accommodations and dining are available at the following:

Blue Moon Motel, 310 Mowat Drive, on Highway 127, (506) 529–3245, has a dining room. Moderate.

Tara Manor Motor Inn, 559 Mowat Drive on Highway 127, (506) 529–3304, features a heated pool, dining room. Moderate to expensive.

Algonquin Hotel, which dominates the hill in the center of town, (506) 529–8823, is one of the premier resorts in Atlantic Canada, with a golf course, tennis courts, swimming pool, excellent dining room, a lounge with live entertainment, and many services and conveniences. Expensive.

The Pickett Fence, 309 Reed Road, (506) 529–8985, offers accommodations near golf course. Moderate.

Shiretown Inn, in the heart of downtown at 218 Water Street, (506) 529–8877, is the oldest summer hotel in Canada and has fine dining. Moderate.

Shady Maples B&B, 132 Sophia Street, (506) 529–4426, is a charming turn-of-the-century home. Inexpensive.

◀ **The fishing villages along the Fundy coast offer perfect scenes for pictures, whether on canvas, watercolor paper, or film. Here you have everything— seagulls, floating mists, rock headlands, charming villages, and the ever- present sea.**

Pansy Patch B&B, 59 Carleton Street, (506) 529–3834, a storybook home, serves waffles and maple syrup for breakfast. Inexpensive.

Rossmount Inn, on Highway 127, (506) 529–3351, is a favorite inn with knowledgeable travelers. It has an excellent dining room. Moderate to expensive.

Smugglers Wharf Restaurant, 225 Water Street, (506) 529–3536, offers seafood and a nice view of the bay. Moderate.

Conley's Lighthouse Restaurant, Patrick Street, (506) 529–3082, located right on the wharf, serves excellent seafood. Moderate.

To get to **Grand Manan Island** take Highway 776, off Highway 1, to **Blacks Harbour** ferry terminal, (506) 657–3306. Ferries sail throughout the year, making four or five trips each way daily during the summer months. Crossing time is two hours. Vessels hold one hundred passengers and twenty-five autos. During the peak vacation period, there is often a wait to get on board. For information, call (506) 642–7317.

Grand Manan is a large island located closer to the U.S. coast at Maine than to Canada's. Favored as a vacation island with many, it is a prize birding area for ornithologists. Visit the Grand Manan Museum and Walter B. McLaughlin Marine Gallery, featuring local history, geology, ornithology, and marine lore. Open mid June to mid September. Free. You can arrange for tours of the puffin and tern rookeries. For cruises to see the whales, contact Ocean Search, P.O. Box 129, Grand Manan Island, New Brunswick E0G 2M0, (506) 662–8144. In addition to its many nature trails, the island also is a perfect place for beachcombing. And try dulse here—the dried seaweed is an acquired taste but healthful. The best part of Grand Manan, however, is that you can get away from the cares and pressures of the modern world and become more in tune with yourself and the natural world. The Marathon Inn, North Head, (506) 662–8144, is a recommended place to stay, with very good dining, expensive. Other accommodations include the Compass Rose, (506) 662–8570, a cozy inn with delicious home cooking and breakfast included, inexpensive; Grand Harbour Inn, (506) 662–8681, a lovely old inn also offering a heated pool and restaurant, moderate; and Shorecrest Lodge, (506) 662–3216, a comfortable lodge with good home-cooked meals, moderate. Reservations for accommodations on the island are essential.

At **Lepreau,** on Highway 1, en route to Saint John, take Highway 790, and explore a peninsula of fishing villages: Maces Bay, Dipper Harbour, and Chance Harbour. This is a prime area for photography and picnics.

Saint John

Continue on Highway 1 to the city of **Saint John,** New Brunswick's largest industrialized urban area. The Loyalists landed here in 1783 and incorporated Canada's first city in 1785. Saint John has always been an important seaport and shipbuilding and repair center. Trading, finance, and manufacturing are other economic activities. The people of Saint John celebrate their heritage on Loyalist Day (May 18) and during Loyalist Days (mid July). If you are traveling here in August, be sure to take in Festival by the Sea, a national performing arts festival of hundreds of shows and performers. Saint John is an attractive city with many new developments such as Market Square and a revitalized waterfront. There are new commercial buildings in the city center, indicating a healthy economic climate. In 1985 the prestigious Canada Summer Games were held in Saint John. Saint John is a departure point for Nova Scotia across the Bay of Fundy (see page 277).

King Square, in the center of the city, is laid out in the pattern of the British Union Jack. It is a pleasant park for a stroll, and band concerts are occasionally performed. Saint John's Tourist Information Center, (506) 658–2855, provides maps and brochures and conducts tours of the city during the summer.

Barbour's General Store, foot of King Street, is a historic building filled with merchandise of the nineteenth century. Open mid May to mid October. Free.

Pleasant Villa School (Little Red Schoolhouse), next to Barbour's store, is an 1876 schoolhouse furnished with original furniture. Open mid May to mid October. Free.

The Old Loyalist Burial Ground, east of King Square, with graves dating to the 1700s, is located near Barbour's Store.

Carleton Martello Tower National Historic Site, on Fundy Drive at Whipple Street, is a circular stone fortification housing a military museum. Open mid June to mid October. Free.

Fort Howe Blockhouse (circa 1777), on Magazine Street, offers an excellent view of Saint John Harbour.

Alliance Fine Canadian Crafts, at Brunswick Square Skywalk, sells New Brunswick crafted pottery, woodwork, glassware, textiles, and jewelry. Open all year.

Prince William Street is famous for its many crafts stores, antique shops, and art galleries. This street has been designated a National Historic Site.

New Brunswick Museum (Canada's first museum, founded in 1842), 277 Douglas Avenue, is the province's main showcase for exhibits on its heritage (especially its collection on early Indian cultures) and natural history. Open throughout the year. Admission charge.

Market Square, at the foot of King Street, is a handsome complex consisting of a 45,000-square-foot Trade and Convention Centre, a new civic and regional library (there is an art gallery in the library), an enclosed retail mall (with more than seventy shops, restaurants, and lounges), two new full-facility hotels (Hilton and Delta), and a series of enclosed overhead walkways that connect with other buildings in the commercial core of the city. The waterfront area adjacent to Market Square has been made into pleasant promenades. From here you can take a boat cruise of Saint John harbour.

Reversing Falls Rapids is where the Saint John River empties into the harbor. At high tide in the harbor, the flow of water reverses itself. This phenomenon can be viewed from the gorge above, where there is parking and the Tourism Information Centre.

Trinity Church (Anglican), 115 Charlotte Street, has over its west door a replica of the British royal arms carved in 1714, brought here by Boston Loyalists and placed in this church in 1791.

Saint John's Stone Church, 87 Carleton Street, was built in 1825 from ballast brought in English ships. This is the only house of worship in the area designated a "garrison church."

Old City Market, on King Street, is a colorful, frenetic bazaar where merchants hawk their meats, fruits, vegetables, crafts, and what not, and shoppers haggle over price and quality. Open Monday through Saturday, except holidays.

Cherry Brook Zoo, in Rockwood Park, via Highway 100, northeast of the city center, has a collection of live animals from around the world, a nice treat for the kids. Open during the summer. Admission charge.

Old County Courthouse, on Sydney Street, next to the tourist bureau, has an elegant spiral stairway. Open during the summer. Free.

Accommodations in the Saint John area include the following:

Fundy Line Motel, 2149 Ocean Way, West, (506) 672–2493. Moderate.

Island View Motel, Highways 7 and 100, (506) 672–1381. Moderate.

Seacoast Motel, off Highway 100, (506) 672–6442. Moderate.

White House Lodge Motor Hotel, off Highways 1 and 100, (506) 672–1000, has a dining room and lounge. Moderate.

Hillcrest Motel, off Highway 100, (506) 672–5310. Moderate.

Balmoral Court Motel, on Highway 142, (506) 672–3019. Moderate.

Howard Johnson Motor Lodge, off Highways 1 and 100, (506) 642–2622, offers many conveniences, a swimming pool, dining room, and lounge. Expensive.

Keddy's Motor Inn, off Highways 1 and 7, (506) 657–7320, popular with travelers, features a swimming pool and a good restaurant. Moderate to expensive.

Delta Brunswick Inn, 39 King Street (downtown), (506) 648–1981, has fine accommodations, a dining room, lounge, sauna, swimming pool, and perfect location. Expensive.

Holiday Inn, 350 Haymarket Square, (506) 657–3610, is comfortable and has a dining room and lounge. Moderate.

Park Plaza, 607 Rothesay Avenue, (506) 633–4100. Moderate.

Shadow Lawn Inn, in Rothesay, via Highway 100, is about fifteen minutes from Saint John, (506) 847–7539. Shadow Lawn, a top choice for excellent accommodations and superb dining in the Saint John area, is located in a pretty private-school town and well known throughout Canada. Reservations are a must. You might very well rub elbows with a prime minister or premier here. Moderate to expensive.

Hilton International, next to Market Square, on the waterfront, (506) 693–8484, has a hard-to-beat location with sweeping harbor views, swimming pool, sauna, lounge, and a dining room that features New Brunswick specialties, such as lobsters and fiddleheads. The Hilton is the best hotel in town. Expensive.

Dining possibilities in Saint John follow:

Grannan's, in Market Square, (506) 634–1555, has a fine reputation for serving excellent seafood. Moderate.

Turn of the Tide, in the Hilton Hotel, (506) 693–8484, highlights seafood, and it has an excellent brunch feast. Expensive.

Top of the Walk, Keddy's Motor Inn, off Highways 1 and 7, (506) 657–7320, lets you dine high above the city. Moderate to expensive.

Mediterranean, 419 Rothesay Avenue, (506) 634–3183, serves good Greek food, also has a cabaret and dancing. Moderate.

The Fundy Coast Continues

In the town of **Hampton,** en route from Saint John to Sussex via Highway 1, is the Kings County Historical Society Museum. Open mid June to the end of September. Admission charge. In Sussex visit the Agricultural Museum of New Brunswick. Open June to September. Admission charge.

Because the Trans-Canada and Highway 1 converge in Sussex, many travelers stop here overnight. The Maples Motel, 1019 Main Street, (506) 433–1558, Fairway Motor Inn, on the Trans-Canada, (506) 433–3470, and Timberland Motel, in Penobsquis, (506) 433–2480, are recommended. All have dining rooms and lounges, and all have moderate rates.

A nice diversion is to take Highway 111 from Sussex to St. Martins, a charming, historic shipbuilding town during the "age of sail" on the Bay of Fundy. Visit the Quaco Museum here. Open June to September. Admission charge. Stay at the Quaco Inn, Beach Street, (506) 833–4772, where rooms are furnished with antiques. It serves hearty breakfasts and home-style dinners. Inexpensive to moderate.

From Sussex you can take the Trans-Canada to Moncton or take a more interesting route, via Highway 114, through *Fundy National Park,* (506) 887–2000, which calls itself the "sea-conditioned" playground. This 80 square mile/205 sq. km. area features camping facilities, picnicking, swimming in a heated pool or in the Bay of Fundy, nature and hiking trails, fishing, boating, golf, extensive interpretation programs, tennis, playgrounds, bowling greens, and many other cultural and recreational programs. Within the park, you can stay at Caledonia Inn & Chalets, (506) 887–2930, and at the Fundy Park Chalets, (506) 887–2808, which has a dining room. Both are moderate in price. In nearby **Alma** consider the Alpine Motor Inn, on Highway 114, (506) 887–2052. Inexpensive.

Follow Highway 114 to **Hopewell Cape,** where you can see the "flowerpots," huge pieces of land sculpted by the sea. To many they look like mushrooms topped by evergreens. Also in this area is the Albert County Museum and the County Court House (local history, agricultural and nautical lore). Open mid June to mid September. Admission charge.

Hillsborough, farther along Highway 114, is the site of the

William Henry Steeves House, home of one of the fathers of the confederation. Open late June to Labour Day. Admission charge. A hand-carved cross at St. Mary's Anglican Church was made from the remains of another recovered from London's Great Fire of 1666.

Take a ride aboard the Salem-Hillsborough Railway. A restored steam locomotive pulls you for 5 miles near the red banks of the Petitcodiac River and the broad Tantramar Marshes. In operation during the summer. Admission charge.

Moncton

Highway 114 will take you right into the center of **Moncton,** a transportation hub of Atlantic Canada, where road and rail lines and air routes converge. It is a lively, modern city that greatly benefits from its cultural duality—French and English. Its attractions include the following:

Magnetic Hill, via Highway 126 and the Trans-Canada (watch for signs), is an illusion that makes you believe your car is being pulled uphill by some mysterious force. Open during the summer season. Free. Adjacent is a wild animal park for the kids. Admission charge. Also in this area is Magic Mountain water theme park, one of Canada's largest, which has water slides, a wave pool, lazy river tube floating, playground, game arcade, minature golf, and other recreations. It also has a gift shop, snack bar, and a restaurant. Well worth a visit when traveling with kids. Open during the summer. Admission charge. Nearby is Wharf Village, a collection of quaint shops and restaurants.

Acadian Museum, off McLaughlin Drive, on the modern campus of the University of Moncton (the most important degree-granting institution of higher learning for French-Acadians in Eastern Canada), has an interesting collection of Acadian artifacts and documents. It has become the premier research center for Acadian studies. Open throughout the year. Free.

Free Meeting House, at Mountain Road, next to the Moncton Museum, is Moncton's oldest building. Open during the summer. Free.

Moncton Museum, 20 Mountain Road, has interesting exhibits relating to local history. The museum shows films and operates a bookstore. Open during the summer. Free.

Bore View Park, off Main Street in the center of the city, is where you can see the tidal bore (the rippling of water heralding the coming of the high tide) rushing up the Petitcodiac River toward Moncton. A sign in the park tells the times the tidal bore arrives from the Bay of Fundy.

Moncton is a popular stopover for those traveling to Nova Scotia, Prince Edward Island, and Québec's Gaspé region. It is also near the province's best warm-water beaches. It is a good idea to make advance reservations for Moncton.

Accommodations and dining include the following:

Skyliner Motel, Trans-Canada, (506) 858–9080, features a dining room. Moderate.

Scenic Motel, Trans-Canada, (506) 384–2478. Moderate.

Magnetic Hill Resort, Magnetic Hill, (506) 858–8878, offers a swimming pool, coffee shop, and lounge. Moderate to expensive.

Howard Johnson Motor Lodge, Highways 2 and 126, (506) 384–1050, features many conveniences, a swimming pool, dining room, and lounge. Moderate to expensive.

Keddy's Motor Inn, Trans-Canada, (506) 854–2210, on the road to warm-water beaches, has a swimming pool. Moderate to expensive.

Elmwood Motel, 401 Elmwood Drive, (506) 388–5096, offers a coffee shop and lounge. Moderate.

Nor-West Court, 1325 Mountain Road, (506) 384–1222. Inexpensive to moderate.

Keddy's Brunswick Hotel, 1005 Main Street, (506) 854–6340, a renovated accommodation with many hotel services, a swimming pool, and a good location. Expensive.

Hotel Beausejour (a Canadian National hotel), 750 Main Street, (506) 854–4344, provides excellent accommodations, services, and restaurants in a convenient location. Expensive.

Rodd's Park House Inn, 434 Main Street, (506) 382–1664, offers a good location, dining room, lounge, and swimming pool. Expensive.

Dining spots in Moncton include the following:

Cy's Seafood Restaurant, 170 East Main Street, (506) 857–0032, is the place for seafood. Moderate to expensive.

L'Auberge, Hotel Beausejour, 750 Main Street, (506) 854–4344, serves seafood, coq au vin, and other specialties. Moderate.

Windjammer, Hotel Beausejour, 750 Main Street, (506) 854–4344, prepares roast beef, Cornish hen, lobster, and fiddleheads elegantly. Expensive.

Vito's, 726 Mountain Road, (506) 858–5003, serves pizza and pasta, chicken cacciatore, and other Italian dishes; it is popular with residents and travelers. Inexpensive.

Chez Jean Pierre, 21 Toombs Street, (506) 382–0332, offers excellent French cuisine in a family inn setting—one of Moncton's best. Moderate to expensive.

Toward Nova Scotia

Highway 6 from Moncton to **Dorchester** is an interesting and scenic drive to the Nova Scotia border or to the Prince Edward Island ferry terminal. En route you will pass through the lovely Acadian villages of Memramcook and Saint Joseph. In Saint Joseph, the Survival of the Acadians National Historic Site, has a visitor's center with exhibits on Acadian survival after their deportation in 1755. Open mid May to mid October. Free.

Dorchester has the Bell Inn (circa 1811), the oldest stone building in New Brunswick. Open June to September. Free. In the center of the village are Keillor House, built in 1813 and furnished with antiques, a carriage house, and a general store. Open June to the end of September. Free. Stay at the Rocklyn Inn B&B, (506) 379–2205. This elegant old home serves full English breakfasts. Inexpensive.

Highway 6 leads to **Sackville,** a pleasant community and home of Mount Allison University, whose campus is the most beautiful in the province. Be sure to visit its Owens Art Gallery. Open all year. Free. During the summer, Mount Allison offers inexpensive accommodations and dining on campus. Call (506) 364–2200. In Sackville you can also visit the nearby Canadian Broadcasting Corporation's international transmitting facilities. See Sackville's Harness Shop, which claims to be the only one in North America still making horse collars by hand. Sackville is where the first Baptist church in Canada was organized. The famous Tantramar Marshes are in this area. These marshes, producing salt-meadow hay for cattle feed, were reclaimed from the sea by the early Acadian dyke system.

One treat of visiting Sackville is to stay and eat at the Marshlands Inn, 73 Bridge Street, (506) 536–0170, an elegant Victorian mansion that serves English-style roast beef with Yorkshire pudding and steak and kidney pie. The bedrooms offer old-fashioned luxury. This is a very popular place for both accommodations and dinner; reservations are essential. Accommodations are moderate; dinner is moderate to expensive. Also in Sackville is the Marshlands Motor Inn, on the Trans-Canada, (506) 536–1327, moderate; the Different

Drummer B&B, 146 West Main Street, (506) 536–1291, inexpensive; and Borden's Restaurant and Motel, on the Trans-Canada, (506) 536–1066, inexpensive to moderate.

At **Aulac,** off the Trans-Canada, is Fort Beausejour National Historic Park. Here are the remains of an eighteenth-century military fortification that was of strategic importance to both the French and the English in their struggle over North America. Open mid May to mid October. Free. There is an excellent view from here of the Cumberland Basin. Nearby is the Drury Lane Steak House, off the Trans-Canada, (506) 536–1252, famous in Atlantic Canada for their beef dishes.

If you are heading for Prince Edward Island, take Highway 16 (a section of the Trans-Canada) to the ferry terminal at Cape Tormentine. En route, at **Port Elgin,** visit the Beachkirk Fibrecraft Museum and Workshop, a lovely church exhibiting and demonstrating the working of flax. It also has displays of fossils and the artifacts of early settlers. Open June 1 to mid September. Free.

Southeast Shores

Most of the communities in this region are French-Acadian, though a number of English-speaking towns are sprinkled throughout. Since most of the people here are fluently bilingual, particularly the Acadians, you should have no language problem. This coast has the best beaches and saltwater swimming in the province. The sand is soft, and the water warm. This region is a very engaging part of the province, where the air and sun invite the pleasure of relaxing indolence.

Highways 15 and 134 take you to the popular coastal town of **Shediac,** which calls itself the "lobster capital of the world" and features plenty of places where you can gorge on these succulent redbacks. In July Shediac celebrates its Lobster Festival. Boat tours and fishing expeditions are available. Nearby Parlée Beach Park has sandy beaches, warm water, and camping, picnic, and recreational facilities. Parlée Beach is a good place for very small children, because the water is shallow and almost tepid. The Hotel Shediac, (506) 532–4405, offers a downtown location, good home cooking; inexpensive to moderate. Other accommodations in town include the Four Seas Restaurant and Motel, 762 Main Street, (506) 532–2585; Chez-François, 93 Main Street, (506) 532–4233, is a lovely inn offering accommodations and excellent seafood; and Neptune Motel, (506) 532–4299. All are inexpensive to moderate in price.

Farther south, via Highways 5 and 950, there are excellent beaches at Cap Pelé, off Highway 15. In nearby **Robichaud** on Highway 15 is the Sportsman's Museum, with exhibits on hunting, fishing, and trapping. Open May to October. Admission charge.

Highway 134 takes you north up the Acadian Coast as far as Richibucto. Highway 11 is the main road from this community to the city of Campbellton. In mid August the International Hydroplane Races are held at **Cocagne,** on Highway 134 (before Richibucto). These unique races attract participants from all over the world.

At **Boutouche,** via Highway 11, visit the Kent Museum, which displays local history and the works of area artists and a century-old restored convent. Both open June to September. Admission charge.

Rexton was the birthplace of Andrew Bonar Law, the only prime minister of Great Britain born outside the United Kingdom. His home is open to the public from the end of June to Labour Day. Free. Visit the Richibucto River Museum, with its exhibits of local history and Indian artifacts. Open July and August. Donation. There are accommodations in nearby Richibucto at Habitant Restaurant and Motel, (506) 523–4421, the best in town, moderate; and Alpen Glow Motel, (506) 523–4300, off Highway 11, inexpensive.

Kouchibouguac National Park, via Highways 11 and 117, (506) 876–2443, offers an extensive area for recreation, with camping, sandy beaches, saltwater swimming, hiking, canoeing, and bird-watching. Highway 117, which goes through the park and along the coast, is a scenic drive to Chatham. At Point Escuminac see the memorial sculpture of local fishermen who lost their lives in the Gulf of the Saint Lawrence.

The Miramichi Basin

Chatham, which can be reached more directly via Highway 11, is at the eastern end of the Miramichi Region. Here the great salmon-fishing Miramichi River flows into the sea. The famous Cunard Steamship Line (which now operates the luxury liner *Queen Elizabeth II*) started in Chatham. Viscount R. B. Bennet, prime minister of Canada and a New Brunswick son, had his law practice in this lovely town. Visit the Miramichi Natural History Museum. Open July and August. Free. Saint Michael's Historical Museum and Lady Chapel Museum are also worth visiting. Open July and August. Free. Saint Michael's Rectory is a national historic site.

One of North America's largest Irish festivals takes place in Chatham in mid July.

The Cunard Restaurant, 32 Cunard Street, (506) 773–7107, serves Chinese and Canadian food. Inexpensive to moderate.

Highway 8, which takes you through the Miramichi Region to the capital city of Fredericton, passes through **Newcastle,** boyhood home of Lord Beaverbrook, the famous newspaper baron and confidant of Winston Churchill. The Old Manse, Beaverbrook's boyhood home, is in the center of town. Guided tours. Open all year. Free.

Highway 11 continues north along Miramichi Bay. At **Bartibog Bridge** is MacDonald Farm Historic Park, depicting the agricultural life in New Brunswick in the nineteenth century. There is a handsome Georgian-style house, furnished with antiques and memorabilia of its builder, Alexander MacDonald, leader of the famed MacDonald's Highlanders during the American Revolutionary War. Visitors are invited to stroll the grounds and see the farming, lumbering, and fishing activities that were the backbone of the local economy. Open late June to early September. Admission charge.

Acadian Coastal Region

Highway 11 now enters what is considered the heart of French-Acadian country. At **Tabusintac** is the Tabusintac Museum (local history). Open July and August. Free.

Tracadie, meaning "ideal place to camp" in Micmac, is the site of the unusual Tracadie Historical Museum at Academie Sainte Famille, which tells the story of those who dedicated their lives to a leper colony that was once here. Open mid June to mid August. Admission charge. Accommodations in Tracadie include the Motel Boudreau, (506) 395–2244, moderate. There are fine beaches in a provincial park at nearby Val Comeau.

Shippagan, an active fishing center, is set on the end of this large peninsula. The Shippagan Marine Center, off Second Avenue, opened in 1982 and features one of the largest marine displays in Eastern Canada. Open throughout the summer. Admission charge. Be sure to see the extensive peat moss areas, where tours of cutting and processing operations are available during the week. You can also hire boats and gear for deep-sea fishing expeditions. A bridge leads from Shippagan to **Lamèque Island**. From there you can take the car ferry to **Miscou Island,** a tranquil island with a nice beach. Here is land's end on this coast of the province.

Caraquet, on Highway 11, is the site of Village Historique Acadien, a re-creation of eighteenth- and nineteenth-century French-Acadian life in Atlantic Canada. There are homes with accurate period furnishings, barns, workshops of a blacksmith, cobbler, printer, cartwright, weaver, and shingler, stores, a church, and marshes with dikes. The costumed staff work the traditional crafts and chores of their ancestors, and they answer your questions about early Acadian life. A visitors' center has a cafeteria serving Acadian dishes, also displays of artifacts and audiovisual presentations about the village and Acadian history. The treat is to be able to walk through the village streets and absorb the ambience of a time long gone. The Village Historique Acadien is a major attraction in New Brunswick that should not be missed. Open the beginning of June to the end of September. Admission charge. For more information, call (506) 727–3467. The nearby Boutique du Village sells Acadian handicrafts—weaving, pottery, sculpture, recorded music, books. Open mid June to end September.

Also in Caraquet is the less ambitious but nonetheless interesting Acadian Museum. Open June to mid September. Admission charge. Sainte Anne-du-Bocage Shrine is a historic and religious monument to the Acadians who settled this area after their expulsion. Open throughout the year. Free. In August Caraquet is the site of the largest Acadian festival in Atlantic Canada, highlighted by the blessing of the fishing fleet, folk singing and dancing, traditional foods, a talent show, and the grand Evangeline and Gabriel Ball. Deep-sea fishing and boat tours can be arranged in Caraquet.

Recommended accommodations in the area include Hotel Paulin, (506) 727–9981, small, homey, and comfortable, inexpensive; Motel du Village, (506) 727–4447, moderate; Auberge de la Baie, (506) 727–3485, moderate to expensive; and Motel Colibri, (506) 727–2222, which also has entertainment, moderate. For fine dining, the Hotel Paulin is noted for its fresh seafood and fabulous desserts, moderate to expensive.

At Grand Anse visit the Popes' Museum, where portraits of all the pontiffs are displayed, along with many religious objects of historic significance. Open June to early September. Admission charge.

From Caraquet follow Highway 11 to Bathurst, an industrial and mining center and a convenient place to obtain accommodations for the Acadian Festival when the peninsula is all booked. Visit the Herman J. Good Memorial Museum, which has a large collection of military artifacts. Open July and August. Free. Other points of interest in the Bathurst area are Papineau Falls, site of an early home of settler Nicholas Denys, and Tetagouche Falls.

Accommodations and dining in the Bathurst region include the following:

Atlantic Host Motor Inn, on Highway 11, (506) 548–3335, is one of the best in the area, with swimming pools, a dining room, and lounge. Moderate to expensive.

Danny's Motor Inn, off Highways 11 and 134, (506) 546–6621, is popular with travelers and has the best dining room in town. Moderate to expensive.

John's Motel, off Highways 11 and 134, (506) 546–5726. Inexpensive.

Ron's Motel, Highway 134, (506) 546–3391, features a swimming pool and dining room. Moderate.

Kent Motel, Highway 134, (506) 546–3345, has a beach and coffee shop. Moderate.

Fundy Line Motel, off Highway 11 on 855 Ste. Anne Drive, (506) 548–8803, features a dining room and lounge. Moderate.

Keddy's Motor Inn, 80 Main Street, (506) 546–6691, offers a beach, dining room, and lounge. Moderate to expensive.

La Fine Grobe, in the village of Nigadoo, on Highway 134, (506) 783–3138, just a few miles north of Bathurst, is one of New Brunswick's most creative restaurants. Many gourmets consider it to be the province's best. La Fine Grobe is operated by chef Georges Frachon, a native of Grenoble, France, and Hilda Lavoi, of Acadian stock. During the tourist months they operate the restaurant. In off-season they make exquisite crafts and teach weaving and pottery. Once you book a table, it is yours for the entire evening. All the ingredients of every dish are fresh, with herbs plucked from their own garden. The menu is broad—from chateaubriand to seafood caught in local waters—and so is the selection of wines. The restaurant is furnished Acadian style (blond pine) and overlooks the Bay of Chaleur. Also in Nigadoo is a wild game farm that is popular with children.

The Restigouche Uplands

The Restigouche Uplands, via Highway 11, extend along the south shore of the Bay of Chaleur. **Dalhousie** has one of New Brunswick's largest paper mills. Visit its Chaleur Area History Museum. Open during the summer. Free. Inch Arran Park has swimming. You can take a ferry here to Québec's Gaspé region.

Campbellton is the commercial center of this northeastern region of New Brunswick. It is also an outfitting center for the great salmon-fishing rivers, such as the Restigouche. See the cairn at Riverside Park, off Highway 134 on the Bay of Chaleur, commemorating the last naval battle of the Seven Years' War. And visit the Restigouche Gallery on Andrew Street. Open throughout the year. Free. *Sugarloaf Provincial Park,* near the city, has one of the few Alpine slides in eastern Canada—fun for all members of the family.

Accommodations and dining in Campbellton are available at Fundy Line Motel, Roseberry Street, (506) 753–3395, moderate; Caspian Motel, 26 Duke Street, (506) 753–7606, one of the best in town, with a dining room and lounge, moderate to expensive; Howard Johnson Motor Lodge, 157 Water Street, (506) 753–5063; offering a dining room, lounge, and swimming pool, expensive; and Idlewilde Motor Court, Highway 134, (506) 753–4665, inexpensive. For Chinese and Canadian dishes, try Chateau Inn Restaurant, 122 Roseberry Street, (506) 759–8059. Inexpensive to moderate.

Campbellton is the gateway to Québec's Gaspé region. A bridge here leads to Pointe-à-la-Croix, Québec.

Highway 134 takes you to Matapédia, Québec, where you can take Highway 132 across the Gaspé peninsula to Mont-Joli on the Saint Lawrence River, which leads to Québec City.

Highway 17 west from Campbellton leads to access roads (from Saint-Quentin and Five Fingers) to *Mount Carleton Provincial Park,* a secluded natural area, rich in game and birds. Highway 17 west continues to Saint-Léonard and the Saint John River Valley.

CHAPTER 13

Nova Scotia

Nova Scotia Today

Nova Scotia (New Scotland) calls itself "Canada's ocean playground," a justifiable boast. Much of its appeal is found along the 4,625-mile/7,400-km. coastline of fine beaches, inspiring maritime scenery, and quaint fishing and farming villages. Along Nova Scotia's shore you can swim, sail, photograph, paint, hike, fish, scuba dive, dine on fresh seafood, and poke around unique and historic places. Wherever you travel in Nova Scotia, you are never more than 35 miles/56 km. from the coast.

On the map, Nova Scotia looks like a giant lobster, with Cape Breton Island, pointed toward Newfoundland, as its snapping claw. Some 350 miles/560 km. long, the province slants northeast/southwest on the globe. Its shores are touched by all of the region's major bodies of water—the Atlantic, the Bay of Fundy, and the Gulf of Saint Lawrence. During the age of sail, Nova Scotia's main highway was the sea, used by explorers from Europe, settlers, pirates, conflicting empires, fishermen, and traders. Halifax has long been a key portal into North America for millions of immigrants, ranking on the East Coast with Boston and New York. Today supertankers and container ships arrive from all over the world and make intensive use of Nova Scotia's deep-water ports and modern terminal facilities. Commercial fishing (cod, lobster, swordfish, scallops) remains a vital factor in the economy, as do other traditional activities, such as mining, lumbering, and agriculture.

Since the end of World War II, Nova Scotia's service and manufacturing sectors have grown rapidly. Tourism is a principal source of income, and Nova Scotia is one of the most popular travel destinations in Atlantic Canada. Halifax, the provincial capital, is Atlantic Canada's premier city in sophistication, business, culture,

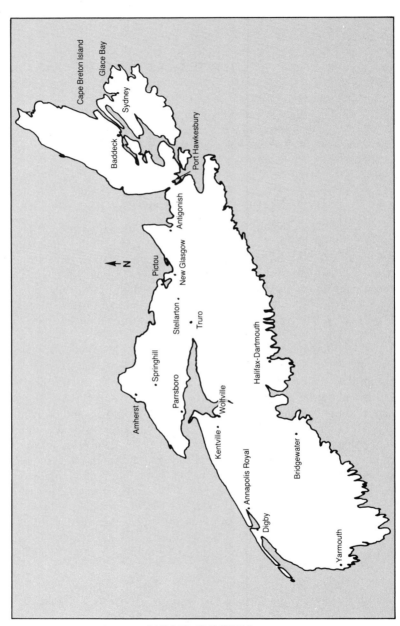

NOVA SCOTIA

education, and medicine. The province's small towns are among the prettiest in all of Canada, reminding one of New England, whence came many of the early settlers.

Much of the rolling interior of Nova Scotia is forested in spruce, pine, hemlock, sugar maple, and birch. This verdant landscape is accented by numerous freshwater lakes, streams, and rivers, offering perfect conditions for salmon and trout angling and wilderness camping, hiking, and canoeing. The 100-mile/160-km. long Annapolis Valley is beautiful and fertile. Its chief crop is apples, and in spring white blossoms cover the valley. The Apple Blossom Festival, in late May and early June, draws enthusiasts from Eastern Canada and the United States to see nature's display and to enjoy the many events.

Cape Breton Island, distinct in place and state of mind, takes up a third of the land area of Nova Scotia. This large island, of dramatic mountains rising from the sea and convoluted fjords, is connected to mainland Nova Scotia by causeway at the Strait of Canso. On the island is Cape Breton Highlands National Park and its famous Cabot Trail, an autoroute that skirts the sides of steep mountains and dips in and out of lush valleys and charming fishing villages.

Sable Island, located in the Atlantic 200 miles east of Halifax, is also a part of Nova Scotia. The island is famous for its erratic sand shifts (which have snagged and wrecked many ships), its wild horses, and its proximity to oil and natural gas fields.

A Wee Bit of History

It is said that the Vikings were the first European visitors to the shores of Nova Scotia. But except for a runic stone in a Yarmouth museum and some old Indian legends, there is little proof of any Norse settlement on Nova Scotia soil (though there is solid evidence of Viking presence in Newfoundland).

John Cabot took possession of Nova Scotia for England when he landed on Cape Breton Island in 1497. Sieur-de-Monts and Samuel de Champlain established the first permanent European settlement north of Florida, when they founded Port Royal in the Annapolis Valley in 1605. Champlain also established a social club, L'Ordre-de-Bon-Temps, which still exists.

In 1621 King James I of Great Britain made Nova Scotia Britain's first colony in the New World, a royal province to strengthen his hold over this vast area, which also included much of what is now New Brunswick. He granted the province a royal coat of arms in 1625, and Nova Scotia became the first Canadian province to have its own flag (the Scottish lion rampant, similar in some respects to Scotland's).

Sir William Alexander, a Scotsman, was empowered by King Charles I to colonize the land then known as Acadia (the name probably originated with the sixteenth-century explorer Verrazzano) and to settle New Scotland (Nova Scotia) with British families. He also had the power to grant certain colonists a Scottish order of knighthood, creating the baronets of Nova Scotia, a title still inherited by some Scottish families. A few traveled to the New World to see if their 24-square mile/61-sq. km. domains had any promise; none of them lingered long in the wilderness.

The French were more successful in settling Nova Scotia. Families from Normandy and Brittany cultivated the land and reclaimed more from the sea by building dikes. In 1755 most of these French-Acadians were expelled from Nova Scotia by the British as being unreliable subjects, and their highly productive lands were taken over by New England planters. Grand Pré, with its well-known statue of the tragic Evangeline, is today a national historic site and attracts thousands of visitors annually to this charming area of the Annapolis Valley. Many Acadians later returned to Nova Scotia, and their descendants now live in French-speaking communities such as Church Point, the Pubnicos, Chéticamp, and Isle Madame.

The English built the city of Halifax in 1749 as a military outpost to checkmate the stronghold of Louisbourg, a massive French fortress on Cape Breton Island that blocked entry into the Gulf of Saint Lawrence and the heartland of Canada. Today Halifax is Atlantic Canada's leading city. Louisbourg, which was razed by victorious British and New England forces after 1759, has been rebuilt since the 1960s at a cost of more than $24 million into one of the most impressive historical attractions in all of North America. It is the largest historical reconstruction in Canada and second largest (next to Williamsburg, Virginia) in North America.

German and French Protestants settled in and around Lunenburg, one of the loveliest towns on the Atlantic coast, where they became famous as enterprising fishermen and boat builders, a reputation they continue to earn. The world-famous racing and fishing schooner *Bluenose* was their most noteworthy creation; its graceful form appears on the Canadian 10 cent piece and on the label of a local beer. The Irish first came to Nova Scotia in the eighteenth century. Alexander McNutt, a visionary of sorts, felt that the New World would be a new start for his oppressed people. The great potato famine of the mid-nineteenth century brought many thousands more Irish into the province.

Another important group of people to settle in Nova Scotia came not from the British Isles but from the thirteen colonies of the United States (Nova Scotia then was considered the fourteenth colony). During and after the American Revolution, more than 25,000 United Empire Loyalists (including about half the living graduates of Harvard College) sought to establish a new life in British-governed Nova Scotia rather than to become citizens of a republican United States. Historians have called their migration the largest single movement of educated and cultured families in British history. The Loyalist settlement of Nova Scotia reinforced British domination of the province and upgraded all aspects of life, particularly economic enterprise and education. Before the arrival of the Loyalists, however, there had been strong sentiment in the province, particularly among former New Englanders, that Nova Scotia should join the other colonies in their cause against Great Britain. The long distance between Nova Scotia and Washington's armies, the harassing of the province's small ports by American privateers, and the strength of the British fleet in Halifax prevented this union.

Blacks (slave and free) were first brought into Nova Scotia by the Loyalists. Later, many thousands more came via the Underground Railroad. Others arrived from the British West Indies. Until the late 1960s, the Halifax-Dartmouth area had the largest concentration of blacks in Canada. Today, Toronto is the center of black life in the country.

The Scot, dressed in a colorful tartan and playing the spine-tingling bagpipe, most symbolizes the people of Nova Scotia. Both Protestant and Roman Catholic Scots fled their beloved country because of famine and political oppression, most particularly during the Highland clearances of the late eighteenth and early nineteenth centuries, when people were driven from their homes and replaced by cheviot sheep. Hardy Highlanders settled in the Cape Breton, New Glasgow–Pictou, and Antigonish areas of Nova Scotia. Their influence on the life and culture of Nova Scotia has been profound. The annual gathering of the clans, the Highland games, and various Gaelic celebrations re-create the passionate heritage of a proud

people. When you come into the province at Amherst, be sure to stop at the border and listen to the kilted piper as he plays the haunting music of the Scots. Every fourth summer, since 1979, the province hosts the International Gathering of the Clans, when clan members from all over the world participate in Scottish activities throughout the province.

But the true native people of Nova Scotia are the Micmacs, who inhabited the area for hundreds of years before Cabot set foot on the soil. Today they live in a few settlements, mostly on Cape Breton Island, and try to make progress in our modern society while retaining some of their traditional ways. Although most Nova Scotians are of the ethnic and racial backgrounds already mentioned, recent immigrants from other European countries, such as Poland and Italy, have added an even richer cultural diversity. Regardless of their background, Nova Scotians use a familiar Gaelic greeting with their guests: "Ciad Mile Failte!" (a hundred thousand welcomes).

A Place of Firsts

Nova Scotia may not be Canada's richest or most populous province, but it has honored itself by having the first Roman Catholic church in America and the first drama written and staged in America. It was the first British overseas colony with responsible government. It had the first school, common law courts, Protestant church (still used for worship), representative assembly, post office, newspaper and freedom of the press, circulating library, Masonic home, English university, legal trade union, and institute of science in Canada.

How to Get to Nova Scotia

By Car

Take Trans-Canada Highway 104 from Moncton, New Brunswick, to Amherst, Nova Scotia. Nova Scotia's roads and highways are paved, well maintained, with good signs. The hundred-series highways are high-speed roads designed for commerce and quick travel.

◀ Neil's Harbour is a quintessential Nova Scotia fishing village, located at the far end of Cape Breton Island. Not far from here John Cabot landed in 1497 and staked claim to Nova Scotia for the English king.

To experience the real Nova Scotia, to see the scenery and historic sites, to experience the festivals, to find the country inns, antique shops, parks, and campgrounds, motorists should leave the superhighways and drive the secondary roads, the seaside routes, even the unpaved country and coastal roads that frequently lead to interesting, off-the-beaten-track places.

Rental cars—Tilden, Hertz, Avis, and others—are available at airports and cities.

By Ship

Car ferries operate from the following points to various parts of Nova Scotia (advance reservations are a must):

Portland, Maine (crossing time eleven hours). The M/S *Scotia Prince* is a cruise/car liner that sails every evening from Portland and arrives the following morning in Yarmouth; it departs Yarmouth in mid morning and arrives Portland in early evening. It operates from May through October. Boarding is at the International Ferry Terminal on Commercial Street in Portland. For more information and reservations, call Prince of Fundy Cruises toll-free: Maine (800) 482–0955; rest of United States, (800) 341–7540; Nova Scotia, New Brunswick, Prince Edward Island (800) 565–7900; for rest of Canada, it's a toll call, (902) 742–5164.

Bar Harbor, Maine (crossing time six hours). The M/V *Bluenose* sails out of Bar Harbor every morning during the summer, arriving in Yarmouth in mid afternoon; it departs Yarmouth in the late afternoon and arrives in Bar Harbor that evening. This schedule is in effect from May to the end of October, with reduced schedule in the winter. The *Bluenose* features cabin accommodations, comfortable lounges, sun decks, a cafeteria, bar, newsstand, casino, and duty-free shop. It accepts autos, campers, trailers, trucks, and bikes. For more information and reservations, call Marine Atlantic at these toll-free numbers: northeastern United States except Maine, (800) 341–7981; Maine, (800) 432–7344; Ontario and Québec, (800) 565–9411; New Brunswick, Nova Scotia, and Prince Edward Island, (800) 565–9470. From all other areas, call (902) 742–3513.

Saint John, New Brunswick (crossing time two and a half to three hours). The M/V *Princess of Acadia* leaves downtown Saint John three times daily Monday through Saturday, two times on Sunday (with a reduced schedule in the winter), for Digby, Nova Scotia, across the Bay of Fundy. For more information and reservations, call Marine Atlantic at the preceding numbers.

Wood Islands, Prince Edward Island. Car ferries operate on this run from Wood Islands, Prince Edward Island, to Caribou (near Pictou), Nova Scotia, as long as the Northumberland Strait remains free of ice. Service is on a first-come basis (no reservations).

By Air

Air Canada and Canadian Airlines International and their affiliate carriers (Air Nova and Air Atlantic) have daily service to Halifax, Yarmouth, and Sydney, Nova Scotia. Contact your local travel agent for more information.

By Bus

You can travel from the United States to Nova Scotia on Greyhound; to Portland, Maine, and via the ferry M/S *Scotia Prince* to Yarmouth; to Bar Harbor, Maine, and via the ferry *Bluenose* to Yarmouth; to the New Brunswick border and via SMT Eastern Limited bus to Saint John and then on the *Princess of Acadia* to Digby, or on to Amherst for connection with Acadian Lines. From Québec, you can travel on Voyageur buses to New Brunswick, connect with SMT, and then with Acadian.

By Rail

Take Canada's VIA Rail service from Toronto, Montréal, or other cities to reach Halifax and other Nova Scotia points. There is daily service to and from Halifax. VIA Rail also serves southern and northern Nova Scotia, through the Annapolis Valley, from Halifax to Yarmouth, and to Sydney on Cape Breton Island.

General Information

Time zone: Atlantic

Telephone area code: 902

Climate and Clothing

The usual tourist season in Nova Scotia is from late May to late October. The best period to visit the province is from late June to about mid October. While July and August are the warmest months and the most popular with visitors, many people who know Nova Scotia feel that early September to mid October is one of Nova Scotia's most glorious times. The days are usually warm, crystal clear, and

278

invigorating; the nights are cool and stimulating. There is more color to the landscape, and the sea is a magnificent Prussian blue with lighter gradations. There are also fewer tourists competing for choice accommodations and dining spots. One drawback of this season is that many attractions close down, and festivals diminish in number. But the off-season is harvest time, and the farms overflow with good things to eat. Nova Scotia is generally not a destination for winter vacationers, though Halifax has become the convention center of Atlantic Canada, drawing delegates to meetings throughout the year.

Nova Scotia has a temperate climate. The temperature in Halifax, for example, averages 72°F/22°C in July and 31°F/0°C in January. In the spring and early summer there can be periods of fog along the immediate coast. If you do get caught in the fog, try exploring the interior, where the sun is sure to be shining.

You can rely on seasonal clothes, with warm sweaters and tweeds for cool evenings. Formal clothes are not necessary for evening dining, even at the better restaurants.

Tourist Information

For more information on Nova Scotia, including free brochures and maps (Nova Scotia Tourism will also help you book reservations for accommodations, ferries, and transportation), call Check In—the Nova Scotia Reservation and Travel Information System—toll-free at these numbers:

Continental United States: (800) 341–6096

Nova Scotia, Prince Edward Island, and New Brunswick: (800) 565–7105

Newfoundland and Québec: (800) 565–7180

Central and Southern Ontario: (800) 565–7140

Northern Ontario, Manitoba, Saskatchewan, Alberta, British Columbia, Northwest Territories, and the Yukon: (800) 565–7166

Halifax and Dartmouth: (902) 425–5781

Tourist information can be obtained at provincial information centers at Portland, Maine, Yarmouth, Amherst, Pictou, Antigonish, Halifax downtown, Post Hastings, Annapolis Royal, Digby, Wood Islands, Prince Edward Island, and the Halifax Airport terminal.

Major Events

During the summer season, all kinds of festivals and events happen in many communities almost every day; thus, Nova Scotia was appointed Canada's official "Festival Province." The list that follows is only partial. Most festivals consist of parades, theater, sporting events, handicraft displays, music, games, and abundant offerings of local foods. These happy doings attract large crowds, and it is therefore necessary to book your lodgings (for example, in Antigonish during the Highland Games) well in advance. Reservations are also necessary for many theatrical and musical events where seating is limited. On the other hand, you need not stay overnight in a festival-crowded town: Just drop in for the day's events, enjoy, and then move on to your next destination. If you have trouble finding a place to sleep, most towns have a tourist bureau to solve your problems and make you feel welcome.

May
Scotia Festival of Music, Halifax
Apple Blossom Festival, Annapolis Valley

June
Children's Festival, Baddeck
Shelburne County Lobster Festival
Nova Scotia Forestry Exhibition, Windsor
Multicultural Festival, Halifax/Dartmouth
Down East Jamboree, Musquodoboit Harbour
Nova Scotia Tattoo (also into early July), Halifax
Privateer Days, Liverpool

July
Canada Day Celebrations, throughout the province
Gathering of the Clans and Fishermen's Regatta, Pugwash
Festival Acadien de Clare, Clare
Pictou Lobster Fisheries Carnival, Pictou
Maritime Old Time Fiddling Contest, Dartmouth
Scottish Festival and Highland Games, Halifax
Lunenburg Craft Festival, Lunenburg
Maritime Old Time Jamboree, Dartmouth
Hector (Scottish) Festival, Pictou
Chester Summer Festival, Chester
Centre Bras d'Or Festival of the Arts (mid July to end August), Baddeck
Antigonish Highland Games, Antigonish
Cherry Carnival, Bear River

Seafest, Yarmouth
Festival of the Tartans, New Glasgow
Acadian Days, Grand Pré
Nova Scotia Bluegrass and Oldtime Music Festival, Ardoise in Hants County
Digby Scallop Days (into early August), Digby
Halifax and Dartmouth Natal Days (last weekend July into August), Halifax

August

Western Nova Scotia Exhibition, Yarmouth
Le Festival de l'Escaouette, Cheticomp
Grand Prix Hydroplane Races, Dartmouth and Chester Yachting Race week, Chester
Nova Scotia Gaelic Mod, South Gut St. Ann's
Lunenburg Folk Harbour Festival, Lunenburg
Sam Slick Days, Windsor
Buskers Festival, Halifax
Sand Castle and Sculpture Festival, Clam Harbour Beach
Nova Scotia Provincial Exhibition, Truro
Yarmouth International Air Show, Yarmouth

September

Shearwater International Air Show, Shearwater
Nova Scotia Fisheries Exhibition and Fishermen's Reunion, Lunenburg
Oktoberfest, Tatamagouche
International Town Criers' Competition, Halifax
Hants County Exhibition (agriculture), Windsor

Provincial Parks and Campgrounds

Parks for picnicking and other daytime activities are maintained by the government. They are typically located off principal roads and highways throughout the province. Watch for the picnic table sign. Some of these wayside stops provide access to swimming and hiking areas; all have water, picnic tables, and toilet facilities.

Most government-operated campgrounds provide basic services (water, firewood, tables, toilets, and fireplaces). Some have more extensive services, such as electrical hookups, showers, sewage disposal, organized activities, and so on. They are, by and large, situated in wooded areas or near other beautiful natural sights, such as the ocean. The camping season begins in early May and extends into October, though some campgrounds close after Labour Day. Fees are nominal. For more information on these and the large number of privately operated campgrounds in Nova Scotia, call Nova Scotia Tourism at the telephone numbers given earlier in this chapter.

Sports

For a moderate day rate, you can charter a boat for deep-sea fishing and its skipper, with bait and gear provided. Tuna is a major sports fish off Nova Scotia's Atlantic coast. No licenses are required, except for sea trout, salmon, and striped bass. Licenses are required for all freshwater angling.

Hunting is also a passion: deer, black bear, partridge, pheasant, grouse, woodcock, and goose. All visiting hunters must employ guides. For complete information on regulations, licenses, and outfitters for both both fishing and hunting, call Nova Scotia Tourism.

Nova Scotia also offers excellent canoeing, ocean boating, windsurfing, golfing, shipwreck diving, river rafting, wilderness excursions, bike touring, hiking treks, ocean and lake swimming, downhill skiing, cross-country skiing, snowmobiling, and tennis. Information on organizations providing services and locations for these sports can be obtained through Nova Scotia Tourism.

Accommodations

Good accommodations are abundant throughout Nova Scotia. They range from plush hotels and world-famous resorts to hotels, motels, tourist homes, Bed and Breakfasts, farm vacations, and campgrounds. The provincial government inspects all accommodations, which must meet strict standards of cleanliness and safety.

During the summer tourist season, Nova Scotia accommodations all do a brisk business. Advance reservations are a must, particularly for Halifax and those communities in which major festivals are taking place.

The government of Nova Scotia has established the Check Inns service, where you can reserve accommodations by calling Nova Scotia Tourism toll-free.

Nova Scotia Farm and Country Vacations

Here is your chance to live with Nova Scotia country people, to be part of their families. You are invited to eat at their tables, and their food is the best because they raise most of it. You can do chores and participate in the activities of the family and the local community. You can stay for an overnight or for the entire summer. You can come up yourself or with your family, whatever your race, ethnic group, or religion. The accommodations and the meals are inexpensive—the best value going. For more information on the location of the farms, contact Nova Scotia Tourism.

Dining

Nova Scotia's best cuisine is based on native foods: fresh fruits and vegetables, fish (cod, halibut, swordfish, haddock, and flounder), shellfish (lobster, scallops, and clams), homemade soups and chowders, and hot-from-the-oven pies and bread. Occasionally you come across Scottish oatcakes, scones, shortbread, and haggis (oatmeal mixed with ground organ meats, sometimes soaked in whiskey, and baked in a sheep's stomach), and French-Acadian rapi-pie, a pork and potato concoction. Halifax offers Nova Scotia's largest concentration of excellent restaurants, and there are many other restaurants with fine reputations scattered throughout the province.

Liquor can be purchased at government-operated stores in major towns and all cities Monday through Saturday. You can also buy liquor in restaurants, bars, and cabarets. The minimum drinking age is nineteen.

Touring Nova Scotia

Exploring

Nova Scotia offers a great deal of diversity to the traveler, and the constant problem is not having enough time to do everything. Here are some suggestions that will make your Nova Scotia holiday more enjoyable.

Visit the small coastal and rural villages. Many times this means traveling on narrow dirt roads, but the fine scenery and the quiet, simple, and unhurried way of life are worth the effort. After all, that's what vacations are for. Talk to the people, and you will hear stories not told in any book, about ship disasters and valiant

men and women. Find out who does the carving or weaving in the town or village—you may find some excellent values. In many communities you can also purchase fresh fish and lobster, home-baked cakes and breads, and newly harvested fruits and vegetables. These are personal discoveries that you will never find in any guidebook, no matter how comprehensive.

One of the most interesting aspects of talking with the local people is hearing the various English dialects (and French in the Acadian towns). Some of them may sound like foreign or ancient languages. And Nova Scotia's sense of peace and harmony is very difficult to find in our modern world. Many of the villages and the surrounding scenery are a feast for the eye; a camera or a sketch book is a must. It is also in the off-the-main-road places that you will find the empty bit of coastline (empty of what passes for human civilization) or the quiet nook where you can be by yourself in the midst of a magnificent natural world.

Nova Scotia's road system is divided into nine theme trails to make touring more interesting: the Evangeline Trail, the Glooscap Trail, Halifax-Dartmouth, the Lighthouse Route, the Sunrise Trail, the Marine Drive, the Cabot Trail, the Fleur-de-Lis Trail, and the Ceilidh Trail. Each is well marked, and distinctive signs highlight major attractions en route.

Yarmouth to Halifax via the Evangeline Trail

The Evangeline Trail, Highway 1, from Yarmouth to Windsor, runs along the coast of the Bay of Fundy and through the Annapolis Valley. Explore the English and the French-Acadian fishing and farming settlements. There are plenty of antique shops along the way as well as places to buy local crafts, produce, and home-baked goods.

Yarmouth serves as terminal for the *Scotia Prince* and *Bluenose* car ferries from Portland and Bar Harbor, Maine, and is thus a major gateway to and from the province for thousands of visitors each year. Yarmouth airport also receives visitors traveling Air Canada. Settled in 1761 by New England families, it is western Nova Scotia's center for commerce, shopping, and distribution. It is a good place to get your bearings when you arrive and to buy

◀ **At Grand Pré National Park, visit the old Acadian chapel (the Church of Saint Charles) and see the lovely statue of Evangeline, the heroine immortalized by Longfellow. This is, after all, the original land of the Acadians, who were sent into their diaspora by the British.**

last-minute gifts (fine woolens and English bone china) before you leave. Be sure to visit the Fire Fighters Museum at 451 Main Street, which has thirty-four engines, including two 1840 Hunneman engines and an 1880 Silsby steamer. Open throughout the year. Admission charge. The Yarmouth County Historical Society Museum, 22 Collins Street, features an old runic stone, found in 1812 and said to have been scribbled on by Leif Eriksson himself. Open throughout the year. Admission charge. While waiting for the ferry, take the road out of Yarmouth Light on Cape Forchu. You will go by some tiny fishing hamlets and end up at a dramatic granite headland marking the entrance to the harbor.

Because of the large number of people passing through Yarmouth, be sure to reserve lodgings ahead. Here are several Yarmouth lodgings and restaurants for you to consider:

Capri Motel, 577 Main Street, (902) 742–7168, offers a swimming pool, dining room, and lounge. Moderate.

Rodd's Colony Harbour Inn, adjacent to the ferry terminal, (902) 742–9194, offers a convenient location, good rooms, restaurant, and lounge. Moderate.

Rodd's Grand Hotel, 417 Main Street, (902) 742–2446, provides full hotel services, one of the best in the area. A good dining room features beef and seafood dishes. Moderate to expensive.

Mermaid Motel, 545 Main Street, (902) 742–7821, offers swimming pool and restaurant. Moderate.

Lakelawn Motel, 641 Main Street, (902) 742–3588, serves breakfast. Moderate.

The Gables Bed and Breakfast, 55 William Street, (902) 742–4404. Moderate.

Manor Inn, in Hebron, a few miles north of Yarmouth on Highway 1, (902) 742–2487, was once the grand lakeside mansion of a shipping tycoon. It has beautiful lawns, shade trees, and a rose garden. Rooms are available in the mansion and adjacent building. It offers an excellent dining room, lounges, and various recreations. A memorable place to stay. Expensive.

Captain Kelly's Kitchen, 557 Main Street, (902) 742–9191, a very popular restaurant, is conveniently located in an old mansion. Seafood and beef dishes are prepared with skill. Moderate.

Harris's Seafood, north of the center of town on Highway 1, (902) 742–5420, is open for lunch and dinner until 11:00 P.M. Some knowledgeable travelers consider Harris's to be one of Atlantic Canada's best seafood restaurants. Moderate.

The Austrian Inn, in the Dayton area, (902) 742–6202, offers savory meat and seafood dishes. Moderate.

After leaving Yarmouth, you'll pass through **Hebron,** with its marvelous display of white, pink, and blue lupines growing alongside the highway in June and covering nearby fields. Then you'll enter a district known as **Clare** (or the **French Shore,** because of the string of French-Acadian towns). Here you'll have sweeping views of the rural countryside and the waters of the Bay of Fundy; the French villages are charming and accented with large churches. Be on the lookout for places selling fresh bread and side roads leading to the Fundy shore for a picnic (the water there is too cold for swimming).

In **Meteghan** visit La Vieille Maison, an eighteenth-century Acadian house, furnished with artifacts from that period. Open daily late June to Labour Day. Admission charge.

Church Point claims to have the largest wooden church (Saint Mary's) in the world, and it is well worth a few clicks of your camera. Inside is an excellent museum of early church vestments and furnishings and of historical documents. Open late June to about mid September. Free. Next to the church is Sainte Anne's College, a degree-conferring institution with students of mostly French-Acadian descent. The annual Acadian Festival of Clare in July is well worth attending. Two restaurants in town specializing in Acadian cuisine and seafood are Tides-Inn-Marée Haute Restaurant, and Restaurant Le Casse–Croûte.

You won't miss seeing the great stone church in **Saint Bernard** because it so dominates the landscape. It was built by the parishioners and seats one thousand.

Weymouth was founded by Loyalists from Massachusetts in 1783. Wood products are manufactured here, and hydroelectric energy is produced on the Sissiboo River.

Digby is a popular town with tourists and an important shipping point. Its harbor opens on the Bay of Fundy. The car ferry *Princess of Acadia* provides a shortcut between Nova Scotia and Saint John, New Brunswick. Digby has one of the largest scallop fleets in the world, and the tiny scallops they catch are absolutely delicious. If you're in Digby in early August, enjoy the Scallop Days Festival. For a good view of the Annapolis Basin, go to the top of the hill near the high school or to the lighthouse at Point Prim, north of town. The Admiral Digby Museum has furnishings, maps, and photographs of local interest. Open Monday through Friday afternoons, mid June to mid September. Free. The area offers hunting, angling, saltwater fishing, and superb golf at the Pines Resort. Take a side trip to Smith's Cove, a favored resort area, or out to Brier's Island, land's end on Digby Neck (via Highway 217). At the dam on the Great Basin of Annapolis, you can see a tidal rise of 21 to 28 feet/6.4 to 8.5 m. twice every twenty-four hours. For accommodations and dining try the following:

Admiral Digby Inn, French Shore Road, (902) 245–2431, has a heated swimming pool, dining room, and lounge. Moderate to expensive.

Hedley House Motor Hotel, at Smith's Cove, (902) 245–2585, offers various recreational facilities, including a beach. Moderate. Its dining room overlooks the water and provides good food and fine service. Moderate.

Mountain Gap Inn and Resort, at Smith's Cove, (902) 245–2277, features various recreational activities on twenty-five acres, a dining room and lounge. Moderate.

The Pines Resort Hotel, near the center of town, (902) 245–2511, is a complete resort, one of the best in Atlantic Canada. Expensive. Its main dining room serves well-executed, varied cuisine and is the best place in town to eat. Moderate to expensive.

For good, wholesome country cooking, have a meal at the Bon E Lass, on Highway 1, in Smith's Cove.

Bear River calls itself the "Switzerland of Nova Scotia": A bit of exaggeration must be tolerated here. At any rate, the town is well worth a visit to see its quaint shops (many of which sell local handicrafts) set on stilts on the Bear River (a prime striped bass estuary). Don't miss the Dutch windmill, built by local artisans and featuring a tea room. In July enjoy the Cherry Carnival.

Visit Old Saint Edwards Church Museum in **Clementsport,** built like a wooden sailing ship (with hand-hewn timbers and wood peg fasteners) and once used as a lighthouse. Open during the summer. Free. **Upper Clements** has a wildlife park (with lynx, fox, bear, and cougar). Open mid May to mid October; free.

Annapolis Royal, first settled in the seventeenth century, is one of the most charming towns in Nova Scotia. It has tree-lined streets and handsome old homes. The town's central attraction is Fort Anne, a national historic park with fortifications and ruins dating to 1710. Open April to late October. Free.

A major renewal and redevelopment project has refurbished numerous historic attractions and created new ones at Annapolis

Royal. Three museums—the O'Dell Inn (a Victorian stagecoach inn), the Pickels and Mills store, and McNamara House—have been redecorated. The Adams-Ritchie House, believed to be the oldest building of British origin in Canada (circa 1712), has been salvaged, and forty-nine other houses and buildings have been earmarked for restoration. A waterfront walkway has been constructed; other projects in the downtown area are planned. The restored King's Theatre, on St. George Street, puts on comedies and musicals during the summer.

On the causeway between Annapolis Royal and Granville Ferry, Nova Scotia's massive tidal power project is under construction. This hydroelectric power installation will generate electricity from the tides of the Bay of Fundy. This power, approximately fifty million kilowatt hours of electricity per year, displacing about eighty thousand barrels of foreign oil, is serving the needs of Nova Scotia.

The Annapolis Royal Historic Gardens attract many visitors. The ten-acre site fronting the Allain River features three theme areas designed and planted to represent seventeenth-century Acadian, eighteenth-century British, and Victorian periods of the community's past. Admission charge. There is an excellent Victorian-style dining room here, complete with gazebo and patio overlooking the gardens.

Accommodations and dining are available at the Royal Anne Motel, west of town on Highway 1, (902) 532–2323, with twenty units and a dining room, moderate; Bread and Roses Country Inn, 82 Victoria Street, (902) 532–5727, an excellent Bed and Breakfast place in a fine old home, moderate; and the Moorings, Granville Ferry, (902) 388–0295, on the road to Port Royal but also convenient to Annapolis Royal, another good Bed and Breakfast, inexpensive. The Garrison House Inn, on St. George Street, (902) 532–5750, is an historic lodging offering fine accommodations and dining, moderate. Newman's Restaurant, on St. George Street, (902) 532–5502, is a top place for gourmet food, moderate. The Queen Ann Inn, 494 Upper St. George Street, (902) 532–7850, is well known for its buffet suppers, homemade soups, and seafood chowders, moderate.

In **Granville Ferry,** visit the North Hills Museum, which has a fine collection of Georgian furniture, ceramics, silver, and glass. Open daily mid May to mid October. Free. From Granville Ferry watch for the signs to Port Royal. The Port Royal National Historic Park, a reconstruction of Champlain's 1605 settlement, at the exact location, is one of the most important historical sites in all of Atlantic

Canada. It offers visitors a real sense of what life was like in this speck of European civilization set in a vast wilderness. Open April to the end of October. Free.

Kejimkujik National Park is located off Highway 8, which passes through Annapolis Royal. Kejimkujik is a vast inland area of forest, lakes, and streams. It offers camping, hiking, boating, canoeing (rentals available), swimming, fishing, and nature walks. Also see the interesting Indian pictographs. Open throughout the year. Free.

The Evangeline Trail now moves through the agriculturally rich **Annapolis Valley.** The valley is flanked on both sides by high hills (called mountains by Nova Scotians in this part of the province). Be on the lookout for the many roadside stands selling fresh fruits and vegetables, wonderful for munching while you travel or for the evening meal if you're bringing your own cooking gear. In season you can pick your own fruits and vegetables at some farms.

Bridgetown, in the midst of farming and dairying country, is a manufacturing center. Stop in at the James House, circa 1837, for tea and a look at historical displays. Open July and August. Free. There's also a public swimming pool in town. Accommodations and dining are available at the Bridgetown Motor Hotel, 83 Granville Street, (902) 665–4491, which features a pool, sauna, and dining room, moderate. Dine at the Revere, 38 Queen Street, for seafood and Sunday buffets.

Lawrencetown is where the Annapolis County Agricultural Exhibition takes place in August. Land surveying and photogrammetry is taught here, attracting students from all over Canada. It is also headquarters for fishermen and hunters, where they can pick up canoes, equipment, and guides.

At **Middleton** visit the Annapolis Valley MacDonald Museum, which has a large collection of old clocks. In **Wilmot** some of the Loyalist descendants of John Alden and Priscilla Mullins (of *Mayflower* and Plymouth Colony fame) settled. **Kingston** is home for the Kingston Bible College and Nova Scotia's largest steer barbecue, held on the second Saturday of July. Canada's largest antisubmarine air base is located at **Greenwood.** At **Auburn** is Saint Mary's Church, circa 1790, with walls plastered with mussel shells and windows carried by foot soldiers from Halifax.

Kentville is the shire town (administrative center) of Kings County and the largest community in the valley. The Canada Department of Agriculture Research Station, specializing in poultry and horticulture, is here, and you are welcome to visit its beautiful grounds. Open throughout the year. Free. The town also has a public swimming pool and tennis courts. The Annapolis Valley Apple Blossom Festival is centered in Kentville, and Rhododendron Sunday is celebrated here in June with magnificent floral displays. For accommodations and dining, try Allen's Motel, Highway 1, (902) 678–2683, with a dining room and picnic area, inexpensive; Sun Valley Motel, 905 Park Street, (902) 678–7368, featuring a coffee shop and convenience to recreational facilities, inexpensive; and Auberge Wandlyn Inn, in Colbrook, Highways 1 and 101, (902) 678–8311, the best in the area, with many facilities and services, including a dining room and lounge, moderate.

A few miles outside of Kentville is **Starr's Point,** which has the Prescott House, a fine example of Georgian architecture, with an exceptional garden. It's worth the side trip. **Blomidon Look Off** offers a spectacular panoramic view of Minas Basin and four Nova Scotia counties. The nature trail system at **Cape Split** is one of the most popular in Nova Scotia.

Lovely **Wolfville** is named after a Connecticut settler, Judge Elisha DeWolfe. In town is the well-known Acadia University, founded by the Nova Scotia Baptist Education Society in 1838. You will enjoy strolling through its tranquil campus. Visit the free Wolfville Historical Museum, with its collection of artifacts relating to the early New England planters. Open mid June to mid September. Free. Wolfville was the center for the old Acadian country, before the Acadians were sent into exile by the British. Nearby are **Grand Pré** and **Grand Pré National Historic Park,** a reconstruction of an old Acadian chapel (the Church of Saint Charles) holds a museum of artifacts and paintings commemorating the Acadian settlement and expulsion (1675–1755). This beautifully landscaped site is pictured in Longfellow's poem *Evangeline,* and a stunning statue of the lovely lady stands in front of the chapel. A bust of Longfellow is nearby. Open early April until Labour Day. Free. Grounds open all year. On a nearby hill is the old Church of the Covenanters, which was built in the 1790s by New England planters. It is noted for its unique pew boxes, sounding boards, and a pulpit that rises halfway to the ceiling. Be sure to explore the surrounding countryside to see the land that the Acadians reclaimed from the sea by constructing dikes. Through their system of dikes, they created extremely productive agricultural land from an area of wet marshes. Also here is the

Grand Pré Estate Vineyard in the Annapolis Valley. Visitors are welcome to tour the vineyard and taste the wines produced at this facility.

Area accommodations and dining facilities include the following:

Victoria's Historic Inn, 416 Main Street, Wolfville, (902) 542–5744, a fine old inn near Acadia University with a dining room, tea garden, and art gallery. Moderate.

Blomidon Inn, 127 Main Street, Wolfville, (902) 542–2291, the home of a former shipowner, has seven fireplaces, four-poster mahogany beds, hand-crafted quilts, and antiques. It also has a fine dining room. Moderate.

Old Orchard Inn, Highway 101, Greenwich, (902) 542–5751, features many recreational facilities, a fine dining room and lounge, entertainment. Expensive.

Roselawn Cottages, 32 Main Street, Wolfville, (902) 542–3420, has housekeeping cottages and efficiency units. Moderate.

Chez La Vigne, 17 Front Street, (902) 542-5077, excellent fresh seafood and homemade desserts. Moderate.

Grand Pré's Evangeline Motel, Highway 1, Grand Pré, (902) 542-2703, near the national historic park, serves breakfast and lunch. Inexpensive to moderate.

On the road from Grand Pré is the town of **Hantsport.** Here is the Churchill House and Maritime Museum, dating from 1860 and housing an excellent collection of shipwrights' tools, ship models, and other seafaring objects. Hantsport was the home of William Hall, R.M., son of a Virginia slave and the first black to win the Victoria Cross.

Windsor is the site of Fort Edward Blockhouse, the oldest such structure in Canada. Built in 1750, it was a major assembly point in the expulsion of the Acadians. Open June 1 to Labour Day (Canadian). Free. Don't miss the Haliburton House, former home of Judge Thomas Chandler Haliburton, creator of the funny Sam Slick stories. His Victorian house, called Clifton, is furnished with fine antiques and set on twenty-five beautifully landscaped acres, including gardens. Open mid May to end October. Free. Windsor is a pleasant town in which to relax before Halifax, your next major stop. Windsor also has King's-Edgehill, one of the top private prep schools in the country.

On your way to Halifax, you should consider visiting **Mount Uniacke,** which has the stately Uniacke House, one of the finest mansions in all of Atlantic Canada. Open mid May to end October. Free.

Yarmouth to Halifax via the Lighthouse Route

An alternate route from Yarmouth to Halifax, Highway 3, along the south coast of Nova Scotia, is known as the Lighthouse Route because of the numerous offshore lighthouses and beacons, which for centuries have guided the fishing boats and marine traffic to safety along the indented shore. The Lighthouse Route signs point to the picturesque seafaring communities that are strung along the coast like pearls between Yarmouth and Halifax. It is here that one truly experiences the effects of the Atlantic Ocean on the Nova Scotian way of life.

The coastline here is famous for its many beaches, granite coves, beautiful fishing and sailing villages, and the hardy people who inhabit them. This is a most scenic route. Explore the side roads to see all facets of the maritime way of life and the special environment of the sea. It's special even in the fog.

Near Yarmouth is a place known as the "House of Four Peoples." Here Paul Revere, a hero of the American Revolutionary War, received his Mark degree in the York Rite of Freemasonry.

Tusket, one of the first towns out of Yarmouth, was founded by Dutch Loyalists from New York and New Jersey. It is said to have been Leif Eriksson's capital of Vinland, but there is no real proof that this ancient Viking ever had his "great house" here.

Outside Tusket is the road that will take you down a scenic peninsula to **Wedgeport,** a port famous for its tuna fishing fleet and tuna tournaments. You can hire a boat here. The peninsula is inhabited mainly by French-Acadians.

The **Pubnicos** (West, Middle West, Lower West, East, Middle East, and Lower East) are small farming and fishing towns, with an Acadian citizenry. See the Acadian Museum of Yarmouth County in **West Pubnico.** Open during the summer. Free.

Take a tour of **Cape Sable,** the most southerly area on Nova Scotia, via Highway 330. Visit the Archelaus Smith Museum of maritime lore. Open July to mid September. Free.

Barrington has places for swimming and trout fishing. It was settled by people from Cape Cod and Nantucket in 1760, many of them progeny of the *Mayflower* Pilgrims. Barrington has the oldest Nonconformist church in Canada. Visit the Old Meeting House, the only surviving New England–style meeting house in Nova Scotia.

Open mid June to late September. Free. And take in the exhibits at the Cape Sable Historical Society. Open July to the end of August. Free.

Shelburne was one of the major Loyalist settlements. About 10,000 New Yorkers, most of them aristocrats, started a new life in Canada here, creating North America's fourth largest city in one settling. It's a lovely old town with many fine buildings. You'll want to linger a bit. Shelburne is also known as the birthplace of yachts. Donald MacKay, the great Boston clipper-ship builder, learned his craft in Shelburne. Visit the Ross Thompson House (circa 1784), a Loyalist-era store and home. Open mid May to end October. Free. And see the shipbuilding and genealogical exhibits at the Shelburne County Museum. Open throughout the year. Free.

For accommodations and dining in Shelburne, try the comfortable Cape Cod Colony Motel, Water Street, (902) 875–3411, which has a breakfast room, moderate; Loyalist Inn Limited, Water Street, (902) 875–2343, with a snack bar and dining room, moderate; and the Hamilton House on Main Street, (902) 875–2957, recommended for fresh seafood, steaks, and chowder, moderate.

At **Jordan Falls,** look for the road on the right that will take you to **Lockeport.** Lockeport has a fine beach and fishing boats for hire. The town was founded by people from Plymouth, Massachusetts. Visit the Little School Museum, July to Labour Day. Free.

Port Mouton offers white sand beaches and seafood dining from local catches. Sieur-de-Monts gave the town its name because of sheep lost overboard during a visit in 1604.

Liverpool has a swashbuckling past. It was a main port for privateers. There is good canoeing and salmon fishing in the nearby Medway River and a beach for swimming at Battery Point. Visit the Simeon Perkins House, featuring nineteenth-century furnishings. Open mid May to end October. Free. The Perkins House, formerly a rectory, was once occupied by a relative of the great American patriot Daniel Webster. A fish hatchery in town might be of interest to children. Highway 8 from Liverpool leads to Kejimkujik National Park.

For accommodations and dining in the Liverpool area, try Lane's Privateer Motor Inn, at the east end of Liverpool Bridge, (902) 354–3456, which offers canoe rental, boat launching, and a dining room. Moderate. White Point Beach Lodge Resort, on Highway 3, (902) 354–3177, has good accommodations, dining, live entertainment, fishing, biking, swimming, and many other amenities and recreations. Moderate to expensive. Mersey House Restaurant, 149 Main Street, (902) 354–5783, serves a broad menu of continental dishes, seafood, steaks, and English pub lunches. Moderate.

Bridgewater is an industrial center and grows Christmas trees for the Canadian and American markets. There are plenty of stores in town for your shopping needs. Visit the De Brisay Museum and Park, which has an extensive collection of old coins and artifacts of the early settlers. Open throughout the year. Free. Also visit the Wile Carding Mill, a mid-nineteenth-century woolen mill. Open mid May to the end of September. Free. At **La Have,** a side trip via Highway 332, is the Fort Point Museum, part of the 1632 Fort Saint Marie de Grace National Historic Site. Open July and August. Free.

Bridgewater accommodations and dining include Best Western Bridgewater Motor Inn, 35 High Street, (902) 543–8171, with a swimming pool and dining room, moderate; The Mariner Inn, 324 Aberdeen Road, (902) 543–5545, with a swimming pool and dining room, moderate; Auberge Wandlyn Inn, 50 North Street, (902) 543–7131, with a good dining room, lounge, and many conveniences, moderate to expensive.

Highway 332 also leads to **Riverport** and the *Ovens Natural Park*. In the mid 1800s there was a gold rush here, and you can see monuments, caverns, and a museum associated with that feverish period. The best part of the Ovens is hiking along the high cliffs with the sea crashing below. Well worth the side trip. Open end of May to about mid September. Free.

Take Highway 3 or continue on 332 to **Lunenburg,** the most important seafaring town on this coast outside of Halifax. This was the home of the famous racing schooner *Bluenose*, a replica of which you can see in Halifax from May to October and in Lunenburg during the rest of the year. The original *Bluenose* was champion (1921–46) of the International Schooner Races. Settled by people from Germany, France, and Switzerland, Lunenburg still reflects the Germanic influence. The noteworthy Victorian architecture suggests that this is a hard working but prosperous place. Don't miss the Fisheries Museum of the Atlantic, which consists of three vessels you can board: the dragger *Cape North*, the rum-runner *Reo-2*, and the schooner *Theresa E. Connor*. This museum also has exhibits in various waterfront buildings and films in the Ice House Theatre. Open mid May to end October. Admission charge (special rates for children, school groups, and so on). Poke around in the interesting shipyard where a replica of the H.M.S. *Bounty* was built. Visit

beautiful Saint John's Church (Anglican), founded by royal charter in 1754. If you can, attend the Nova Scotia Fisheries Exhibition and Fisherman's Reunion in September.

From Lunenburg, a nice, short drive via Highway 3 takes you to the fishing village of **Blue Rocks**. The scenery around here is wonderful for the artist and the photographer, for picnickers and people in love.

In **Blockhouse**, via Highway 3A, visit the Roaring 20's Museum, a private collection of antique automobiles. Open mid May through September. Admission charge. In **Parkdale**, via Highway 10 and New Germany, see the Parkdale-Maplewood Museum for historical artifacts and exhibits focusing on the German heritage of the area. Open during the summer. Free.

Accommodations and dining in Lunenburg include the comfortable Belroy Motel, near the high school and fairgrounds, (902) 634–8867, which has a comfortable dining room, moderate, and Bluenose Lodge, 10 Falkland Street, (902) 634–8851, offers good accommodations and features a popular dining room specializing in heaping fisherman's platters, moderate. Also in town are the Compass Rose, 15 King Street, (902) 634–8509; Lion Inn, 33 Cornwallis Street, (902) 634–8509; Chillingsworth, 52 MacDonald Street, (902) 634–3701; the Boscowan Inn, 150 Cumberland Street, (902) 634–3325; and Ashlea House, 42 Falkland Street, (902) 634–3455. All these guest places are inexpensive to moderate. Lobster suppers are served at the Dolphin of Lunenburg, on Pelham Street. The Rum Runner Inn, on Montague Street, overlooking the Fisheries Museum, serves lobster and other seafood. Yellow Dragon, also on Montague Street, is the town's Chinese restaurant.

In pretty **Mahone Bay,** via Highway 3, three churches stand side by side, a striking ecclesiastical formation that provides a perfect subject for your camera. In town are handicraft shops: Suttles and Seawinds, Birdsall and Worthington Pottery, The TeAzer, The Whirligig, and Amos Peweters. Accommodations in Mahone Bay include the Sou'Western Inn, on Main Street, (902) 624–9296; and Bayview Pines Country Inn, Rural Road 2 at Indian Point, (902) 624–9970. Both places are moderate. Zwicker's Inn, on Main Street, (902) 624–8045, is well known for food prepared with care, creativity, and the freshest ingredients, moderate. Also in town is the Cape

◀ You can come on board these vessels when you visit the important fishing town of Lunenburg, where the famous racing schooner *Bluenose* was built.

House Inn, on Highway 3, (902) 624–8211, a restored settlers home overlooking the bay, serving good country food for lunch and dinner. In the bay itself is **Oak Island,** where the pirate Captain Kidd is supposed to have buried a treasure beyond imagining. Though people have dug on the island for decades (some quite scientifically), the treasure remains the old cutthroat's secret. Best Western Oak Island Inn and Marina, located between Mahone Bay and Chester, (902) 627–2600, offers fine accommodations and dining, also boat cruises to and tours of Oak Island. Moderate.

Chester, via Highway 3, set at the end of a peninsula, has long been a refuge for the affluent and retired high-ranking military. Chester is a pleasant, beautiful place, with a fine golf course, ferry trips to the Tancook Islands, and an excellent puppet theater. The best accommodations in town are at the Windjammer Motel, off Highway 3, (902) 275–3567, which has a well-known restaurant. Moderate. The Captain's House, 129 Central Street, (902) 275–3501, offers good accommodations and fine seafood dining, with a splendid view of the harbor. Moderate. The Galley at South Shore Marine, at Marriotts Cove, serves home-style cooking and seafood. Moderate. The Rope Loft Dining Room overlooks the harbor and offers seafood, steak, pasta, and salads. Moderate. There is an amusing story of how the women of Chester saved the town from an attacking U.S. ship in 1782. With their husbands absent, the women wore scarlet-lined skirts over their dresses and shouldered broomsticks and children played the drums, causing the ship to withdraw because they thought a full British garrison was there.

The Ross Farm, on Highway 12, north of Chester at **New Ross,** is Nova Scotia's official agricultural museum, designed to preserve the agricultural heritage of Nova Scotia and to foster an appreciation of early rural life. A restored nineteenth-century farm, Ross Farm uses the old methods of farming, including teams of oxen. Open mid May to mid October. Admission charge.

Back on Highway 103, turn off at Highway 333 to go directly to the Peggy Cove area or stay on Highway 103 and be in Halifax in a few minutes.

Amherst to Halifax and Cape Breton Island

Amherst is the overland gateway from Canada and the United States into Nova Scotia and the geographical center of the Maritime Provinces. More people come into Nova Scotia through Amherst than through any other portal. If your route to the province is entirely by land (via New Brunswick), the Trans-Canada Highway will bring you through this nice community, with accommodations, shops, and restaurants. It is a strategic stopover before going farther into Nova Scotia or to Prince Edward Island.

The town is named after Baron Jeffery Amherst, who also gave his name to a college in Massachusetts. Be sure to visit the Nova Scotia Tourist Bureau facility at the border, where a kilted bagpiper welcomes you. You can see the famous Tantramar Marshes from viewpoints in town. From Amherst it is easy to get to Cape Breton Island via the Trans-Canada Highway 104 or to Halifax via the Trans-Canada to Truro and then Highway 102.

Auberge Wandlyn Inn, at the Victoria Street exit of the Trans-Canada, (902) 667–3331, offers many conveniences, a dining room, and a lounge. Moderate.

Amherst Shore Country Inn, on Highway 366, (902) 667–4800, is the best restaurant in this part of Nova Scotia—Spanish tomato soup, sole with rice and pecan filling, Flemish Dijon chicken, blueberry flan, fresh fruit Romanoff. Moderate to expensive.

Emerald Palace Restaurant, 85 Victoria Street, (902) 667–3371, serves Chinese and Canadian food. Inexpensive to moderate.

Bird's Family Restaurant, in downtown, serves fresh baked breads, seafood, meat dishes, and sandwiches. Inexpensive.

At **Minudie,** via Highways 302 and 242, overlooking the Cumberland Basin and a short trip from Amherst, is the Amos Seaman School Museum, with its collection of memorabilia commemorating the life of a successful nineteenth-century merchant and industrialist. Open early July to early September. Free.

Also near Amherst, at **Nappan,** via Highway 302, is the Canada Department of Agriculture Experimental Farm. Open throughout the year, with picnic facilities. South of Nappan along Highway 302 a tidal bore, a singular wave in advance of the high tide, occurs on the Maccan River near the village of Maccan.

Highway 242 leads to the small Cumberland Basin community of **Joggins,** famous for its fossil fields and cliffs, where relics of prehistoric times may be picked up along the beach and in the fields, and fossilized plants may be seen embedded in the 150-foot/46-m. sandstone cliffs. This is a protected site, and interested parties must secure a permit (free of charge) from the Nova Scotia Museum in Halifax.

Via the *Glooscap Trail* (Glooscap is the man-god of the Micmac Indians), Highway 2, visit **Springhill,** exit 5 off the Trans-Canada. Springhill, in a beautiful location, is most widely known for the tragedies that have taken place in its coal mines. Its number 2 mine is the deepest in Canada. In 1881, 125 miners lost their lives, and in 1956, 39 miners died. In 1958, the entire world listened as another Springhill disaster claimed 76 lives. You can tour a (safe) real coal mine, with experienced miners as guides, and see industry exhibits at the Miners Museum. Open May 1 to the end of November. Admission charge. Springhill is also the hometown of Anne Murray, one of North America's most popular singers. The new Anne Murray Center was opened in 1988. It tells the story of Anne's fabulous career.

Parrsboro, on the Minas Basin, via Glooscap, Highway 2, is a very pretty town of tree-shaded streets and the old homes of a hardy seafaring breed. This is a good place to see the Bay of Fundy's extreme tides (the highest in the world), with large cargo ships resting on the red muddy bottom at low water. The area around the town is a rock hound's haven, where amethysts, agates, and other minerals can be found with a little diligence. Visit the Geological Museum, with its impressive collection. Free. And take Highway 209 out to the beautiful headland of Cape Spencer for the scenery and perhaps the discovery of a rare gemstone. The Maple Inn, 17 Western Avenue, (902) 254–3735, is recommended for accommodations and dining, as is the Glooscap Motel, on Highway 2, (902) 254–3135, which serves breakfast. Both are moderate. My Place Dining Room on Church Street serves home cooking, and so does the Stowaway on Main Street. Both are inexpensive.

Highway 2 from Parrsboro leads to the **Five Islands** area, five small islands in the Minas Basin. The scenery here is a photographer's delight. There is overnight camping in the area at a provincially operated park.

Not far from Great Village, at **Londonderry,** on a side road off Highway 2, is the Mines Museum, showing artifacts of mining operations in that area. Open May 1 to the end of September. Free.

Highway 2 will take you into **Truro,** where you can connect with the Trans-Canada for Cape Breton Island or to Highway 102, the fast track to Halifax. But do take time to see Truro, a manufacturing city, with underwear one of its chief products and home of the Nova Scotia Agricultural College, on Bible Hill, and the province's Teachers' College. Enjoy the Olympic-size pool and pleasant parks here. Visit the Colchester Historical Society Museum (human and natural history). Open throughout the year. Admission charge.

Truro accommodations and dining are available at the following places:

Berry's Motel, 73 Robie Street, (902) 895–5823, is comfortable and serves breakfast. Moderate.

Best Western Glengarry Motel, 150 Willow Street, (902) 893–4311, features a swimming pool, spacious grounds, dining room, and lounge. Moderate.

Keddy's Motor Inn, 437 Prince Street, downtown Truro, (902) 895–1651, has many conveniences, a dining room, and a lounge with entertainment. Moderate.

Palliser Resort, off Highway 102 at exit 14, (902) 893–8951, has good accommodations and dining. Moderate.

For delicious Italian specialties cooked to order, call the Paesanella, on Bible Hill, (902) 893–7011, for orders to go; for steaks, try the Glengarry Motel's dining room. Both are priced moderate.

Just below Truro off Highway 102, en route to Halifax, is a provincial wildlife park at **Shubenacadie,** which has many birds and animals common to Nova Scotia, including a small herd of Sable Island ponies. Because the animals are wild, parents are advised to supervise their children so that they will not get injured or molest the animals. There are picnic facilities here. Open mid May to mid October. Free. Shubenacadie also has a Micmac Indian reserve and roadside stands selling Indian handicrafts.

In **Walton,** via Highway 215, is the Walton Museum (local history). Also on Highway 215, in **Maitland,** is the Lawrence House, home of the late William D. Lawrence, member of Parliament and builder of the largest full-rigged wooden ship in Canada. Highway 14, off Highway 102, leads to the South Rawdon Museum, in **South Rawdon,** which has exhibits of the local temperance movement. Open mid June to mid September. Free.

If you're heading straight to Cape Breton Island from Amherst, you can take the Trans-Canada (Highway 104) to the causeway at the Canso Strait. However, a more scenic route is the *Sunrise Trail* (Highway 6), which runs parallel to the Trans-Canada and along the Northumberland shore. The Sunrise Trail gives you access not only to interesting towns and villages, but also to beaches with the warmest water in Nova Scotia.

Highway 6 is a major road out of Amherst. It passes through **Pugwash,** the birthplace and summer home of industrialist Cyrus Eaton, and original site of the internationally known Thinkers' Conferences, which brought outstanding people from all over the world to this lovely community. Pugwash offers good bathing in warm waters, fishing, and golf.

Continue on to **Wallace,** the birthplace of Simon Newcomb, a world-renowned astronomer and mathematician.

At **Tatamagouche** is the Sunrise Trail Museum, which includes material belonging to the giantess Anna Swann. Open throughout the summer. Admission charge. There are many fine beaches in this area.

Highway 311 will take you to the Balmoral Grist Mill at **Balmoral Mills,** where you can see nineteenth-century machinery grind wheat, oats, and barley into flour. Open mid May to end October. Free. Nearby, on Highway 326, in **Denmark,** is the Sutherland Steam Mill (circa 1894), which manufactured carriages, wagons, doors, and sashes. Open daily mid May to mid October. Free.

At **Pictou,** via Highway 6, take time to visit the Hector National Exhibit Centre, where exhibits show the settlement of Nova Scotia by Highland Scots. The *Hector*, a decrepit Dutch ship, is famous in Canadian and Scottish history for bringing thirty-three families and twenty-five unmarried men to start a new life in the New World of 1773. This was the time of the Highland clearances, when Scots were being evicted from their ancient lands and replaced with profitable sheep. The *Hector* settlers faced a difficult time in the hostile wilds of Nova Scotia (the plight of the *Mayflower* Pilgrims seems tame in comparison), but they survived, and their progeny have flourished in Canada. Open mid May to mid October. Admission charge.

Also see Pictou's Mic Mac Museum, which celebrates the survival of the first people of Nova Scotia. Here is one of the largest archaeological discoveries of its kind in eastern Canada—an ancient Indian burial ground. Open mid June to mid September. Admission charge. The Northumberland Fisheries Museum is located in the old Pictou railway station and features items relating to the Northumberland fisheries. Open during the summer. Free. The 1806 Thomas McCulloch House is the former home of the Reverend T. McCulloch, minister, author, educator, ornithologist, and founder of Pictou Academy. Open mid May to end October. Free. In early July Pictou holds its Lobster Carnival.

In Pictou, accommodations and dining are available at comfortable MacKean's Holiday Cottages, on Highway 6, (902) 485–6147, offering housekeeping cottages with and without fireplaces, moderate, and L'Auberge, 80 Front Street, (902) 485–6900, which has good accommodations and dining, moderate. For dining, the New Consulate Restaurant on Water Street serves European and North American cuisines, moderate.

From Pictou you can reach **Caribou,** which has frequent daily ferry service to Prince Edward Island.

If you are heading for Cape Breton Island, continue on the Trans-Canada. **New Glasgow** and **Stellarton,** sister towns, off the Trans-Canada, are industrial and mining centers. New Glasgow's Pictou County Historical Museum displays its fine collection of old Trenton glassware. Nearby is the *Samson,* the first steam locomotive used in Canada. Open July 1 to Labour Day. Admission charge. Stellarton's Mining Museum and Library details the coal mining history of this area. Open mid June to the end of September. Free. At **MacPherson Mills,** via Highway 347, is MacPherson's Mills and Farm Homestead, a water-powered grist mill and restored farm complex. Open June to September. Free.

In New Glasgow, accommodations and dining are available at the Heather Motor Hotel, exit 24 off the Trans-Canada, (902) 752–8401, with a gift shop and dining room, moderate; Peter Pan Motel Limited, 390 Marsh Street, (902) 752–8327, with a heated swimming pool, dining room, and coffee shop, moderate; Sundowner Motel, exit 23 off the Trans-Canada, (902) 752–8496, with a children's play area, swimming pool, and picnic area, moderate; and the comfortable Tara Motel, exit 25 off the Trans-Canada, (902) 752–8458, which serves breakfast, moderate.

If you have a few extra hours to spare, take Highways 245 and 337 around Cape George to **Antigonish.** You will pass through quaint villages clinging to the edge of the sea. Don't miss the beautiful rolling hills, fields carpeted with colorful wildflowers, and high cliffs rising from the sea. This is a good route for backpacking and cycling. You'll want to linger a while here.

Antigonish is a Roman Catholic Scottish community. It is primarily a university town, the home of Saint Francis Xavier University and the world-famous Coady International Institute, where students from all over the world learn how to organize cooperatives, credit unions, and adult education programs in their own countries. The Antigonish movement has taught millions of poor people to become "masters of their own destiny." You are welcome to visit this beautiful campus. Also see Saint Ninian's Cathedral, inscribed in Gaelic: "Tigh Dhe" (House of God). Antigonish's famous High-

land Games, in mid July, are the biggest Scottish bash in eastern Canada. In-town accommodations are difficult to get during the games, but you can stay in surrounding towns and come into Antigonish for all the events.

Accommodations and dining are available at the following places:

Best Western Claymore Inn, Church Street, (902) 863–1050, has a heated swimming pool and dining room. Moderate.

Dingle Motel, on the Trans-Canada, (902) 863–3730, is a comfortable accommodation. Moderate.

Auberge Wandlyn Inn, 158 Main Street, (902) 863–4001, offers fine guest amenities and dining. Moderate.

Lobster Treat, on the Trans-Canada, is a top Atlantic Canada eatery specializing in lobster and steak. Moderate. Call (902) 863–5465. Also try Wongs, on Main Street, for Chinese food, and the Venice Restaurant, on College Street, for Italian, Greek, and Eastern specialties. Both inexpensive to moderate. The Goshen Restaurant, on Highway 104, (902) 863-3068, serves seafood and steaks in a Scottish setting. Moderate.

Take the Trans-Canada to **Auld Cove,** where you will cross the Canso Strait on the causeway to Cape Breton Island. There is a round-trip toll to pay when you cross the causeway.

Cape Breton Island

Once you cross the causeway, you enter into a very special part of Nova Scotia, considered by countless visitors to be the most dramatically beautiful part of the province. After touring its famous Cabot Trail and the Bras d'Or Lakes region, it is easy to understand why so many visitors make it a *must* on their itinerary. Cape Breton offers not only awesome scenery, reminiscent of the Highlands of Scotland, and pretty villages, but also significant historical sites, from John Cabot's landing in 1497 to the strong French presence at Fort Louisbourg, now resurrected from rubble. It is said that Cape Breton was once the western coast of what is now Scotland and was moved by continental drift. More Gaelic is spoken here than in Scotland.

◀ **The Highland Games at Antigonish are the Scottish version of the World Series, where cabers are tossed, swords danced over, and bagpipes skirled to the delight of thousands. Nova Scotia is also host for the International Gathering of the Clans. This is the province for you if you have Scottish blood in your veins or if you love the taste of haggis and shortbread.**

Port Hastings is your first town on Cape Breton. If you want to pull in here, you can find accommodations at Keddy's Motor Inn, junction of Highways 104 and 105, (902) 625–0460, which offers a convenient location and a dining room, moderate to expensive; Skye Motel, junction of Highways 104 and 105, (902) 625–1300, also offering a dining room, moderate; or Auberge Wandlyn Inn, off Highway 105, nearby in Port Hawkesbury, (902) 625–0320, with many conveniences, a dining room and lounge, moderate to expensive.

At Port Hastings, the Trans-Canada becomes Highway 105 to Sydney.

On your way to the Cabot Trail, which begins at Baddeck, take a side trip to the Nova Scotia Highland Village Museum at Iona, via Highway 223. This unique museum portrays the life of the early Scottish settlers in the province, with a carding mill, forge, country store, school, and settler's home. It's on a beautiful site overlooking the majestic Bras d'Or Lakes. The Highland Heights Inn, on Highway 223, (902) 622–2360, is recommended for accommodations and dining. Moderate.

The Cabot Trail

Baddeck itself is the premier resort town on the Bras d'Or Lakes. Here Alexander Graham Bell lived, and he and his beloved wife are buried at their estate, Beinn Bhreagh (not open to the public). One of the highlights of a Cape Breton visit is Baddeck's magnificent Alexander Graham Bell Museum, (902) 295–2069, which tells a comprehensive story of the great man's life and exhibits some of his inventions: aircraft, hydrofoil, and, of course, the telephone. Open July to Labour Day. Free. Also visit the Victoria County Archives and Museum. Open during the summer. Free. The children will love Cabotland, a family park of exciting rides, Micmac basket weaving, animals for touching, and picnic area. At **South Gut Saint Ann's** is the well-known Gaelic College of Celtic folk arts and Highland crafts (classes in bagpipes, band drumming, and Highland dancing, handwoven tartan goods, and so on). Also here is the Giant MacAskill Highland Pioneers Museum. Open during the summer. Free. There are beaches for swimming in the Baddeck area.

Accommodations and dining in Baddeck include the following:

Inverary Inn Resort, Shore Road, (902) 295–2674, one of the very best on Cape Breton, offers a fine dining room featuring Scottish fare (reservations suggested) and a private beach. Moderate to expensive.

Gisele's Motel, Shore Road, (902) 295–2849, is comfortable and has a good dining room. Moderate.

Cabot Trail Motel, on Highway 105, (902) 295–2580, overlooks Bras d'Or Lakes and serves breakfast. Moderate.

Silver Dart Lodge, off Highway 105, near the center of town, (902) 295–2340, is a renovated mansion overlooking the lake, with a fine dining room, lounge, swimming, biking, and other amenities. Moderate to expensive.

Telegraph House, Chebucto Street, (902) 295–9988, convenient to the Trans-Canada, has a dining room. Moderate to expensive.

Trailsman Motel, off Highway 105, west of Baddeck, (902) 295–2413, offers a swimming pool and dining room. Moderate.

Baddeck Lobster Suppers are held daily at the Canadian Legion Hall (902) 295–3307. Also try H&H Steak House, Shore Road, and Wong's Restaurant on Chebucto Street.

It is no exaggeration to call the Cabot Trail one of the most beautiful drives in North America. It is 184 miles/294 km. of dramatic vistas of mountains, cliffs, forests, and the Gulf of Saint Lawrence and the Atlantic Ocean. The trail starts and ends in Baddeck, and the traveler is advised to follow it clockwise for the best views and the security of hugging the sides of the mountains while driving up and down some of the steep and curvy stretches. The road is a good one, but your car should be in working order to be safe on the steep grades.

The Cabot Trail runs through the beautiful Margaree Valley and meets the Gulf of Saint Lawrence at the fishing village of Margaree Harbour. From Margaree Harbour to the town of Chéticamp, you will pass through French-Acadian fishing settlements: Watch for local craft items such as ship models and hooked rugs.

En route to Margaree Harbour, stop at **North East Margaree** and visit the Salmon Museum, featuring fishing techniques and exhibits devoted to the Atlantic salmon. Open mid June to mid October. Admission charge. In **Margaree** see Scottish, Indian, and Acadian handicrafts at the Museum of Cape Breton Heritage. Open mid June to mid October. Free.

There are fine accommodations and dining at the Margaree Lodge, Margaree Forks, (902) 248–2193, moderate. The Duck Cove Inn, Margaree Harbour, (902) 235–2658, provides guides and equipment for deep-sea and freshwater fishing, a dining room, and lounge. Moderate. Margaree Harbour's Whale Cove Summer Village, (902) 235–2202, offers housekeeping cottages, fishing, and a sandy beach. Moderate. The Normaway Inn, Margaree Valley, (902) 248–2987, has been a favorite place with travelers for accommodations and dining since 1928. The inn also offers live entertainment, tennis, and salmon fishing. Moderate.

Chéticamp, an Acadian fishing settlement, makes a good overnight stop before going on through Cape Breton Highlands National Park, which starts just north of town. Chéticamp and the surrounding countryside offer many excellent opportunities for the photographer—sea, islands, and mountains, and the harbor filled with fishing boats, nets, and lobster traps. Visit huge Saint Peter's Church with its ornate interior and the nearby Acadian Museum with its many interesting exhibits and weaving demonstrations. Open throughout the summer. Free. The Dr. Elizabeth LeFort Gallery and Museum should also be seen. Admission charge. Whale and bird watching trips operate from town. Accommodations and dining in Chéticamp include the following:

Acadian Motel, on the Cabot Trail (Highway 19), near the church, (902) 224–2640. Moderate.

Fraser Motel Cottages, Main Street, (902) 224–2411. Inexpensive.

Merry's Motel, on the Cabot Trail (Highway 19), in town, (902) 224–2456, is comfortable. Inexpensive.

Ocean View Motel, Main Street, (902) 224–2313. Moderate.

Park View Motel, on the Cabot Trail (Highway 19), at the entrance to the park, (902) 224–3232, has a dining room and lounge. Moderate.

The Harbour Restaurant offers seafood and steaks. The dining room at **Laurie's Motel** and **Restaurant Acadien** are also good dining places in town.

Cape Breton Highlands National Park, (902) 285–2270, covers 370 square miles/962 sq. km. and lies between the Gulf of Saint Lawrence and the Atlantic Ocean. The Cabot Trail winds along the mountain sides, reaching an elevation of 1,492 feet/455 m. at French Mountain, and descends into valleys in which fishing villages, such as **Pleasant Bay,** are nestled. Beachside Motel and Restaurant in Pleasant Bay, (902) 224–2467, offers accommodations and dining. Moderate. The Black Whale Restaurant serves seafood. The views along the Cabot Trail are breathtaking, and there are a number of turnoffs where you can stop and be inspired. The park offers excellent fishing, camping, hiking, beaches, and, at Ingonish Beach, a great golf course.

At **Cape North** visit the North Highlands Community Museum, which portrays the history of this area. Open mid June to mid October. Free. Also in Cape North, swing off the Cabot Trail and follow the road to Bay Saint Lawrence for good views of Nova Scotia's northern end. Try a swim in Aspy Bay and the Cabot Strait.

At **Neil's Harbour,** where the Cabot Trail runs along the Atlantic, is an English-speaking fishing settlement and one of the best places on Cape Breton Island to photograph the maritime way of life—the people, the village, and the sea coming in against the dark cliffs. The drive from Neil's Harbour to **Ingonish** is a very dramatic one of steep grades and magnificent vistas, reminding many people of the Highlands of Scotland. Good beaches and fishing can be found along this route.

Ingonish Beach is part of Cape Breton Highlands National Park and the site of one of the finest eighteen-hole golf courses in all of North America. In addition there are sand beaches, campgrounds, picnic areas, tennis courts, hiking trails, and many other attractions, including a fine anchorage for even the largest vessels. Cape Smokey has a modern ski facility (tows and a lodge) for winter visitors; the lift also operates in the summer. Because of the popularity of Ingonish Beach, the campgrounds are always full, so plan accordingly. Camp sites can be reserved in advance. The world-famous Keltic Lodge, off the Cabot Trail, (902) 285–2880, operated by the provincial government, offers guests excellent accommodations and some of the finest cuisine on Cape Breton Island, swimming in a heated saltwater pool, entertainment, and many other activities. The setting of the resort, on a headland jutting out to sea, the access to the national park golf course, and the serenity of the environment make the lodge one of the most popular in Atlantic Canada. It is usually booked to capacity several months before the start of the season, but there are always last-minute cancellations and travelers without reservations should give it a try. Expensive. Alternative accommodations on the Cabot Trail are Cape Breton Highlands Bungalows, (902) 285–2000, moderate, and the Glenghorn Resort, (902) 285–2049, moderate.

From Ingonish Beach you can continue on the Cabot Trail back to Baddeck or you can connect with the Trans-Canada and head to the city of Sydney and then to Fort Louisbourg, the most impressive manmade attraction on Cape Breton.

The Sydney Area

Sydney is Nova Scotia's second largest city, an industrial and steel-making center. It's a convenient base from which to explore the area's many attractions, such as Louisbourg National Historic Park, and to stop in before taking the Newfoundland ferries at North Sydney. Sydney can also be reached by air from Halifax.

In Sydney itself, visit Saint Patrick's Church, the oldest Roman Catholic church on Cape Breton. It has an interesting historical collection. Open June to mid October. Free. The Cossitt House, built in 1787, is considered the oldest home in the city. Open mid May to end October. Admission charge.

Accommodations and dining in Sydney include the following:

Ramada Mariner Hotel, 300 Esplanade, (902) 562–7500, is Sydney's best, new place of accommodation, offering suites, dining, a lounge, exercise facility, and many other services and amenities. Expensive.

Holiday Inn Sydney, 480 Kings Road, (902) 539–6750, is modern with many conveniences, a dining room and lounge. Expensive.

Keddy's Motor Inn, 600 Kings Road, (902) 539–1140, is comfortable and has a dining room. Moderate.

Vista Motel, 140 Kings Road, (902) 539–6550, features a game room and dining room. Moderate.

Auberge Wandlyn Inn, 100 Kings Road, (902) 539–3700, is near the center of the city and has a good dining room. Moderate.

Jasper's Restaurant, 1167 Kings Road, (902) 564–6181, provides a varied family menu and children's specials. Inexpensive to moderate.

Joe's Warehouse, 424 Charlotte Street, (902) 539–6686, is great for beef and steaks. Moderate.

Le Petit Jean, 233 Esplanade, (902) 539–4671, is one of the best French restaurants on Cape Breton. Moderate to expensive.

At nearby **Glace Bay,** via Highway 4, tour deep coal mines and visit a miner's village at the Miners Museum. Open during the summer. Admission charge. In Sydney Mines, via Highway 305 from **North Sydney,** is the Princess Colliery, where you can plunge

Fortress Louisbourg National Historic Park is one of Canada's largest ▶ historic reconstructions. When it was first built, even King Louis XIV complained of high cost. Yet for many years the fortified town helped to protect his vast empire in North America. It was destroyed by the British and American colonists in 1760 and reconstructed in our time.

hundreds of feet into coal mines that go beneath the ocean floor and travel in pit cars once used by miners. Open during the summer. Admission charge. **Port Morien,** near Glace Bay, is the site of the French Mine, one of the earliest coal mines in North America. Here you can see an exposed seam of coal along the rugged shore, fossils of 200-million-year-old trees, and artifacts from shipwrecks. Open during the summer. Admission charge. For good dining by candlelight, the Miners' Village Restaurant in Glace Bay is recommended.

Fortress Louisbourg National Historic Park, via Highway 22, in **Louisbourg,** is one of Canada's largest historic reconstruction projects. In its day, Fortress Louisbourg was the French king's bastion against the British in North America. It protected French fishing interests and trade routes in the North Atlantic and the Canadian hinterland via the Gulf of Saint Lawrence. Although it had many conveniences for its civilian and military population, life at Louisbourg was harsh, particularly in the winter. The fortress was subject to repeated attacks and sieges by British and New England forces, until it was destroyed by the British in 1760, not long after General Wolfe took Québec. At any rate, to see the reconstruction from a distance (you leave the visitors' center by park bus—no autos in the restoration) is to be confronted with an apparition from the past. To step into its confines (and be stopped at the main portal by guards who ask if you are an English spy!) is to enter another age. Fortress Louisbourg is not just a defensive enclosure, like the Halifax Citadel, but a fortified settlement containing ramparts, private homes, barracks, storehouses, barns, a governor's palace, a chapel, streets, taverns, a blacksmith shop, waterfront docks, and so on. Here people dress in the costumes of the eighteenth-century inhabitants: soldiers on patrol, housewives cooking meals and doing various chores, craftsmen making the implements necessary for industry and survival. You can also come in the evening, when the inhabitants pay no attention to you and speak only in French. It's an eerie feeling—almost as if you're intruding on the business of ghosts. Fortress Louisbourg is a marvelous experience for everyone; it's as important to visit as riding the Cabot Trail. The park's visitor center has an audiovisual presentation of the history of the fortress, exhibits of artifacts, and a gift shop. Open June to the end of September. Admission charge.

While in the fortress, dine eighteenth-century style at the L'Epée Royale, where authentic French recipes are served in the style and atmosphere of the period, moderate to expensive. For more affordable fare, try the Hôtel-de-la-Marine, also in the fortress.

In the town of Louisbourg visit the Sydney and Louisbourg Railway Museum. Open June to Labour Day. Free. Anchors Aweigh Restaurant and the Grubstake Restaurant are additional dining places in town.

North Sydney is the terminal port for those wishing to take the ferries to Newfoundland. The passenger car and freight-carrying ships sail daily for Port-aux-Basques throughout the year and for Argentia during the summer. Recommended accommodations in North Sydney are the Clansman Motel, on Peppett Street, (902) 794–7226, moderate, and the Highland Motel, 530 Seaview Drive, (902) 794–4530, moderate.

To move on from Cape Breton Island, take the Trans-Canada to Baddeck and Port Hastings. Or take a more scenic way via Highway 4, which runs along the shores of the beautiful Bras d'Or Lakes and next to the East Bay Hills. You'll come to **Saint Peter's** on a small spit of land separating the Bras d'Or Lakes and Saint Peter's Bay, which flows out into the Atlantic Ocean. Saint Peter's is a charming historic town, with excellent views of both bodies of water. Visit the Nicholas Denys Museum. Open June to the end of September. Admission charge.

As you drive along Highway 4, consider swinging off onto Highway 320 and then 206 to explore the French-Acadian area of **Isle Madame.** Go as far as the village of **Arichat**: The panoramas of the sea and landscape make this side trip well worth while. While in Arichat, see the LeNoir Forge, an eighteenth-century blacksmith shop with a working forge. Open during the summer. Admission charge. Continue on Highway 4 to Port Hawkesbury and Port Hastings and then cross the causeway at Canso Strait to mainland Nova Scotia.

CHAPTER 14

Halifax

Halifax Today

In many ways, Halifax is the perfect medium-sized city: It has nearly everything it needs and far fewer problems than most other North American cities. A city built on a human scale, it blends urban sophistication and the natural environment. Most people who come to Atlantic Canada do so to shed themselves of their cities. Halifax is one city to be savored—allow at least two days.

Halifax, now with more than 120,000 inhabitants in a metropolitan area of 300,000 people, came into existence as a British military outpost in 1749. Lord Cornwallis founded it, but his interests were more in developing a strategic base to protect British interests against the French than in building a substantial city. His garrison town, the first Canadian community settled primarily by the English, was named in honor of the Earl of Halifax. Cornwallis commenced construction of the Citadel, a star-shaped fortification set on a high hill that continues to dominate the city. During the American Revolution, Halifax was a solid, secure British bastion in the North Atlantic and a place of refuge for fleeing Loyalists. Only the quicksilver ships of American privateers, playing cat and mouse with the British, dared to harass Nova Scotia seacoast towns.

The military commanders of Halifax were well prepared for attack from the French and from the Americans, but the Citadel has never yet fired a shot in anger. One of the more illustrious British commanders of Halifax was the Duke of Kent, Queen Victoria's father and a generous benefactor to Halifax. The ornate town clock, which sits on the brow of Citadel Hill and still keeps good time, is one of his gifts to the city.

◀ Halifax town crier tells visitors about the happenings of the day at the city's Historic Properties.

CITY OF HALIFAX

On December 6, 1917, during World War I, Halifax became victim of one of the worst explosives disasters of history. The *Mont Blanc*, a French freighter loaded with munitions, collided with the *Imo*, a Norwegian vessel meant to carry relief supplies for war victims in Belgium. The explosion flattened the north end of the city and damaged buildings throughout the city. Some 2,000 people were killed, 9,000 injured; 1,600 buildings in the blast area were totally destroyed, 12,000 others severely damaged. It was a $50 million loss. Today there is very little evidence of this horror, but Haligonians (as the people of Halifax call themselves) remember not only the pain of the event but also the millions of dollars worth of relief supplies that came from the United States.

In World War II Halifax played an important role as a staging area for the Allied convoys that sailed the North Atlantic route against the Nazi U-boat "wolf packs." The broad Bedford Basin was packed with Allied ships, soldiers, and military cargo. This effort helped to save Great Britain and made possible the Allied victory over Germany. Halifax is now the base for the Canadian Atlantic fleet and headquarters of the commander of the Maritime Command of the Armed Forces of Canada. The commander is responsible for the surveillance and control of the oceans around the country and for supplying NATO forces, which make Halifax a major port of call. The city has the oldest naval dockyard in North America, and you can see many modern warships via land and water tours of the city.

As a year-round ice-free port, Halifax also plays an important role in Canada's civilian maritime activities, such as scientific research, which includes the world's third largest oceanographic center, the Bedford Institute; shipping; and the many other businesses associated with the sea. Samuel Cunard, one of the city's leading citizens in the nineteenth century, ran his steamship line from Halifax. Insurance, banking, and international trade have flourished here. Manufacturing also employs many Haligonians. Halifax is also the provincial capital, and most government agencies and departments have their main offices in the city.

Leading universities, such as Dalhousie and Saint Mary's, and first-rate hospitals, such as Victoria General and Children's, add to the community's high quality of life. The large concentration of research facilities includes the Bedford Institute of Oceanography, Dalhousie School of Medicine, and Federal Department of Fisheries and Oceans. Live theater, art galleries, museums of all kinds, a symphony orchestra, and professional sports provide bountiful cultural enrichment to residents and visitors alike. An increasing number of first-rate hotels and restaurants, boutiques specializing in everything from dolls to expensive furs to Scottish tartans, and ultramodern shopping centers can be found throughout Halifax. Handsome old homes and beautiful parks and gardens bespeak a city of tradition, civility, and elegance.

Halifax prides itself on many firsts:

The first parliament legislature in Canada (1819);

The highest ratio of educational facilities to population in North America;

The first postal service in North America (1752, Halifax to New York City);

Britain's first overseas cathedral (St. Paul's, 1750);

The first newspaper in Canada (*Halifax Gazette*);

The first and oldest saltwater ferry service in North America.

Bring comfortable shoes, for Halifax is a walking city. The weather is similar to Boston's, though usually a few degrees cooler in the summer. Haligonians are proud of their city and of their province, and their British-style reserve is mixed with a warm outgoing nature. You will more likely experience friendly interest than cold indifference.

How to Get to Halifax

By Car

Take Highway 101 from Windsor; 103 from Lunenburg; 102 from Truro; 118 through Dartmouth; or 107 from Marine Drive.

By Rail

Passenger trains connecting from major cities in Canada arrive and depart at the VIA Rail station, located off Hollis Street.

By Bus

Acadian Lines provides direct service throughout the province and connecting service to other provinces in the Atlantic region. MacKenzie Bus Lines provides service for the Atlantic route, from Halifax to Yarmouth.

By Air

Halifax International Airport is located off Highway 102, a thirty- to forty-minute drive from Halifax center. The airport is situated on high ground and not subject to the dense fogs of coastal areas. It is the main air terminus for Atlantic Canada, and there are connections to other parts of the region (Newfoundland, New Brunswick, Prince Edward Island, and so on). The major carriers are Air Canada and Canadian Airlines International, and their affiliates Air Nova and Air Atlantic.

Rental cars—Hertz, Avis, Tilden—are available at the airport and downtown locations. There is frequent bus service from the airport to downtown Halifax hotels. Private taxis are available but expensive.

General Information

Time zone: Atlantic

Telephone area code: 902

Police: local, dial 4105

Medical emergency: Victoria General Hospital, (902) 428–2110

Help line: (902) 422–7444, a twenty-four-hour service to provide assistance to those in need, also to communication services to the deaf

How to Get Around Halifax

The Central Area

Halifax is a peninsula, shaped like a foot sticking into the water. Its toe, at the Halifax harbor, points to the sea. Its heel juts into the Bedford Basin. Its sole forms the narrows, with the city of Dartmouth on the other side. The top of the foot forms one bank of the 3-mile/5-km. North West Arm. Halifax is, therefore, almost completely surrounded by water, and the central city runs along the sole to the toe of this imaginary foot. Barrington, Lower Water, and Hollis are the major streets running through the business and shopping areas in the central city. Perpendicular to these runs Spring Garden Road, the most fashionable shopping street in the central area. Two good landmarks to use are Citadel Hill and Scotia Square (a complex of tall office and hotel buildings). The area from Citadel Hill to Point Pleasant Park (at the toe) is fairly easy to get around, and you should have little trouble on foot or in a car. Some of the outlying neighborhoods can get confusing. Stick to marked routes or stop and ask directions; people want to help and do so by providing accurate directions.

Halifax and its sister city Dartmouth comprise a metropolitan region of 300,000 people. The two cities are connected at the narrows by the Angus L. Macdonald Bridge and at the Bedford Basin by the A. Murray Mackay Bridge. There is also frequent ferry service to Dartmouth from Lower Water Street in Halifax.

Transportation Within the City

Taxi cabs are available at hotels, shopping centers, and other high-traffic areas.

Public buses stop at convenient locations, but drivers accept only correct change.

Ferry service to and from Dartmouth is located at the new terminal, off Lower Water Street, and operates every half hour throughout the day and every fifteen minutes at peak times. This is a cheap and pleasant way to ride around the harbor and see Halifax from the water, as sailors have for generations. Dating from 1752, it is the oldest operating saltwater ferry service in North America.

Guided Tours and Cruises

Gray Line, (902) 454–9321, provides a tour of the city. They pick up passengers at all major hotels. Also available are Halifax Double Decker Tours, (902) 420–1155, and Harbour Walk Tours, (902) 422–6591. To see Halifax from the water, call Halifax Water Tours, (902) 423–1271, or the famous sailing schooner *Bluenose II*, (902) 422–2678. Cruises depart from Privateers' Wharf at Historic Properties.

Tourist Information

For brochures, maps, answers to questions, and help with hotel reservations, visit Tourism Halifax, (902) 421–8736, in Old City Hall at the corner of Duke and Barrington streets on the Grande Parade; also the provincial information centre, (902) 424–4247, at the Old Red Store at Historic Properties.

For toll-free telephone information on Halifax, including free brochures and maps (Nova Scotia Tourism will also help you book reservations for accommodations, ferries, and transportation), call Check Inns—the Nova Scotia Reservation and Travel Information System—toll-free at these numbers:

◄ Halifax is Atlantic Canada's largest and most dynamic city. Here are excellent accommodations, dining, attractions, and entertainment for the entire family.

Continental United States, (800) 341–6096
Nova Scotia, Prince Edward Island, and New Brunswick, (800) 565–7105
Newfoundland and Québec, (800) 565–7180
Central and Southern Ontario, (800) 565–7140
Northern Ontario, Manitoba, Saskatchewan, Alberta, British Columbia,
Northwest Territories, and the Yukon, (800) 565–7166
Halifax and Dartmouth, (902) 425–5781

Major Events

Festival Acadien de Halifax, late April and early May
Children's Festival of Nova Scotia, late May
Scotia Festival of Music, late May and early June
Greek Summer Fest, early June
Multicultural Festival, mid June
Nova Scotia Tattoo, late June to early July: This spectacular event features dancers, singers, bagpipers, military bands, drummers, and gymnasts. It is a memorable experience for the entire family. For ticket information, call (902) 427–6953.

Canada Celebrations, July 1
Grand Prix Hydroplane Races, early August
Metro Scottish Festival and Highland Games, early July
Halifax Natal Day, last weekend of July into early August: Halifax and Darmouth celebrate their birthdays with sports events, shows, fairs, parades, and fireworks.

Harbourfest Celebration, early August: This festival celebrates the city's close relationship with the sea and features parades, fireworks, and many entertainments.

Buskers, mid August: International street performers gather from around the world for neary two weeks, offering one of North America's most exciting family outdoor events.

International Town Criers' Competition, mid September
Atlantic Winter Fair, early to mid October

Attractions

Citadel Hill (Halifax Citadel National Historic Park), built in 1828, is on the same site as the bastion built under orders by Lord Cornwallis in 1749. This stone fortress offers the best view of the

323

city and the surrounding country in all directions. By law no building can be built higher than the Citadel. It has interesting museums on Halifax history, a fifty-minute audiovisual show, guided tours, and military exhibits. Open throughout the year. Free.

Historic Properties, on the waterfront, are refurbished old warehouses containing attractive promenades with boutiques, restaurants, pubs, and offices. Historic Properties gives you a sense of what the waterfront was like in the olden days but with many modern conveniences. At Privateers' Wharf, for example, you will find the schooner *Bluenose II*, which provides cruises on the harbor. It is a perfect place for strolling, browsing, and spending money. Open throughout the year.

Halifax Public Gardens, Spring Garden Road, have pleasant walks among exotic imported flowers, trees, and shrubs. At the entrance is a bust of Sir Walter Scott, and across the street stands a statue of Robert Burns. These are Canada's oldest public gardens, and their design is based on that of St. James Park in London, England. Open throughout the year. Free.

Maritime Museum of the Atlantic, on the waterfront near the ferry terminal, has displays of maritime history, the merchant navy, and the history of wooden sailing ships of the Atlantic. The showpiece of the museum is the *Acadia*, Canada's first hydrographic survey vessel, now a national historic site, tied up alongside the building. This fine museum also contains the Halifax Explosion Memorial and a special exhibit on the ill-fated luxury liner *Titanic*. Open daily throughout the year.

Nova Scotia Museum, 1747 Summer Street, houses extensive natural history and anthropological collections relating to the province. Open throughout the year. Free.

Province House, Granville Street, is Nova Scotia's seat of government and the country's oldest provincial legislative building (1819). It is an interesting example of colonial Georgian architecture. Open throughout the year. Free.

Saint Paul's Anglican Church, Grand Parade, is the city's oldest building (1749), mother church of the Protestant churches of Canada in general and of the Anglican church of Canada in particular. King George II is its royal founder. Known as the Westminster Abbey of Canada, this exquisite wooden church has many memorials relating to famous Canadians, Loyalists, and British. Saint Paul's should not be missed, and there is always a warm welcome for all visitors.

Dalhousie University, at the end of University Avenue, is one of Canada's premier institutions of higher learning. It was founded in a rather odd way: A British military expedition extracted taxes from the citizens of Castine, Maine, to establish in Halifax a college modeled after Edinburgh University. The impressive campus features a modern library and arts center.

Maritime Command Museum, Admiralty House, C.F.B. Stadacona, Gottingen Street at Almon Street, has a fine exhibition of military and maritime artifacts. Open throughout the year. Free.

Public Archives of Nova Scotia, corner of University Avenue and Robie Street, has historical documents, a genealogical section, and an art gallery, exhibits of coins, stamps, prints, and paintings. Open throughout the year. Free.

Little Dutch (Deutsch) Church, Brunswick Street, built in 1758 for use by German Evangelical Lutherans, is nicknamed the "chicken coop church."

Round Church, Brunswick Street, was built at the instigation of the Duke of Kent who didn't want the devil to catch him in a corner.

Saint Matthew's Church, Barrington Street, opened in 1859, has a rose window that is a copy of the one at Chartres and a pew for the lieutenant governor. Guided tours are available in the summer.

Fort McNab National Historic Site, on McNab's Island in the harbor—reached by ferry (902) 422–9523—was established in the nineteenth century as one of the most important fortifications protecting the British naval station at Halifax and the city itself. In addition to viewing these old fortifications, visit the beaches, nature trails, and bike paths on the island.

Point Pleasant Park, at the south end of Young Avenue and at the toe of the peninsula, is a safe, wonderful, natural preserve, where you can jog, enjoy the tranquillity of the woods and the nearby sea, and visit old fortifications, such as the Prince of Wales Tower, built in 1798 by the Duke of Kent. Cars are not permitted in the park. There is a public beach and a nature trail. Open throughout the year. Free.

Saint Mary's University, Robie Street, founded by the Jesuits, is the oldest English-speaking Roman Catholic university in Canada. Its astronomical observatory is open to the public.

University of King's College, at Coburg Road on the Dalhousie Campus, founded in 1789, is the oldest university in the Commonwealth outside the United Kingdom itself.

Visual Art Exhibitions

Halifax is Atlantic Canada's thriving center for the visual arts. Some of the places in the city where you can see contemporary painting, sculpture, and crafts follow:

Nova Scotia College of Art and Design, Duke Street

Art Gallery of Mount Saint Vincent University, off the Bedford Highway

Art Gallery of Nova Scotia, Old Dominion Building, Hollis Street

Dalhousie University Art Gallery, Dalhousie Arts Centre

Dresden Gallery, 1539 Birmingham

Manuge Gallery, 1674 Hollis Street

School of Architecture Gallery, Technical University of Nova Scotia, 5410 Spring Garden Road

Zwicker's Gallery, 5415 Doyle Street

Recreational Sports

The metropolitan area has a number of public and private golf courses, tennis courts, swimming pools, and fitness facilities. There are also jogging routes and water sport areas. Your hotel concierge will be happy to make suggestions and reservations. Most major places of accommodation also have swimming pools and various recreational and exercise facilities.

Accommodations

There are plenty of rooms in Halifax, but they are always in great demand by business travelers, politicians, delegates to conventions, and tourists. This cannot be repeated enough: Please reserve ahead. Use Nova Scotia's free Check Inns service to help you (see page 279):

Halifax Sheraton, at Historic Properties on Upper Water Street, (902) 421–1700, is one of the city's finest hotels. It overlooks the harbor and is adjacent to Historic Properties and the Convention Centre. This Sheraton offers restaurants, lounges, shops, swimming pool, and many other guest amenities. Moderate to expensive.

Airport Hotel, opposite Halifax airport, (902) 873–3000, features a restaurant and lounge. Moderate to expensive.

The Delta Barrington Inn, 1875 Barrington Street, (902) 429–

7410, a Delta Hotel, features a good location and many conveniences, including dining facilities. Expensive.

Chateau Halifax, Scotia Square, (902) 425–6700, is a good convention hotel, with all hotel conveniences and an excellent location. Expensive.

Citadel Inn, 1960 Brunswick Street, (902) 422–1391, offers all hotel conveniences. At this writing, it's the best in Halifax. Moderate to expensive.

Holiday Inn Halifax Centre, 1980 Robie Street, (902) 423–1161, is one of Halifax's best, with a fine dining room and entertainment. Expensive.

Hotel Nova Scotian, 1181 Hollis Street, (902) 423–7231, next to the VIA Rail station, provides fine accommodations and an excellent main restaurant. Expensive.

Cambridge Suites Hotel, 1583 Brunswick Street, (902) 420–0555, located in expensive downtown Cambridge, offers several sizes of suites and many fine amenities at reasonable prices. This is a new place of accommodation. Ideal for families who want to be in the center of everything. Moderate to expensive.

The Halliburton House Inn, 5184 Morris Street, (902) 420–0658, was built in 1820 and was the home of Sir Benton Halliburton, former Chief Justice of the Supreme Court of Nova Scotia. Halliburton House offers fine accommodations and breakfast. Moderate to expensive.

The Prince George Hotel, 1725 Market Street, (902) 425–1986, offers fine accommodations and dining and a lounge with live entertainment. There is a swimming pool and exercise facility. Moderate to expensive.

Lord Nelson Hotel, South Park Street, across from the Public Gardens, (902) 423–6331, is in a fashionable area and carries an establishment aura. It features many conveniences. Moderate.

Keddy's Halifax, St. Margaret's Bay Road, (902) 477–5611, offers good accommodations, dining, and recreational facilities, overlooking Chocolate Lake. Moderate.

During the summer, these local universities offer inexpensive accommodations in their dormitories for families, couples, and singles:

Dalhousie University, (902) 424–8840.

Saint Mary's University, (902) 420–5486.

Mount Saint Vincent University, (902) 443–4450.

Technical University of Nova Scotia, (902) 429–8300.

Dining

Halifax offers some of the best dining in Atlantic Canada and the greatest variety of restaurants, from very elegant affairs to the usual fast-food places;

Old Man Morias, 1150 Barrington Street, (902) 422–7960, has become the top Greek restaurant in the Canadian Maritimes, with traditional roasted lamb dishes a specialty of the house. Moderate to expensive.

Bentley's Bistro, 5411 Spring Garden Road, (902) 423–6618 (part of Fat Frank's culinary empire), offers fancy salads, desserts, and more, San Francisco style. Moderate.

Clipper Cay, Historic Properties, (902) 423–6818, offers seafood specialties and an eighteenth-century atmosphere overlooking the harbor. Moderate to expensive.

McKelvie's, 1680 Lower Water Street, (902) 421–6161, located in the popular waterfront area, serves tempting seafood dishes. Moderate.

Suisha Gardens, Maritime Centre, (902) 422–1576, offers Japanese cuisine and a steak ceremony. Moderate to expensive.

Five Fishermen, 1744 Argyle Street, (902) 422–4421, features a fresh catch of the day and home-baked rolls, prepared by French and Swiss chefs. Moderate to expensive.

Scanway Restaurant, at the Courtyard on Dresden Row, (902) 422–3733, a casual Scandinavian setting where delicious seafood, steaks, and desserts are served. Moderate to expensive.

Thackery's, 5407 Spring Garden Road, (902) 423–5995, prepares seafood, chicken, roast beef, and steak. Moderate to expensive.

Pepe's, 5680 Spring Garden Road, (902) 429–7321, is a popular city-center dining room, specializing in seafood. Moderate to expensive.

Le Bistro, 1333 South Park Street, (902) 423–8428. Fine French cuisine in a café setting. Moderate.

Voila, 5140 Prince Street, (902) 422–2210. A new French restaurant that has captured the palates of Haligonians and visitors to the city. The emphasis is on traditional haute cuisine and fine wines. A comfortable, elegant restaurant. Tables are set with linen and crystal. One of the best dining places in Halifax. Expensive.

Fat Frank's, 5411 Spring Garden Road, (902) 423–6618, is considered one of Canada's best gourmet restaurants, with an excellent wine cellar. Expensive.

Gondola, 5175 South Street, (902) 423–8719, offers good Italian food and ambience. Moderate.

Mother Tucker's, 1668 Lower Water Street, (902) 422–4436, is a relatively inexpensive prime roast beef, baked potato, and salad place. Inexpensive to moderate.

L'Evangeline, Hotel Nova Scotian, 1181 Hollis Street, (902) 423–7231, is an elegant, special treat for haute cuisine. Expensive.

Duffy's Bar and Grill, upstairs in Spring Garden Place, (902) 421–1116, serves superior steaks; cuts and trims U.S. choice grade prime beef at your table. It is cut to your order, and you pay only for the final weight. Moderate to expensive.

42nd Street, 1567 Grafton Street, (902) 425–4278, is Halifax's only New York–style café and grill. Moderate to expensive.

Historic Feast Company, at Simon's Warehouse at Historic Properties, (902) 420–1840, takes you back to the mid-nineteenth century for food, theater, music, and song. Moderate.

Privateer's Warehouse, Historic Properties, (902) 422–1289, is an old-time pub featuring seafood and a jazz club. Moderate.

Café San Marco, at Prince and Grafton Street, (902) 420–8330, well prepared northern Italian cuisine. Moderate to expensive.

Entertainment

On any given day, during the summer, entertainment abounds in Halifax—festivals, theater, music, and more. Hotels provide listings of current events. There is enough going on to make your stay fun and enjoyable.

Theater

The Halifax Metro Centre, 5284 Duke Street, (902) 421–8005, a huge new arena, holds many entertainment and sporting events throughout the year. One of the most spectacular of these is the Nova Scotia Tattoo, which runs for about a week in early July.

Neptune Theatre, 5216 Sackville Street, (902) 429–7300, is the top place to see live drama in Atlantic Canada, and it features leading Canadian, British, and American players.

Cunard Street Theatre, Cunard near Gottigen, (902) 421–1902, is the Neptune's second stage, operated by the Nova Scotia Drama League.

Night Spots

For after-hours relaxation, Halifax has bars, lounges, discos, and evening night spots (ask your hotel's concierge for suggestions on what's hot in town):

Thirsty Duck, 5472 Spring Garden Road, is the place for traditional pub entertainment and fun.

Misty Moon, 1595 Barrington Street, presents national and international rock and blues acts.

J. J. Rosy's, at Historic Properties, is the largest pub in Atlantic Canada.

My Apartment, 1740 Argyle Street, offers glitzy decor and ambience for sparkling people who enjoy dancing to rock.

Middle Deck, at Historic Properties, is excellent for jazz; try Lower Deck (same location) for British public house bawdy songs and potent brews.

Several cinemas around town show first-run films. The National Film Board Theater, 1572 Barrington Street, (902) 426–6001, shows excellent Canadian films for free.

Shopping

Scotia Square and the new Park Lane are the city's main downtown shopping malls. Each contains more than one hundred shops, restaurants, and services. Halifax's high fashion street is Spring Garden Road. There are many interesting shops and restaurants at the Brewery on Lower Water Street; Maritime Mall and Barrington Place on Barrington Street; Historic Properties on the Water Front; Founders Square at the corner of Hollis and Prince streets; Spring Garden Place on Spring Garden Road; and the Courtyard on Dresden Row. All these shopping areas are in downtown Halifax.

Side Trips

Dartmouth

You can visit Halifax's sister city by taking the ferry or going over the Macdonald or the Mackay bridges. Dartmouth (population 65,000) is primarily a bedroom community for Halifax, but it has several interesting attractions. The Dartmouth Heritage Museum, 100 Wyse Road, has historical exhibits and the re-created study of Joseph Howe, one of Nova Scotia's foremost patriots. Open throughout the year. Free. The Historic Quaker Whaler's House (circa 1785), 57 Ochterloney Street, has items relating to early Nantucket whalers who lived in the city. Open only in the summer. Free. The Bedford Institute of Oceanography, located in the north end of the city, is the country's leading scientific center for marine research. Dartmouth is called the city of lakes: It has twenty-three of them. Seven have public beaches and are stocked with speckled trout.

Cole Harbor, via Highway 207 on the Marine Drive out of Dartmouth, is the site of the Heritage Farm Museum, 471 Poplar Drive, which depicts the area's agricultural traditions. Open late May to early October. Free.

Cape Sambro

Take Highways 253 and 349 for a pleasant drive through small towns and fishing villages. The views of the ocean are lovely, and there are plenty of spots to picnic, hike, photograph, or paint pictures. Near **Purcell's Cove** is *York Redoubt National Historic Park* and its fortifications. This is a choice morning or afternoon excursion from Halifax, a chance to get away from the city briefly and return with a sharper appetite.

Peggy's Cove

Take Highway 333 for one of the most popular side trips from Halifax (or from Yarmouth via the Lighthouse Route). On the way to Peggy's Cove, be sure to take the secondary roads that lead to Terence Bay, Prospect Harbour, and East Dover to see authentic fishing villages where the people still live by old ways and virtues. This journey to a different world is quite a contrast to the sophistication of Halifax and immensely appealing. Peggy's Cove looks like a nineteenth-century fishing village. Modern structures cannot be built here. It is an ideal place to photograph fishing shacks and boats, lovely little St. John's Anglican church, a majestic lighthouse, and rock cliffs on a thundering ocean. The lighthouse, no longer functioning as a navigational beacon, serves as a post office during the summer. The postmaster sells stamps decorated with a picture of this famous lighthouse. Also in Peggy's Cove is a carving in the side of a huge granite boulder by the late William E. deGarthe. The Finnish artist worked in the village for many years. DeGarthe's carving portrays thirty-two Peggy's Cove fishermen, their wives and children, a guardian angel with spread wings, and the mythological "Peggy" for whom the village is named. There are also two de-

Garthe murals inside St. John's Church. You can find inexpensive to moderate motels and restaurants in the Indian Harbor area if you want to spend more time in the area. Candleriggs, in Indian Harbour, (902) 624–9973, offers hearty Scottish breakfasts, lunch, Scottish tea, dinner, and weekend champagne brunch, also fine Nova Scotia handicrafts. Be sure to explore the strange geological terrain around Peggy's Cove, a vestige of the great glaciers.

To Cape Breton Island via Marine Drive

You can reach Cape Breton Island, one of the prime tourist areas in all of Atlantic Canada, from the Halifax-Dartmouth area by taking Highway 107 from Dartmouth and then Highway 7 along the Atlantic coast, passing through or near such scenic villages as Seaforth, Musquodoboit Harbour, Jeddore, Clam Harbour, Sheet Harbour, Port Dufferin, Ecum Secum, and Liscomb. Along the way, enjoy the attractions, explore charming fishing villages, take beach walks or plunge into the saltwater, and just relish the maritime landscape. You can reach Cape Breton in a day from the Halifax area, or you can linger awhile.

At **Musquodobit Harbor** is the Musquodobit Railway Museum, with its displays of railroad history in a 1917 Canadian National Railway station. Open June through August. Free.

The Fisherman's Life Museum at **Jeddore Oyster Pond** shows you how inshore fishermen live and work. Since most of the fishermen in the province are independent operators or members of cooperatives working the inshore waters, this is a worthwhile museum to visit to understand an important aspect of Nova Scotia life. Open mid May to mid October. Free.

If you want to stay at a special resort, make reservations at Liscombe Lodge in **Liscomb Mills**, (902) 779–2307. Liscombe Lodge offers fine accommodations and meals, canoe rentals, hiking trails, swimming, fishing, deep-sea charters, boat tours, many conveniences, and recreational features. Moderate to expensive.

Sherbrooke is the site of the historic Sherbrooke Village, a restored nineteenth-century lumbering, shipbuilding, and gold-mining community. There are demonstrations of various crafts and trades of the period, a general store, courthouse, jail, school, post office, church, blacksmith shop, and other interesting buildings. Open mid May to end October. Admission charge.

Highway 7 will take you to the Trans-Canada Highway 104 at Antigonish. Take the Trans-Canada to the causeway at the Canso

Strait (Port Hawkesbury) and Cape Breton Island. En route you might take exit 37 to Highway 16 for a side trip to **Guysborough,** a pretty town with tree-lined streets, elegant homes, a golf course, and the Old Court House Museum, featuring local history. Open June 1 to mid September. Free. Highway 16 ends at the Cape of Canso. In the town of **Canso** is the Canso Museum, housed in the restored Whitman House. Open during the summer. Free.

An alternative and faster route from Halifax to Cape Breton Island follows Highway 102 and the Trans-Canada. This drive takes about five hours from the Halifax area. Be careful of your speed, as the Royal Canadian Mounted Police strictly enforce speed limits.

CHAPTER 15

Newfoundland-
Labrador

Newfoundland-Labrador Today

The land mass of Newfoundland-Labrador is vast. Labrador, the most easterly extension of mainland Canada, occupies 110,000 square miles/286,000 sq. km., with its lamb-chop shape bordered by the Province of Québec on the west and south and the Atlantic Ocean on the north and east. Nearly 40,000 people inhabit Labrador, mostly along the coast and in modern interior settlements that are involved with mineral and hydroelectric development or with the military. Most of the interior of Labrador is a wilderness where very few people have set foot.

The island of Newfoundland, where more than 560,000 people live, is 43,000 square miles/112 sq. km. in area and shaped like an arrowhead pointing westward into the Gulf of Saint Lawrence. This island is separated from Labrador to the north by the Strait of Belle Isle, with the Atlantic Ocean to its east and south. It is the most easterly part of North America, only 1,800 miles/2,880 km. from the coast of Ireland. Most of the people of the island live along its coasts. St. John's is the capital city, with a population of 150,000. Much of Newfoundland's interior is forested, and the paper and pulp industries are important factors in the economy. Fishing is the mainstay of the economy and has been ever since Newfoundland was discovered centuries ago.

History and Culture

How many towns do you know with names such as Bumble Bee Bight, Jerry's Nose, Blow Me Down, Too Good Arm, Empty

◀ Newfoundland-Labrador delights in the folkways of its fishing people—their songs, stories, crafts, and speech.

335

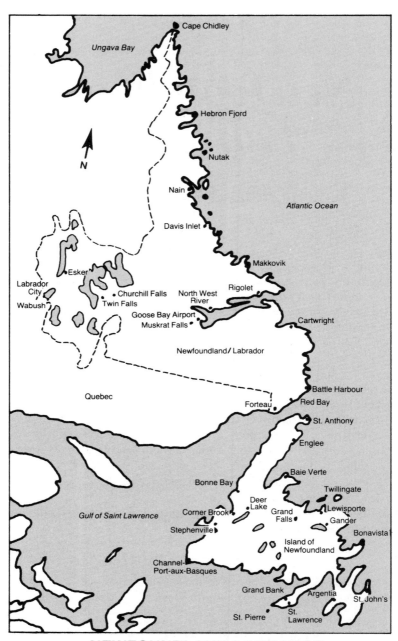

NEWFOUNDLAND-LABRADOR

Basket, or Heart's Desire? One place in North America not only takes these names seriously but has many others just as poetic—and that's Newfoundland.

Newfoundland was discovered long before the rest of Atlantic Canada. At L'Anse aux Meadows, Helge Ingstad, a Norwegian scientist, found the first proof of a Viking settlement in this northern tip of Newfoundland. Many earlier scholars had assumed that the Vikings had discovered North America and sailed along its coasts, but Ingstad uncovered the scientific evidence. Those who think Columbus discovered the New World will have to be content with a hero who came in second.

From A.D. 1000, when the Vikings were in Newfoundland, until the time of John Cabot's first record of the island, Basque and Portuguese fishermen evidently came to the Grand Banks for the fat cod that have always been so abundant here.

When Cabot claimed Newfoundland for the king of England in 1497, the island's long history as an English fishing and defensive stronghold began. Even at that time fishing vessels came not only from England but also from Portugal, Holland, and France. While there was much activity in the offshore waters and at the shore stations where the catches were prepared for shipment to Europe, no colonization was attempted.

In 1610 John Guy established his Sea Forest Plantation in the Cupid's Bay area. While it was not successful, it did attract a number of other Englishmen, who founded their own communities all along the shores of the Avalon Peninsula, today the most populous region of the province.

Sir David Kirke tried to consolidate all these communities in the late 1600s, but his effort failed, and England prohibited settlement of Newfoundland until the beginning of the nineteenth century, instead using this massive island essentially as a fishing station. It was not until 1855 that Newfoundland achieved self-government.

Labrador has been part of Newfoundland since the boundary dispute was settled in 1927, though the province of Québec continues to claim all of Labrador except for a 20-mile/32-km. strip of coastline.

In the 1930s, the fish-based economy of Newfoundland collapsed, and the government was placed in the hands of a royal commission appointed by the British Crown. After the Second World War, Newfoundland showed new economic vigor, and the people were asked to decide on their political future—to remain

under the control of the commission, to return to self-government, or to unite with Canada in confederation. In a 1948 plebiscite the people voted—by only a 2 percent majority—to join with the rest of Canada. Thus, Newfoundland-Labrador, Britain's oldest colony, became Canada's newest province.

The dynamic force behind the confederation movement was former Premier Joseph (Joey) Smallwood, considered the George Washington of Newfoundland-Labrador by many. Through his energetic and often controversial programs, Newfoundland-Labrador, particularly the island part of the province, came out of the sixteenth century and into the twentieth. He diversified the economic base by developing timber and mineral resources and by offering large corporations attractive incentives. Not all of these economic development programs succeeded, but the Smallwood years represented a dramatic attempt to move the province forward.

Today's combined population of Newfoundland-Labrador numbers more than 600,000, and is predominantly English-speaking (99 percent) British, American, Irish, Scottish, and Welsh stock. In addition, the province has a French-speaking population of Acadian descent and peoples of the American Indian and Inuit cultures.

During the Second World War, when a number of Allied military bases were built in the province, Newfoundland was called "the guardian of the Atlantic." The first face-to-face meeting between Winston Churchill and Franklin Delano Roosevelt took place in the waters of Newfoundland. From that meeting issued the Atlantic Charter, which was instrumental in defeating Hitler. Thousands of American troops were stationed in such places as Goose Bay, Argentia, Stephenville, and St. John's. Many American servicemen married Newfoundland women, and some stayed to make homes in their "new found land." In addition thousands of Newfoundlanders have gone to the "Boston States" (their name for the United States) to find jobs and a new life.

While fishing continues to be an important part of the economy and employs a large percentage of the population, lumbering, paper and pulp production, construction, mining, tourism, and a variety of other services are providing more opportunities for the people.

◀ **Most roads in Newfoundland lead to the edge of the sea. Here you can satisfy your craving for lighthouses, icebergs, seabirds, whales offshore, fishing villages, granite cliffs, and the tangy air that blows only off the North Atlantic.**

Tourism facilities are more than adequate and are improving in quality and quantity all the time. A visit to Newfoundland is a different kind of experience—far off on an island where the people speak in a brogue and cling to old-fashioned ways. If you have extra time, travel to Newfoundland and discover for yourself.

Speak the Language

Newfoundland even has its own language. Here are a few examples of their tongue twisters and what they mean:

Angishore	Weak, miserable person
Bannock	Round cake of bread
Blather	Nonsensical talk
Calabogus	Rum, molasses, and spruce beer
Crubeens	Pickled pig's feet
Duckish	The time between sunset and dark
Gansey	Woolen sweater
Gommil	Moron
Gulvin	Codfish's stomach
Gilderoy	Proud person
Jackeen	Rascal
Jinker	Bad-luck person
Kingcorn	Adam's apple
Manus	Mutiny
Mundle	Wooden soup stirrer
Oonshick	Stupid person
Rames	Skeleton
Sadogue	Fat person
Scut	Dirty person
Shooneen	Move backwards
Suent	Graceful
Squabby	Jelly soft
Titivate	To adorn
Vang	Fried salt pork
Yuck	To vomit

And here are some old Newfie sayings:
A fisherman is one rogue, a merchant is many.
Fair weather to you and snow to your heels.
Go to law with the devil and hold court in hell.

In a leaky punt with a broken oar, 'tis always best to hug the shore.

Pigs may fly, but they are very unlikely birds.

You can't tell the mind of a squid.

You are as deep as your grave.

Crazy as a loon.

Deaf as a haddock.

Dirty as a duck's puddle.

Hard as the knockers of Newgate.

Like a birch broom in the fits.

Lonesome as a gull on a rock.

Old as Buckley's goat.

Smoky as a Labrador tilt.

Wide as the devil's boots.

How to Get to Newfoundland-Labrador

By Car and Ship

Take the Trans-Canada to the Marine Atlantic terminal at North Sydney, Nova Scotia. Passenger car, trailer, and truck ferry service to Port aux Basques, Newfoundland, operates daily throughout the year. During the summer, there is also service to Argentia. The vessels include a cafeteria, a bar, and cabins.

For rates and schedules, contact Marine Atlantic, P.O. Box 250, North Sydney, Nova Scotia B2A 3M3, or telephone using these toll-free numbers: (800) 565–9411 from Ontario and Québec; (800) 565-9470 from Nova Scotia, New Brunswick, and Prince Edward Island; (800) 341–7981 from continental United States except Maine; and (800) 432–7344 in Maine; from all other areas, a toll-call, (902) 794–7203.

By Air

Both Air Canada and Canadian Airlines International provide service to Newfoundland cities. Connections can be made in St. John's for service to Goose Bay and Churchill Falls, Labrador. Rental cars—Tilden, Avis, and others—are available at airports.

General Information

Time zone: Atlantic (Labrador) and Newfoundland (Newfoundland)—½ hour ahead of Atlantic time.

Telephone area code: 709

Climate and Clothing

Summers on the island of Newfoundland are pleasant, though the weather can change fast along the Atlantic coast. The Labrador coast is mild to cool in the summer, depending on how far north you go. Winters range from cold in Newfoundland to arctic in Labrador. Giant floating icebergs can be seen in the late spring and early summer off the Atlantic coast. Dense fogs are not uncommon, especially in the late spring and fall. Generally, good weather and pleasant temperatures prevail from late June to the end of September.

Since much of your visit to Newfoundland will be auto touring, casual, comfortable clothes are sufficient. Bring good shoes for hiking, warm jackets and sweaters, and basic rain gear. There is nothing stuffy about the people of Newfoundland-Labrador, so you don't have to worry about dressing up for dinner.

Tourist Information

For more information write the Newfoundland-Labrador Department of Development and Tourism, P.O. Box 2016, St. John's, Newfoundland A1C 5R8. Call toll-free (800) 563–6353 throughout the year.

Visitor Information Centres are located in North Sydney (Nova Scotia), Port aux Basques, Deer Lake, Notre Dame Junction, Clarenville, and Whitbourne. Also in St. John's, Dunville, Marystown, Gander, Twillingate, Grand Falls, Springdale, Corner Brook, and Stephenville/St. George's.

How to Get Around Newfoundland-Labrador

The Trans-Canada Highway 1, the main transportation route on the island of Newfoundland, is 565 miles/910 km. from Port aux Basques to St. John's, fully paved, and well maintained. Road conditions are generally good on other roads, although some stretches are unpaved but driveable.

Coastal Newfoundland and Labrador

The coastal vessels that service the many otherwise inaccessible fishing outports with supplies and mail are the best way to come close to the traditional way of life along the Atlantic coasts of the island of Newfoundland and Labrador. For example, you can sail from Lewisporte to Nain, Labrador, 725 miles/1,166 km. one way (you return more quickly by air from Goose Bay). Space on these ships is limited, and the demand for accommodations is great. Meals are provided on board. For further information, contact Marine Atlantic at the telephone numbers given in the "By Car and Ship" section.

Wilderness Tours and Ocean Cruises

One of the best ways to experience the special world of Newfoundland and Labrador is to go out on the ocean or into the wilderness. The following are several companies that provide such memorable experiences:

Labrador Straits Tours, (709) 931–2332, takes you along the southern Labrador coast with its fishing outport villages, archaeological sites, puffin sanctuary.

Wildland Tours, (709) 722–3335, explores the Avalon Peninsula.

Bontours, (709) 458–2256, runs cruises on Western Brook Pond in Gros Morne National Park.

Ocean Contact Limited, (709) 464–3269, offers whale and bird watching in Trinity Bay area.

Atlantic Marine Ventures, (709) 722–2222, leads diving expeditions off Newfoundland's coasts.

Gander River Tours, (709) 679–2271, runs canoe river expeditions.

Labrador Adventure, (709) 925–3235, offers tours of the Churchill Falls area.

Newfoundland Nature Tours, (709) 754–2052, leads excursions to marine and bird sanctuaries and to archaeological sites.

Tasiujatsoak Wilderness Camp, (709) 896–8505, offers tours to Nain, the most northerly Inuit settlement on the Labrador coast and to the Torngat Mountains.

Sanctuary Boat Charters, (709) 334–2887, takes trips to Witless Bay seabird sanctuary.

Seal Island Boat Tours, (709) 243–2376, runs trips to view harbour seals in St. Paul's Inlet.

Major Events

June

Marystown Days, Marystown
St. John's Day Celebrations, St. John's

Newfoundland Folk Festival, St. John's
Placentia Bay Folk Festival, Placentia

July

Summer Festival, July and August, St. John's (Art and Culture Centre)
Garden Party, St. Fintan's
Conception Bay Folk Festival, Harbour Grace
Hang Ashore Folk Festival, Corner Brook area
Festival of the Arts, Stephenville
Regatta, Southeast Arm, Placentia Bay

August

Une Longue Veillée (folk festival), Cape St. George
Shoal Harbour Day Folk Festival, Clarenville
Regatta Day, Quidi Vidi Lake, St. John's
Bakeapple Festival, L'Anse-Armour
Most of these festivals and events involve parades, sporting events, dancing, and singing, plus a lot of eating and drinking—in short, a great time.

Hunting and Fishing

The province offers some 156,000 square miles/406,000 sq. km. of almost virgin territory, with more than 13,000 square miles/ 34,000 sq. km. of lakes and rivers—a hunting and fishing paradise. Nonresident hunters must be accompanied by a guide, and you must have a permit from the government to use your own airplane for transportation to hunting areas. Moose, caribou, black bear, duck, geese, snipe, grouse, and rabbit are abundant. Salmon (land-locked and Atlantic), trout (speckled and brown), tuna, pike, and char are some of the species popular with sports fishermen.

For more information on outfitters, guides, and regulations, call tourism information at the telephone numbers given above.

Provincial Parks and Campgrounds

Newfoundland is well suited for people bringing their own accommodations (trailers, campers, tents, and the like). Provincial parks are located scenic areas and offer hiking, swimming, fishing, camping conveniences, boating and canoeing areas, historic sites, cultural events, and other features.

The following is a listing of government-operated parks:

Otter Bay Park, on Highway 470, near Isle-aux-Morts
Cheesman Park, on Highway 1, near Cape Ray
Mummichog Park, on Highway 1, near Tompkins
Grand Codroy Park, on Highway 406, near Doyles
Crabbes River Park, on Highway 1, near St. Fintans
Barachois Park, on Highway 1, near St. Georges
Piccadilly Head Park, on Highway 463, near Piccadilly
Blue Ponds Park, on Highway 1, near Corner Brook
Blow Me Down Park, on Highway 450, near Lake Harbour
River of Ponds Park, off Highway 1, near River of Ponds
Pistolet Bay Park, off Highway 437, near Raleigh
Squires Memorial Park, on Highway 422, near Cormack
Sops Arm Park, on Highway 420, near Sops Arm
Flatwater Pond Park, on Highway 410, near Baie Verte
Indian River Park, on Highway 1, near Springdale
Catamaran Park, on Highway 1, near Badger
Mary March Park, on Highway 370, near Buchans Junction
Beothuck Park, on Highway 1, near Grand Falls
Notre Dame Park, on Highway 1, near Lewisporte
Dildo Run Park, on Highway 340, near Virgin Arm
Jonathan's Pond Park, on Highway 330, near Gander
Square Pond Park, on Highway 1, near Gambo
David Smallwood Park, on Highway 320, near Middle Brook
Windmill Bight Park, on Highway 330, near Lumsden
Lockston Path Park, on Highway 236, near Port Rexton
Frenchman's Cove Park, on Highway 213, near Frenchman's Cove
Freshwater Pond Park, on Highway 220, near Lewins Cove
Jack's Pond Park, on Highway 1, near Arnold's Cove
LaManche Park, on Highway 10, near Cape Broyle
Holyrood Pond Park, on Highway 90, near Trepassey

The Canadian federal government operates the following as part of the national park system:

Gros Morne National Park, on Highway 430, north of Deer Lake
Terra Nova National Park, on Highway 1
Newman Sound Campground in Terra Nova National Park
Malady Head Campground in Terra Nova National Park

Accommodations

A number of provincial parks and private campgrounds are near the main roads, and there are adequate motels, although not as many as on mainland Canada. If you are relying on motels, plan to stay in the major cities: Stephenville, Corner Brook, Deer Lake, Gander, and St. John's. Make sure you have advance reservations for St. John's. Also consider staying at hospitality homes, (known in other regions as B & Bs), private homes offering inexpensive, good accommodations and home cooking.

Dining

Cod and pork scraps, cod au gratin, cod tongues, and New-foundland fish chowder are some of the province's traditional dishes. Seal flipper pie is one of the great delicacies. Blueberries are also a favorite food, flavoring many wonderful baked goods. Lobster and salmon dishes are available in many restaurants.

Liquor can be purchased at government stores and in licensed dining rooms and lounges. Try Newfoundland Screech, a potent rum and a provincial tradition.

Touring Newfoundland

One of the lures of Newfoundland is the people, especially those living in the little villages and outposts along the coasts. Many still pursue a way of life that died long ago in the rest of North America. They are humble, religious, lusty, joyful, and very friendly once you make the first move. There are many similarities between the coastal people of Newfoundland and those of Ireland—their attitudes, thick brogues, close-knit families and communities, and strong faith in the will of God. It is the people of Newfoundland and Labrador, plus their magnificent land and powerful ocean, that make this province one of the most unusual places to visit in Atlantic Canada.

The best way to see the island of Newfoundland by car is to get off the ferry at Port aux Basques and get on the Trans-Canada Highway. From Port aux Basques to the capital city of St. John's, use the 565-mile/910-km. Trans-Canada as your primary route but take frequent side trips to explore the countryside and the seacoast, to swim, fish, camp, and boat. Through these side trips you will discover the essence of Newfoundland, while still having the conveniences (accommodations, restaurants, and the attractions in larger communities) on the Trans-Canada not too far away.

Along your route of travel, you will have many opportunities for swimming, boating, fishing, and sight-seeing. Buy fresh home-baked bread and pies, locally grown produce, and newly caught fish and make the most of picnics in beautiful natural surroundings. Discover secluded spots along lakes, streams, in the woods, and along the shores for priceless moments of peace and harmony.

Channel-Port aux Basques to L'Anse aux Meadows

Most travelers enter and leave the province at Channel-Port aux Basques, an important fishing community that traces its history back to 1500 and the Basques who fished in its waters. Visit the Community Museum of Maritime History. Open during the summer. Admission charge. At nearby Rose Blanche Point is a lighthouse built in 1873. Accommodations include Hotel Port aux Basques, (709) 695–2171, and Grand Bay Hotel, (709) 695–2105, both off the Trans-Canada, with dining rooms and lounges, moderate.

Highway 1 extends along the Cape Ray shore, an area with many spectacular views of the ocean crashing against the land, and then through the rich agricultural Codroy Valley to Stephenville. The Codroy Valley has a number of excellent salmon-fishing rivers, and the scenery is enhanced by farms.

During early August, **Stephenville** holds an arts festival, featuring live drama, which has received rave notices from critics. Accommodations include Hotel Stephenville, (709) 643–5176, and White's Hotel-Motel, (709) 643–2101, both off the Trans-Canada, with dining rooms and lounges, moderate.

Take a side trip to **Port-au-Port Peninsula,** which has fine sandy beaches, swimming, and an attractive park. Many of the inhabitants here are of Acadian descent.

Corner Brook, at the mouth of the Humber River, is Newfoundland's second largest city. It is an important transportation and distribution center and its main industry is the giant Kruger Paper Mill. There are many beautiful drives in the Corner Brook area— along the Humber River to the quaint fishing village of *Bottle Cove* and *Blow Me Down Provincial Park*. Here also is the Captain James Cook Monument, a National Historic Site. Cook charted the Bay of Islands in 1764. Accommodations and dining in the center of town or on the Trans-Canada include Hotel Corner Brook, Main Street, (709) 634–8211, with a dining room and lounge, moderate; Holiday Inn, West Street, (709) 634–5381, with a swimming pool, dining room, and lounge, moderate to expensive; Glynmill Inn, Cobb Lane, (709) 634–5181, with a good restaurant, moderate; and Mamateek Motor Inn, (709) 639–8901, with a dining room overlooking the city, moderate.

Deer Lake, located on a lake of the same name, is in a dense forested area and at the junction of the Trans-Canada and Highway 430, which goes up the Great Northern Peninsula to Gros Morne National Park and L'Anse aux Meadows. The trip to L'Anse aux Meadows and back will require about three extra days.

Wiltondale, via Highway 430, is at the entrance of Gros Morne National Park. Here starts the drive up the Great Northern Peninsula. A side trip on Highway 431 from Wiltondale takes you to **Glenburnie** and to **Trout River,** where you have some fine views of the rugged landscape and the water. You can gather clams and mussels at low tide here. *Gros Morne National Park,* (709) 458–2417, reminds some of Norway: imposing mountains and dramatic fjords—some of the most stunning scenery on the island. Bonne Bay and the Long Range Mountains give Gros Morne its special look. Camping, hiking, fishing, and swimming, and interesting fishing villages can be had all along the coast at such spots as Bear Cove, Sally Cove, St. Paul's, and Cow Head (where Jacques Cartier is supposed to have anchored). Boat tours of the coast are offered at Bonne Bay and on Western Brook Pond.

At **Port au Choix,** about midway on the Great Northern Peninsula, is the Maritime Archaic (Red Paint Culture) Indian burial ground, dating back 2340 B.C., and artifacts of the Dorset Eskimos. This national historic park is an important archaeological find. Open mid June to September. Free.

Just above Port au Choix, at the village of **St. Barbe,** you can catch the ferry that crosses the Strait of Belle Isle to Blanc-Sablon, Québec, during ice-free months. The ferry takes cars, trailers, and trucks. From Blanc-Sablon you can drive into Labrador, via Highway 510, as far as **Red Bay.** There are not many miles of road here, but you can boast that you were in Labrador. Accommodations in this part of Labrador include Northern Light Inn, L'Anse au Clair, (709) 931–2332, with a dining room and lounge, moderate, and Barney's Hospitality Home, L'Anse-au-Loup, (709) 927–5634, with home-cooked meals, inexpensive.

L'Anse aux Meadows, via Highway 436, off Highway 430, at the northernmost tip of Newfoundland, is the site of the Viking settlement (A.D. 1000) discovered by Helge and Anne Stine Ingstad. At this national historic site, (709) 623–2108, trained guides explain the excavations. There are replicas here of what this ancient Norse settlement might have been like in the days of the Vikings. What is impressive here is not so much the excavations themselves or the moody landscape, but the feeling of the tremendous struggle for survival that must have consumed the inhabitants. Open June to September. Free. In 1978 L'Anse aux Meadows was declared a World Heritage Site by UNESCO, recognized as one of the world's major archaeological properties.

St. Anthony, via Highway 430, is the largest town on the Great Northern Peninsula and the place for overnight accommodations after seeing L'Anse aux Meadows. St. Anthony is headquarters for the International Grenfell Association, which used to provide medical services (hospitals, nursing stations, and children's homes) to isolated communities on the island and on the coast of Labrador. Dr. Wilfred Grenfell devoted his life to the fishing peoples of these northern coasts at a time when they were neglected even by the government. The Grenfell House is open to the public during the summer, free. While in St. Anthony visit the Grenfell Mission's handicraft center, where you can purchase exquisite hand-embroidered parkas and other beautiful items made by the coastal people. Also visit St. Anthony Museum and Archives at town hall, open during the summer, free. Accommodations include the St. Anthony Motel, (709) 454–3200, with a dining room and lounge, moderate; Viking Motel, (709) 454–3541, with a dining room and lounge, moderate; and Howell's Tourist Home, (709) 454–3402, with home-cooked meals, inexpensive.

To return to the Trans-Canada, backtrack on Highway 430 to Deer Lake.

Grand Falls to St. John's

Grand Falls, 285 miles/456 km. west of St. John's, on the Trans-Canada, is one of the world's largest producers of newsprint. Perhaps the paper you read this morning was printed on a product made in Grand Falls. The Mary March Museum for the study of the Beothuck Indians is also located here. Open throughout the summer. Free. The area around Grand Falls is popular for moose and caribou hunting and salmon and trout fishing. Recommended accommodations in the town include Highliner Inn, (709) 489–5639, with a dining room and lounge; Mount Peyton Motel, (709) 489–2251, with a dining room and lounge; and Car Sans Hotel, (709) 489–5324, with a dining room and lounge. All are moderately priced.

Lewisporte, with its access to Notre Dame Bay, is famous for its lobsters. You can hire boats for sport fishing in the Atlantic. This is headquarters for blue-fin tuna fishing expeditions. Marine Atlantic ferries operate between Lewisporte and Goose Bay and Nain, Labrador. Contact Marine Atlantic for more information (see page 341). Accommodations in Lewisporte are the Brittany Inns, (709) 535-2533, with a dining room and lounge, and Chaulk's Tourist Home, (709) 535–6305. Both are moderate in price.

At **Twillingate,** via Highway 346, in the Long Point area, you can see floating icebergs in the early summer (the *Titanic* was sunk by icebergs off the waters of Newfoundland). This is a rare opportunity to take photos of a natural phenomenon that very few people see. Visit the Twillingate Museum, open during the summer, admission charge. Long Point Lighthouse in this area was built in 1876. Highway 331 runs along Gander Bay and connects with Highway 330, which takes you to the city of Gander on the Trans-Canada.

Gander is famous in aviation history as the last refueling point for transatlantic flights (and for flights coming from Europe to North America). Gander International Airport, known as the "crossroads of the world," was a major military base during the Second World War, when thousands of Allied flights went through here on their way to Europe. Today, because modern aircraft have a longer range, Gander's importance as a refueling stop has diminished.

Accommodations are available at the Albatross Motel, Highway 1, (709) 256–3956, with a dining room and lounge, moderate; Airport Inn, Highway 1, (709) 256–3535, with housekeeping units, inexpensive; Holiday Inn, Highway 1, (709) 256–3981, with a swimming pool, dining room, and lounge, moderate; and Hotel Gander, Highway 1, (709) 256–3931, with a dining room and lounge, moderate.

The Trans-Canada cuts through *Terra Nova National Park,* (709) 533–2801, on Bonavista Bay. This is one of the most popular parks in the province because of its natural beauty, dramatic coastline, and many attractions. You can hike trails in the company of a trained naturalist or go off by yourself. Moose, black bears, and other wildlife move about freely. At the edge of the sea you can watch herds of whales cavorting and many different species of birds wheeling overhead. There are lakes and streams for swimming and fishing, ample areas for camping and picnics, and a nine-hole golf course. Terra Nova, like Gros Morne on the west coast, is one of Newfoundland's great natural attractions, and it should not be missed. Accommodations in this area are at Weston's Terra Nova National Park Chalets, (709) 533–2296, which offers full facilities. Moderate.

Eastport, via Highway 310, on the northern edge of the park, is a farming town, where you can purchase fresh vegetables, home-baked bread, and jam. It has a sandy beach for a plunge in the cold Atlantic.

There is an interesting museum of local history at **Salvage,** where you can purchase weaving made to order. Open throughout the summer. Free. Savor the locally smoked salmon while touring or relaxing on the beaches at **Sandy Cove** and **Happy Adventure.**

Cape Bonavista, via Highway 230, is reputed to be the landfall of John Cabot on June 24, 1497. The lighthouse on Cape Bonavista, first used in 1843, is now a provincial historic site. Continue on Highway 230 to **Trinity,** one of the oldest settlements in Newfoundland, discovered by Gasper Corté Real in 1500. Saint Paul's Church here was built in 1734. Trinity was where the first smallpox vaccination was administered in North America. Visit the Trinity Museum. Open throughout the summer. Free. In town the oldest known fire engine in North America is on display.

In the Trinity Bay area, the Trans-Canada is joined by Highway 210, which leads down the Burin Peninsula. **Marystown** is a center for the building of fishing vessels (Newfoundland "longliners"), and in **Fortune** you can catch the ferry for the French islands of Saint Pierre and Miquelon. Ferries operate from mid June to mid September.

The islands of **Saint Pierre** and **Miquelon** are a department of France. They are among the last vestiges of the once-great empire France commanded in the New World. Miquelon, the larger of the two islands, is mostly uninhabited, except for some fishing stations in the summer. Saint Pierre is a thriving fishing and supply center and serves as a quarantine station for cattle shipped to North America from Europe. The islands drew international attention in 1967 when General Charles de Gaulle visited on his way to Montréal.

The architecture in Saint Pierre is unmistakably French. The buildings that fringe General de Gaulle Square give one the feeling

of being in Brittany. Fine wine and expensive French perfumes are sold here at bargain prices, though the bargains are not what they once were. Accommodations are in charming French-style guest houses, and the chefs here conjure up the best cuisine this side of Montréal. Issuing stamps is another key industry, and the products of these islands are highly regarded by philatelists around the world. Visit the post office in the center of town and see its impressive collection of stamps. Free. Also in the center of town is the local museum, which has artifacts from shipwrecks and a guillotine, once used to behead a murderer. Open throughout the summer. Admission charge. Every July 14 Bastille Day is celebrated with the same joyous passion as on the French mainland. This is a grand time for parades, sporting events, fireworks, dancing, eating, and drinking. Another popular celebration is Jacques Cartier Day, the first Sunday in August. For more information, contact the French Government Tourist Office, 610 Fifth Avenue, New York, NY 10020; (212) 757–1125.

St. John's

The Trans-Canada, Highway 1 leads into **St. John's** on the Avalon Peninsula, the largest city in the province and its capital. St. John's is the easternmost city of North America and one of the oldest inhabited ports of the continent. Cabot is said to have named it in honor of Saint John in 1497. It has one of the great ice-free harbors on the North Atlantic. The French and the English struggled over it for close to four centuries. The English were victorious, and St. John's and the rest of Newfoundland came under their control in 1762, where they stayed until the province joined Canadian confederation in the 1940s.

Newfoundland Historic Trust tours of old St. John's depart from the Hotel Newfoundland at 10:00 A.M. and 2:00 P.M. Elaine Dunne Tours, (709) 579–9352, provides guided tours of historic St. John's and excursions to Cape Spear National Park, Petty Harbour, and along scenic Marine Drive. Cruises from St. John's harbor to Cape Spear, the most easterly point in North America, operate mid June to mid September. During this two-hour sail, you can jig for

◀ **St. John's, Newfoundland, has been an important port throughout its history. During World War II, large convoys of merchant ships sailed from here over the North Atlantic route to aid beleaguered Great Britain's fight against Hitler.**

cod and squid and see blue and humpback whales. For information and rates, call Harbour Charters, (709) 754–1672.

St. John's attractions include:

Signal Hill National Historic Park, on high cliffs, offers some of the best views of the harbor, the city, and the sea. At Signal Hill the last military engagement between the French and the English for the possession of the Atlantic coast took place. The remains of old gun emplacements and fortifications are still evident in the terrain at the Queen's Battery. At Cabot Tower, Guglielmo Marconi received the first transatlantic wireless signal on December 12, 1901. Signal Hill and its tower were the last landmarks for Charles Lindbergh before he crossed the ocean on his historic transatlantic flight. Nearby is Gibbet Hill, where criminals were hanged. The park's visitors center has exhibits on the history of the city and the province. Open throughout the year. Free.

Newfoundland Museum, on Duckworth Street, contains artifacts of the Beothucks (the original inhabitants of Newfoundland), the Inuit, and the Naskaupi. The museum also has models of early vessels and plans of French fortifications. Open mid June to mid September. Free.

Newfoundland Museum at Murray Premises, Water Street, formerly the Confederation Building Museum, has many interesting items relating to Newfoundland's military and maritime past. (St. John's was a major port for North Atlantic convoys during World War II.) Open throughout the year. Free.

Confederation Building, Prince Philip Drive, is the seat of government for the province. Open throughout the year. Free.

Colonial Building, on Military Road, the former seat of government (circa 1850), now serves as the provincial archives and is open to the public. Free.

Government House, on Bannerman Road, a handsome mansion, is the residence of the lieutenant governor, a native Newfoundlander appointed by Queen Elizabeth. Not open to the public.

Anglican Cathedral, on Church Hill, is a fine example of ecclesiastical architecture, with a Gothic nave and beautiful stained-glass windows. A small museum tells the story of the various fires the city has suffered.

Basilica of Saint John the Baptist, on Military Road, with its familiar towers, dominates the city from its hillside. The interior is very ornate but uplifting, especially on a foggy day. Fishermen from Portugal's White Fleet (no longer in existence) gave the statue of

Our Lady of Fatima in appreciation for many years of friendship. A convent and Catholic school buildings are clustered around the basilica.

Garrison Church (Saint Thomas), on Military Road, dating back to 1836, is another venerable place of worship. This church was used by the British military.

Commissariat House, on Kings Bridge Road, is an exceptional Georgian-style structure, furnished with period English china, silver, paintings, and Brussels carpets. A major restoration was made possible by the provincial government and the Newfoundland Historical Society. Open throughout the summer. Free.

War Memorial, on Water Street, commemorating Newfoundlanders who gave their lives in the two world wars and in Korea, is said to be on the spot where Sir Humphrey Gilbert, in 1583, declared Newfoundland a possession of Queen Elizabeth I.

Quidi Vidi Lake and Battery, at Quidi Vidi Village, within St. John's City, via Forest Road, is a provincial historic site overlooking a charming fishing village. Open mid June to mid September. Free. At nearby Quidi Vidi Lake the annual St. John's Regatta is held every August, a major event of boat races, entertainment, games, and food.

Arts and Culture Centre, at the corner of Allandale Road and Prince Philip Drive, is an attractive, modern facility featuring contemporary Canadian painting, sculpture, and crafts. The complex contains a library, gift shop, gourmet restaurant, and theater, where many major dramatic and musical productions are presented. For schedule and ticket information, call (709) 576–3901. Nearby is the campus of Memorial University.

Bowring Park, on Waterford Bridge Road, is the city's most popular place for a stroll and for the kids to let off steam. It has many beautiful statues, including the *Fighting Newfoundlander* and *Peter Pan*.

Memorial University Botanical Garden at Oxen Pond, via Mount Scio Road at Pippy Park, features acres of forest, bog and fen, heathland, alder thicket, and wild gardens. Open from May to end of November. Free.

Accommodations are available at the following:

Radisson Plaza Hotel, 120 New Gower Street, (709) 739–6404, is St. John's best, offering excellent accommodations, gourmet dining, lounge, swimming pool, and fitness center. Expensive.

The Stel Battery, Signal Hill Road, (709) 726–0040, offers comfortable rooms in a good location, dining room, and lounge. Moderate.

Airport Inn, Airport Road, (709) 753–3500, features a beauty salon, dining room, and lounge. Moderate to expensive.

Hotel Newfoundland, Cavendish Square, (709) 726–4980, is the grande dame of city hotels, offering good accommodations and dining and an excellent downtown location. Expensive.

Kenmount Motel, Elizabeth Avenue, (709) 726–0092, is comfortable, with a dining room and lounge. Moderate.

Lester Hotel, 12 Blackmarsh Road, (709) 579–2141, offers a sauna, dining room, and lounge. Moderate.

Holiday Inn Government Centre, 180 Portugal Cove Road, (709) 722–0506, has a restaurant and lounge with live entertainment and a swimming pool. Expensive.

The following are recommended for dining:

Newman's, at the Radisson Plaza Hotel, (709) 739–6404, offers classical cuisine in an elegant room. Expensive.

The Cabot Club, at the Hotel Newfoundland, (709) 726–4980, serves fine food in a congenial room overlooking the harbor. Expensive.

Explorers', at the Fishing Admiral, 203 Water Street, (709) 753–6203, is a top place for lobster and prime rib of beef. Moderate to expensive.

Victoria Station, 288 Duckworth Street, (709) 722–1290, offers an eclectic menu of pasta, sushi, seafood, and terrific desserts. Moderate to expensive.

Biarritz on the Square, 188 Duckworth Street, (709) 726–3885, serves Cajun cuisine. Moderate.

Act III, Arts and Culture Centre, (709) 754–0790, is a top gourmet restaurant in a high-brow setting. Expensive.

Woodstock Colonial Inn, on Highway 60, (709) 722-6933, expertly prepares traditional Newfoundland dishes, such as seal flipper pie. Moderate to expensive.

St. John's has several pubs, such as Erins on Water Street for Irish music, in which to relax and enjoy some Newfoundland style. Ask the concierge at your hotel for suggestions on what's currently tops in town.

Your best shopping buys are Newfoundland handicrafts: colorful hooked mats made by outport women, pine furniture, pottery, Labradorite jewelry, hand-knit woolens, Inuit soapstone carvings, Grenfell parkas, painted tiles, crochet work, silk batik, Torbay knit-

ting, and fishermen's mitts. In downtown St. John's you can purchase quality handicrafts at the Salt Box, Duckworth Street; Livyers, Duckworth Street; the Newfoundland Weavery, Duckworth Street; Winmill Woolens, at Murray Premises; Nonia, Water Street; and the Cod Jigger, Duckworth Street.

There are handicraft places in most towns and villages throughout the island. For unusual value be on the lookout for handicrafts being sold at the artisan's own home.

The Avalon Peninsula

From St. John's you can easily tour the Avalon Peninsula. Start with Highway 20 to Torbay, where the English forces, under General Amherst, landed to recapture St. John's from the French. **Pouch Cove** is a pretty fishing village leading to **Cape St. Francis,** a dramatic headland graced with a lighthouse. Marine Drive leads back to St. John's and goes along a wild coastline through a number of traditional fishing villages.

Highway 1, the Trans-Canada, heading west from St. John's meets Highway 100, which leads to the west coast of the Avalon Peninsula and the towns of **Argentia** and **Placentia.** Placentia Bay is where Churchill and Roosevelt signed the Atlantic Charter in 1941. Visit *Castle Hill National Historic Park* to see the seventeenth- and eighteenth-century French and English fortifications. There is ferry service to and from Argentia from North Sydney, Nova Scotia, in the summer (contact Marine Atlantic for details; see page 341).

From St. John's you can also take the Trans-Canada west to Highway 60. In **Topsail** you will have an excellent view of Conception Bay and its islands. **Holyrood** is a base for blue fin tuna expeditions. The famous American artist Rockwell Kent once lived in **Brigus,** as did Captain Bob Bartlett, who accompanied Commodore Perry on his 1909 Arctic expedition. **Cupids** is where John Guy attempted his ill-fated Sea Forest Plantation in 1610.

Port de Grave Peninsula, via Highway 72, has some of the best coastal scenery and picturesque fishing villages in the province. **Hibb's Cove** has the Fishermen's Museum and Art Centre. **Har-**

◄ Many Newfoundland fishing outports (villages) are built so close to the edge of the sea that homes and work sheds stand on stilts above the high-tide mark. Cod is the prime catch, and it is amazing how many delicious dishes Newfoundlanders can make out of this fish, using even the cod's cheeks and tongue.

bour Grace was visited by pirate Peter Easton in the seventeenth century. A "pirate's fort" stood on the site of the local museum in the old customs house. Here are Saint Paul's Anglican Church, the oldest stone church in Newfoundland, and the oldest jail built in Canada. Harbour Grace is the birthplace of Sir Thomas Roddickton, professor of surgery, governor of McGill University, and a member of Parliament. In 1932 Amelia Earhart left Harbour Grace to fly solo over the Atlantic, the first woman to do so. In **Heart's Content** the first successful transatlantic cable was landed in 1866. Visit the Communications Museum, depicting the role of this community in the development of modern communications. Open throughout the summer. Free.

Another tour from St. John's follows the southern shore, Highway 10, to **Petty Harbour, Bay Bulls,** and **Witless Bay.** During the summer, take a boat tour to view bird colonies (gannets, puffins, kittiwakes, razorbills) on coastal islands. There is a beautiful waterfall in **La Manche** and a provincial park for camping and picnics. From **Ferryland** Sir David Kirke ruled Newfoundland in the seventeenth century. Sir George Calvert was a Ferryland resident, too. An old lighthouse and high cliffs mark this ambitious settlement, which failed because of the cold winters. In **Renews** Roman Catholics secretly celebrated the Mass at a time when it was prohibited by the Protestant rulers of the colony. A grotto commemorates the place where these early settlers kept their faith alive.

Trepassey was another starting point for early transatlantic flights. In 1928 Amelia Earhart flew from here to Southampton, England, as a passenger. Trepassey is now the site of a tower that serves as a long-distance navigational aid for aircraft and ships. Willow ptarmigan is a popular game bird for hunters in this area, and salmon-fishing expeditions go out from Trepassey.

A short but memorable side trip from St. John's is to *Cape Spear National Historic Park*, via Highway 11. Cape Spear is the easternmost spit of land on this continent, a desolate but beautiful place that has been hammered for eons by weather and the sea. A lighthouse and gun emplacements nearby protected Allied military bases on the island during the Second World War. Stand on the cliffs of Cape Spear. Just the Atlantic separates you from Europe: The entire North American continent lies behind you.

CHAPTER 16

Prince Edward Island

Prince Edward Island Today

Perhaps it is the ferry trip across the Northumberland Strait that does it—cutting that psychological tie to the problems and cares on the mainland—because visitors to Prince Edward Island (P.E.I., as it is affectionately and familiarly called) feel a sense of peace and renewal almost as soon as they set foot on its luxurious red shore. Of all the Atlantic Canada provinces, P.E.I. is the most manicured, almost as if an expert English gardener carefully tended its landscape every day. Nearly every town and village seems clipped from a romantic postcard, and even Charlottetown, the province's capital city, is small, intimate, and pretty. P.E.I. is an island gem set off Canada's east coast in the Gulf of Saint Lawrence.

The island is compact, only 140 miles/224 km. long and 4 to 40 miles/6 to 64 km. wide. You are never far from the sea, and P.E.I. has some of the best warm-water beaches in the Atlantic region. Even people from the other Atlantic provinces come to P.E.I. for their vacations. A typical day could easily include trout fishing in an inland stream in the morning; a picnic on the coast for lunch, followed by a refreshing swim; golf on a championship course in the afternoon; and a lobster dinner, followed by harness racing or live theater in the evening.

P.E.I., with 2,184 square miles/5,678 sq. km., is the smallest of Canada's ten provinces and is largely devoted to agriculture. Besides being Canada's principal grower of seed and table potatoes, it produces large crops of strawberries and various vegetables. Hogs, sheep, poultry, and dairy cattle are also important. Lobster, oysters,

361

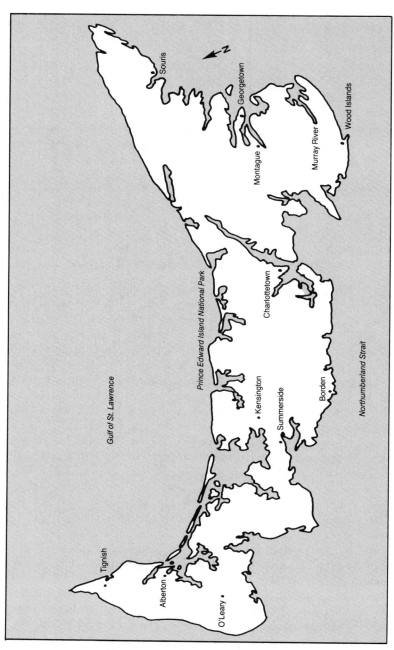

PRINCE EDWARD ISLAND

mussels, scallops, clams, tuna, and Irish moss bring additional income for the islanders. Increasing numbers of people are being employed in various service industries, including government, education, medical care, and tourism. Tourism, one of the most important elements in P.E.I.'s economy, is a well-developed and organized industry here, all of which benefits the visitor.

P.E.I., one of Canada's most densely populated provinces (though it scarcely feels that way), has close to zero population growth. Many of the young people are moving to more industrialized areas on the mainland. The young, however, make the move from this Canadian Camelot reluctantly and plan for the day when they can return permanently. The current population is 124,000, with the greatest concentration in the Charlottetown area.

History and Culture

Jacques Cartier, who discovered P.E.I. for the French in 1534, said of it, "All this land is low, and most beautiful to see." The Micmacs, its original inhabitants, called the island "Abegweit." The British first dubbed it "Island of Saint John," but later changed their minds and named it Prince Edward Island, after Queen Victoria's father. P.E.I. is also called the "garden of the gulf" and the "million-acre farm."

Most of the early settlers of P.E.I.—the English, Scots, Irish, and Acadians—sought refuge from hard times in their native lands. Leaders from the Canadian provinces gathered in 1864 in Charlottetown to discuss a political and economic union of British North America, making P.E.I. the birthplace of Canadian confederation, though the island itself did not enter the confederation at this time. Until 1873, the people of P.E.I. had limited self-government but were at the mercy of absentee English landlords who collected rents from lands most of them never saw. In 1873 P.E.I. joined the Confederation of Canadian provinces and did an astounding thing for that time: The provincial government bought the land back from the landlords and sold it to the people—a successful example of land reform that has not been duplicated in many places.

How to Get to Prince Edward Island

By Car and Ship

From New Brunswick you can take the Trans-Canada to Cape Tormentine, where the CN Marine ferry will take you and your car across the Northumberland Strait to Borden, P.E.I. During the summer, there are hourly departures from each terminal. The crossing takes about forty-five minutes, and there are a snack bar and cafeteria on board. Ferries operate year-round, but at the peak of the season, expect a wait in the terminal staging area before boarding. Tourism officials advise making the crossing in late evening or early morning to avoid delays.

From Nova Scotia, the Trans-Canada takes you to the ferry at Caribou, which sails to Wood Islands, P.E.I., from May to December. There is frequent service from both terminals. The crossing time is seventy-five minutes, and there is a cafeteria on board.

By Air

Both Air Canada and Canadian Airlines International, through their affiliate carriers, provide connecting service to the Charlottetown airport from major Canadian and U.S. cities.

Rental cars (Tilden, Avis, and others) are available at the airport, in Charlottetown, and in Summerside. There is taxi service from the airport to Charlottetown.

By Bus and Rail

VIA Rail has bus service to and from P.E.I. VIA Rail buses connect with passenger trains in Amherst, Nova Scotia, and in Moncton, New Brunswick.

Several bus companies provide tours of P.E.I. from the United States and mainland Canada. Check with your travel agent for details.

General Information

Time zone: Atlantic

Telephone area code: 902

Police emergency: (902) 566–7100

Medical emergency: Charlottetown, (902) 566–6111

Climate and Clothing

Prince Edward Island's summer weather is usually perfect for all activities. The natural air-conditioning of sea breezes usually discourages fog and suffocating humidity. The winters here are cold.

Because of the lack of heavy manufacturing or mining, there is little air pollution, except that created by cars and trucks—a modern malady of any inhabited place.

Casual and sporting clothes of all types can be used on a P.E.I. vacation. Business suits and cocktail dresses can be worn in better restaurants and to the theater, but there is very little fuss over dress codes. You should bring some warm jackets and sweaters for cool days on the beach and for evenings.

Tourist Information

Information and reservations can be obtained by calling P.E.I. Visitor Services toll-free at (800) 565–9060 from the eastern United States; (800) 565–7421 from the Maritime provinces (May to October); (800) 565–0243 from Ontario (except area code 807), Newfoundland, and Québec. From all other locations, call (902) 368–4444. You can write P.E.I. Visitor Services at P.O. Box 940E, Charlottetown, P.E.I. C1A 7M5.

For your convenience, the province has tourist information centers at Aulac, New Brunswick (en route to Cape Tormentine), and Caribou, Nova Scotia, as well as on P.E.I. at Borden, Brackley Beach, Cavendish, Charlottetown (in Oak Tree Place), Pooles Corner, Portage, Souris, Stanhope, Wilmot, and Wood Islands.

Major Events

P.E.I. has many activities and special events throughout the summer. These include country or harvest fairs, special exhibitions of art and handicrafts, concerts, theater, yacht races, and top entertainment from the mainland. There's also harness racing at the Charlottetown Driving Park and at the Summerside Raceway.

Here are some of the top festivals on P.E.I.:

June

Natal Day Celebrations, Charlottetown
Charlottetown Festival, Charlottetown, May to October
Irish Moss Festival, Tignish

July

Summerside Centennial Yacht Club Race, Summerside
Confederation Centre Art Gallery and Museum Summer Exhibition, Charlottetown, July to September

Strawberry Festival, Orwell Corner
Irish Folk Festival, Woodstock
Souris Regatta, Souris
Lobster Carnival and Livestock Exhibition, Summerside
Potato Blossom Festival, O'Leary
Fiddle and Stepdancing Festival, Montague
Northumberland Fisheries Festival, July and August

August

Oyster Festival, Tyne Valley
Highland Games and Gathering of the Clans, Eldon
Country Days and Old Home Week, Charlottetown
Gold Cup and Saucer Parade, Charlottetown
Prince County Exhibition, Alberton
Crapaud Exhibition, Crapaud
Harvest Festival, Kensington
P.E.I. Ploughing Match and Agricultural Fair, Dundas
Blueberry Festival and Homecoming, St. Peters
Harvest of the Sea, Basin Head

September

Acadian Festival, Abrams Village
Egmont Bay and Mont Carmel Agricultural Exhibition, Abrams Village
Green Gables Open, Green Gables Golf Course, Cavendish

Sports

Hunting and Fishing

While hunting is primarily restricted to shooting birds and small game (goose, black duck, grouse, partridge, and snowshoe hare), fishing (salmon, rainbow trout, and eastern brook trout) is a major sport on the island. Ponds, lakes, rivers, estuaries, and streams offering good opportunities are all over the island. Licenses are required for freshwater fishing.

P.E.I. is one of the world's centers for tuna fishing; some giants weighing more than a thousand pounds have been caught in its waters.

◀ Inexpensive farm vacations are a holiday treat for city folk on Prince Edward Island.

The season generally begins in July, but the larger tuna are normally landed during September and October. Tuna boats and gear are for hire. Charters can be booked up to a season in advance.

Deep-sea fishing for cod, halibut, hake, mackerel, and herring is popular with many visitors. It's a great experience for landlubbers both young and old.

Golf

Here are some of the most beautiful and challenging courses in Atlantic Canada:

Belvedere Golf and Winter Club, Charlottetown, (902) 892–7838, eighteen holes, par 72.

Brudenell River Provincial Golf Course, Roseneath, (902) 652–2342, eighteen holes, par 72.

Glen Afton Golf Course, Nine Mile Creek, (902) 675–3000, eighteen holes, par 72.

Green Gables Golf Course, Cavendish, (902) 963–2488, eighteen holes, par 72.

Mill River Provincial Golf Course, Mill River, (902) 859–2238, eighteen holes, par 72.

Rustico Resort, Rustico, (902) 963–2357, eighteen holes, par 72.

Stanhope Golf and Country Club, Stanhope, (902) 672–2842, eighteen holes, par 72.

Summerside Golf Club, Summerside, (902) 436–2505, eighteen holes, par 72.

Provincial Parks and Campgrounds

Here is a listing of provincial parks with campgrounds:
Jacques Cartier Park, off Highway 12, near Alberton
Mill River Park, on Highway 162, near O'Leary
Cedar Dunes Park, on Highway 14, near O'Leary
Green Park, on Highway 12, near Tyne Valley
Linkletter Park, on Highway 11, near Summerside
Cabot Park, on Highway 20, near Kensington
Strathgartney Park, on the Trans-Canada, near Charlottetown
Lord Selkirk Park, off the Trans-Canada, near Eldon

Prince Edward Island is home to some of the best harness racing in East-▶ ern Canada. Islanders are proud of their horses, and years of training and driving skills show up in every race.

Brudenell River Park, on Highway 3, near Georgetown
Northumberland Park, on Highway 4, near Wood Islands
Campbell's Cove Park, on Highway 16, near Elmira
Red Point Park, on Highway 16, near Souris
Crow Bush Cove Park, Highway 350, at West St. Peter's
Panmure Island, Highway 347, north of Gaspereaux.

The following, in P.E.I. National Park, are operated by the Canadian federal government as part of the national park system:

Cavendish Campground, on Gulf Shore Road
Rustico Island Campground, on Gulf Shore Road
Stanhope Campground, on Gulf Shore Road

Most government campgrounds provide basic services (water, firewood, tables, toilets, fireplaces, and so on). Some have more extensive services, such as electrical hookups, showers, sewage disposal, and organized activities. They are all situated near woodlands, fishing streams, or saltwater beaches. Some, such as Brudenell River Park, have superior golf courses. Most provincial parks are open from June to Labour Day, and fees are nominal. For more information on these and privately owned campgrounds, contact P.E.I. Visitor Services.

Accommodations

Prince Edward Island has ample accommodations of all kinds (hotels, motels, resorts, campgrounds, private homes, and farms). The demand for them during the summer is heavy, however, and reservations are advised.

If you are traveling in New Brunswick or in Nova Scotia, use the toll-free "Dial-the-Island" information and accommodation reservation system: (800) 565–7421, from mid May to end October.

P.E.I. was one of the originators of the inexpensive farm vacations, where you can live and relax with a farm family. You and your family can share in the daily life of a farm family and their community. The food is wholesome, ample, and well prepared, the accommodations clean, comfortable, and homelike. Discover the true essence of this special island, at a very reasonable price. For more information, call P.E.I. Visitor Services.

Dining

One of the best ways to dine in P.E.I. is at a church or community supper. Here's a chance to fill up on good homemade food without spending a great deal of money. You can have hot or cold lobster (the specialty of the island), ham and beef plates, potato salad, cole slaw—and all the fresh-baked pies, breads, and cakes you can handle.

P.E.I. is famous for its vegetables, oysters, and lobsters. Islanders are masters in the preparation of chowders. P.E.I. has a number of fine restaurants, especially in Charlottetown. Be sure to check the dining room at your hotel or motel: Many innkeepers pride themselves on their delicious fare.

The following is a listing of popular lobster suppers available around the island throughout the summer season:

Brackley Beach Lobster Suppers, Brackley Beach
Cardigan Lobster Suppers, Cardigan
Fisherman's Wharf Lobster Suppers, North Rustico
New Glasgow Lobster Suppers, New Glasgow
New London Lions Lobster Suppers, New London
Saint Ann's Church Suppers, Hunter River (probably the most famous of them all)

Liquor is sold by the bottle in government store outlets located in major population centers, open Monday through Friday. Licensed restaurants and lounges sell liquor by the glass. The legal drinking age in P.E.I. is nineteen.

Touring Prince Edward Island

P.E.I. is small enough that you are never far from warm-water beaches. Charlottetown, on the southern shore of Prince Edward Island, is convenient to all areas of the island. The Trans-Canada Highway 1 is the province's main highway, extending from Borden through Charlottetown to Wood Islands. P.E.I. is organized into three scenic drives: the Kings Byway through King County, the Blue Heron through Queens County, and the Lady Slipper through Prince County. Attractions on these theme roads will keep the family busy and entertained. Pick up a free copy of the official P.E.I. tour guide at any visitor information center. This publication highlights area attractions, history, and special events. Also be sure to take less-traveled roads and discover more of the island. Take time to picnic, swim, hike, and make the effort to get to know the people.

A word of warning: During wet weather, be careful driving on unpaved roads—the red clay surface gets slick and slippery.

Charlottetown

One of your first destinations will be the island's lovely capital and only city, Charlottetown. This community dates back to the early eighteenth century, when it was known as Port Lajoie, under the French regime. After coming under British control in 1763, it was renamed in honor of Queen Charlotte, consort to King George III. In 1864 the Fathers of Canadian Confederation met in Province House to formulate the union of the provinces of British North America.

Charlottetown is more like a medium-sized town than a city, where you can walk to most places of interest. If you prefer to ride, Abegweit Tours, (902) 894–9966, uses an authentic London double-decker bus for comprehensive tours of Charlottetown and limousine service for the north and south shores. Island Horse and Buggy provides carriage tours of the city and its major attractions. Free, one-hour, guided walking tours of Old Charlotte Town leave Province House beginning at 10:00 A.M. Call (902) 894–5552 for more information. Bike rentals are available at MacQueen's Bike Shop at 430 Queen Street.

The most important attraction in the city is the Charlottetown Festival, a series of outstanding theatrical events held at the main stage of the *Confederation Centre of the Arts,* at the corner of Queen and Grafton streets, during the summer. The most popular show in the festival is *Anne of Green Gables,* a wonderful musical comedy about a red-haired, misfit orphan girl who unexpectedly arrives in a small P.E.I. town and turns it head over heels. Millions of people throughout the world have read the story of Anne or seen her on television, and now you have a chance to see Anne on stage. This is delightful entertainment for all ages, with a highly professional cast, orchestra, and settings. *Anne* is the mainstay of the festival, but each year it alternates during the week with new, original productions. The Cameo Cabaret, at the David MacKenzie Theatre, opposite the Confederation Centre, puts on original productions, on a smaller scale but no less entertaining. The Cabaret is fully licensed (drinks are served). These festival productions play to packed houses. For information and reservations, call (902) 566–1267.

In addition to its handsome main theater, the Confederation Centre, a complex of five buildings, has an impressive art gallery and museum, featuring paintings by Robert Harris (a famous island artist), the Poole Porcelain Collection, and contemporary Canadian painting and crafts; restaurant and gift shop; the Provincial Library and Archives; and Memorial Hall. Open throughout the year. Free.

Province House National Historic Site, next to the Confederation Centre, contains the restored Confederation Chamber, where the Fathers of Confederation started the country on its way to self-government. Confederation Chamber is open for public viewing. Province House continues to serve as the seat of P.E.I.'s government. Open throughout the year. Free.

Beaconsfield, 2 Kent Street, former mansion of a shipbuilder, is now the headquarters of the P.E.I. Heritage Foundation. Beaconsfield is an elegant old house with nicely landscaped grounds and historical displays on the main floor. Open throughout the year. Donations accepted. Here also is the province's center for genealogical research. You are invited to trace your family roots through a Master Name Index, Family Files, and Vital Statistical Records. For more information contact or visit the Prince Edward Island Museum and Heritage Foundation at Beaconsfield, 2 Kent Street, Charlottetown, P.E.I. C1A 1M6, (902) 892–9127.

Victoria Park, overlooking the harbor, is a fine place for a walk, offering forty acres of lawns, wooded groves, and playing fields.

Government House (circa 1835), on Pond Road near Victoria Park, is the residence of the province's lieutenant governor. Not open to the public.

Saint Dunstan's Basilica, on Great George Street, the seat of the Roman Catholic diocese, has a marvelously ornate interior.

Saint Paul's Anglican Church (established 1747), 203 Richmond Street, is P.E.I.'s oldest Protestant church.

Saint Peter's Anglican Church, Rochford Square, has murals by famed island artist Robert Harris.

Saint James Kirk (Presbyterian), 35 Fitzroy Street, has relics from Iona, Scotland, and beautiful stained-glass windows.

Great George Street Gallery, 132 Richmond Street, exhibits the latest work of local and regional artists. Open throughout the year. Free.

Project Harbourside has restored the historic wood and brick buildings along the waterfront and converted them into offices, shops, and restaurants.

Harness races are held daily at Charlottetown Driving Park during the summer.

Recommended accommodations include the following:

373

Dundee Arms Motel, 200 Pownal Street, (902) 892–2496, is an inn furnished in antiques, whose dining room has been featured in *Gourmet* magazine. Moderate to expensive.

Inn on the Hill, 150 Euston Street, (902) 894–8572. Moderate to expensive.

Kirkwood Motor Hotel, 455 University Avenue, (902) 892–4206, features a bilingual staff and a swimming pool. Moderate to expensive.

Best Western MacLauchlan's Motel, 238 Grafton Street, (902) 892–2461, has housekeeping units, a sauna, dining room, and lounge. Moderate to expensive.

Rodd's Royalty Inn, on the Trans-Canada, west of the city, (902) 894–8566, has excellent accommodations in a new section, a tropical swimming pool, restaurant, and lounge. Expensive.

CP Prince Edward Hotel, 18 Queen Street, (902) 566–2222, is the best large hotel on the island, offering all deluxe hotel amenities, including indoor swimming pool, fitness facility, sauna. Its Lord Selkirk dining room is elegant, with good food and service. The Prince Edward also has facilities for meetings and conventions. Expensive.

Auberge Wandlyn Inn, on the Trans-Canada, northwest of the city center, (902) 892–1201, offers a heated pool, dining room, and lounge. Moderate to expensive.

Rodd's Confederation Inn, on the Trans Canada in West Royalty, (902) 892–2481. Moderate to expensive.

For dining the following places are recommended:

Casa Mia, 186 Prince Street, (902) 892–8888, serves steaks, Italian dishes, Greek salads, lobster. Moderate.

Lord Selkirk Dining Room at CP Prince Edward Hotel, 18 Queen Street, (902) 566–2222, serves gourmet fare in an elegant environment. Expensive.

King Palace Restaurant, 159–161 Queen Street, (902) 894–9644, specializes in Szechuan, Mandarin, and Polynesian food. Moderate to expensive.

Caesar's Italy, University Plaza, (902) 892–9201, is the city's pasta emporium for good Italian cooking. Moderate.

Samuel's at the Inn on the Hill, 150 Euston Street, (902) 894–8572, specializes in halibut steak, filet mignon, and homemade desserts. Moderate.

The Carvery at the Wandlyn Inn, Trans Canada in West Royalty, (902) 892–1201, an "all you can eat" buffet, with roast beef, turkey, and ham. Moderate. The Governor's Feast, also at the Wandlyn, is dinner theater Victorian style.

Ye Olde Dublin Pub, 131 Sydney Street, (902) 892–6992. Your name does not have to be Murphy to enjoy the pub food and rollicking entertainment served in this historic building. Inexpensive to moderate.

Canton Café, 73 Queen Street, (902) 892–2527, is a favorite spot for Chinese food. Moderate.

Off Broadway, 125 Sydney Street, (902) 566–4620, is the place for crêpes and good soups. Inexpensive to moderate.

Dundee Arms Hotel, 200 Pownal Street, (902) 892–2496. Its highly regarded dining room has a colonial ambience, and specialties include Malpeque oysters and fresh seafood. Expensive.

Claddagh Room, 131 Sydney Street, (902) 892–9661, is an excellent seafood restaurant. Moderate to expensive.

Shop in Charlottetown at Oak Tree Place, University Avenue, north of the city center, or Charlottetown Mall, on the Trans-Canada, north of city center. Confederation Court Mall is located on Grafton Street, across from the Confederation Centre of the Arts. At West Royalty Industrial Park is British Woolen Knitters, and on 77 Water Street is the Company Store, offering various goods at factory-outlet prices. There are many interesting little shops in downtown selling English china, woolen goods, antiques, and P.E.I. handicrafts.

The Kings Byway Drive

By taking the Trans-Canada Highway 1 east and crossing the Hillsborough Bridge, you enter the scenic Kings Byway Drive.

From the top of Tea Hill you'll have a splendid view of Governor's Island and the Northumberland Strait. In this lush farm country the strawberry is the king crop. Many farms allow you to pick your own baskets of the fruit. The strawberry season on P.E.I. is July.

At the wildlife sanctuary in **Orwell** a great variety of shorebirds, including the blue heron, can be seen on the tidal flats. Orwell Corner Historic Site is a small, rural community that has been restored to its nineteenth-century appearance. Open late May to late September. Admission charge.

A side trip via Highway 207 leads to **Belfast,** founded by Scottish Highlanders under the leadership of the Earl of Selkirk. Saint John's Kirk, built in 1823, has a Christopher Wren–style tower and memorials to Selkirk's daughter.

Eldon, back on Highway 1, was also founded by Scots and now holds its annual Highland Games and Gathering of the Clans in early August. The Lord Selkirk Pioneer Settlement, off Highway 1, depicts the life of the early inhabitants. Open mid June to mid September. Admission charge. This area also has an early French-Acadian cemetery. Stop and enjoy the excellent beach at *Lord Selkirk Provincial Park.*

Wood Islands is the location of ferry service to Caribou, Nova Scotia. Both P.E.I. and Nova Scotia have tourist information offices in the terminal area. The P.E.I. office has a gift shop featuring island-made crafts, and there are a beach and other diversions while you wait your turn to board the ferry. Northumberland Sailing Adventures offers schooner cruises out on the strait. The Meadow Lodge Motel, 2 miles/3 km. west of the terminal, (902) 962–2022, offers good accommodations in the Wood Islands area, moderate. Also in the area, on Highway 4, is The Netherstone, (902) 962–3200, moderate. The Netherstone's dining room is one of P.E.I.'s best.

The P.E.I. portion of the Trans-Canada Highway ends at Wood Islands. The Kings Byway Drive continues via various highway numbers. Look for the signs bearing the royal crown.

A side trip via Highway 18A takes you to the Log Cabin Museum near **Murray Harbour.** It contains farm and household artifacts going back two centuries. Open July 1 to Labour Day. Admission charge. In nearby **Gladstone** is the Pioneer Cemetery, dating from 1854, and Fantasyland Provincial Park. Fantasyland has large statues of favorite storybook characters, live deer, a miniature log fort, and recreational equipment for the kids. Open late May to mid September. Free.

Shumates Toy Factory and the Free Church of Scotland, built in 1867, are in **Murray River.** Deep-sea and tuna fishing expeditions go out from the town's wharf, and there is good canoeing here.

A long stretch of white sand beach with sweeping dunes graces **Murray Harbour North.** Take Highway 347 to *Panmure Island Provincial Park* for excellent red and white sand beaches and a look at the Panmure Head Lighthouse.

Take a side trip via Highway 4 to *Buffaloland Provincial Park,* in **Milltown Cross,** home of a herd of bison and deer that roams freely over its hundred acres. Open throughout the year. Free. Also in Milltown Cross is Moore's Migratory Bird Sanctuary, where you can bike or hike natural trails, fish for trout, and see Canada geese and other waterfowl. Open June to mid September. Admission charge.

One of the province's oldest sandstone cottages is at **Lower Montague,** on Highway 4. At **Montague,** P.E.I.'s third largest town, is the Garden of the Gulf Museum, 6 Main Street, South, featuring artifacts of early pioneer life, an Indian stone collection, and a gun collection. Open late June to mid September. Admission charge. In late July the folks here hold their annual Garden of the Gulf Fiddle and Stepdancing Festival. Fine accommodations and seafood dining can be had at Lobster Shanty North, on Highway 17, Main Street, (902) 838–2463, moderate. This town also has a number of curio and antique shops in which to poke around. In nearby Little Sands, on Highway 4, is Bayberry Cliff B&B, (902) 962–3395. This comfortable, artist-designed accommodation is set on a high cliff overlooking the Northumberland Strait, highly recommended, moderate. Watson's Lakeside Cottage, in New Perth on Highway 3, (902) 838–2658, moderate.

At **Pooles Corner,** at the junction of Highways 3 and 4, be sure to stop in the King's Byway Interpretive Centre, which has many interesting displays relating to the past and present of King County and a staff to answer your questions. Open June to mid October. Free. Kingsway Motel, at Highways 3 and 4, (902) 838–2112, moderate.

Brudenell River Provincial Park is one of the best recreational facilities on the island, with an eighteen-hole championship golf course, tennis courts, trail rides, boating, a resort, a supervised beach and pool, and many special programs. Good accommodations and dining are at Rodd's Brudenell Resort, Highway 3, 3 miles/5 km. west of Georgetown, (902) 652–2332, moderate to expensive.

Deep-sea and tuna fishing expeditions can be chartered at **Georgetown,** reached via Highway 3. The town's many historic buildings create an Old World charm. You can buy fresh fish and lobster at Georgetown Seafoods Limited. The King's Playhouse is located here, offering repertory theater from July through August, (902) 652–2053. De Roma Cottages, off Highway 3, (902) 687–2845, are recommended accommodations, moderate.

There are reports of buried treasure at **Abells Cape,** via Highway 310, and a mystery. Charles Flocton, an American actor, bought the cape and wished to be buried there. But through circumstances beyond his control, Flocton was forced to accept San Francisco as his final resting place—that is, until several years after his death, when a casket engraved with the name of Charles Flocton washed up on the Abells Cape shore.

At **Dingwells Mills,** via Highway 2, is Johnny Belinda Pond, named after the character created by writer Elmer Harris. *Johnny Belinda*, the story of a young deaf and mute girl, was set in this area and ran for 320 consecutive performances on Broadway. Harris made his summer home at **Fortune Bridge,** via Highway 2.

Farther along Highway 2, in **Rollo Bay** the Saint Alexis Church has a bell dating from the old French regime, given to the parish in honor of the first white child born on the island. Rollo Bay puts on its annual Fiddler Festival in mid July.

Souris ("mouse" in French) is the island's fourth largest town. Accommodations in the area include the Higland Inn, Lea Crane Drive, (902) 687–3758; Hilltop Motel, Main Street, (902) 687–3315; Souris West Motel, on Highway 2, 1 mile/2 km. west of Souris, (902) 687–2676; Wind Surfer Motel, on Lower Rollo Bay Road, (902) 687–2339. All are in the inexpensive to moderate price range.

Souris is a terminus for the passenger and car ferry service to the **Iles-de-la-Madeleine (Magdalen Islands),** which operates April 1 to the end of January, depending on weather and ice conditions. The crossing time is five hours. For sailing schedule and fares, call (902) 687–2181. See Chapter 10 for information on the islands.

In the **Kingsboro** area visit the Basin Head Fisheries Museum, with displays and photographs telling the story of fishing and lobstering in P.E.I. waters. Open late May to late September. Admission charge. A side trip to **Elmira,** via Highway 16A, brings you to the old Elmira Railway Station, which depicts early railroading days on the island. Open late May to late September. Free.

East Point, via Highway 16, is the last community on this end of the island. From East Point Lighthouse you may be able to see the distant shore of Cape Breton Island on a clear day. Here the waters of the Gulf of Saint Lawrence and the Northumberland Strait converge. From this point the Kings Byway extends west along the Gulf of Saint Lawrence.

North Lake is considered by many sportsmen and women the tuna fishing capital of the world. You can charter fishing expeditions from North Lake Harbour and buy fresh seafood at the wharf.

Saint Andrews, via Highway 2, farther down from North Lake, was the site of Saint Andrews College, the island's first institute for higher learning, founded by Bishop Angus MacEachern in 1831. At **Saint Tereasa,** a side trip via Highway 22 brings you to Saint Cuthbert's Church, built from a design by famed island architect William Harris. **Scotchfort,** a pleasant rural community on Highway 22 was settled in 1772 by Scottish Roman Catholics.

The Highway 6 section of the Kings Byway takes you to the *Prince Edward Island National Park,* (902) 892–0203, and its **Dalvay** to **Brackley** beaches, the most popular saltwater bathing area in Atlantic Canada. At the entrance to the park is Dalvay-by-the-Sea mansion, now a well-known resort, built in 1896 by Alexander Mac-Donald, once the president of Standard Oil. The Dalvay-by-the-Sea Hotel, (902) 672–2048, offers good accommodations and fine dining, plus tennis courts, lawn bowling, and beautiful grounds; expensive. There are many cottage accommodations and small restaurants in the communities along the national park and with easy access to the beaches. Stanhope Beach Lodge and Motel, (902) 672–2047, for example, is recommended for a stay and for its all-you-can-eat lobster smorgasbord; moderate to expensive. There is a challenging golf course in **Stanhope.** Windsurfing P.E.I. rents equipment. The annual Windsurfing P.E.I. Championships are held here in late August.

In **West Covehead,** on Highway 6, is Saint James United Church (circa 1837), a fine example of early colonial architecture.

Visit the Spoke Wheel Car Museum in **Dunstaffnage.** Open June to end of September. Admission charge. The East River Speedway has stock car races on Wednesdays, from May to September. After passing through **Parkdale,** the Kings Byway ends where it started, in Charlottetown.

The Blue Heron Drive

The Blue Heron Drive also starts and finishes in Charlottetown. It loops around the midsection of the island, through Queens County. Follow Highway 15 from Charlottetown to Brackley Beach (if you have followed the Kings Byway to this area, continue along the coast on Highway 6 instead of going back to Charlottetown). For accommodations, try Shaw's Hotel and Cottages, on Highway 15, (902) 672–2022, expensive.

Take a side trip via Highway 25 to **York** and its Jewell's Gardens and Pioneer Village, an antique-glass museum and children's barn set in beautiful landscaping. Open mid June to mid October. Admission charge.

At **Oyster Bed Bridge,** via Highway 6, you can canoe on the Wheatley River and watch shorebirds, including the great blue heron, in the mud flats. Let the children spin their wheels at the go-cart rides. Open the end of June to September. Admission charge. Rustico Resort Trail and Pony Rides has horseback treks.

A side trip, via Highway 243, leads to the Farmers' Bank in **South Rustico,** one of the first "people's banks" in Canada, chartered in 1864. Next to the bank is Saint Augustine's Church, built in 1838, and the old Belcourt Lodge, a former convent. Also in South Rustico is Jumpin Jacks' Old Country Store Museum. Open July and August. Donations appreciated. Grant's Trail Rides offers horseback treks in the area from mid June to Labour Day.

North Rustico is the site of Santa's Woods, a fun treat for the children. Open June 1 to mid September. Admission charge. In North Rustico you can hire boats and gear for deep-sea fishing and buy freshly caught lobster. Accommodations include the following: North Rustico Motel and Lodge, on Highway 6, (902) 963–2253, moderate; St. Lawrence Motel, on Gulf Shore Road, (902) 963–2053, moderate; the Breakers by the Sea, on Highway 6 in Rusticoville, (902) 963–2555, moderate; the Pines Hotel, on Highway 6 in Rusticoville, (902) 963–2029, moderate; Rustico Resort, on Highway 242, off Highway 6 in South Rustico, (902) 963–2357, moderate.

Cavendish has been immortalized by Lucy Maud Montgomery's popular *Anne of Green Gables* books. In the Cavendish area you can visit several "Anne" attractions, including the Green Gables House, on Highway 6, where the best-known story is set. Open mid May to mid October. Free. Bilingual guides are provided.

Other family attractions in Cavendish include Royal Atlantic Wax Museum, at the junction of Highways 6 and 13, which displays life-size, costumed historical figures. Open late May to end September. Admission charge. Visit Rainbow Valley, an extensive recreational area featuring Anne of Green Gables Land, Children's Farm, boating lakes, and a gift shop. Open early June to mid September. Admission charge. Cavendish also has an excellent eighteen-hole golf course adjacent to Anne of Green Gables. Also in this attraction-packed area is the Enchanted Castle, housing fairyland scenes. Open from mid June to Labour Day. Admission charge. King Tut's Tomb and Treasures, open mid June to Labour Day. Admission charge. Sandspit, a mini-racing car track, open late June to early September. Admission charge. Cranberry Village, open late June to early September. Admission charge. Great Northern Merchants, at Cavendish Boardwalk, is the place for shopping, offering a wide assortment of goods at factory-outlet prices.

Recommended accommodations are Cavendish Beach Cottages, in National Park, (902) 963–2025, moderate; Cavendish Lodge and Cottages, on Highway 6, (902) 963–2553, moderate; Cavendish Motel, at the junction of Highways 6 and 13, (902) 963–2244, moderate to expensive. Also Anne Shirley Motel and Cabins, at Highway 6 and 13, (902) 963–2224, moderate; Bay Vista Motor Inn, on Highway 6, (902) 963–2225, moderate; Lakeview Lodge and Cottages, on Highway 6, (902) 963–2436, moderate; Parkview Farm Tourist Home and Cottages, on Highway 6, (902) 963–2027; Silverwood Motel, on Highway 6, (902) 963–2439, moderate; and White Eagle by the Sea, on Gulf Shore Road, (902) 963–2361, moderate to expensive.

Visit the P.E.I. Marine Aquarium in **Stanley Bridge,** via Highway 6. Open mid June to mid September. Admission charge. Also visit the Cavendish White Water Jet Skis, open late June to early September. Admission charge. Cap'n Bart's Adventure Park, open July to Labour Day. Admission charge. And the P.E.I. Marine Aquarium, open mid June to mid September. Admission charge.

New London is the birthplace of author Lucy Maud Montgomery, who wrote *Anne of Green Gables.* On display at her home are her wedding dress and personal scrapbooks. Open mid June to Labour Day. Admission charge. Stop in Memories Gift Shop, across from the author's birthplace. In Park Corner on Highway 20 is Anne of Green Gables Museum at Silver Bush; Lucy Maud Montgomery's home during her adult life. This museum has the largest collection of personal possessions belonging to the author. Open June to October. Admission charge.

Take a side trip, via Highway 234, to **Burlington** to see one of P.E.I.'s most unusual attractions, the Woodleigh Replicas, scaled-down versions of the Tower of London, Anne Hathaway's cottage, and Dunvegan Castle. Open late May to mid October. Admission charge. Nearby is Burlington Go-Karts. Open late May to September. Admission charge.

In **French River,** back on the Blue Heron Drive, via Highway 20, is the Yankee Hill Cemetery, containing the bodies of American sailors who drowned off the coast in the fierce gale of 1851. Anne's House of Dreams, based on the Montgomery books, depicts the home of Anne and Gilbert as newlyweds. Open early June to early October. Admission charge.

Malpeque Bay is famous for its oysters, which can be bought fresh here or in restaurants all over the island. Include a visit to the Malpeque Gardens, famous for their dahlias and roses. Open late June to mid October. Admission charge. For accommodations, try Malpeque Harbour Cottages. Call (902) 836–5203. Moderate.

Saint Mary's in **Indian River** is one of P.E.I.'s most beautiful rural churches, designed by William Harris. The handsome interior was also designed by Harris.

The Blue Heron Drive now passes near the communities of Summerside and **Borden,** which is the main ferry terminus for the island.

At **Cape Traverse,** via Highway 10, a national historic monument tells of the ice-boat service that connected the island to the mainland in the nineteenth and early twentieth centuries.

Victoria is one of P.E.I.'s most picturesque coastal villages. The Victoria Playhouse puts on various theatrical productions— comedy, drama, romance, (902) 658–2025. Victoria Sailing Excursions provides cruises on the Northumberland Strait.

At **De Sable,** the House of International Dolls exhibits its extensive collection, including characters from Charles Dickens books. Open mid June to Labour Day. Admission charge.

A side trip on the Trans-Canada from De Sable takes you to **Bonshaw** and its Car Life Museum. Open late May to Labour Day. Admission charge. The Bonshaw 500 is an exciting go-cart place for the kids. Open mid May to late September. Admission charge. **New Haven** is the site of the P.E.I. Fairyland, which features miniature golf, a fairytale forest, miniature train, and boating pond. Open mid June to early September. Admission charge. Accommodations are available at Strathgartney Country Inn, on the Trans-Canada, (902) 675–4711. Inexpensive.

The Blue Heron Drive now leads to *Fort Amherst National Historic Park,* which stands on the site of Port Lajoie, the first capital of the island. The Visitor Centre has an audiovisual presentation on the history of the fort and the surrounding area. There are the remains of eighteenth-century earthworks and an excellent view of Charlottetown. The park is a great place to picnic. Open June 1 to mid October. Free. Nearby is the MicMac Indian Village, a re-creation of Indian life on the island. A shop sells authentic Indian handicrafts. Open June to October. Admission charge.

From Rocky Point, the Blue Heron Drive continues along the scenic coast, passing through **New Dominion, Cornwall,** and **West,** and concludes in Charlottetown.

The Lady Slipper Drive

The Lady Slipper Drive begins and ends in **Summerside**, the second largest community on the island. Its new waterfront development area has a good-size shopping center, a marina, the Marine and Fisheries Training Centre, and the Eptek National Exhibition Centre. The Eptek Centre contains the P.E.I. Sports Hall of Fame and a gallery featuring both contemporary art from the island and traveling exhibitions. Open throughout the year. Free. Summerside is a charming coastal town with tree-lined streets and many historic buildings. There are harness racing and eighteen-hole golf in the area. The annual Summerside Lobster Carnival is an eight-day festival of games, entertainment, and good eating held in mid July. Vagabond Boat Charters provides cruises on the Northumberland Strait, sailing near lighthouses and islands. Summerside Raceway has harness races on Wednesday nights during the summer.

Accommodations are available at the following places:

Cairns' Motel, 721 Water Street, (902) 436–5841, is centrally located. Moderate.

Best Western Linkletter Inn, 311 Market Street, (902) 436–2157, serves buffets during the week. Moderate.

MacQuarrie's Lighthouse Motel, 802 Water Street, (902) 436–2992, is centrally located. Moderate.

Quality Inn—Garden of the Gulf, 618 Water Street, (902) 436–2295, offers a heated outdoor pool and other recreation. Expensive.

Sunny Isle Motel, 720 Water Street, (902) 436–5665, is centrally located. Moderate.

For dining, try Brothers Two Restaurant, on Water Street, next to Quality Inn, (902) 436–7674. Downstairs is P.E.I.'s most unusual dining experience, the Summer of '61 Feast. For a set price, you dine on Malpeque oysters, steamed clams, seafood chowder, lobster, scallops, fillet of sole, an array of salads, and homemade bread. You are entertained with song and dance by professionals in a 1960s high school–reunion setting. It is an excellent value considering everything you get. Advance reservations are a must.

From Summerside the Lady Slipper Drive goes through **Saint Eleanors.** At the Canadian Forces Base is an Argus Aircraft (antisubmarine patrol) mounted on a pedestal. Open throughout the year. Free.

At **Miscouche,** at the junction of Highways 2 and 12, is one of the most photographed churches on the island, Saint John the Baptist. The Acadian Museum of P.E.I., via Highway 2, displays its extensive collection of church, household, and agricultural artifacts, including many items of historical and genealogical interest. Open July 1 to September. Admission charge. In 1884, in Miscouche, a national French-Acadian congress selected the official Acadian flag (tricolor and yellow star) that now flies in many parts of the region.

There is warm-water bathing and picnicking at the provincial park in **Union Corner.**

The Eglise Notre Dame in **Mont Carmel** is noted for its beautiful twin spires and its lavish interior. Mont Carmel's Le Village-des-Pioneers-Acadiens re-creates an early French settlement, including a church, store, house, barns, and blacksmith shop. The settlement's Etoile de Mer restaurant serves traditional Acadian food. Open mid June to mid September. Admission charge. La Cuisine à Mémé is P.E.I.'s French dinner theater—music, skits, and Acadian food—(902) 854–2227.

The coastline is interesting in the **Cape Egmont** area: Red sandstone cliffs and strange rock formations have been carved by the sea and the weather. At Cape Egmont is the Six Gables Bottle House, via Highway 11, a building made from more than eleven thousand bottles, with a rock and flower garden. Open early June to early October. Admission charge.

Abrams Village is the home of the well-known Acadian singer Angele Arsenault. Visit Le Centre d'Artisanat for locally made handicrafts. Saturday night dances are held at the Club 50.

There is another handsome church in **Egmont Bay—Eglise Saint-Philippe-et-Saint-Jacques.**

Farther along the Lady Slipper Drive is the pretty rural community of **Coleman.** Its old Free Church of Scotland was where the Reverend Donald MacDonald preached his hell and brimstone sermons. The railway station dates back to the late nineteenth century. Shop for fresh vegetables and flowers at the old School Market.

Take a side trip to **O'Leary,** via Highway 140 and 148, to visit the O'Leary Museum, where several buildings display local history. Open June 1 to September. Admission charge. In late July O'Leary holds its annual Potato Blossom Festival (the town is in one of the best potato-producing areas on the island).

On Highway 2, 36 miles/57 km. west of Summerside, is Rodd's Miller River Resort, (902) 859–3555, which has a golf course, tennis courts, canoeing, windsurfing, and many other recreations. Moderate.

Back on the Lady Slipper Drive, via Highway 14, there is a fine sandy beach at **West Point**. Captain Kidd is said to have buried a treasure near the lighthouse at **Cape Wolfe**. Note the red-stained rocks here. According to Micmac legend, an Indian maiden was dashed against the rocks by an angry god. There have been sightings of a full-rigged ghost ship in flames in the **Burton-Campbellton** area.

The harvesting and drying of Irish sea moss is big business in the **Miminegash** area. Sea moss is used in many foods, such as ice cream and chocolate milk, and in shampoos, cosmetics, and ceramic glazes. The Marine Plants Experimental Station here will show you how Irish moss grows and tell you about its benefits. Open throughout the summer. Free. Fresh fish and lobster can be bought at the dock in both Miminegash and at Skinners Pond.

The northernmost tip of P.E.I. is at **North Cape**. The sandstone at this point washes away at a disconcerting rate of 3 feet/1 m. a year. Visit the Atlantic Wind Test Site, via Highway 14, where windmills are tested as an alternative energy source. Open throughout the year. Free.

Tignish is one of the world's biggest producers of canned lobster meat. Its fisheries, the canning operation, the credit union, the store, and the gas station are all owned cooperatively by the local people. There are also two blacksmith shops here and a good-natured ghost named Blimphey.

Jacques Cartier Provincial Park, in the **Kildare Capes** area, features an excellent sandy beach and a long line of sand dunes. In the community of Kildare is the P.E.I. Miniature Railway, on South Kildare Road, a scaled-down passenger-carrying train that travels through a nice rural countryside. Open June to early September. Admission charge.

At the pleasant town of **Alberton** is the Alberton Museum (local history), on Church Street. Open late June to Labour Day. Admission charge. Also visit Leavitt's Maple Tree Craft Shop, where you can see local craftspeople make beautiful items from maple and other woods. Open throughout the year. Free. Accommodations are available at the Westerner Motel, on Highway 12, (902) 853–2215. Moderate.

A side trip, via Highway 152, to **Northport** takes you to the Craft of Taxidermy Shop, opposite Alberton Wharf, the island's one and only. Open June to September. Free. Also visit the Sea Rescue Park, which features a restored sea rescue station and lifeboat, beach, and picnic area.

Freetown was where the first land purchase was made by local residents. Before the historic Land Purchase Act of 1853, most of the land on the island belonged to absentee British landlords.

A side trip via Highway 173 takes you to **Milligan's Wharf,** where you can buy mackerel and lobsters in season. Another side trip, via Highway 163, goes to the Micmac reservation on **Lennox Island.** Visit the Indian church: Much of its interior ornamentation was made by the local Micmacs. Stop in the Indian arts and crafts shop. Open June to late September. Fresh Malpeque oysters can be purchased on Lennox Island at Burleigh Brothers, a large oyster-farming operation that provides tours for visitors.

The Lady Slipper Drive continues to **Port Hill,** via Highway 12, which has a fine provincial park on the former Green Park estate of shipbuilding tycoon James Yeo. An excellent museum depicts nineteenth-century shipbuilding activities on P.E.I. You can wander in a re-created early shipyard and see a partly completed full-size vessel. Open mid June to Labour Day. Admission charge. The park itself offers an excellent beach, picnic area, and nature trail.

In **Grand River,** on Highway 12, is beautiful Saint Patrick's Church, also designed by William Harris.

The Lady Slipper Drive goes through **MacDougall,** via Highway 12, meanders along the Grand River, and comes to an end at Travellers Rest in the Summerside area at Highway 1A.

INDEX

Abbreviation Key:

394

HIGHWAY SIGNS

TRANS CANADA
HIGHWAY

PROVINCIAL
ARTERIAL HIGHWAY

TRUNK
HIGHWAY

COLLECTOR
HIGHWAY

GAS

FOOD

LODGING

PICNIC
TABLES

CAMP
GROUND

TRAILER
PARK

TELEPHONE

PROVINCIAL
TOURIST
INFORMATION

HOSPITAL

SCHOOL
CROSSWALK

SCHOOL
ZONE

TURN

KEEP
RIGHT

SIGNALS
AHEAD

MAXIMUM
SPEED AHEAD

MAXIMUM
SPEED

NO TURNS

TURN
RIGHT

NO RIGHT
TURN

TURN

NO U TURNS

TRUCK
ROUTE

NO HEAVY
TRUCKS

DO NOT
ENTER

RAILWAY
CROSSING

HIDDEN
INTERSECTION

PLAYGROUND

YIELD THE
RIGHT OF WAY

FULL
STOP

DIVIDED
HIGHWAY BEGINS

DIVIDED
HIGHWAY ENDS

SLIPPERY
WHEN WET

HILL

PAVEMENT
NARROWS

NARROW OR
ONE LANE BRIDGE

ONE WAY STREET

ADVISORY
SPEED

BUMP

LOW CLEARANCE

STOP AHEAD

MEN WORKING

SHARP CHANGE
OF ALIGNMENT